PENGUIN BOOKS

CAN WE HAVE OUR BALLS BACK, PLEASE?

Julian Norridge is an award-winning journalist and a BAFTA- and Emmy-nominated programme maker and writer. He lives in Putney. This is his first book.

CAN WE HAVE OUR BALLS BACK, PLEASE?

How the British invented sport

JULIAN NORRIDGE

PENGUIN BOOKS

PENGUIN BOOKS

Published by the Penguin Group
Penguin Books Ltd, 80 Strand, London WC2R ORL, England
Penguin Group (USA) Inc., 375 Hudson Street, New York, New York 10014, USA
Penguin Group (Canada), 90 Eglinton Avenue East, Suite 700, Toronto, Ontario, Canada M4P 2Y3
(a division of Pearson Penguin Canada Inc.)
Penguin Ireland, 25 St Stephen's Green, Dublin 2, Ireland (a division of Penguin Books Ltd)
Penguin Group (Australia), 250 Camberwell Road, Camberwell, Victoria 3124, Australia
(a division of Pearson Australia Group Pty Ltd)
Penguin Books India Pvt Ltd, 11 Community Centre, Panchsheel Park, New Delhi – 110 017, India
Penguin Group (NZ), 67 Apollo Drive, Rosedale, Auckland 0632, New Zealand
(a division of Pearson New Zealand Ltd)
Penguin Books (South Africa) (Pty) Ltd, Block D, Rosebank Office Park, 181 Jan Smuts Avenue,
Parktown North, Gauteng 2193, South Africa

Penguin Books Ltd, Registered Offices: 80 Strand, London WC2R ORL, England

www.penguin.com

First published 2008
Published in paperback 2009
This revised and updated edition published 2012
001

Copyright © Julian Norridge, 2008, 2012

Typeset by Rowlands Phototypesetting Ltd, Bury St Edmunds, Suffolk
Printed in Great Britain by Clays Ltd, St Ives plc

978-0-7181-9393-5

www.greenpenguin.co.uk

ALWAYS LEARNING   **PEARSON**

For my father, Bobby Norridge, who gave me my love of sports. And to the women in my life – Susan, Helen, Zoë, Pippa and Jessica – who have had to put up with it ever since.

CONTENTS

ACKNOWLEDGEMENTS

A multitude of people have contributed to the writing of this book, many of them unknowingly. I am grateful to all the authors whose books I have shamelessly rifled. I'd like to single out the late Sir Derek Birley, not so much for information as inspiration. I have received valuable assistance from the librarians of the Rugby Football Union, the All England Lawn Tennis and Croquet Club and the Amateur Rowing Association. The staff of the London Library have been endlessly patient and helpful. At Penguin, Georgina Laycock and Alice Dawson have done everything to make the writing of the book as painless as possible and Georgina came up with endless useful and creative suggestions. I am grateful to Tim Waller for correcting so many of my mistakes – those that remain are, of course, entirely my responsibility. Many thanks too to my ever enthusiastic agent, Laura Morris. I have received valuable advice and suggestions from Anwer Bati, Donald Carroll, Michael Williamson, Gavin Weightman and my brother Simon Norridge. Above all I must thank my wife Susan not only for putting up with nine months of obsession, but positively encouraging it.

MAPS

British Sites of Historical Sporting Interest

Scotland inset

Republic of Ireland inset

England & Wales

Aintree
First Grand National run in February 1839

Rhiwabon, Denbighshire
Birthplace of Major Walter Clopton Wingfield, inventor of lawn tennis

WALES

Camarthenshire
Birthplace of John Graham Chambers, founder of the Amateur Athletics Club

Badminton, Gloucestershire
Where the game was invented... or renamed

Dublin
Birthplace of Thomas Doggett, founder of the first ever rowing race, 1716

Galway
The first mention of hockey appears in the Galway Statutes in 1527

REPUBLIC OF IRELAND

Cork
Home of the first ever sailing club, founded in 1720

Plymouth Hoe
Where Drake finished playing bowls before defeating the Armada

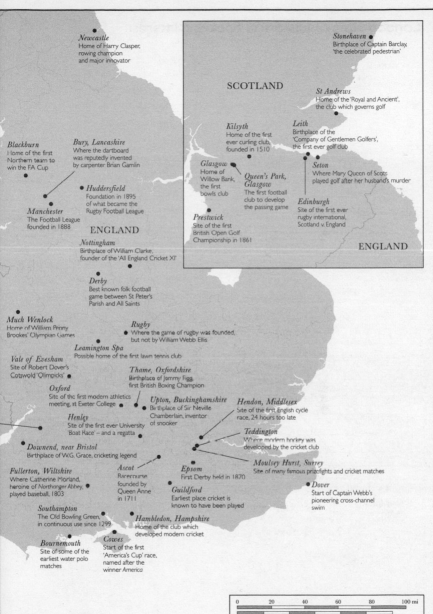

Newcastle
Home of Harry Clasper,
rowing champion
and major innovator

Stonehaven
Birthplace of Captain Barclay,
'the celebrated pedestrian'

SCOTLAND

St Andrews
Home of the 'Royal and Ancient',
the club which governs golf

Blackburn
Home of the first
Northern team to
win the FA Cup

Bury, Lancashire
Where the dartboard
was reputedly invented
by carpenter Brian Gamlin

Kilsyth
Home of the first
ever curling club,
founded in 1510

Leith
Birthplace of the
'Company of Gentlemen Golfers',
the first ever golf club

Huddersfield
Foundation in 1895
of what became the
Rugby Football League

Glasgow
Home of
Willow Bank,
the first
bowls club

**Queen's Park,
Glasgow**
The first football
club to develop
the passing game

Seton
Where Mary Queen of Scots
played golf after her husband's murder

Manchester
The Football League
founded in 1888

Prestwick
Site of the first
British Open Golf
Championship in 1861

Edinburgh
Site of the first ever
rugby international,
Scotland v. England

ENGLAND

ENGLAND

Nottingham
Birthplace of William Clarke,
founder of the 'All England Cricket XI'

Derby
Best known folk football
game between St Peter's
Parish and All Saints

Much Wenlock
Home of William Penny
Brookes' Olympian Games

Rugby
Where the game of rugby was founded,
but not by William Webb Ellis

Leamington Spa
Possible home of the first lawn tennis club

Vale of Evesham
Site of Robert Dover's
Cotswold 'Olimpicks'

Thame, Oxfordshire
Birthplace of Jammy Figg,
first British Boxing Champion

Oxford
Site of the first modern athletics
meeting, at Exeter College

Upton, Buckinghamshire
Birthplace of Sir Neville
Chamberlain, inventor
of snooker

Hendon, Middlesex
Site of the first English cycle
race, 24 hours too late

Henley
Site of the first ever University
'Boat Race' – and a regatta

Teddington
Where modern hockey was
developed by the cricket club

Downend, near Bristol
Birthplace of W.G. Grace, cricketing legend

Moulsey Hurst, Surrey
Site of many famous prizefights and cricket matches

Fullerton, Wiltshire
Where Catherine Morland,
heroine of Northanger Abbey,
played baseball, 1803

Ascot
Racecourse
founded by
Queen Anne
in 1711

Epsom
First Derby held in 1870

Dover
Start of Captain Webb's
pioneering cross-channel
swim

Guildford
Earliest place cricket is
known to have been played

Southampton
The Old Bowling Green,
in continuous use since 1299

Hambledon, Hampshire
Home of the club which
developed modern cricket

Bournemouth
Site of some of the
earliest water polo
matches

Cowes
Start of the first
'America's Cup' race,
named after the
winner America

0	20	40	60	80	100 mi

0	25	50	75	100	125	150 km

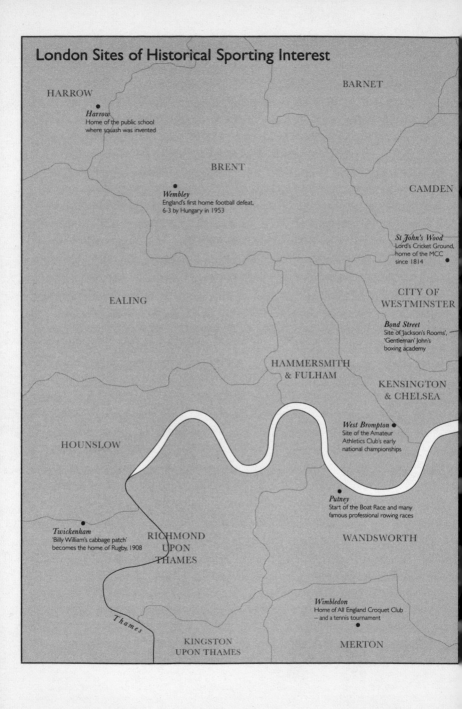

London Sites of Historical Sporting Interest

HARROW

● Harrow
Home of the public school
where squash was invented

BARNET

BRENT

● Wembley
England's first home football defeat,
6-3 by Hungary in 1953

CAMDEN

St John's Wood
Lord's Cricket Ground,
home of the MCC
since 1814 ●

EALING

CITY OF
WESTMINSTER

Bond Street
Site of 'Jackson's Rooms',
'Gentleman' John's
boxing academy

HAMMERSMITH
& FULHAM

KENSINGTON
& CHELSEA

West Brompton ●
Site of the Amateur
Athletics Club's early
national championships

HOUNSLOW

● Putney
Start of the Boat Race and many
famous professional rowing races

● Twickenham
'Billy William's cabbage patch'
becomes the home of Rugby, 1908

RICHMOND
UPON
THAMES

WANDSWORTH

Thames

Wimbledon
Home of All England Croquet Club
— and a tennis tournament
●

KINGSTON
UPON THAMES

MERTON

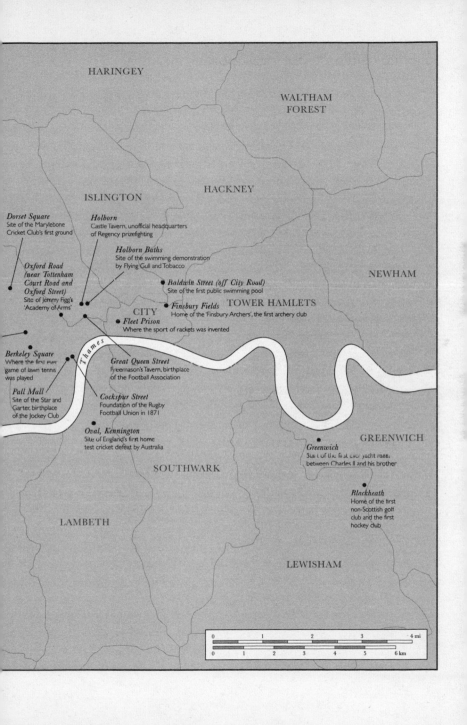

HARINGEY

WALTHAM
FOREST

HACKNEY

ISLINGTON

Dorset Square
Site of the Marylebone
Cricket Club's first ground

Holborn
Castle Tavern, unofficial headquarters
of Regency prizefighting

Holborn Baths
Site of the swimming demonstration
by Flying Gull and Tobacco

NEWHAM

*Oxford Road
(near Tottenham
Court Road and
Oxford Street)*
Site of Jemmy Figg's
'Academy of Arms'

● *Baldwin Street (off City Road)*
Site of the first public swimming pool

● *Finsbury Fields* TOWER HAMLETS
Home of the 'Finsbury Archers', the first archery club

CITY
● *Fleet Prison*
Where the sport of rackets was invented

Berkeley Square
Where the first ever
game of lawn tennis
was played

Great Queen Street
Freemason's Tavern, birthplace
of the Football Association

Pall Mall
Site of the Star and
Garter, birthplace
of the Jockey Club

Cockspur Street
Foundation of the Rugby
Football Union in 1871

Thames

Oval, Kennington
Site of England's first home
test cricket defeat by Australia

GREENWICH

Greenwich
Start of the first ever yacht race,
between Charles II and his brother

SOUTHWARK

Blackheath
Home of the first
non-Scottish golf
club and the first
hockey club

LAMBETH

LEWISHAM

| 0 | | 1 | | 2 | | 3 | | 4 mi |
| 0 | 1 | 2 | 3 | 4 | 5 | 6 km |

INTRODUCTION

IN THE BEGINNING, there were games. There always have been. As soon as our ancestors found they could spare a bit of time from hunting and gathering, they started playing around with whatever came to hand – sticks, stones, spears, each other – and competing. As Jonathan Swift said: 'Most sorts of diversion in men, children and other animals are in imitation of fighting.'

Over the centuries, games proliferated and spread. But they were mainly localized affairs, played between local people or local teams. If there were any rules – and often there weren't – they tended to be different from town to town and village to village. Quite often they were agreed between the contestants on the day. What the British did between the middle of the eighteenth century and the end of the nineteenth was to enable this localized game-playing to become globalized sport. They made it possible for a soccer team from Brazil to play one from France on equal terms; for a Russian tennis player to compete against a South African. The British didn't invent every modern sport, but they did invent most of them. Above all, they established the idea of sport that could be played around the world.

So how and why did this happen? The how is relatively easy. The British codified sets of rules according to which the different types of contests should be conducted. With the rulebooks came referees and umpires to see that the rules were observed, and regulatory bodies, both national and international, to ensure the orderly administration of each sport (and to keep an eye on the referees and umpires).

The why is a little more complex. You could just say that during those 150 years, the British were inventing the whole of the modern world. They were energetic, imaginative and creative. So is it any wonder that during that period they also invented modern sport? Well, yes. But there's more to it than that.

A game of two phases

You can roughly divide the development of sport in Britain into two phases. One took place from the middle to late eighteenth century, the other from the middle to late nineteenth century. The two are very different because Britain, in particular England, went through a huge change in the intervening years. The social historian Harold Perkin put it like this: 'Between 1780 and 1850 the English ceased to be one of the most aggressive, brutal, rowdy, outspoken, riotous, cruel and blood-thirsty nations in the world and became one of the most inhibited, polite, orderly, tender-minded, prudish and hypocritical.'

It has been called, rightly or wrongly, a 'civilizing' process. Its causes were complex. They included industrialization, mass migration from the countryside to the new cities, the growth of Empire and the development of international trade. It reflected the emergence of a new, respectable, socially aspiring and socially exclusive middle class which made the feel of the sports that developed in the nineteenth century very different from those that emerged in the eighteenth.

I think Perkin may have been a little harsh on the seventeenth century. Yes, it was rowdy, outspoken, riotous and probably cruel, but it was also fun-loving and open in an almost innocent way. The class system was markedly less rigid in England at that time than in the rest of Europe. The landed gentry, who felt secure both financially and socially, were willing to fraternize with the lower orders. A duke was happy to play cricket in a team captained by his gardener. The Prince of Wales entertained a pugilist to dinner at his house. The owner of a racehorse could develop a close working relationship with his groom or jockey. This had an effect on how early sport developed.

Follow the money!

So what began the process of regulation? In any investigation it's always wise to bear in mind the sage advice of Deep Throat in Watergate: Follow the money! In the eighteenth and much of the nineteenth centuries, most of the money belonged to the aristocracy and the landed gentry. And what many of them liked doing with their money more than anything else was . . . gambling. Joseph Strutt, in his *Sports and Pastimes of the People of England*, says that by 1801 (when the book was published) gambling had 'attained to a gigantic stature'. But the activities on which the rich – and the poor when they had the chance – wagered at this time were not always what we would now expect.

Consider this. Two teams of highly paid professionals, effectively owned by very rich men, are playing a game for a purse of 1000 guineas – the equivalent of nearly £100,000 in today's money. They are being watched by a large and raucous crowd, many of whom are drunk and nearly all of whom have money on the outcome. This is cricket in 1777.

Bowls, which these days we think of as an activity best accompanied by tea and chocolate biscuits, was also the cause of much rowdiness and reckless betting. Most bowling greens were attached to 'common drinking houses', which led Joseph Strutt to conclude that 'their play is seldom productive of much benefit, but more frequently becomes the prelude to drunkenness'.

Horse racing has always been the preserve of the rich, but by the eighteenth century it took place in front of large and appreciative crowds who, then as now, enjoyed having a flutter. 'Even horse-racing,' lamented Strutt, 'which anciently was considered as a liberal sport, and proper for the amusement of a gentleman, has been of late years degraded into a dangerous species of gambling, by no means the less deserving of censure, because it is fashionable and countenanced by persons of the highest rank and fortune.'

Such distinguished personages were also frequently the patrons of professional runners. One nobleman would pit his 'running footman' against the champion of another, generally for a sizeable purse. The race would be advertised, the crowds would come, bets would be laid. They might do the same for their watermen. Professional boxing was run on much the same lines, although boxers had the muscle to have more say in – and take more profit from – their exertions.

It was these frequently rowdy activities that were the first to be regulated. Partly at least because the rich wanted to know exactly what they were betting on. The earliest rules to be formulated – in 1743 – were for boxing, or prizefighting as it was then known. Golf, always an egalitarian game, followed shortly afterwards. The first arguably national sporting body was the Jockey Club, set up around 1750 to regulate horse racing. The Marylebone Cricket Club, which from the outset became the (not very efficient) guardian of the laws of cricket, was founded in 1787.

Boxing, horse racing and cricket were, in the main, sports which the upper classes paid the lower classes to conduct on their behalf (though many a lord enjoyed having a go at all three – including boxing, under controlled conditions). But there were no amateurs or professionals at this stage, because such a distinction had not yet been conceived of. It was the gentry who promulgated the rules in most cases – though not for boxing – because they had the natural authority; but they were generally just following developments which had been fashioned by the players they paid.

The rich also enjoyed games that they most definitely did play themselves. They delighted in riding, hunting, hawking and other such country pursuits. But they also indulged in (and wagered heavily on) sports which are more widespread today, such as golf, sailing and bowls. What became the Royal and Ancient Golf Club of St Andrews was founded in 1754 and continues to be the arbiter of the rules of the sport. The first yacht club was founded in 1775 by the Duke of Cumberland, younger brother of George III. Every grand house had a bowling green.

Then there were the sports of the common people. They played cricket, of course, and bowls. Skittles was popular in pubs, as were quoits and similar games. At fairs and festivals there would be running and jumping, various field sports such as putting the shot, and different kinds of folk wrestling in different parts of the country. There were a number of stick-and-ball games, the precursors of hockey, and above all, especially on high days and holidays, there was football.

Folk football was probably the most anarchic, raucous and violent game of all. From the Middle Ages onwards, it was beloved by the masses and by the gentry, many of whom were happy to roll up their breeches and wade in. The rules, such as they were, varied from place to place; but most participants would have paid them scant regard even if they had known what they were. The fact that there were occasional fatalities seemed no reason to curtail such a traditional and enjoyable activity – until towards the end of the eighteenth century.

It was the beginning of the 'civilizing' process. Shopkeepers became fearful for their premises (the game was often played right through the streets of a town or village), magistrates became concerned about chaos on the public highway and for the first time the forces of law and order had the power and the numbers to put a stop to such riotous behaviour. That's why Strutt could say in 1801 that football of late years 'is but little practised'.

The story of how this game – and others – was transformed and revived is the beginning of the second stage of the development of British sport. And it started with a sea change in the nature of some uniquely British institutions which were certainly not open to the football-loving masses.

Enter the public schools

In the early part of the nineteenth century, public schools were in a lamentable state. Conditions were appalling, education was basic, brutality was rife and pupil rebellions were common. In the early 1840s, the future prime minister, Lord Salisbury, described how a boy called Troughton Major, drunk on ten pints of beer, had held a burning candle in a fellow Etonian's mouth. 'Really now Eton has become perfectly insupportable,' he wrote glumly to his father. 'They kicked me and pulled my hair and punched me and hit me so hard as ever they could for twenty minutes; and now I am aching in every joint and hardly am able to write this.' Not surprising, then, that numbers had fallen dramatically. In 1835, Charterhouse was down to 99 pupils. By 1844, Harrow had just 69.

Change was brought about in large part by the man who took over as Headmaster of Rugby School in 1828, Dr Thomas Arnold. He played a key role in the civilizing process. He saw the public school as the perfect vehicle for initiating the emerging middle classes, newly enriched by industrialization, into the attitudes and aspirations of a reformed upper class. Their children would become the colonial administrators and governors, the senior churchmen, the politicians, statesmen, lawyers and professionals of booming British society.

Arnold himself cared little about what his pupils did on the playing field. But his disciples quickly adopted the view that there was no better way to achieve his aims than through team sports. In his classic novel *Tom Brown's Schooldays*, set at Rugby, Thomas Hughes has a master talk

'The conversation during the match': an original illustration from Tom Brown's Schooldays

to Tom about team sport – he was talking about cricket, but it could have been any other team game – as follows: 'The discipline and reliance on one another which it teaches is so valuable, I think ... it ought to be such an unselfish game. It merges the individual in the eleven; he doesn't play that he might win, but that his side may.' Substitute 'country' or even 'empire' for 'side' in that last phrase and you get the idea.

But for the team to win, you had to have competition. And for competition to work, you needed rules. That is what each public school, starting with Rugby, set about trying to devise. And that is what drove the second phase of the development of sport.

Fair play and muscular Christianity

These rules were underpinned by two new concepts. One was the idea of fair play. The Victorians were not renowned for their sense of fairness towards the urban poor or the industrialized working class – read Dickens – nor towards the 'natives' of the colonies. But among the aspiring middle class, at school or within society at large, fair play was seen as essential. Failure to conform to convention, to do the right thing, was thought to be potentially disastrous. Remember some of the words that Perkin used: the Victorian English were inhibited, polite, orderly and prudish. But they could also, as our story will show, be deeply hypocritical.

The other new concept was that sport was good for you, not just physically but also spiritually. Sport became idealized. Instead of being fun and a great way to gamble, it was decided that it developed 'character'. Competition was fine, but winning was not everything. Playing the game was what it was all about. The new idea was called 'muscular Christianity'. The ruthless determination of the 'professional' sportsman was reviled. The idea of the gentleman amateur, who played sport for sport's sake, began to emerge.

The rules

To allow these gentlemen to continue to play their beloved games, a problem needed to be overcome. In the mid-nineteenth century, before the advent of cheap rail travel, most competition was within each public school – between 'houses' or whatever organizational unit the school espoused. The rules were all different – and there was no reason to standardize them. But when these young men left their public schools and went on to Oxford and Cambridge, they wanted to continue playing the sports they loved and which they felt were so honourable and worthwhile. In order to play with and against people who'd been to other schools, they needed to agree a new set of regulations. That is how the rules of many modern sports – football, rugby, hockey, athletics, rowing and many others – came into existence. They were devised so that gentlemen amateurs could go on playing the games they loved. This was the rationale for the sports of the second phase.

Some sports took the idea of the gentleman amateur to extremes. Rowing, for instance, excluded not just professionals but anyone who earned his living through manual labour. Grace Kelly's father, who built much of Philadelphia, was banned from rowing at Henley because he had once been apprenticed to a bricklayer. Hockey players went to a different extreme. Their game, they said, was designed to be played as a recreation by gentlemen as gentlemen; therefore they banned any kind of organized competition, a ruling which lasted until after World War II.

The sports of the first phase were developed because they were fun and because they offered great opportunities for gambling. Most of the sports of the second phase were developed because they were good for your character, at least if you were a gentleman. The two were not mutually exclusive, of course. People who played cricket or who boxed might well think what they did was character-building, while those who played rugby or hockey might also have had a lot of fun. But the difference affected the attitudes of those who ran the sports.

Those gambling-based sports which had been regulated early on – boxing, horse racing, cricket, golf and sailing – always tolerated the idea of the professional (though the gentlemen (amateurs) and the players (professionals) had to use different changing rooms at Lord's until the 1950s). A few of the second-phase sports, notably football and rugby league, quickly gave in to the idea of professionalism. But many others, such as tennis, athletics, rowing, swimming and rugby union, insisted on maintaining their treasured amateur status until long after World War II.

Market forces and the emergence of sport as a major global business eventually forced them to change. But a question remains. Did the differing attitudes which helped shape the sports the British gave to the world eventually have an impact on our ability to play them in the fiercely competitive environment of today?

I.
BOXING

The bulldog breed

BOXING, WROTE THE early sporting journalist Pierce Egan, who was to become as famous in his day as the champions he wrote about, had 'raised the valour and manly intrepidity of the English nation, eminently conspicuous above all others!'

Without it, he went on in his first book, *Boxiana* (1812), the English character might 'act too *refined* and the thoroughbred bull-dog degenerate into the *whining* puppy! Not for the British the long knives of the Dutch, Italian stilettos or French or German sticks and stones – in England the FIST only is used . . . The fight done, the hand is given in token of peace . . . As a national trait we feel no hesitation in declaring that it is wholly – *British*!'

And so, for nearly two centuries, it was. From around 1680, prize-fighting, as the bare-knuckle game was properly called, was a major sport in Britain and in no other country. Even the Americans did not embrace the fight game until well into the nineteenth century, and then it was mainly under the influence of immigrants from England and Ireland.

For much of this time, the sport was technically illegal, but this only seemed to add to its attractions. It was supported by royalty (even the King attended a fight in the early days), by members of the aristocracy and by Government ministers. It was fêted by poets such as Pope, Swift, Keats and Byron, by writers such as Dr Johnson and William

Hazlitt and by artists including Hogarth, Blake, Turner, Gillray and the Cruikshank brothers. It was given wide coverage by the emerging popular press. Sporting men at all levels of society found it hugely popular and the prizefighters themselves were among the most notorious celebrities of their day.

This devotion to the ring allows Britain to claim that it invented the modern sport of boxing. But of course the basic idea goes back rather further . . .

Round one

Boxing began when the first person raised his fists in play – or in anger – against someone else. There is some evidence that it existed as a sport 6000 years ago in modern-day Ethiopia, then spread to Egypt and the Mediterranean. The earliest images we have are from Sumerian relief carvings in the third millennium BC. There are some Egyptian images of

Ancient boxer, from a fragment of pottery
found at Knossos, around 1600 BC

bare-fisted fights. A vase from Minoan Crete (around 1500 BC) shows boxers with helmets (health and safety?) and what look like metal plates attached to their fists (maybe not!). A relief sculpture from Egyptian Thebes 150 years later shows boxers fighting in front of spectators.

The Greeks took a while to warm to the sport. It didn't become an official Olympic event until 688 BC, at the 23rd Olympiad. The rules were that contestants wore oxhide thongs to protect their hands, there were no interruptions or 'rounds' and the fight went on until one man admitted defeat by lifting a finger or alternatively collapsed in a heap.

Homer recounts a contest in the *Iliad* – the first of many literary accounts of boxing. A challenge is put before the Achaians, designed to attract the two men who are 'the best among you'. The winner is to walk away with a 'hard-working jenny' – a female donkey – while the loser gets a two-handed goblet. (Clearly Homer hadn't foreseen *Antiques Roadshow*.) Up steps 'huge and powerful' Epeios, son of Panopeus. He dares anyone to challenge him, giving an inviting picture of what he'll do to anyone who does:

> I will smash his skin apart and break his bones on each other.
> Let those who care for him wait nearby in a huddle about him
> To carry him out, after my fists have beaten him under.

Only Euryalos, 'a godlike man', takes up the challenge. Encouraged by his second – 'the spear-famed son of Tydeus' – he pulls on the boxing belt and dons thongs 'carefully cut from the hide of a ranging ox'.

> The two men, girt up, strode into the midst of the circle
> And faced each other, and put up their ponderous hands at the same time
> And closed, so that their heavy arms were crossing each other,
> And there was a fierce grinding of teeth, the sweat began to run
> Everywhere from their bodies. Great Epeios came in, and hit him
> As he peered out from his guard, on the cheek, and he could no longer
> Keep his feet, but where he stood the glorious limbs gave.

Statue of a seated boxer, first century BC:
note the strapping on his arms and fists.

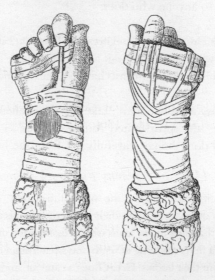

Drawing of similar strapping on the right hand
of a statue of a boxer from Sorrento.

As in the water roughened by the north wind a fish jumps
In the weed of the beach-break, then the dark water closes above him,
So Euryalos left the ground from the blow, but great-hearted Epeios
Took him in his arms and set him upright, and his true companions
Stood about him, and led him out of the circle, feet dragging
As he spat up the thick blood and rolled his head over on one side.

(From Book XXIII of Homer's *Iliad*, translated by Richmond Lattimore)

Which sounds pretty much like a modern bout, although there must be doubts about Euryalos' defensive skills and it's not clear that Epeios' apparent sportsmanship is quite credible after what he said in his challenge.

Over the centuries, the simple thong was reinforced with a hard leather strip over the knuckles that was designed to cut opponents. The Romans added metal studs to create the *cestus*. During the Republic even aristocrats started fighting, but this was eventually banned by Augustus. Under the Empire, boxing ceased to be a sport and became instead a gruesome entertainment for the masses. An even nastier hand-covering was developed, a vicious, spur-like device called a *myrmex*, or 'limb piercer'. Fights between gladiator slaves were often to the death.

In the fourth century AD, with the rise of Christianity and the decline of the Empire, these cruel excesses were finally abolished. Pugilism in Europe seemingly disappeared – at least there is no formal record of it – until it re-emerged in London 1300 years later.

Here I am, Jemmy Figg from Thame

In 1681, the *Protestant Mercury* reported on a formal boxing bout which took place in London. By 1698, we know that regular bouts were being staged at the Royal Theatre in London. These were bare-knuckle fights, with virtually no rules. Fists were the main weapons but wrestling was also allowed: a man could grab and throw his opponent, then jump on him and continue pulverizing him while he was down.

The boxers, who were often local champions, fought for an agreed purse. Numerous side bets were placed by their supporters and the enthusiastic crowds. It was a rumbustious and brutally crude activity and quickly became immensely popular.

The first person to introduce a measure of artfulness to the sport was James Figg. He was born in Thame in Oxfordshire sometime around 1695, probably the son of poor farmers. We know that by 1714 he was in London studying under the well-known 'Master of the Noble Science of Defence', Timothy Buck of Clare Market. Before the end of that year Figg himself had qualified as a 'master'.

James Figg, the first Champion of England: he made boxing
a matter of skill rather than brute force

At the time, the 'Noble Science' embraced not just fisticuffs but swords and cudgels or quarterstaffs. Figg seems to have been highly proficient at all three. Years later, the Marquis de Bretagne recalled seeing a 'certain Prize fighter called Figg, who handles a broad Sword with the greatest Dexterity of any Man alive'. Figg seems to have practised his art and made his name by appearing at fairs, including the famous one at the Bowling Green in Southwark. 'Here I am, Jemmy Figg from Thame – I will fight any man in England' was the cry with which he used to attract the crowds to his booth.

In 1719, possibly under the patronage of the Earl of Peterborough, he opened an 'academy of arms' near his house in Oxford Road, just off Oxford Street and not far from what is now Tottenham Court Road. His business card, which may have been designed by the young

James Figg's flyer for his 'Academy of Arms' in Oxford Road,
signed by the young William Hogarth.

William Hogarth, read 'James Figg. Master of the Noble Science of Defence on the right hand in Oxford Road near Adam and Eve Court – teaches gentlemen the use of the small backsword and quarterstaff at home and abroad'.

Figg's influence on boxing was huge. He adapted his skill at fencing for use in the ring, teaching his pupils to parry and cross-punch just as a fencer parries and ripostes. For the first time, boxing became a matter of skill rather than pure brute force. His pupils ranged from aspiring professional prizefighters to gentlemen about town who came to learn the manly arts and watch the top fighters of the day exhibiting their talents.

That same year Figg declared himself to be Champion of England, an informal but far from idle claim as he had already beaten all the other major fighters of the time. In his career he is believed to have fought more than 270 bouts and lost only one of them. These fights were talked up in a style that would make Muhammad Ali proud. In one newspaper advertisement, one of Figg's most frequent challengers, Rowland Bennet of Ireland, said that having seen Figg practise, he was 'fully persuaded that if the proper method is executed against him, he (like Sampson with his hair off) is like other men'. In the ensuing battle, Figg behaved like Samson with his hair on and duly won.

The only person ever to beat Figg was a pipe-maker from Gravesend called Ned Sutton. Figg immediately claimed that he had been ill and challenged Sutton to a rematch, which he won. Sutton in turn then called for a third deciding bout. Like many of Figg's fights, it was a 'trial of skill', which involved all three disciplines, rather than a 'trial of manhood', where only fists were used. The antagonists fought first with swords 'to first blood', then with fists and finally with cudgels. The event drew a large crowd, including the Prime Minister, Sir Robert Walpole, the poets Pope, Swift and Colley Cibber, and many ladies of fashion – this despite the fact that boxing was technically illegal at the time. When the fighting started, Figg spilt his own blood first with his own sword, which didn't count, and then cut Sutton's shoulder. In the fisticuffs battle the momentum swung back and forth until finally Figg prevailed. And in the cudgels contest Figg quickly broke Sutton's knee, which brought the matter to a swift conclusion.

Figg also acted as a fight promoter, including a spectacular 'battle' in 1733 between the Lincolnshire drover John Whitacre and a Venetian gondolier, which was watched by George II from a specially con-structed royal box. Figg retired from active fighting in 1730 and died in 1734, still only in his late 30s.

Jack Broughton and his rules

After Figg's retirement, one of his leading pupils, George Taylor, claimed the Championship. But he wasn't to be Champion of England for long. Within a couple of years he was defeated by the great Jack Broughton, who was to become known as the 'Father of English Boxing'.

Broughton's first sporting achievement had nothing to do with the ring. In 1730, he won London's annual rowing race in which six watermen who have just completed their apprenticeship vie for the prize of 'Doggett's Coat and Badge'. (The race, which continues today, is

Jack Broughton, Champion and author of the first
written rules applied to any British sport

one of the world's oldest sporting events.) At the time, Broughton was plying his trade as a ferryman from Hungerford Stairs, on the north side of the Thames where Hungerford Bridge now stands. We don't know when he began training at James Figg's academy, but by the

1730s he was taking on and defeating some of the leading prizefighters of the day.

After he won the Championship, Broughton became the major attraction at Taylor's Booth for a number of years. He attracted some influential patrons, including the Duke of Cumberland, the younger son of George II. In February 1741, Broughton was challenged for the title by a relative unknown, a former coachman from Yorkshire called George Stevenson. Broughton was backed as ever by Cumberland, but Stevenson was taken up by the Duke's older brother, Frederick, Prince of Wales. This royal rivalry gave the bout an added edge and attracted a massive amount of attention.

The fight took place at Taylor's Booth in Tottenham Court Road. A large crowd gathered outside. When the doors opened, the pit where the common people stood was quickly filled. Then a cheer went up as the Duke of Cumberland arrived in the gallery, accompanied in uniform by Captain John Godfrey (who six years later published the first book on boxing, *A Treatise upon the Useful Science of Defence*) and a crowd of supporters, including several ladies. They sat on one side. Shortly afterwards they were followed by the Prince of Wales and his favourites, including, according to a contemporary report, 'a bevy of easy-virtued ladies' whose eyes betrayed the effects of last night's dissipation. They took their seats on the opposite side.

At noon a trumpet sounded to announce the start of the main event. Stevenson and then Broughton made their entrance onto the stage. Broughton was nearly six feet tall, with a powerful, muscular frame. Stevenson was shorter but broader and more heavily built. Broughton made the first move, feinting and then trying to throw a right, but Stevenson jumped back to avoid the blow. The crowd was accustomed to Broughton's skills, but few had expected Stevenson to be almost a match for them. The fight continued at a breathless pace for more than half an hour – there were no rules and so no rounds at that time. Captain Godfrey, who was acting as Broughton's umpire, later recounted the story.

*The fight between Broughton and Yorkshire coachman George
Stevenson, who died of his injuries within a month*

After a most desperate conflict of thirty-five minutes, both being against the
rails, and the Coachman attempting to get the whip-hand of Broughton, the
latter, by his superior genius, got such a lock upon Stevenson as no math-
ematician could have devised a better. There he held him by this artificial
lock, depriving him of all power of rising or falling, till, resting his head
for three or four minutes upon his [Stevenson's] back, he found himself
recovering, then loosed his hold. By this manoeuvre Broughton became as a
new man, and on setting to again he gave the Coachman a tremendous blow
as hard as any he had given him in the whole battle, so that he could no
longer stand, and his brave, contending heart, though with reluctance, was
forced to yield.

When the coachman fell and didn't get up, a distraught Broughton is
said to have cried 'Good God. What have I done? I've killed him. So
help me God, I'll never fight again.' Stevenson did indeed die within
the month.

Two years later, with the help of his rich backers, Broughton opened his own amphitheatre and boxing academy. And, perhaps in reaction to the Stevenson incident, he laid down a set of rules 'to be observed in all battles on the stage'. They were 'agreed by several gentlemen at Broughton's Amphitheatre, Tottenham Court Road, August 16, 1743'. This was a historic moment. These were the first written rules to be applied to any sport. Broughton only intended them to govern bouts taking place in his amphitheatre, but they were quickly adopted by most other venues and continued to be the basic rules of boxing for the next 100 years.

They were still pretty crude. The rules allowed wrestling moves provided they were above the belt (it was forbidden to seize an opponent 'by the ham, the breeches or any part below the waist'); they also permitted hitting below the belt and hair-pulling. But they ruled out hitting a man when he was down or when he was on his knees. They also provided for a 'square of a Yard' to be chalked in the middle of the stage; when a man was knocked down, his seconds had half a minute to get him back up to the mark or 'he shall be deemed a beaten man'.

Broughton's other great innovation was the introduction of 'mufflers' – the precursor to boxing gloves – for use when sparring in order to protect his frequently aristocratic pupils 'from the Inconveniency of black Eyes, broken Jaws and bloody Noses'. In his teaching, Broughton built on the innovations of James Figg to develop a much more scientific approach to boxing. His own defensive skills were said to be so great that he was hardly ever struck during a match.

Undefeated, Broughton went into semi-retirement in the mid-1740s, concentrating on teaching and promoting matches. But in 1750 he was persuaded back into the ring to face a butcher called Jack Slack, who was claimed to be the grandson of James Figg. Broughton said he accepted the challenge because Slack had insulted his manhood. Another more pressing reason might have been that his patron, the Duke of Cumberland, thought he could make a lot of money on the match. Broughton started well but after fourteen minutes he received a blow above the nose which caused his eyes to swell shut. According to Pierce Egan, Cumberland shouted: 'What are you about, Broughton?

You can't fight. You're beat.' Broughton bravely replied: 'I can't see my man, your Highness; I am blind, but not beat; only let me be placed before my antagonist, and he shall not gain the day yet.' But it wasn't to be. Cumberland lost £10,000 on the bout and Broughton never fought again.

But he went on teaching for another twenty-five years. He was also a Yeoman of the Guard and was almost certainly the John Broughton who, as one of the King's bodyguards, was with George II at the Battle of Dettingen in 1743, the last time an English monarch led his army into battle. He died on 8 January 1789 and was buried in Westminster Abbey.

The language of boxing

The world of prizefighting has given the English language many familiar phrases, some obvious, some less so. The obvious ones include delivering 'a knockout blow'; doing something devious, which is seen as 'below the belt'; taking advantage by 'hitting someone when they're down'; and someone in difficulties who is 'on the ropes'. You can also proclaim yourself as a contender by 'throwing your hat into the ring'.

The less obvious ones are more complex. Under Jack Broughton's rules, a line was scratched or marked in the centre of the surface of the ring. At the beginning of each round each fighter had to put his toes up against this line to prove he was fit to continue – hence the expressions 'up to the mark' and 'up to scratch'. In the early days, the purse or prize money that was being fought for was hung on one of the posts that marked out the ring, which were known as stakes. Hence such expressions as 'stake money', 'playing for high stakes' and 'stakeholder'. If a fight was inconclusive, the referee would indicate that it was over by pulling up the posts which formed the ring. This was called 'drawing the stakes'. Which is the origin of the term 'draw'.

Regency Boximania

In 1750, the year Jack Slack took the title from Broughton, an Act of Parliament reaffirmed that prizefighting was illegal. It was viewed by the courts as an affray or an assault. This was not decreed for the benefit or protection of the poor fighters. It had much more to do with a widespread nervousness in the second half of the eighteenth century about large, unruly gatherings. The law continued to be widely ignored, but its reiteration may have had something to do with bringing about a temporary decline in interest among the gentry around this time.

A more likely reason was that for the next thirty years, prizefighting was plagued by corruption. Fight after fight was thrown and it became a dangerous sport for a man of fashion – or anyone else – to risk his money on. But, in the 1780s, the sport underwent a revival when Tom Johnson took over as champion. He was seen as a decent man and an accomplished fighter and won support from members of the aristocracy and William Windham MP, a friend of Dr Johnson and a future cabinet minister. More to the point, during his era the sport once again began to attract the attention of royalty, in the portly form of the Prince of Wales and his two younger brothers, the Dukes of York and Clarence.

As prizefighting was still illegal, the princes had to be very circumspect. But there is strong evidence that the Prince attended a number of fights between 1786 and 1788. There have even been suggestions that he arranged fights himself and gave active support to his 'chairman' – as in the man who carried his sedan chair – Tom Tring. It seems almost certain that he attended the important fight in which 'Gentleman' John Jackson beat Tom Futrell (sometimes spelled as Fewterel) in 1788 – his presence is recorded in a print by James Gillray. But his active involvement was about to be curtailed. In August 1788 he was present at a fight near Brighton in which one of the participants died. William Windham, who was also there, took swift action to limit the potentially damaging publicity but further royal attendance at fights was seen to be too dangerous. And this nervousness was made all the greater later in the year when, in the words of Sir Derek Birley in *Sport and the Making of Britain*, George III 'aroused hopes of a Regency by stepping from his coach in Windsor Great Park and addressing an oak tree as the King of Prussia'.

James Gillray's print of the fight between Tom Futrell (left) and 'Gentleman' John Jackson. The Prince of Wales is in the front row, just behind Jackson

The support of rich patrons was to be vital to the sport over the next forty years, which many regard as prizefighting's golden age. As well as royalty and nobility, patrons came from the landowning gentry and the world of business. Because fights were technically illegal, they couldn't be widely advertised. No advance tickets could be sold and gate receipts were therefore unpredictable. Prize money, which could range from fifty pounds to a thousand or more, had to be put up beforehand. This was the role of the private patron. He put up the stake and pocketed the proceeds if his man won, though he would generally pay his champion a percentage. The two fighters then split the money taken at the door.

The fighters

The men who actually fought in the prize ring, however, were mainly from the unskilled working class. Big Ben Brain, who beat Tom Johnson to become champion in 1791, was a 'coalheaver' from Bristol. When he became too ill to defend his title – he died in 1794 – the championship passed to Daniel Mendoza from a Jewish immigrant family in the East End. He favoured the 'scientific' method of boxing, using his feet to get out of trouble, and early in his career he opened a

*Gillray print of Daniel Mendoza: he favoured
the 'scientific' method of fighting*

boxing academy and wrote a book called *The Art of Boxing*. Pierce Egan thought him unrivalled in teaching his art. He wasn't so masterful at finance, however, and was in and out of debtors' prison. He went on fighting until he was 55 and died in relative poverty.

Subsequent champions included Jem Belcher, a popular and courageous boxer, again from Bristol and a butcher by trade. His brother

Tom was also a respected fighter and later became the landlord of the Castle Tavern in Holborn, which became the *de facto* headquarters of boxing. Jem lost his title to fellow Bristolian Hen Pearce (inevitably known as the 'Game Chicken') in 1805, not long after he lost an eye in a rackets game. Pearce was succeeded by John Gully, another butcher, who subsequently gave up the game and his craft to become in turn a coal dealer, bookmaker, racehorse owner and Member of Parliament.

Tom Cribb, who became known simply as 'The Champion', was a sailor who also originally hailed from Bristol. As we shall see, he fought some memorable fights and was later the landlord of the Union Arms in Panton Street near Haymarket, where, now renamed after him, you'll find his achievements are still celebrated. His successor was Bill Neat, yet another butcher from Bristol, who went back to his trade after he was defeated by fellow butcher Tom Spring (real name Winter, but clearly an optimist) from Fownhope in Herefordshire. Spring was regarded by Egan as the last champion of the golden age. When he retired in 1824, he took over the licence of the Castle Tavern from Tom Belcher.

Two fighters stand out from the solid British working-class background of most of the top boxers of the day. Bill Richmond was never champion but he had a long and successful career and became almost a father figure in the world of prizefighting. Two things about him were remarkable. One was that, almost alone among fighters, he had completed an apprenticeship – as a cabinetmaker. He was a skilled craftsman. The other was that he was black. He was a former slave from near New York who was brought to England as a servant of the Duke of Northumberland. When he began in the London ring in 1804 he lost his first two fights but then, apart from a defeat by Tom Cribb, he won the next eleven. He was renowned for his ability to punch and then withdraw. He became a successful teacher – Pierce Egan said he was 'intellectual, witty and well-informed'. He was a careful and resourceful man who later became the successful landlord of another important boxing pub, the Horse and Dolphin in St Martin's Lane.

Bill Richmond, a former slave who became
a renowned prizefighter and teacher

But he is probably best known as what we would now term the manager of another former slave, Tom Molyneaux from Virginia, who had won his freedom through boxing. His challenge to Tom Cribb for the championship in December 1810 was seen almost as an assault on the national character. It had not been a good year for Britain. The King had gone mad again and Wellington was bogged down in Spain in the war against Napoleon. Defeat for Cribb would be a further blow to the country's dented morale. In front of a large and hostile crowd at Copthall Common near East Grinstead, Molyneaux started well and seemed to have the upper hand. At the end of the twenty-eighth round Cribb was unconscious and in no shape to come up to the mark. But his wily second immediately lodged a complaint of foul play with the far from impartial referee, Sir Thomas Ap Rhys. By the time it was dismissed after a lengthy argument, Cribb was back on his feet and Molyneaux, more used to the warmth of Virginia than the frost of a December night in Sussex, was shivering with cold. Cribb took just five

The end of the battle between Tom Cribb and Tom Molyneaux:
note the look of shock on Bill Richmond's face

more rounds to finish him off. British honour, if it could be called that, had been saved.

The second exception was 'Gentleman' John Jackson. As the son of a successful builder, he was a member of the middle class and in his career he was to milk every ounce of advantage he could from this status. He first made his mark by defeating Tom Futrell in the presence of the Prince of Wales in 1788. Nine months later he was defeated by the relatively unknown George Ingleston, 'the Brewer', when he slipped on a wet floor and broke a bone in his leg. He offered to continue tied to a chair, but his opponent declined. He didn't fight again for six years but when he did it was against Daniel Mendoza for the championship. He won in just eleven minutes, in part by grabbing Mendoza's imprudently long hair and pulling him onto the punch.

It is what he did next that marks Jackson out. After just three fights, he retired from the ring to set up a boxing academy at 13 Bond Street. 'Jackson's Rooms' were grander than anything seen before and quickly attracted a clientele from the aristocracy and the gentry. Lord Byron was among his pupils and used to refer to him as the 'Professor of Pugilism'. On the strength of his success Jackson became known as the 'Commander-in-Chief' of the prize ring. Whenever he attended a fight, which he did often, it was customary for him to be asked to act as referee. He was, said Pierce Egan 'the link that keeps the whole chain together'.

From 1802 onwards, he began organizing gloved exhibition bouts at the Fives Court in St Martin's Lane. These events were held for the 'benefit' of individual fighters. The bill might start with novices trying to catch a patron's eye, then minor fighters who were paid a small sum

The Fives Court in St Martin's Lane, where exhibition bouts with gloves were organized: three shillings for the rabble and a guinea for gentlefolk

for their appearance and finally the leading fighters of the day, who appeared for the benefit of their colleague (and in the expectation of the favour being returned). The most elegant and 'scientific' were Tom Belcher and Bill Richmond. The court could hold up to 1000 people. The general public paid three shillings a head while the elite, who had their own balcony, contributed a guinea. The exhibitions were highly popular because they offered a convenient location free from pros-ecution and you could buy a ticket in advance. Egan called the Fives

Court 'an animated inspiring lounge for the nobility and the heavy swells and ... an attraction in general to the public'. And they had a real impact: they lent the sport respectability, they introduced new fighters and they helped develop the skills which were to form the basis of modern boxing.

In 1814, after Napoleon had abdicated and was exiled to Elba, several allied sovereigns were invited to London by the Prince Regent. John Jackson helped organize and present an exhibition of gloved fisticuffs at Lord Lowther's house in Pall Mall, attended by Alexander, Tsar of all the Russias, the King of Prussia and his three sons and Marshal Blücher, who had led the allied forces. Tom Belcher, Tom Cribb, Bill Richmond and Jackson himself took part. That same year, Jackson helped found the Pugilistic Club, which included the Royal Dukes of York and Clarence and 118 other noblemen and gentlemen. They each subscribed an annual amount to provide guaranteed but fairly modest purses for forthcoming fights, supporting but by no means replacing private backers.

The club met at Jackson's Rooms and was committed to promoting fair play and exposing corruption. But it also liked a bit of a flourish. It had its own ring stakes, which were painted with the letters PC; while

'Jackson's Rooms' in Bond Street, where Byron learned boxing
from the man he called the 'Professor of Pugilism'

its members enjoyed wearing a uniform of blue and buff, with yellow kerseymere waistcoats with 'P.C.' engraved on their buttons. The club was almost certainly modelled on the Jockey Club and the MCC, which regulated two of the other major gambling sports of the day, racing and cricket. But unlike them – and under a very different kind of pressure – it was not long-lived.

One of Jackson's last acts was to provide eighteen prizefighters – including himself, Tom Cribb, Tom Belcher, Bill Richmond and Tom Spring – to guard the entrance to Westminster Abbey at the coronation of George IV in 1820. Just who they were guarding the entrance against is not clear – some have suggested supporters of the King's much-abused wife, Caroline of Brunswick. We don't know. What we do know is that the pugilists were dressed as 'pages'. They must have been quite a sight.

The Fancy

The eclectic, eccentric, rumbustious collection of people from all strata of society who were devoted to bare-knuckle fighting – or 'milling' as it was often called – were universally known as 'the Fancy'. So what would they have experienced? What was a prizefight like in the era of 'Regency Boximania'?

The preliminaries involved raising the stake money, lodging it with a stakeholder and drawing up the articles of agreement that would govern the fight, always based on Jack Broughton's rules. Once everything was settled, word about the fight would spread among the aficionados from all levels of society who followed the sport, 'the Fancy'. But, for fear of alerting the magistrates, no details would be given of where the bout would take place until the last moment. This was almost always, again for fear of the law, in the countryside. Moulsey Hurst and the surrounding area near Kingston in Surrey was popular, particularly with the Pugilistic Club. It was also convenient for the Duke of Clarence's estate at Bushy Park. But often the Fancy had to go much further afield.

A day or two before the fight the location would become available at the well-known sporting pubs in London, such as Tom Belcher's Castle in Holborn and Bill Richmond's Horse and Dolphin in St Martin's Lane. Occasionally, a starting point for the journey would be specified and at some unholy hour of the morning legions of the Fancy would gather, some armed with fishing rods, shotguns or other such props to disguise their true purpose. Crowds of 20,000 to 30,000 were quite common, so for hours beforehand the roads to the location would be packed with coach and fours, post-chaises, vehicles of all descriptions, riders and pedestrians representing all levels of society.

'It was a union of all ranks,' wrote Egan of the crowd at one big fight, 'from the *brilliant* of the highest class in the circle of the CORINTH-IANS, down to the *Dusty Bob* gradation in society; and even a *shade* or two below that. Lots of the UPPER HOUSE; the LOWER house, and the *flash* house. Proprietors of splendid parks and demesnes; inmates from proud and lofty mansions; groups from the most respect-able dwellings; thousands from the peaceable cot – and myriads of *coves* from no houses at all; in a word, it was a *conglomeration* of the *Fancy*.'

Sometimes bouts were held at racecourses, where spectators could use the grandstand. On other occasions special stands could be put up because the organizers were confident there would be no magisterial interference. This didn't necessarily imply corruption; many magis-trates were sympathetic to the noble art. One observer at the second fight between Cribb and Molyneaux noticed that 'all the magistrates in the county of Rutland were there'. (They'd just held one of their regular administrative meetings nearby.) But more often than not there were no seats, just standing room for spectators and an outer circle of carriages, wagons and riders on horseback.

In the centre there were often two rings, one inside the other. The outer ring had several purposes. It served as a crowd-break and was patrolled by professional pugilists to keep the unruly mob at bay. It was also where the backers and their swell friends watched the fight. And it accommodated the two umpires – usually gentlemen, one appointed by each fighter – and the referee. Unlike boxing today, the referee at a prizefight was only there to adjudicate in a dispute between the

The typical layout of a prizefight in the Regency period:
this one is between John Gully and Bob Gregson

umpires. Because there were so few rules, the umpires' main task was timekeeping. Under Broughton's rules, a round ended when one of the fighters fell, so it might last anything from a few seconds to half an hour. The umpires' job was to make sure the fallen man was back up to the mark at the end of thirty seconds. Not surprisingly, rounds got shorter as the fight wore on.

The inner ring, which could range in size from 18 to 48 feet square, was for the boxers and their seconds. Each fighter was allowed a 'kneeman', on whose leg he would sit between rounds (stools came in much later), and a 'bottleman', who had water and a sponge and maybe a flask of brandy for emergencies. When the fighters first arrived, generally decked out in the kind of finery that befitted a glamorous celebrity, they would ostentatiously throw their hats in the ring, both as a challenge and to let the crowd know they were there. Then they would repair to their carriages to strip. Prizefighters always fought bare-chested.

The fights were to the finish – there was no points system. In the early days the likes of Jack Broughton would take their stance and stand their ground; fighters then tried never to step back. They would exchange punches with their opponent and then close and try to wrestle him to the ground with a trip or a 'cross-buttock' throw. An alternative was to trap a man in a hold called a 'suit in chancery', which involved grabbing his head in one arm while pummelling him with your other hand, often in the neck, which was very vulnerable to a bare fist. Early in the nineteenth century, fights became much less static. Boxers such as Jem Belcher and Bill Richmond were constantly on the move, trying to find openings for attack while avoiding being hit. These skills were refined in the exhibitions at the Fives Court.

But no matter how scientific the game became, bare-knuckle fighting always had horrendous effects. In one way it's surprising how few deaths there were in the ring in top-flight fighting (although many more were reported in minor provincial battles). But a lot of boxers died within a few months from injuries they'd suffered in a bout. Many more probably died from the cumulative effects of their time in the ring: frequently they were said to have died from drink, but this was an era when the concept of being 'punch drunk' was unknown. Few fighters could manage more than a dozen bouts in their career and the sensible and successful ones fought much less. The lucky ones – John Jackson, John Gully, Tom Belcher, Tom Cribb, Bill Richmond and Tom Spring – lived to a prosperous old age. But the casualty rate among the majority inevitably meant that, in the dawn of a less raucous and more law-abiding era, the days of the prizefight were numbered.

The last great fights of the (somewhat stretched-out) Regency era were Tom Spring's two battles with the Irish champion Jack Langan. The first, a grand event at Worcester racecourse in January 1824, was attended by a reported 30,000 people. The fight survived several crowd invasions before Langan finally succumbed in the seventy-seventh round. The rematch a few months later in a field near Chichester lasted a mere seventy-six rounds. Langan lost again and the feeling began to spread that an era was over. Later in the year Egan declared that prizefighting 'may be said to be at an end; the Beaks will have little if any more trouble to interrupt it'. A rival journalist said that if thrown fights and corruption were not ended, 'the consequences must be fate-ful'. Support from the great and the good went into decline, John Jackson closed his rooms and the Pugilistic Club was dissolved.

But the fight game was not ready to die.

The London Prize Ring rules

In 1838 the British Pugilists' Protective Association, a much-needed body if ever there was one, introduced what were called the London Prize Ring rules. But they were, for the most part, a cop-out. They fixed the size of the ring at 24 feet square; decreed that a fallen fighter should come to the mark within thirty seconds unaided (but then gave him an extra eight seconds before he was declared beaten); and kicking, gouging, butting with the head and low blows were all declared fouls. But the basic brutality of the bare-knuckle fight was left unreformed.

James 'Deaf' Burke, the first champion to fight
under the London Prize Ring rules in 1839

The 'New Rules' were first used in a championship fight in 1839 between James 'Deaf' Burke, the reigning champion who had skipped off to America (a growing trend) after a contest in which his opponent had died, and one William Thompson from Nottingham, known as Bendigo. Thompson claimed this was because he was one of triplets who had been known as Shadrack, Meshack and Abednego, but the records show he was actually one of twins. Bendigo won after Burke contravened the new rules by butting him. Maybe not surprising, because Bendigo had a record of provoking fouls – he had previously beaten the respected champion Ben Caunt with a similar stratagem. He subsequently faced Caunt again, and was given the decision after the referee seems to have been intimidated by his supporters, known as Nottingham 'lambs'. When he retired, Bendigo first followed the fighters' stereotype of taking to drink, but then saw the light and became an evangelist. He used to admit that when necessary he still used his skills, but claimed he was now fighting Beelzebub. When he tried to explain this to Lord Longford, the forebear of another pious

Bendigo: he won his fights in part by having his supporters
– the Nottingham 'lambs' – intimidate the referee

campaigner, the good lord replied: 'I hope you fight him more fairly than you did Ben Caunt, or my sympathies will be all with the devil.'

Prizefighting stumbled on for a few more years until a new hero emerged. Tom Sayers from Brighton was just 5 ft 8 in tall and weighed less than 11 stone but made up for his size with skill. He started fighting in 1849 and suffered just one defeat – to the ageing but accomplished Nat Langham, the leading boxer of the day. In 1857, Sayers demolished 'the Tipton Slasher', Bill Perry, who weighed in at 14 stone 6 lb, to become the undisputed champion. But his most famous fight was to take place three years later. It was highly significant for the future of boxing, for two reasons.

The first was the nationality of his opponent. John Carmel Heenan, a giant of a man, was an American. The fact that he had come over to Britain to challenge the champion – this was in effect the first World Championship fight – was an early indication that the future of boxing was about to shift across the Atlantic. It was by then firmly established in urban centres such as New York, Boston and Philadelphia. For many years the fledgling sport had been dominated by expatriate British fighters who found it easier to ply their illegal trade there. But now America was beginning to produce its own top-flight pugilists.

The other distinction the fight could claim was the extraordinary difficulty the organizers had in staging it. When news of it first broke, it created a tremendous stir in the newspapers. Then the Derby police found Heenan in his training quarters and bound him over to keep the peace. Word soon got out that the fight was still on, but no one knew where or when. In late January, *The Times* suggested it would take place 'privately' on 16 April in Suffolk, which immediately necessitated a change of venue. The *Sporting Life* then warned its readers to expect a 'tremendous journey' in mid-April. Questions were asked in Parliament and the Prime Minister, Lord Palmerston, a well-known supporter of 'manly sport', urged the opposition to be moderate.

On 15 April the sporting journal, *Bell's Life*, gave the names of sporting establishments where 'excursion tickets' could be bought for the fight. A deal had been done with the South Eastern Railway Company to run a special train that would stop between stations near the border between Hampshire and Surrey. In the end two trains were needed, using all sixty-three of the company's carriages. They left London Bridge at 4 a.m. but found the police lining the track to prevent the train stopping. They finally came across an unguarded stretch near Farnborough. The Fancy jumped off and followed the ring-maker (without whom the fight could not proceed) across the fields. 'Many,' according to Sir Derek Birley, 'fell in a ditch full of stagnant water.'

The fight itself was a typically brutal affair. After thirty-six rounds, Sayers seemed exhausted, but Heenan couldn't finish him off. Out of frustration, he appeared to start strangling his opponent, at which point the crowd invaded the ring. The referee and, in a half-hearted way, the police, tried to stop the fight, but the crowd wouldn't let them. After a few more rounds both men collapsed together and a draw was declared, which left no one happy. In America, James Gordon Bennett, the only newspaper magnate ever to have a swear-word named after him, claimed that Sayers's camp was just trying to save its money. William Makepeace Thackeray, on the other hand, claimed that Sayers had had the best of it. A rematch was mooted but the Home Secretary made it clear it would bring an immediate prosecution. Sayers never fought again, and it looked as though prize-fighting too might be on its last legs.

The Marquess of Queensberry rules

One place where boxing remained popular was in the public schools. Thomas Hughes devotes a chapter to it in *Tom Brown's Schooldays* to counter 'the cant and twaddle that's talked of boxing and fighting with fists nowadays'. He saw it as the British way of accepting responsibility. This was certainly the view of John Graham Chambers, who was to become an important figure in British sport. He came from a Welsh landowning family and was educated at Eton and Cambridge, where he was a distinguished athlete and oarsman. By the time he left Cambridge in 1865, his father had run into financial problems and he was forced to take paid employment, as a journalist and sports administrator.

The following year he founded the Amateur Athletics Club, with the aim of establishing an authoritative body for athletics which would play a similar role to the MCC in cricket. Chambers regarded boxing as a form of athletics and wanted to include bouts at three weights in the club's annual sports meeting in 1867. He worked out some rules for these contests and persuaded his Cambridge contemporary the Marquess of Queensberry to donate cups for the winners – and put his name to the rules. Those rules have been the basis for the modern sport of boxing ever since.

They were a considerable achievement. Most sporting regulations, such as the Laws of Cricket controlled by the MCC, simply reflected what the players were already doing. Chambers's rules broke new ground. The most important innovation, if perhaps the most obvious in retrospect, was that contestants should always wear 'fair-sized boxing gloves'. Rounds were to be three minutes long, with a minute between each round. (This put an end to the practice of boxers stopping a round by dropping on one knee to give themselves a breather; it thus put more emphasis on skill and footwork.) If a man fell, he had ten seconds to get back up or lose the fight. No wrestling or hugging was to be allowed. For amateur fights, Chambers decreed that there should be just three rounds and that the referee should award points to decide the winner if there was no knockout. There were no such restrictions for the professional game. Fights – or 'Contests of Endurance' as the rules called them – could continue until only one man was left standing.

Following the publication of the Queensberry Rules, amateur boxing in Britain thrived. Boxing was seen as a character-builder. The YMCA took it up, as did church clubs and an array of charitable boys' clubs. A lot of former bare-knuckle pugilists happily found themselves work as 'Professors of Boxing' for the keen new amateurs. In 1880, the Amateur Boxing Association was formed and swiftly set up a popular championship. It was a model that would be successfully exported around the world.

But the professionals dithered. Most found that to get work beyond the fairground boxing booths they had to be willing to fight under both rubrics. At the highest level, the impetus had now firmly switched to

America. In 1882 the Irish-born American John L. Sullivan, the 'Boston Strongboy', was declared world champion after a bout fought under London Prize Ring rules. He was challenged by the British prizefighter Charley Mitchell in 1883 but, despite being felled once, ended the bout by knocking his opponent out of the ring. Mitchell managed a draw in a rematch in France but failed to get his revenge in a decider in Madison Square Gardens because Sullivan turned up too drunk to fight.

John L. Sullivan, 'an insolent bully whose prodigious strength carried him to victory . . . despite drink and lack of training'

Sullivan always preferred the London Rules game and in 1889 he defended his title against Jake Kilrain in the last bare-knuckle fight to be staged in America. But the bout led to endless legal ramifications. By this time London Rules fighting was illegal in every state and Sullivan had to pay large amounts to settle the legal actions brought against him. Which is why, when called upon to defend his title against 'Gentleman' Jim Corbett in 1892, he insisted on the Queensberry Rules. It didn't work. Corbett, who was living evidence that a big man

'Gentleman' Jim Corbett, thought by many
to be the greatest boxer ever

could still be highly scientific and skilful, defeated him to claim the championship. Unusually for a boxer, Corbett had a college education. He also worked during his career as an actor. He was in turn played by Errol Flynn in the 1942 Hollywood film *Gentleman Jim*, based on his autobiography.

The last bare-knuckle fight on British soil took place in 1885, between the champion Jem Smith and challenger Jack Davis. Smith won easily, but hardly anyone turned up to watch. Prizefighting was out cold. The Queensberry Rules were in the ascendant. Over the ensuing years they were to bring cheap, legal entertainment to the masses and help many a working-class boy out of the ghettos of Britain's expanding industrial cities. Many of them were good fighters and a few even became world champions at the lighter weights. But for the last century or more the sport has been dominated by America.

Ironically, Jim Corbett lost his heavyweight title in 1897 to Bob Fitzsimmons, who was brought up in New Zealand but had been born in Helston in Cornwall. It was to be nearly 100 years before there was

another British-born world heavyweight champion in the shape of
Lennox Lewis, who won the WBC title in 1993 – a long wait in a sport
which was once seen as being quintessentially British.

2.
HORSE RACING

WHAT DISTINGUISHES HORSE racing from almost every other sport is that it hasn't changed very much since it first began way back when. The basic idea remains the same: the horse that gets to the finishing line first wins. So how come the British can lay claim to inventing the sport – at least the modern sport that would be recognized by any punter today? Therein lies the story . . .

The ancient world

The first racing horses were introduced into Eastern Europe and North Africa by the Hyksos invaders who conquered Egypt around 1674 BC. We know very little about them except that they possessed a superior breed of horse, much faster than anything known in Europe or most of Asia Minor at the time. One consequence was the development of the chariot as a weapon of war. By the time the Hyksos disappeared back into the depths of history around 1567 BC, the Egyptians had become devoted to the chariot. So in turn did the Minoans on Crete and the Greeks of Mycenae. At some point, someone somewhere started racing them.

The first description of a chariot race that we have is from Homer. At the funeral of Patroclus, who was killed by Hector before the walls of Troy, Achilles organized a race for half a dozen two-horse chariots. It was won, after divine intervention, by Diomedes. His rather more worldly prize was 'a lady'. Homer makes it clear that at this time horses were rarely ridden – they were too small. Instead, they were driven. Not long after Homer's time, the Greeks learned from the Libyans how to drive a chariot with four horses abreast. This new chariot was called a *quadriga*, and in 680 BC *quadriga* races were introduced into the twenty-fifth Olympiad. In 648 BC, the year of the thirty-third games, the first bareback ridden race was introduced. Both two- and four-horse chariot racing and ridden races remained an important and popular part of the Olympics until the games petered out under the Roman Empire towards the end of the fourth century AD. Chariots were also used from very early on in Britain. Archaeologists have found Iron Age chariot tracks and the remains of axles throughout the country. Caesar noted the Britons' skilful use of chariots in battle rather than for entertainment in his report of his invasions of Britain in 55 and 54 BC.

Legend has it that the first horse race in Rome took place soon after the city had been founded by Romulus. To increase the population he settled a bunch of fugitives, exiles and general ne'er-do-wells on the Capitoline Hill and made them citizens. But they had no women. Romulus declared a great horse race in honour of Neptune and invited

Votive relief from the Acropolis Museum showing a four-horse chariot called a quadriga, *introduced around the seventh century BC*

their neighbours, the Sabines. When they arrived, he told his men to seize the women and make them their wives. The subsequent paintings of the rape of the Sabine women never seem to show the racecourse.

Chariot racing became a hugely popular sport at the Circus Maximus in Rome and later at circuses throughout the Empire. Pliny claimed the Circus Maximus, as enlarged by Julius Caesar, could hold 260,000 spectators, all seated. It was probably finished on time too. The Circus was shaped like an elongated D, square at one end and round at the other, with a long island in the middle. The contestants would charge out from the starting stalls at the square end (a concept not seen again for nearly two millennia) and race around the circuit seven times. Each lap was probably six furlongs or so. According to Livy, eggs were placed on pillars to show the contestants and the spectators how many laps had been completed. They must have been big eggs to be seen by a crowd that size.

During the Republic and the early Empire, the contestants were amateurs, from the best Roman families. But from around the middle of the first century AD, the professionals took over. They enjoyed the same kind of celebrity as modern football players and behaved about as badly. Each contestant represented one of four factions – Veneta, Prasina, Albata or Russata; or Blue, Green, White and Red – and wore the appropriate colours. The drivers could make a fortune but they also took enormous risks – not just from accidents but from skulduggery. Death in the Circus was not uncommon. The story goes that one race meeting during the decline of the Eastern Empire ended in a riot that cost 30,000 lives.

The barbarians who took over the Roman Empire would have inherited the circuses and probably the horses. Almost certainly they continued racing but there are no written records. The same is probably true in Britain and the rest of Northern Europe. One place we know there was racing was Ireland. It would take place mainly at an *aenach*, or fair, the most sporting of the traditional gatherings. The greatest centre of racing, from the middle of the third century AD, was the Curragh of Kildare, where the annual fair was the Aenach Colmain (or Aenach Lifé, the fair of the Liffey) which lasted for several

Illustration from the Book of Kells *showing a horseman
riding bareback but with bit and bridle: around AD 700*

days. The races at the Curragh were ridden rather than driven.
Ancient Irish laws, of which we have copies, make it clear that an
established 'fair-green' could be used for horse racing without fine or
charge, no matter who owned the land, with no compensation payable
for any damage caused by galloping horses. Indeed, so important
was racing to the Irish, it seems, that pagan Irish heaven promised
unlimited racing.

The Middle Ages

After William the Conqueror arrived in Britain in 1066, the main duty
of the horse seems to have been hunting rather than racing. The King
sequestered large areas of forest across the country for the use of himself and his cronies. But racing of a kind was also going on. Before the
end of the twelfth century, we have a clear report from the monk
William Fitzstephen (the biographer of Thomas à Becket, whose death

he witnessed in Canterbury) of a regular event which took place at Smithfield Market, then just outside the City of London. It involved 'hackneys and charging steeds' and the aim was to demonstrate the quality of the horses being offered for sale.

When a race is to be run by this sort of horses, and perhaps by others which, in their kind, are also strong and fleet, a shout is immediately raised and the common horses are ordered to withdraw out of the way. Three jockeys, or sometime only two, as the match is made, prepare themselves for the contest ... The horses on their part are not without emulation; they tremble and are impatient, and are continually in motion. At last, the signal once given, they start, devour the course, and hurry along with unremitting swiftness. The jockeys, inspired with the thought of applause and the hope of victory, clap spurs to their willing horses, brandish their whips, and cheer them on with their cries.

It is widely believed that knights brought many Arabian horses back from the Crusades which they then proceeded to race, for prizes that were most likely donated by the king. King John is said to have imported many Eastern horses for hunting purposes and established a major royal stud at Eltham, south-east of London. Many of his successors, most notably Henry III and Richard II, were fans of racing.

Elsewhere in Europe, the most famous races took place in Italy for the Palio, an elaborately embroidered banner. The oldest and grandest took place – and still takes place – in Siena. What happens today is probably not too far removed from what happened in medieval times. Two races take place each year. Each horse represents one of the city's seventeen *contrade,* or wards, and rivalry is fierce. There is only room for ten horses to compete in each race and there are several days of plotting and negotiation before the event to decide which three *contrade* will be allowed to run twice each year. Horses, chosen largely for their uniform mediocrity, are allocated by lot to the successful ten. The bareback jockeys who will ride them are mercenaries who will be paid a small fortune and are consequently expected to deliver.

On the morning of the race each horse is taken to the parish church of its ward to be blessed, an extraordinary sight in itself. Then, in the afternoon, city officials dressed in full medieval dress lead a colourful procession of the horses and their supporters through the narrow streets to the Campo, the city's sizeable main square, where thousands have been waiting for hours in the baking sun. The narrow course runs round the outside of the square, covered in sand, with mattresses in the corners to prevent fatal injury. In the early evening the runners and riders emerge at the starting area and begin a ritual milling-about. Theoretically they are trying to get into the right position to start but everyone knows they are actually trying to offer and attract last-minute deals – bribery is not only legal, it's expected. The rules for the race itself are simple: jockeys are not allowed to grab their rivals' reins but everything else is permitted. Suddenly the race begins – three times around the square in a ninety-second explosion of jostling, shoving, pushing, blocking and whipping. At the end, all the riders gallop straight out of the Campo pursued by frenzied supporters. The winning *contrada* is presented with the Palio. Losing jockeys can often be seen being frog-marched by their ward officials to an inquisition, and often something worse. Meanwhile the victors begin a victory parade through the streets of the medieval city, complete with trumpets and drums, which will go on late into the night. In Siena, some things never change.

The Sport of Kings ... and Queens

Back in Britain, after the instabilities brought on by the War of the Roses had settled down, the young Henry VIII embarked on a programme of importation to improve the stock of horses at the royal stud at Eltham, a programme which started well but then seems to have run into problems. At the same time, he kept a separate stable at Greenwich just for racehorses and employed between two and four stable lads to ride them. It is most likely they were used in informal 'matches' for wagers with gentlemen of the court. Henry's daughter Elizabeth also liked racing, and set up a new and rather more efficient stud at Tutbury in Staffordshire, which was run with advice from Prospero d'Osma from Naples, an expert in the new skill of scientific horse breeding.

Over the same period, starting with Chester in 1511, 'municipal' racecourses were being set up in cities and towns around the country. Kiplingcotes, Croydon, Salisbury, Carlisle, Richmond in Yorkshire and Doncaster all had courses for annual races by the end of the century. Courses had also been established across Scotland. In almost every case the prize offered for 'the horse, which with speedy running, then should rune before all the others' was a silver bell, paid for by the local municipality. Which probably explains why the victor had to return it by the time next year's race came around.

James I, when he was still only James VI of Scotland, had raced horses. But his real interest was hunting and that is what led him, almost by accident, to make his greatest contribution to British racing. He discovered Newmarket. He came across the verdant plane of Newmarket Heath and decided that it would be an ideal spot for hunting. At first, he rented the Griffin Inn in the town for £100 a year, even though he was only ever there for a few weeks. Then, in 1610, he built a palace. Not very well, as it turns out, because it fell down almost immediately. But in 1613, Inigo Jones built him another one, along with some stables which became the pride and joy of not only James but also his son Prince Henry (who was to die before he could succeed to the throne).

Most of the horses in the stables were for hunting and tilting, but there were also racehorses. In 1619, just a couple of weeks after his Queen had died of dropsy, James stayed so long at a horse race at Newmarket that he had to stop off to sleep at an inn on his way back to London. Three years later, there was another race at Newmarket which was to take on a major, and probably unwarranted, significance. On 8 March 1622, the Duke of Buckingham's horse Prince lost the first recorded race across Newmarket Heath to an unknown horse owned by Lord Salisbury. It was for a purse of £100 and has long been said to be the first time that gambling and racing had been brought together at what was to become the spiritual home of racing.

*A view of one of the many local race meetings
that flourished between 1680 and 1740*

But that's probably not entirely true. It's hard to imagine any race taking place at this time that didn't involve gambling. Match races for money had existed for centuries. And certainly in the early seventeenth century gambling was rife among the upper classes. At his Twelfth Night party in 1608, James I refused to admit anyone who didn't have £300 in cash in their pocket for wagers – that's over £30,000 at today's values. Around the same time, we're told that Lord Pembroke lost £2000 – £200,000 today – in one evening of unlucky wagering. This gambling fever was to have a profound effect on the development not just of racing but of much early British sport.

Meanwhile, municipal horse racing across the country was flourishing, with the emergence of even more new courses. Silver bells were being replaced by gold and silver cups as prizes as a way of attracting a better class of horse, and sometimes the winner even got to keep the prize. Doncaster had a grandstand by the early seventeenth century and Lincoln had a roped-off home straight. Kiplingcotes came up with a set of rules covering subscriptions, weights, fouls, weighing in and out and subscriptions. Racing was beginning to look like an organized sport. And it's odds on that side bets were universal, although of course they were never mentioned in the municipal records.

Then came Oliver Cromwell and the puritan Commonwealth. In 1649 Charles I, who was more of a huntsman than a racing man but still maintained the racing stables at Newmarket, lost his head. The Council of State subsequently forbade racing throughout the land. Cromwell broke up the royal studs, but interestingly kept some of the best horses for himself. Many noblemen, including Lord Fairfax who had commanded Cromwell's New Model Army but had disapproved of the King's execution, retired to their estates and quietly got on with breeding horses in expectation of better times to come.

Restoration – they're off again

Amid scenes of great rejoicing, Charles II returned to London on 29 May 1660 to claim his throne. Eight days later, he appointed James D'Arcy to be the Master of the Royal Stud. This showed a sense of priorities that was to characterize much of his reign. And this may well have been just what his subjects needed. Certainly the country could hardly wait to get back to racing. The courses at Chester, Croydon and Windsor were soon in action again and new ones opened, including Epsom, where Charles went racing for the first time as King in 1661.

Newmarket reopened in the spring of 1663, but for some reason Charles did not make it there until 1666. But after that, for the next eighteen years, he visited two or three times a year, for two or three weeks each time. The old royal palace had been gutted during Cromwell's time, so Charles bought 'an old wretched house of my Lord Thomond's' in the middle of town and a little later the Greyhound Inn next door and set about building a new one. It was not, by all accounts, well conceived. The Duke of Tuscany, clearly a demanding guest, said after a visit that it 'does not deserve to be called a king's residence'. But Charles was probably too busy racing, attending cockfights, eating, drinking, gambling and entertaining his several mistresses (Nell Gwyn used to rent a little house just across the road from the palace) to worry too much.

The ungrateful Duke of Tuscany was not the only foreign dignitary to visit the town. When Charles was in residence, he was attended by a large part of the court and many hangers-on. Ambassadors were regularly received. The fashionable set in turn attracted numerous merchants, many of the most expensive kind, as well as entertainers, gaming-room proprietors, brothel keepers and related vagabonds.

But the racing was the real attraction. The Duke of Tuscany described the scene on the Heath: 'The racecourse ... extending to a distance of four miles over a spacious level meadow, covered with very short grass, is marked out by tall wooden posts, painted white.' The Duke watched a 'match', a race between two horses who were led out 'by the men who were to ride them, dressed in taffeta of different colours'. They started slowly, but gathered pace until they were at full speed. The King and his attendants were watching on horseback; as the race reached its climax, they galloped alongside. 'Trumpets and drums, which were in readiness for the purpose, sounded in applause of the conqueror.' But Charles also rode in races, with considerable gusto. Sir Robert Carr, in a despatch to Whitehall, reported that: 'Yesterday his majestie rode himself three heats and a course and won the Plate, all fower were hard and nere run, and I doe assure you the king wonn by good Horseman Ship.'

The Plate that Charles won that day was his own Newmarket Town Plate, which he had established even before he first went to Newmarket as King. It was a race between a number of competitors rather than just the two who would normally take part in a match. And it had formal rules (unlike a match, where the way the race was to be run was simply agreed between the parties when they agreed to the contest). The course for the Plate was specified, it was to be four miles long and the jockeys would ride at 12 stone (168 lb). Certain acts were proscribed: 'Item – Every rider that layeth hold on, or striketh any of the riders, shall win no plate or prize'. Such rules implied a judge to ensure they were observed – a role which Charles often played himself in later years. This race and other 'plate races' being set up around the country were the precursors of modern racing and paved the way for the formal regulation of the sport in the next century.

Charles's last visit to Newmarket was in the spring of 1684. He died the following year. His successor James II liked racing but had little time to spare – he was too busy trying to convert the country back to

*Racing at Windsor on 24 August 1684, the last meeting attended
by Charles II before his death the following year*

Catholicism. But one thing did change during his reign: for the first time, professional riders were allowed to compete in some races. Previously, horses had been ridden by their owners or by their grooms (who were also known as jockeys).

Dour William of Orange, imported in the 'Glorious Revolution' of 1688 to save the country from Catholicism, had none of Charles's *joie de vivre*, but he was a prodigious gambler and maintained the royal racing establishment at Newmarket. He also revitalized the royal studs, including reopening the stud at Hampton Court. One of his horses won a famous victory over the outstanding horse of the day, Lord Wharton's Careless, because he was carrying the lowest weight possible – a feather – as opposed to Careless's nine stone. The King's horse was called Stiff Dick. In her lively history of Newmarket, Laura Thompson points out that such names were not uncommon. Others she cites include Cream Cheeks, Broad Bottom, Spanker and Bloody Buttocks.

Queen Anne loved racing as much as any male monarch. During

her reign, the first formal meeting was held at York and in 1711 she
founded Royal Ascot, not for the fashion – she was plain and continually pregnant (at least eighteen times: but none of her children survived
infancy) and had no time for such frivolities – but for the racing. She
also maintained the royal racing establishment at Newmarket and kept
on the dominating figure that William had appointed to be 'Keeper
of the Running Horses'. William Tregonwell Frampton was possibly
the world's first professional racehorse trainer. Under four successive
monarchs, he kept the royal horses at his stables and organized the
royal racing schedule. He set up many matches, some involving royal
horses and some his own, on which he bet heavily. Far more heavily,
in fact, than he should have been able to afford on his modest
salary, which suggests that he was a canny and successful gambler.
His position and skills earned him the not wholly fond sobriquet of
'Father of the Turf'.

There are many stories about Tregonwell Frampton, none of them
flattering and most apocryphal. One, however, might just be true.

William Tregonwell Frampton, 'Keeper of the Running
Horses' at Newmarket under four sovereigns

A Yorkshire baronet called Sir William Strickland brought his horse Old Merlin down to Newmarket for a match with an unnamed horse from Frampton's stable. Because Northern and Southern racing rarely met, it was quietly suggested there should be a trial before the race. Old Merlin won – just. But what the Newmarket insiders knew was that Frampton had put an extra seven pounds of weight on his horse. Massive amounts of money were poured onto the local mount. In the real race, Old Merlin won once again. His trainer, one Heseltine, had clearly heard all the stories about Frampton, apocryphal or not. He too had put an extra seven pounds on his horse. As a result, according to legend, fortunes and estates were lost. And the North's victory was celebrated in drinking songs for years to come.

Thoroughbred

In 1715, a horse was foaled which was to change everything. Flying Childers, a beautiful bay with four white socks, was 'allowed by Sportsmen to be the fleetest horse that ever ran at Newmarket, or, as generally believed, that was ever bred in the World'. In a race against Fox, one of the best horses of the day, Flying Childers gave him a stone in weight and still won by two furlongs. He won every race he ever started. He showed what a truly great thoroughbred racehorse could be. Since then, the sport has never stopped trying to find his like.

It was only in England at this time that horses were being bred specifically for racing – and what every English breeder wanted were horses of Arabian stock. The concept of the 'thoroughbred' was first mentioned by the Earl of Bristol in a letter to his son in 1713: 'thro'-bred English horses are allowd to surpass most of ye same species'. Flying Childers was one of the first thoroughbreds and possibly the greatest there has ever been. But his father, or sire in racing parlance, was a horse of even greater significance. He was found by Thomas Darley, a merchant in the Syrian city of Aleppo, and shipped back to England for his father Richard, who ran a stud farm in Yorkshire. He was called simply the Darley Arabian. Recent research has suggested that 95 per cent of modern racehorses are direct descendants of his.

The Darley Arabian was one of the three so-called 'Foundation Stallions' from whom all modern racehorses throughout the world are directly descended in the male line, though he was obviously the most prolific. The earliest was the 'Byerley Turk', who was captured by one

*The Darley Arabian, bought in Aleppo in 1704: research suggests
that 95% of modern racehorses are descended from him*

Captain Byerley when the Hungarian capital Buda was taken from the Turks in 1686. It is believed that Byerley subsequently rode him at the Battle of the Boyne in 1690, where William III finally defeated his predecessor and challenger James II. Afterwards, the horse was sent to stud. The other foundation stallion was the 'Godolphin Arabian', who was improbably said to have been found by an English trader called Edward Coke pulling a water cart in Paris. It is more likely that he was originally given to Louis XV by the Bey of Tunis, was then bought by Coke and eventually handed on to Lord Godolphin.

It was never planned that these three horses, which never raced themselves, should be the progenitors of all subsequent thoroughbred

*The Byerley Turk, the earliest of the three 'Foundation Stallions', captured by
Captain Byerley when Buda was taken from the Turks in 1688*

*The Godolphin Arabian, foaled in 1725, with his constant companion, Grimalkin
the cat: after Grimalkin died, he tried to kill any cat that he saw*

racehorses. It just happened. But once the idea of thoroughbreds had been developed, planning, record-keeping and regulation became inevitable. There was too much money at stake for it to be otherwise.

The Jockey Club

In the first half of the eighteenth century, horse racing exploded. According to one contemporary report, 'there is scarce a village so mean that has not a bit of plate raised once a year for the purpose'. In these local affairs, hunters, ponies, carthorses and even donkeys were raced. The 'sport' was rough and ready, to say the least. Prizes were small, races were fixed, officials were bribed, dishonesty held sway. Or so the story goes. This was not what the Sport of Kings was meant to be about.

And, of course, there was no regulation. In 1740, Parliament stepped in and passed 'An Act to restrain and prevent the Excessive Increase of Horse Racing'. It was aimed at little meetings which encouraged idleness, impoverished the 'meaner subjects' of the King and were damaging the breed. It decreed that there should be no races for a prize of less than £50, a substantial sum way beyond the pocket of most villages. An exception was made for Newmarket and Hambleton in Yorkshire, because that is where the great and the good – including, of course, many Parliamentarians – did their racing. The Act also laid down minimum weights, designed to encourage the breeding of stout horses.

From 1727, this great profusion of racing had been recorded for the first time. John Cheny of Arundel published the first sporting calendar: *An Historical List of all Horse-Matches Run, And of all Plates and Prizes run for in England (of the value of £10 and upwards) in 1727*. It included a large number of pedigrees, so for the first time the history of the new thoroughbreds could be traced. Cheny toyed with the idea of starting a separate Stud Book, but he died in 1750 before he could carry out his plan. But his calendar was an important first step towards bringing some sense of order to racing.

In 1751, a successor publication included a small announcement. It said that at Newmarket on 1 April 1752 there was to be run 'A Contribution Free Plate, by Horses the Property of the Noblemen and Gentlemen belonging to the JOCKEY CLUB at the *Star and Garter* in *Pall Mall*, one heat on the Round Course, weight eight Stone, seven Pound'. This was the first mention of an institution that was to govern racing for the next 250 years.

We don't know exactly when the Jockey Club was formed, or who the first members were. But we can be pretty sure that they didn't set themselves up to be a regulatory body. The Star and Garter in Pall Mall was the favoured meeting place of the sporting aristocrats of the day and plays an important role in the development of the two other great gambling sports of this time – boxing and cricket. The 'noblemen and gentlemen' met there for three purposes: to drink, to eat and above all to gamble. They were not natural administrators.

One of them was undoubtedly William, Duke of Cumberland, the second son of George II, who was known as the 'Butcher of Culloden' for his brutal suppression of the Stuart uprising in 1746. We know he was a member of the Jockey Club because he won a Jockey Club plate in 1754. He was an efficient if brutal soldier but, after defeat at the hands of the French in 1757, he gave up military life to devote himself full-time to racing and gambling. He gambled all day and every day. The sight of him carefully placing his huge belly under the card table every night, with his stake money in a pile in front of him, led the writer and social observer Horace Walpole, in a memorable phrase, to describe him as 'the prodigal son and the fatted calf both'. He died of obesity in 1765, just 44 years of age, but not before leaving an important legacy to racing.

Another early member of the Club was Lord March, later the last Duke of Queensberry. In his youth he was a fine rider and an excellent judge of horses who made a number of successful matches – not always fairly. One such in 1750 was against a horse owned by an irascible Irish peer. March's horse won the race but then it came to light that his jockey had slipped some of his weights to an accomplice before the start and replaced them just before the weighing-in after the race.

When March shrugged off the allegation and refused to apologize, the Irishman challenged him to a duel. The two men met at sunrise the next morning, 10 June. As pistols were being prepared, a large coffin arrived inscribed: 'William Douglas, Earl of March, born November

'Old Q', the last Duke of Queensberry: he would sit on the balcony of his house ogling passing women

5th 1725, died June 10th 1750.' It was too much for March, who made a grovelling apology and withdrew.

He would gamble on anything except, it seems, his own life. He once wagered that he could despatch a letter fifty miles in an hour. The bet was won by enclosing the letter in a cricket ball which was then thrown around a circle by twenty-four expert fielders. On another occasion he bet that he could 'produce a carriage with four running wheels and with a man in it, to be drawn by four horses, nineteen miles in one hour.' He designed the vehicle and had it made by Wright of Long Acre. The race against the clock took place on Newmarket Heath in 1750 before a vast crowd. The carriage achieved the distance with six and a half minutes to spare and March won 1000 guineas. Throughout his life he is said to have won nearly a quarter of a million pounds. He had his best year at Newmarket when he was 63 and then retired to his house in Piccadilly to devote himself to his other great passion, the lusts of the flesh. He became known punningly as 'Old Q' (from the French word *queue*, meaning tail, which also has a sexual connotation) and was

The 'Chaise Match' at Newmarket in August 1750: Old Q's carriage
covered nineteen miles in an hour, winning him 1,000 guineas

rumoured to be still indulging in 'unspeakable orgies' until not long before his death at nearly 90.

Another Jockey Club member was the third Duke of Grafton, who seemed to prefer racing to his day job of being Prime Minister. He once sent a message to his cabinet colleagues that he wouldn't be able to make a meeting because he was running a horse in a match at Newmarket. Another racing Prime Minister was Charles Wentworth, the last Marquis of Rockingham. He had no great reputation as a politician – a contemporary joke was 'The Ministry sleeps and the Minister's Rocking'em' – but was something of a legend as a gambler. He once bet five hundred pounds that he would find five geese to beat Lord Orford's five turkeys in a walking match between Norwich and London. As far as we know, the actual race never took place.

No, these men weren't natural administrators, but they were

immensely powerful. As racing proliferated, it became clear that a consistent set of rules was needed, along with an appeal body whose decisions would be accepted as final. It was probably inevitable that the Jockey Club, which had quickly established a headquarters for itself at Newmarket, would come to meet these needs. In 1757, the first dispute was submitted to the Club for arbitration. The following year, the first general order of the Jockey Club was published: that two pounds overweight was the maximum permitted unless declared, and failure to declare meant disqualification. At first these rules were only meant to apply to racing at Newmarket, but such was the prestige of the Jockey Club that they were quickly adopted by nearly all other racecourses. Nonetheless, the Club's influence did not become irrevocable until the emergence of one of racing's most important figures.

The Dictator of the Turf

Sir Charles Bunbury was born in 1740, at Mildenhall in Suffolk, not far from Newmarket, where his father was vicar. He became the MP for Suffolk when he was just 21 and a year later married Lady Sarah Lennox, the beautiful daughter of the second Duke of Richmond who had been unsuccessfully wooed by the young George III. But it seems Sir Charles had little interest in either politics or his socially ambitious young wife, preferring instead to devote his time to racing. He became Steward of the Jockey Club when he was 28 and a few years later his wife finally despaired of him and went to live with Lord William Gordon. Sir Charles seems briefly to have flirted with the idea of challenging Gordon to a duel, but his friends rather ungallantly pointed out that it was best to deal with known poachers on his manor in the correct sequence – in which case Gordon would come in tenth on the list.

He was much more successful at developing racing. He dominated the sport for many years, even when not officially in office – he was known as the 'perpetual president'. Under his leadership, the Jockey Club became the undisputed governing body of the turf throughout the

*Sir Charles Bunbury, the first 'Dictator of the Turf', who made the
Jockey Club the undisputed governing body of horseracing*

country. He reformed and modernized the sport and turned it into
something much more akin to racing as we know it today. But he is
probably best known for taking on, on behalf of the Jockey Club, the
powerful figure of the Prince of Wales in a mysterious incident known
as 'the Escape Affair'.

The Prince, later to be the Prince Regent and then George IV,
always had a mixed relationship with racing. He started buying horses
when he came of age in 1784 and within two years was so badly in debt
that he was forced to close much of his home at Carlton House and
sell off most of his horses at ludicrously low prices. Then Parliament
baled him out by paying off his debts, and his father – by now too
mad to care – increased his allowance. As a consequence the Prince
didn't just restock his stable, he doubled the size of it. He was reckless
but not unskilful – between 1788 and 1792 he won 185 races, including
the Derby. But one purchase he may have come to regret involved a
yearling he had bred but had been forced to sell for £800 when he

was broke. The new owner called the horse Escape after he avoided injury when he put his fetlock through his loose box. He went on to show great promise, so the newly solvent Prince bought him back for £1500.

The famous affair began on 20 October 1791. Escape was due to be ridden by the Prince's regular jockey Sam Chifney at Newmarket in a field of four over two miles. He was 2–1 on favourite but came in last. Disappointed, the Prince decided to run him again the next day over four miles in a field of six that included two of the horses who had just

Rowlandson cartoon of the Escape affair: the horse is hobbled by a royal banner, while the Prince of Wales plans his bet for the following day

beaten him. This time Escape was a 5–1 outsider but Chifney brought him home an easy winner. This did not look good.

Chifney, a brilliant but disreputable rider, subsequently said he had warned the Prince before the first race not to back Escape because he didn't think he was fit. He had not had a 'sweat' – the then fashionable process of working a horse hard covered in heavy clothing to prepare him for a race – for a fortnight. But he supported the Prince's decision to run him again the next day because the exertions of the first race would have 'opened his pores' and made him ready for the four-mile race, a distance he preferred. Both Chifney and the Prince had strongly backed the horse in the second race, which made things look even worse. The Jockey Club was up in arms.

The Prince accepted Chifney's version of events and asked whether he'd be willing to be questioned by Sir Charles Bunbury and the other two Jockey Club stewards. The interview duly took place and Bunbury subsequently travelled to Carlton House to tell the Prince that if he allowed Chifney to ride his horses again, 'no gentlemen would start against him'. The Prince refused to be intimidated and said that rather than sacrifice his jockey, he would leave the turf. He then compensated the ruined Chifney by settling £200 a year on him for life.

Many think that Bunbury was out to destroy Chifney, who was widely believed to be less than honest, regardless of whether Escape had been held back or not in that first race. But the consequences of the incident are known. Sam Chifney, the world's first successful professional jockey, sold the prince's generous annuity for a lump sum, spent all the money and died in the debtors' prison at the age of 53. The Prince returned to the turf, winning 107 races between 1800 and 1808, but he never returned to Newmarket. The Jockey Club emerged as a much stronger and more powerful institution which had shown itself capable of standing up to the heir to the throne.

The emergence of modern racing

Under Sir Charles Bunbury, the nature of racing changed considerably. First, the type of races run underwent a transformation. Before, there were essentially 'matches' – races between two horses with their owners putting up the prize money; and 'plates' – where a number of horses competed for a set prize, carrying weights set according to their age. As the eighteenth century wore on, new ideas began to emerge.

One didn't last long. These were called 'give and take' races, where horses carried different weights according to their size. Not a very sensible notion and dead before the end of the century. More interesting was the idea of handicap races. They began with 'matches', where two owners who wanted to run horses of differing abilities against each other would agree, often over a cordial dinner, on a weight differential. Sometimes a third person decided the handicap. Then an interesting ritual ensued. The two owners and the handicapper each put a set amount of money into a hat. The handicapper would come up with a proposal. The two owners would put their hands in their pockets and, on a given signal, bring them out closed. They would open them simultaneously. If they both had money in them, the match was made and the handicapper pocketed the money in the hat. If neither hand had money in it, there was no match but the handicapper still took the hat money. But if only one hand contained money, there was still no match but the owner who was willing to take the risk scooped the pool. It took rather longer for the sport to work out how to handicap a multiple horse race: the first was the Oatlands Stakes at Ascot in 1791.

But the biggest innovation was the sweepstake. The problem with a match was that if you won, you had yourself put up half the prize money. But if twenty owners each agreed to put in £50 each, you had a prize well worth racing for and you had only put in a small percentage. The benefit to owners was obvious. The idea was introduced around the time of the founding of the Jockey Club in 1750. It grew quickly. The redoubtable Admiral Rous, a central figure in racing in Victorian times, calculated that in 1762 there were 449 matches, 38 sweepstakes and 205 plates. By 1843, there were 86 matches, 897 sweepstakes and 191 plates.

But the match took a while to die. In 1799, one of the greatest ever was held at Newmarket between Hambletonian and Diamond. Hambletonian was a Northern horse, owned by Sir Harry Tempest Vane and ridden by Sam Chifney's successor as leading jockey, Frank Buckle. Diamond was owned by Joseph Cookson and ridden by Dennis Fitzpatrick, the first Irish professional jockey to ply his trade in England. He was seen as the best horse in the South but still received three pounds from Hambletonian. The race was for a massive 3000 guineas. The crowd was huge and side-betting was estimated at between 200,000 and 300,000 guineas. After just over four miles of intense racing, Hambletonian was adjudged to have won by half a neck. Sir Harry was made so ill by all the excitement that he never raced again.

The greatest racehorse of the second half of the century was Eclipse, who was bred by the Duke of Cumberland just before his death in 1764 and is his great legacy to horse racing. Rumour of his startling ability had leaked out before his first race, in which his odds were 4–1 on. The norm in those days was to race in heats: the first horse to win two heats was declared the winner. Eclipse won the first heat easily. At this point, according to legend, the great Irish adventurer and gambler Colonel Dennis O'Kelly became involved. He was so frustrated by the odds being offered on Eclipse for the second heat that he said he'd bet on the placings of all the runners. His prediction became one of the most famous sayings in racing: 'Eclipse first, the rest nowhere.' He was betting that the rest of the field would be so far behind they would be beyond the 'distance post' – 240 yards from the finish line. This meant they were beyond the theoretical limit of the judges' vision, so they couldn't be placed. It seems that for the first three miles of the race, Eclipse was happy to gallop alongside his four fellow runners. Then his jockey let him go. He comfortably won by more than the 240 yards needed for O'Kelly to win his bet.

O'Kelly subsequently bought Eclipse, who went on to win eleven races and seven walkovers – people were too afraid to challenge him. He then went to stud, where he not only made a fortune for O'Kelly but also ensured the future of the most important male line of all, that of the Darley Arabian.

The emergence of men such as Dennis O'Kelly and Richard Tattersall, the owner of the great bloodstock auctioneers and of the century's second greatest stallion, Highflyer, marked a significant development. The two greatest horses of the day, Eclipse and Highflyer, were now owned not by reckless, fickle aristocrats but by businesslike and knowledgeable professionals. O'Kelly wanted 'speedy and jady' Eclipse to breed with the daughters of 'hard and stout' Highflyer, while for just the same reasons Tattersall wanted Highflyer to breed with the daughters of Eclipse. The results were a new kind of thoroughbred for a new kind of racing.

Two things happened. Horses started racing younger, at lower weights. And races became shorter. At the beginning of the century, few horses raced before they were five years old, and six was more common; and they generally raced over four miles. By the end, the norm was two- and three-year-olds racing for less than two miles. There were two reasons: racing at a younger age meant a faster return on investment; and shorter races were more exciting to watch and pulled in bigger crowds. Youth and speed became the fashion. Many would argue that the constant refinement of the thoroughbred made this inevitable. But the process was certainly helped along enthusiastically by Sir Charles Bunbury and the Jockey Club.

It was also during Bunbury's time that the season began to take on the shape that we know today. The five 'classics' were founded: the St Leger (1776), run at Doncaster and named after local grandee Lieutenant General Anthony St Leger; the Oaks (1779), run at Epsom and named after Lord Derby's country house; the Derby (1780), also at Epsom, named after the lord but only, the story goes, after he won the toss of a coin against Bunbury (Sir Charles had the consolation of winning the first race with his horse Diomed); the Two Thousand Guineas (1809), and the One Thousand Guineas (1814), both run at Newmarket. All five races were (and still are) for three-year-olds and run over courses ranging from a mile to one mile six furlongs.

Racing as we know it today was under way. The atmosphere was changing too. It was no longer a jolly romp. There were now, following in the stirrups of Sam Chifney, growing numbers of professional jockeys. There were professional trainers. There were rigorous and knowledgeable owners such as O'Kelly and Tattersall. There were professional administrators at the Jockey Club. James Weatherby's *Racing Calendar*, which had emerged triumphant after a brief period of competition following the death of John Cheny in 1750, became the official journal of the club. In 1790, Weatherby announced the beginning of the *General Stud Book*, recording the pedigree of all racing thoroughbreds. The turf was becoming an industry.

Scandal

By the nineteenth century, the pattern of flat racing was well established. But it still had its ups and downs. The first half of the century saw endless scandals. The lowest point was the Derby of 1844, the most extraordinary race in the 200-year history of the event. The favourite was the victim of foul riding, the second favourite was nobbled and one of the runners in this race for three-year-olds was a six-year-old who broke his leg and had to be put down. The race was won by Running Rein, except it wasn't, because Running Rein was in fact a horse called Maccabeus, a four-year-old who had previously been declared dead.

The scandal was uncovered largely by the efforts of Lord George Bentinck, a successful owner and the reforming manager of the new racecourse at Goodwood. He was no stranger to sharp practices himself. (His cousin, the diarist Charles Greville, said of him after his death: 'Oh for the inconsistency of human nature, the strange compound and medley of human motives and impulses, when the same man who crusaded against the tricks and villainies of others did not scruple to do things quite as bad as the worst of the misdeeds which he so vigorously and unrelentingly attacked!' With a cousin like that . . .)

But in the case of Running Rein, Bentinck was probity personified. He persuaded the owner of the horse which came second, Colonel Jonathan Peel (brother of Sir Robert), to lodge a formal objection. As a result, the prize money was withheld. The owner of Running Rein sued Peel and the matter was brought before the courts. 'Our case was admirably got up,' wrote Charles Greville in his diary, 'owing in great measure to the indefatigable activity and the intelligence and penetration of George Bentinck, who played the part both of attorney and policeman in hunting out and getting up the evidence.'

Bentinck became a national hero and was dubbed the second Dictator of the Turf. He was awarded a large sum of money, raised by subscription from the grateful racing community, which he promptly gave to the Jockey Club to start a fund for the distressed dependents of jockeys and grooms. Shortly afterwards, he gave up racing for a career in politics. He died of a heart attack two years later at the age of 46.

Steeplechasing

The major change in the nineteenth century was the growth of steeple-chasing. Its origins are obscure. The Tudors indulged in something called a 'wild-goose-chase', a match across country in which the horse in front after the first furlong could lead his opponent where he liked. If the follower fell too far behind or refused to take some suicidal jump, the leader was declared the winner. It was cruel and dangerous and for these reasons fell out of fashion. The earliest steeplechase 'matches' were between hunters ridden by their owners across country to some visible point, such as a steeple. But in the early days these were slow and sedate affairs because hunters and hounds were slow.

Then, in the 1760s, a new, much faster breed of foxhound was introduced. This encouraged the use of thoroughbreds, seven-eighths- and three-parts-bred horses in hunting, which made real racing possible. In 1790, there was a nine-mile 'match' near Melton Mowbray for 1000 guineas. The same year, the first multiple cross-country race was held. In 1804, a three-horse steeplechase became the first to be ridden in colours. But the biggest innovation came in 1794, when a race was held at Newmarket over a mile with five-foot bars every quarter of a mile. This was the first time fences had been built on a racecourse, but the idea was to take a long while to catch on.

In 1830, Thomas Coleman came up with the idea of an out-and-back course through the countryside, beginning and ending conveniently close to his pub called the Turf Hotel near St Albans. This was obviously much better for spectators. In 1835, the Cheltenham Grand Annual Steeplechase was started. A similar race followed in Aylesbury the next year. And in 1836, a Mr Lynn set up the 'Grand Liverpool Steeplechase' near his Waterloo Hotel in the Liverpool suburb of Aintree. The race was a success and was won by Captain Becher, one of the best jump jockeys of the day, on The Duke. But

Lynn was no entrepreneur and lost most of his money. Racing at Aintree was taken over by a committee which included Lord George Bentinck and a number of other racing notables. Their first race was in February 1839 over four miles, with two circuits and twenty-nine

A steeplechase held near St Albans in 1832, as depicted in Pierce Egan's Book of Sports

fences. Captain Becher on Conrad fell into a brook on the first circuit, remounted and fell into it again the second time around. It has carried his name ever since. This was the first Grand National, although it wasn't given that name till 1847. Appropriately it was won by a horse called Lottery.

Steeplechasing grew rapidly around the middle of the century. Minor courses were 'got up by innkeepers, for the good of their houses', and made possible by the expansion of the railways. But it was rough and ready. There were no rules and it attracted many 'sharpers' excluded from the flat by the resurgent authority of the Jockey Club. In 1857 one Fothergill Rowlands, known as 'Fogo' or 'Fog', tried to do something about this. He organized a 'Grand National Hunt Steeplechase' at Market Harborough, supported by four local hunts. It failed but was important because he laid down a set of rules: the 'Harborough Act'. Subsequent attempts at Market Harborough and then at Cheltenham were much more successful: because the races were believed to be honest, they were immensely popular.

Suddenly there was a wider demand for rules to cover the whole of the emerging sport. Various suggestions were put forward by members of the Jockey Club. Even Admiral Henry Rous, a long-standing Steward of the Jockey Club and the third and last Dictator of the Turf, offered refinements. In 1863 the 'Grand National Hunt Steeplechase Committee' was formed. It quickly started arbitrating in disputes and, because its decisions were seen as sensible and fair, its authority grew.

Dog racing

Dog racing grew out of the ancient sport of coursing, which involved dogs, usually greyhounds, chasing live game. It was first written about at length by the Greek philosopher Arrian in the second century AD. In the Middle Ages, hare coursing became popular among the nobility in Britain – the first formal rules were written at the behest of Elizabeth I. But by the late nineteenth century, sensibilities were changing and the idea of using a live hare became increasingly unacceptable. The first attempt to use a mechanical one took place in a field near the Welsh Harp pub in Hendon in 1876 over a straight track of 450 yards. There were two problems: first, the length of the track meant no one could see the whole race; second, there were none of the swerves and changes of direction there had been with a live hare, so the race was won by the fastest dog. As dogs generally run true to form, this made the races predictable. What was needed was a circular or oval track. This idea was mooted in England in 1890, but funds were not forthcoming. The idea was eventually taken up in America in 1909, so modern dog racing was born in the USA. The first track in Britain was opened at Belle Vue in Manchester in 1926.

Admiral Henry Rous (left), the last Dictator of the Turf,
with racehorse owner and gambler George Payne

It was reconstituted by the Jockey Club in 1866, mostly with Club members, and the following year was given control over hurdle races. In 1888, the first official Steeplechase Calendar was published. There were many problems still to be overcome, but the basis of the new branch of racing had been established.

Exports

By the late nineteenth century, the English had been exporting their unique style of racing to countries around the world for almost two hundred years. Wherever the idea caught on, there was an immediate demand for English horses. In 1730 a tobacco planter from Hanover County in Virginia called Samuel Gist imported Bulle Rock, a son of the Darley Arabian, into the United States. In 1751, Colonel Benjamin Tasker of Maryland imported Selima, by the Godolphin Arabian out of a daughter of Flying Childers. These were just the well-bred tip of a large iceberg.

The French too loved English horses, both for hunting and, from the late eighteenth century, for racing. A few French aristocrats bought English horses and raced them in England. Soon they were taking them home to race and to breed, and attracting attention from English owners as well. In 1783, both Lord March and Lord Derby had runners in the royal park of Vincennes. 'We have copied the races from the English,' wrote one French observer. 'The *jockei* who is going to ride is made to fast, to weigh less ... We go to the Plaine des Sablons to watch skinny animals run covered in sweat.' You can almost hear the disdain, but it was the fashion, so it had to be obeyed. By 1789, French-bred horses of pure English blood were already running and winning. Then came the Revolution.

In 1805, Napoleon tried to rekindle racing by decree, as part of a breeding programme to promote French horses such as the Percheron rather than English thoroughbreds. After Waterloo, Louis XVIII continued the programme, but it didn't really work. The peasants wanted horses that earned their keep rather than animals ridden for fun. But help was at hand. In 1825 or thereabouts, one Thomas Bryon started an organization in the Rue Blanche in Paris clumsily called 'The English Jockey Club and Pigeon-shooting Club'. A few members were English, most were French. In 1833, the club spawned the Jockey Club and the *Société d'Encouragement pour l'Amélioration des Races des Chevaux en France*. By 1834, the *Société* was running thoroughbred races at Chantilly. All the trainers and jockeys were English.

Meanwhile, English thoroughbreds were being exported to kick-start modern racing in Italy, Germany and the Austro-Hungarian Empire. In 1876, the Hungarians had the cheek to send a horse called Kisber to Epsom to win the Derby, but at least both his parents were English. English bloodstock also travelled to South Africa, Australia and New Zealand, and then indirectly to India, South America and countries even further afield.

It was inevitable that these exports would come back to haunt the English. The Irish were the first. In 1845 an Irish-bred horse called

Le turf

In his 1972 book, *The History of Horse Racing*, Roger Longrigg includes a little paragraph on the language of French racing which is an eloquent indication of the sport's origins:

'In 1896,' he wrote, 'every horse on *le turf* went, with *le pedigree* in *le Stud-Book*, from *le stud-groom* to *le head-lad* and *le stable-boy*; it travelled in *le box* to be ridden by *le jockey* or *le gentleman-rider* in *le handicap* (made by *le handicapeur*), *le steeplechase*, or some other event in *le Racing-Calendar*. If *le crack*, as seen by *le tout*, it was unlikely to be made *l'outsider* by *le book-maker*. It was backed by *le sportsman* for *le pony* (25 louis) or *le fifty*, unless it had *le walkover* or *le pickpocket* had been busy. When *le starter* dropped his flag, the horse ran to *le winning-post*, if a victim neither of *le doping* or *être broken-down*. After winning it was *all-right*, and the successful punter celebrated with *l'oueské* or *le clarett*.'

The Baron won the St Leger. In 1847, a horse called Matthew won the Grand National and established Irish horses as a major force in English steeplechasing. The first horse to win the National twice was Abd-el-Kader (yes, he was Irish) in 1850 and 1851. From 1889 to 1899, every Grand National except one was won by an Irish-bred horse. (Unbelievably, the exception was a Shropshire horse called Father O'Flynn.) Strangely, it wasn't until 1907 that an Irish-trained horse – Orby, owned by the American racketeer Richard 'Boss' Coker – won the Derby. This was a cause of much celebration in Ireland and Irish America. An old lady reportedly said to Coker's stable manager: 'Thank God and you, sir, we have lived to see a *Catholic* horse win the Derby.'

But at least Ireland was, at that time, still part of Britain. The French were different. They began their raid on English racing in 1854 but were at first rebuffed. Then came Comte Frédéric de Lagrange and his horse Gladiateur. In 1865, they won the St Leger, the Derby and the Two Thousand Guineas – the English Triple Crown, only the second horse to do so. An ebullient Frenchman wrote: 'For the first time their undisputed sceptre had been wrested from our neighbour's hands; for the first time a foreign horse had beaten the pick of the produce of the United Kingdom ... The French thoroughbred still had a rival, but no longer a master.' The only consolation was that Gladiateur was trained by an Englishman, Tom Jennings, at Newmarket. Racing was fast becoming an international business.

Confirmation was to come from the Americans. Their invasion can be dated to 1897 and was to have a big impact. It began with a jockey from Indiana called Tod Sloan. He shocked England by riding lying along the horse's neck with his knees tucked almost under his chin. People called the style 'monkey on a stick'. They hated it but it worked. Sloan won twenty races on second-rate horses on which, according to the leading English trainer George Lambton, no English jockey would have stood a chance. Hardly surprising, then, that within a year most English riders had adopted the new style. When American trainers flocked into England at around this time, they brought about an equally dramatic revolution in training techniques.

Lonesome Sloan

The American jockey Tod Sloan, who revolutionized racing by inventing the crouching style of riding, gave rise to his own piece of cockney rhyming slang. He was so successful in his first year of racing in Britain, winning twenty races on second-rate horses, that people started saying he was always out on his own. As a result, 'on your own' then became 'on your Tod Sloan', which in turn, in true cockney style, became 'on your tod'.

A matter of life and teeth

As almost everybody knows, the most reliable way of telling a horse's age is to look at its teeth. That is why it's always best to get your information 'straight from the horse's mouth'. It is also why it is not thought polite 'to look a gift horse in the mouth'.

The Americans have played an important part in English racing ever since. The US now has by far the largest bloodstock industry in the world. During one memorable period, four out of five Derby

Tod Sloan from Indiana: his revolutionary riding style
has been copied by all jockeys ever since

winners were American-bred – Sir Ivor (1968), Nijinsky (1970), Mill Reef (1971) and Roberto (1972). The French too have been a constant presence, as have the Irish, who are still dominant in the world of steeplechasing. The British have to work hard these days to compete in the sport they invented. But that is as it should be.

A postscript. In July 2007, a long-standing British tradition finally came to an end. The Jockey Club relinquished its power to regulate the sport to the new and independent British Horseracing Authority. Perhaps the surprise is not that this should have happened but that an elite private club should have held on to these powers for 250 years. But then, that's Britain.

The tote

The automatic totalizator, or 'tote', was invented by the Norfolk-born son of the Primate of New Zealand, who knew nothing about horse racing and had no interest in betting. Sir George Alfred Julius inherited a love of gadgetry and machines from his Archbishop father. After gaining a degree in engineering, he went to work for the Western Australian Government Railways. In response to a minor dispute over votes cast in a local election, he developed an idea for a machine which would accurately count votes without human intervention. But the Government rejected it on the grounds of cost – elections don't happen very often, after all. A friend then asked him if it could be adapted as a 'tote'. Pari-mutuel betting, where all the money bet on a race (minus a commission) is divided among those who backed the winner, had been developed in France in the late nineteenth century, but no one had come up with a quick and accurate way of working out the total. 'At that time I had never seen a racecourse,' Julius said later. 'I found the problem of great interest as the perfect tote must have a mechanism capable of adding the records from a number of operators, all of whom might issue a ticket on the same horse at the same instant.' It took him five years to perfect his machine. He sold the first one to the Ellerslie Racecourse in Auckland, NZ, in 1913. It was a runaway success. Julius went on to sell his tote to racecourses in twenty-nine different countries, including the UK and USA. The last one finally went out of service on 25 September 1987 at the Harringay dog track in London.

3.
CRICKET

Opening the innings . . .

ON NORTH STREET in the centre of the old market town of Guildford
in Surrey, there is a small square, enclosed on three sides. Most of
the surface is marked out as parking spaces, except for an area around
an old tree. On the right is a window shop, on the left a furniture
and home accessories shop called Lombok. Straight ahead is a much
bigger store called Multiyork (Master Furniture Makers). It looks like a
thoroughly nondescript piece of urban landscape.

However, what is now Lombok used to be the Horse and Groom
pub. On 5 October 1974, it was blown up by the IRA, killing five
people. The tree is quite probably the 'Speaking Tree', Guildford's old
version of Speaker's Corner. And the land on which Multiyork now
stands is the first place that we know for certain that cricket, the
quintessentially English game, was ever played.

At the Surrey History Centre in nearby Woking, they keep the
original Guildford Borough Court Book 1586–1675. It's a large and
handsome leather-bound volume commonly known to the staff as
'The Cricket Book'. On page 40 there is a deposition given by one
John Derrick, aged 59, one of the Queen's coroners, in a dispute
about the ownership of this land. It is dated 16 January 1598. In it,
Mr Derrick says he knew the place well. In spidery copperplate, the
book goes on:

And also this deponent saith that hee beinge a scholler in the ffree school did runne and play there at Creckett and other plaies.

It is the oldest written reference to cricket we have. Given his age, it suggests that the young John Derrick was happily playing cricket on this piece of land in the 1550s, during the reigns of Edward VI and Bloody Queen Mary. It's on that land that Multiyork now stands. (And

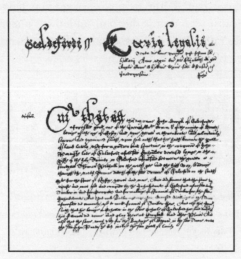

John Derrick's deposition dated 16 January 1598:
the oldest written reference to cricket

there is still a cricket connection: Multiyork's area manager at the time of writing is the father of sometime England wicketkeeper Matt Prior.)

Guildford may be the first place that we *know* that cricket was played, but it almost certainly wasn't the first place that the game was ever enjoyed. The ancient origins of cricket are a mystery. We simply don't know how it began. But we have a pretty good idea of where it started: in the Weald of Kent and the downlands of Sussex and Surrey.

So let's imagine what may have happened. Country boys, perhaps tending sheep, may have whiled away their time by bowling a primitive ball, possibly matted sheep's wool or even a stone, at a target. They probably rolled the ball along the ground, as in the even older sport of bowling. Their opponent stood in front of the target with a stick (an ancient Anglo-Saxon word for staff or stick was *cricc*) and tried to stop the ball reaching it. The target might have been a tree stump or a hurdle gate into a sheep pen. Such gates consisted of two uprights and a crossbar resting on slotted tops. The gate was called a 'wicket' and the crossbar a 'bail'. Ultimately, the wicket may have won out over the stump because dislodging the bail ended all uncertainty. It was also, of course, rather more transportable. But the word 'stump' was retained to describe the uprights of the wicket.

The first known depiction of cricket, drawn by the French artist Gravelot in England in 1611 as a children's book illustration

A romantic notion, and it may even be true. We don't know. Nor do we have any clear idea of when the game started. There is a reference in the Royal Wardrobe Accounts for 1299–1300 of £6 being paid out for the 15-year-old Prince Edward (later Edward II) to play at '*creag*'. Many attempts have been made to relate *creag* to cricket but none have reached any particularly convincing conclusion. There was no further written reference to the game until John Derrick's deposition 300 years later. This may have been because it wasn't very popular or was played only by boys. Certainly it was never singled out for prohibition, unlike other such subversive sports as bowls and football.

But by the early seventeenth century, the dawn of Puritanism, the climate was clearly changing. On Easter Sunday, 1611, Bartholomew Wyatt and Richard Latter of Sidlesham in Sussex made the grievous mistake of playing a bit of cricket rather than going to church. This could not be tolerated. They were dragged before a consistory court in Chichester Cathedral and fined twelvepence and ordered to pay penance. There were many more such cases to come.

In 1629, the Reverend Henry Cuffin, a young curate from the village of Ruckinge in Kent, was censured for playing cricket after evening prayers 'in very unseemely manner with boyes and other very meane and base persons of our parrishe to the great scandal of his Ministerie and offence of such as sawe him play at the said game'. Young Cuffin's response was that he had in fact been playing with 'persons . . . of repute and fashion'. Cricket, it seems, was no longer purely a peasant's game.

On 29 May 1646, in the midst of the Civil War, four gentlemen from Maidstone lost a game of cricket on the common land at Cox Heath, just south of the town, to two young Royalists. We know about it because of a court case. A wager had been laid – for twelve candles – and when the losers refused to deliver, the victors sued. It is the first time that gambling, however modest, had been officially associated with cricket.

As the black cloud of Puritanism spread over the land, cricket became increasingly reviled. In 1654, at the start of the Protectorate, three men from Eltham in Kent were fined twenty-four pence – double the previous penalty – for daring to play cricket on a Sunday. This despite the fact the young Oliver Cromwell is described by Sir William Dugdale, admittedly a Royalist writer, as going up to London in 1617 to indulge in football, cricket, cudgelling and wrestling, and thus 'gaining for himself the name of royster'. Clearly the Lord Protector had outgrown such childish misdemeanours. After all he had also banned Christmas.

Charles II's Restoration in 1660 led to an explosion in all kinds of sporting activity. Forbidden popular favourites such as bear-baiting, bull-baiting and cock-fighting re-emerged. Horse racing, bowls and tennis prospered. And gambling was rife – so much so that an Act was passed in 1664 limiting stakes to £100, the equivalent of around £10,000 in today's money.

By 1668, the landlord of the Ram Inn in Smithfield was paying rates for a cricket field. Thenceforth, publicans and innkeepers were to play a major role in the commercialization of the sport. That same year, the court in Maidstone decided to waive excise duty on the sale of beer 'at an horse race or kricketing'. It's clear that cricket matches were beginning to attract sizeable – and profitable – crowds.

Over the next twenty years, it seems likely that the game grew in popularity – but we hear nothing about it. This is partly because it wasn't the subject of court proceedings any more and partly because the press, such as it was, was still under strict control to prevent the spread of sedition. But in 1696, eight years after the Glorious Revolution installed dour William of Orange on the throne, all press restrictions were lifted. The following year the *Foreign Post* reported that 'The middle of last week a great match at cricket was played in Sussex; they were eleven of a side, and they played for fifty guineas apiece.' Matches such as this were to set the pattern for the game for much of the next century.

The game in 1700

So what sort of game were these new-style gamblers risking their money on? As far as we know there were no set 'Laws of Cricket' – rules were decided between sides on a match-by-match basis and often varied from village to village. There was no set number of players, though eleven or twelve a side seems to have been widely favoured.

Matches were played on rough open ground, a long way from the manicured squares of today. The wickets consisted of two stumps and a bail and seemed to vary a bit in size – they were probably 6 to 8 inches wide and much lower than they are today. They were 'pitched' a fair distance apart – 22 yards may have been common because it represented four 'gads' or 'goads', an important measurement of length in Tudor times equivalent to 16.5 modern feet.

The bowlers bowled the ball – a 'leathern orb' according to a poem by schoolmaster William Goldwin published in 1706 – quite fast underarm along the ground. The batsman stood guard over his wicket with a curved bat a bit like a hockey stick, not a bad shape, as any hockey player will tell you, for hitting a ball coming at you along the ground.

*'An Exact Representation of the Game of Cricket', an engraving
from 1743: note the scorers sitting on the pitch*

There were generally two umpires, one appointed by each side. They stood close to their respective wickets and carried a 'stick'. To score a run the batsman had to touch the umpire's stick. The scorers, who seemingly sat side by side on the field of play, would then register the run by carving a notch on a stick, with every tenth notch being deeper than the rest to make counting easier. Hence in the early days runs were generally known as notches.

There were no boundaries. Because of the roughness of the terrain, scores tended to be low by modern standards. For the same reason, injuries to the shins were frequent. Players wore their ordinary clothes – shirts, breeches and silk stockings – which made it easy to see the bruises swell and the blood flow. It would be more than 100 years before protective clothing was introduced.

But the essence of the modern game was there. Over the next

century, it would evolve into something that we would easily recognize today.

The age of patrons

The 1720 edition of Stow's *Survey of London* mentioned cricket for the first time. It classed it as an amusement of 'the more common sort' of people, along with such vulgar activities as football, wrestling, drinking in alehouses and bell-ringing.

Certainly cricket was very popular among the ordinary folk of Sussex, Surrey and Kent. Regular matches were played between villages on the village green, on common land or on the estate of the local squire. By the eighteenth century the game had acquired a degree of respectability. We know from schoolmaster William Goldwin that it was being played at Eton and that Samuel Johnson played the game at Oxford in 1729.

Cricket's growing popularity among the wealthier classes led to games of a very different kind. What lay behind these 'great matches' was money. The early 1700s were obsessed with speculation. The wealthy were risking their fortunes in new industries, the stock market and investment in the burgeoning colonies. The South Sea Bubble, the stock market crash of the time, burst in 1720. In this atmosphere gambling had become a national addiction. And cricket was seen as a perfect vehicle.

Members of the nobility and the gentry would put together teams taken from their households (many a gardener and groom were employed largely for their cricketing ability), from their tenants or from local villagers. The players would be paid for their exertions, while the patrons would fix the sum of money for which the match – or often a series of matches – would be played.

These 'great matches' were carefully arranged. In 1727, the second Duke of Richmond, one of the most important early patrons, agreed to play two matches against Mr Alan Brodrick, heir to Viscount Midleton. The two men drew up strict 'Articles of Agreement' clarifying the accepted but as yet unwritten rules of the game and specifying in sixteen points how the match would be played. One reads:

that there shall be one umpire of each side; & that if any of the Gamesters shall speak or give their opinion, on any point of the game, they are to be turned out & voided in the match; this not to extend to the Duke of Richmond and Mr Brodrick.

So, one rule for the 'gamesters', another for the patrons.

These matches were played for a modest twelve guineas per match. But as the century wore on, the stakes grew larger and larger. In the 1730s, no less a person than Frederick Louis, Prince of Wales, began to take an interest in the game. He was the eldest son of George II and is known to history as 'Poor Fred' after an epitaph written after his early death at the age of 44:

> Here lies poor Fred,
> Who was alive and is dead:
> Had it been his father,
> I had much rather;
> Had it been his brother,
> Still better than another;
> Had it been his sister,
> No one would have missed her;
> Had it been the whole generation,
> Still better for the nation;
> But since 'tis only Fred,
> Who was alive and is dead, –
> There's no more to be said!

Poor Fred did not come to Britain until he was twenty, when his father succeeded to the throne as George II in 1727. His initial interest in cricket may have been a conscious attempt to 'anglicize' himself (a little later he was indirectly responsible for 'Rule, Britannia', which was given its first performance at his country house). But cricket does seem to have become a genuine enthusiasm. He became a serious patron and an occasional player, although he probably wasn't very good. In July 1735, Poor Fred played a match against a Kent side sponsored by his friend Charles Sackville, the Earl of Middlesex, for the sum of £1000, around £100,000 today. The Prince lost both this and the subsequent return match, even though he fielded Cook of Brentford, one of the best bowlers of the day. So Poor Fred became significantly poorer.

There was another development around this time which was to be a harbinger of the future: the emergence of a 'professional' village club side. The Duke of Richmond gave his support to the village team

'The Game of Cricket': an early engraving showing
two-stump wickets and the umpires with sticks

from Slindon, which was close to his country seat at Goodwood. Two of the Duke's regulars played for the village – his groom Thomas Waymark, who was already well known, and a barber from Surrey called Stephen Dingate. But the core of the team was the three Newland brothers, who were born in the village. Richard Newland was regarded by many as the best player in England. He captained the team for a run of forty-three games with only one defeat.

Newland was a huge draw. In 1743, he led a team of Three of England against Three of Kent in a single-wicket game at the Artillery Ground in London. The names mean little – the teams were simply made up of the best available box-office attractions. In this case Newland's team included a bricklayer and a 'nondescript', while 'Kent' had a clock-maker and a tanner. These ordinary working men still managed to attract a crowd of 10,000. The match was for 500 guineas, presumably put up by the patrons of each side.

In the second half of the century, Slindon's achievements were to be overshadowed by the emergence of another 'professional' village side who not only dominated cricket for the next two decades but also had a lot to do with shaping the modern game.

The Hambledon Club

The motto of the Hambledon Club was 'Wine, Cricket and Song'. In that order. This was not a group of players that got together to enjoy a game – indeed, most of the members were not players and most of the players were not members. This was a social club and the primary aim of the gentlemen who joined was to gamble and to enjoy themselves. An entry in an early club book reads: 'A wet day: only three members present: nine bottles of wine.'

The club was an amalgam of notables from far afield and gentlemen from the surrounding area. According to one count, of the 157 members listed over time, eighteen had titles, six were MPs, two county sheriffs, twenty-seven army and navy officers (of whom ten went on to be admirals – the village is near Portsmouth), four clergymen and, perhaps appropriately, two wine merchants. The earliest minute book which survives is full of references to buying wine. It also lists at the beginning a series of 'standing toasts':

1. The Queen's Mother
2. The King
3. Hambledon Club
4. Cricket
5. To the Immortal Memory of Madge
6. The President

Number 5 has caused much speculation. Who – or what – is Madge? Various theories have been put forward, of varying degrees of scurrility, all of them largely based on speculation. It is probably safer to leave the matter unresolved, to allow the imagination full rein but in private.

A key figure in the club's early history was Richard Nyren, landlord of the Bat and Ball Inn on Broadhalfpenny Down in Hampshire, where the club played in the early days. He had learnt his cricket from his uncle, the great Richard Newland from Slindon. He captained the

The Bat and Ball Inn on Broadhalfpenny Down: landlord Richard
Nyren was both captain and caterer to the Hambledon club

team and was a fine bowler and a pretty good bat. But he was also the interface between the players and the members. He organized the team on behalf of the club and arranged matches for individual members at Broadhalfpenny Down and elsewhere. And he had an eye for business: he provided dinner for a shilling, with port at two shillings a bottle and sherry at three. We don't know how much he charged for wine but we can be sure that there was plenty of it around.

His son John Nyren also played for the club in the later years. But

John's greatest contribution was a memoir he published in 1833, half
a century after the club's glory days, called *The Cricketers of My Time*.
In it he paints charming and affectionate portraits of the players who
dominated cricket for twenty years.

The players that Nyren Sr led were hired hands. Some were reasonably local but many came from the neighbouring counties of Sussex
and Surrey. They were paid on a match-by-match basis, 'four shillings
if winners, and three shillings if losers'. For away matches, they were
paid more than double – seven to nine shillings – at a time when a farm
labourer's wage was eight or nine shillings for a six-day week.

It is unclear exactly how much they were paid for the 'great matches'
which took place every week during the season, usually for £500 but
sometimes for £1000. Their opponents were often teams assembled by
the second generation of patrons of the game: Lord John Sackville, the
third Duke of Dorset; his neighbour from Kent, Sir Horace Mann; and
the Earl of Tankerville from Surrey.

These games were grand affairs. In August 1772, a match took place
at Sir Horace Mann's estate at Bourne Place between his All England
team (which meant he had brought in players from outside his native
Kent) and a team from Hampshire which included several Hambledon
players. Seats and benches were laid out around the ground, booths
erected selling food and drink and grandstands were put up for the
elite, which included many of the grandest figures in the county. It was
estimated that between 15,000 and 20,000 spectators attended on the
first day of the two-day game.

The scene would have been similar at Broadhalfpenny Down and
the other grounds where Hambledon sometimes played – Stoke Down
and later Windmill Down – with refreshment booths, special tents for
grandees and for ladies, and a lodge for club members. At least two
sides of the ground would be packed with the carts and wagons of local
spectators.

An advertisement appeared in the *Hampshire Chronicle* of 22 June
1777, which showed that Richard Nyren's interests spread beyond the
cricket: 'NYREN has laid in a stock of excellent wines and cold provisions, and hopes the air of Stoke Down will, with the Ladies at least,

stand in the place of Marbres, Aspiques, Blanc Manges &c. For good
appetite, there will be a sufficient quantity of beef, ham, chicken and
tarts.'

It is a feature of cricket at this time that it seems to have been well
attended by 'the Ladies'. The Rev. Reynell Cotton, Master of Hyde
Abbey School, Winchester, suggests in the comic cricket song he
composed for the club around 1772, which was later adopted as its
anthem, that their attention might not always be on the game:

> The parties are met, and array'd all in white,
> Famed Elis ne'er boasted so noble a sight;
> Each nymph looks askance at her favourite swain,
> And views him half stripp'd both with pleasure and pain.

But for all these social niceties, the cricket itself was taken very
seriously. It had to be considering the amount of money that was
often at stake. And over the twenty or more years of Hambledon's
dominance, important changes were introduced to the game. Many
stemmed from 1744 when the first attempt was made to bring together
the 'Laws of Cricket' by 'the Cricket Club', probably the London Club,
a collection of gentlemen who then played at the Artillery Ground in
Finsbury and spent much of their leisure time at the Star and Garter
in Pall Mall, the favourite watering hole of aristocratic sporting blades.

The 'Laws' established that the stumps should be 22 inches high and
the bail across them 6 inches. This was higher and narrower than had
been customary and either reflected, or made possible, a new bowling
technique. Instead of trundling the ball along the ground, the extra
height of the stumps made it worthwhile to 'pitch' the ball in front of
the batsman so that it bounced up at him. If he missed, there was now
a lot more of a target to hit.

The legendary Edward Stevens (universally known as Lumpy) was
probably the first to try 'pitching on a length', as this new form of
bowling was called. But it was David Harris who perfected the technique. John Nyren called him the very best bowler of his age: 'His balls
were very little beholden to the ground when pitched; it was but a

touch, and up again; and woe be to the man who did not get in to block them; for they had such a peculiar curl that they would grind his fingers against the bat . . .'

The new technique led to another change. The old curved bat was fine for hitting a ball on the ground, but hopeless at hitting a ball coming up at you 'off a length'. So in the 1750s, the design of the bat

Contemporary sketch of David Harris, who perfected the art of 'pitching on a length'

changed. It became straight and flat at the front, with a distinct shoulder at the top. The design is attributed to John Small Sr. He had a formidable reputation as the best of the early Hambledon batsmen. Of the grand match at Bourne Park in August 1772, the *Kentish Gazette* reported that: 'Lumpy had the honour of bowling out Small, which had not been done for some years.'

The reason it had been such a rare occurrence is that John Small is also credited with another development. Against the old trundling style of bowling, the batsman stood face-on to the bowler. That didn't work against flighted 'length' balls. Instead, the batsman now took guard side-on to the bowler. This enabled him to do what John Nyren had said was so vital against David Harris – 'get in to block them'. In other words, get your foot to the pitch of the ball and stop it. The forward defensive stroke was born.

Another change emerged from a contest between Lumpy and John Small. Five of Kent was playing Five of England in a single-wicket game at the Artillery Ground in London. Small went in last man for England with 14 runs needed to win. His innings lasted two and three-quarter hours and he eventually scored the runs, but not before Lumpy had beaten him three times, only to see the ball go *between* the stumps without removing the bail. This was thought unfair – you might almost say not cricket – and shortly afterwards a third, middle stump was introduced.

The rules of the game evolved as they were needed. When, for instance, Thomas White of Reigate came to the crease at Hambledon with a bat as wide as the wicket, this was not to be tolerated. Richard Nyren, John Small and Thomas Brett, the club's leading bowler, signed a resolution saying the club would not play against anyone with a bat wider than 4¼ inches. It remains the regulation size for a cricket bat today.

The best wielder of the bat in the later Hambledon years was William Beldham, always known as 'Silver Billy'. He came from Farnham in Surrey where he had been trained by Harry Hall, a local gingerbread baker who was an average cricketer but a brilliant coach. Silver Billy remained at the top of the game for forty years. 'No one within my recollection,' wrote John Nyren, 'could stop a ball better, or make more brilliant hits all over the ground. Wherever the ball was bowled, there she was hit away, and in the most severe, venomous style.'

One of the most endearing Hambledon characters was 'The Little Farmer', William Lamborn, the first off-spin bowler. Anyone who has ever bowled underarm will know that leg spin is easy but off spin is fiendishly difficult. Just try it. This is how Nyren describes it: '. . . he had the most extraordinary delivery I ever saw. The ball was delivered quite low, and with a twist; not like the generality of right-handed

William 'Silver Billy' Beldham, a contemporary
sketch of the greatest batsman of his day

'Silver Billy' Beldham in old age: his first
class career lasted for forty years

bowlers, but just the reverse way: that is if bowling to a right-handed hitter, his ball would twist from the off stump to the leg. He was the first I remember who introduced this teazing style of delivering the ball.'

Lamborn's difficulty at first was that he bowled too straight, so that when the ball spun it might beat the bat but it would also miss leg stump. Nyren Sr – 'after a great deal of trouble (for the Farmer's comprehension did not equal the speed of lightning)' – persuaded him to pitch the ball outside off stump so that it spun into the wicket. Once mastered, this new trick proved devastating. Against an All England side, writes John Nyren, '. . . the Little Farmer was appointed one of our bowlers; and, egad! this new trick of his so bothered the Kent and Surrey men that they tumbled out one after another, as if they had been picked off by a rifle corps.'

Another bowling innovation came from Hambledon's Tom Walker, 'an anointed clod-stumper' of extreme rusticity, according to Nyren: 'Tom's hard, ungainly, scrag-of-mutton frame; wilted, apple-john face, (he always looked twenty years older than he really was), his long spider

Hambledon's Tom Walker, 'Old Ever-lasting', who
scored the first recorded century at Lord's

legs, as thick at the ankles as the hips, and perfectly strait all the way down – for the embellishment of a calf in Tom's leg, Dame Nature had considered would be but a wanton superfluity.' Tom Walker was mainly known as a steadfast defensive batsman – his nickname was 'Old Ever-lasting' – but his bowling innovation was what Nyren called 'throwing' and would later be called round-arm. He was too far ahead of his time. A council of his own club decided that it was 'foul play' and he was firmly told not to do it again.

Hambledon's influence on cricket was huge, far larger than anyone would expect from a small village in Hampshire. But then it was no ordinary club. It was an amalgamation of the luminaries of the Star and Garter and the Artillery Ground with some of the best players in the country. But it was not the only club prospering at the time. Others were springing up throughout the Home Counties. And gradually the appeal of cricket was spreading out of its homeland and into Berkshire, Bedfordshire, Oxfordshire, Cambridgeshire, Suffolk, Norfolk, Nottinghamshire, Warwickshire, Yorkshire and even Durham. It was becoming a national English game.

Towards the end of the eighteenth century, another club was to be founded – almost accidentally – which would come to influence not just the national game but the whole of international cricket.

The Mary-le-Bone Club

In 1774 and again in 1788, the 'Laws of Cricket' were revised at the Star and Garter, first by the London Club and then by a 'committee of Noblemen and Gentlemen of Kent, Hampshire, Surrey, Sussex, Middlesex and London'. They weren't trying to lay down universal laws for every cricketer. Instead, they were agreeing among themselves how the games in which they would play, which they would sponsor and on which – most importantly – they would wager large sums of money, should be conducted.

Cricket had become extremely fashionable in London by this time. The old London Club had had its playing headquarters at the Artillery

Ground. But after the untimely death in 1751 of their president, the Prince of Wales – Poor Fred – the fashionable set began to transfer their allegiance to White Conduit Fields in Islington. Now largely covered by the sprawl of King's Cross railway station, it was then in unadulterated countryside, a fact that local publican, Robert Bartholomew, was keen to advertise:

Hot loaves and butter every day, milk directly from the cows; coffee and tea and all manner of liquors in the greatest perfection; also a handsome Long Room from whence is the most copious prospect and envy situation of any now in vogue.

Note: my cows eat no grains, neither any adulteration in the milk or cream. Bats and balls for cricket and a convenient field to play in.

At Hambledon, the members and the professionals had been happy to play together. Indeed, the romantic social historian G. M. Trevelyan, referring to a game in which the future Duke of Dorset played in a team captained by his own gardener, suggested that 'If the French *noblesse* had been capable of playing cricket with their peasants, their chateaux would never have been burnt.' But the White Conduit Club allowed no such social mix. Their rules stated 'none but gentlemen ever to play'.

But their chosen ground was far from being exclusive. On 22 June 1785 the *Daily Universal Register*, the forerunner of *The Times*, suggested, tongue firmly in cheek, that the 'Lordling cricketers who amuse themselves in White Conduit Street' should seek an Act of Parliament to enclose their 'play ground' in order to 'protect themselves from a repetition of severe rebuke which they justly merit, and received on Saturday evening from some spirited citizens whom they insulted and attempted *vi et armis* to drive from their footpath, pretending it was within their bounds'.

Protection from such 'spirited citizens' was clearly needed. In 1786 two of the club members, the Earl of Winchilsea and Colonel Charles Lennox (later the Fourth Duke of Richmond), made an approach to an ambitious young man who was an attendant at the White Conduit Club and often bowled in the practice nets, for the benefit of gentlemen batsmen. They asked him to try to find a private ground closer to the fashionable West End and offered their full financial support if he managed to do so. The attendant's name was Thomas Lord.

*Thomas Lord, founder of the home of
cricket which still bears his name*

Lord's background is remarkable. He was born in Thirsk in Yorkshire in 1755 and his birth certificate said he was the son of 'William Lord, Labourer'. In fact he came from an old Catholic landowning family, but in 1745 his father had supported the Jacobite rebellion and raised 500 horses at his own expense to serve Bonnie Prince Charlie. But after the rebellion was brutally put down by the 'Butcher of Culloden' – the Duke of Cumberland, despised younger brother of 'Poor Fred' who was ironically a leading light at the Star and Garter – William's property was confiscated and he was forced to work as a labourer on the land he had once owned.

The family managed to move to Norfolk when Thomas was a boy

and it was there that he discovered a talent for cricket. When he left school, he headed straight for London. There he secured a job with the White Conduit Club and also managed to set himself up as a wine merchant. He was an entrepreneur.

In response to the approach from Winchilsea and Lennox, Lord leased part of the Portman estate in Marylebone, on the spot which is now Dorset Square. He put up a high fence all around the ground, erected a shed to store equipment, prepared the field as best he could and by May 1787 was ready for business. The first match recorded there was between makeshift county sides for 100 guineas and certainly not for gentlemen only. But enough of the socialites from the White Conduit Club, led by Lord Winchilsea, transferred their allegiance to the new ground for people to start talking before the year was out of 'the Marylebone Club'. All written records of the founding of the club were destroyed in a fire in 1825. But the Marylebone Cricket Club, or MCC as it quickly became known, has always dated its founding to 1787.

The following year the new club issued a further revision of the 'Laws of Cricket'. But once again these were rules to govern their own matches. If other clubs wanted to adopt them, that was their choice, but it was not the object of the exercise. The day when the MCC would be seen as the fount of regulatory rectitude was still in the future.

Within a year or two, the Marylebone Club had overtaken Hambledon as the strongest cricketing force in the land. It had also taken over several of the Hampshire club's former hired hands. On 7 May 1792, Tom Walker – 'Old Ever-lasting' – scored the first century recorded at Lord's for the MCC in a match against Middlesex. His former Hambledon colleague 'Silver Billy' Beldham, still the best batsman in the country, scored the second in the same match.

Forsaken by both its rich patrons and by its best players, Hambledon struggled to continue. The last entry in the minute book, for 21 September 1796, simply says 'No Gentlemen'. The club was wound up shortly afterwards.

A sticky wicket

With its newly established supremacy, the Marylebone Cricket Club should have thrived. But it didn't. This was partly because of the times. The French Revolution had struck fear into the governing class. Poverty was rife, especially in rural areas. Radicalism was spreading. And the country was at war with France. While none of this had much real impact on what Sir Derek Birley calls 'the enjoying classes', it seems to have dented their confidence.

The rich patron was a thing of the past. Gone were the days when two individuals could sponsor a game between 'Kent' or 'Surrey' and an 'All England XI'. Now, a subscription list needed to be posted at Lord's and notices put up at Brooks's and the other fashionable West End clubs asking for guarantors. As a result, the number of matches declined. The MCC played twenty-four games in 1800, but only seven in 1803. So-called 'England' matches dropped from eight in 1800 to two in 1802 and often only one a year for a period after that. The same trend can be seen in 'county' matches.

As a result, Thomas Lord found he couldn't live off the MCC alone. So he let his ground out to anyone who wanted to play, often single-wicket matches for considerable sums. And then he diversified. There were foot races, pigeon-shooting contests, balloon ascents and even hopping races. On more than one occasion, his land was used for the presentation of colours to various regiments.

In 1810 Lord's lease came up for renewal. The continuing expansion of London drove the Portman Estate to demand a much higher rent. But Lord had already rented some alternative fields in what is now Regent's Park. But the members hated it. The MCC played no games there in 1811 or 1812, and only three the year after. But Lord was someone who always enjoyed great luck. Parliament came along and told him they wanted to build the new Regent's Canal right through his cricket pitch. They offered him £4000 compensation and another piece of land in St John's Wood. He snapped it up. The ground that bears his name has been there ever since.

Conflict and corruption

The dominant figure in the MCC around the turn of the century and beyond was Lord Frederick Beauclerk, fourth son of the Duke of St Albans and a great grandson of Charles II and Nell Gwyn. He was the first amateur aristocrat who could play cricket as well as a proletarian professional. And he needed to.

As a younger son, he had inherited little more than a living from the Church of England, eventually as the Vicar of St Albans. (He was not a conventional parson by any means; he once delivered his sermon from the saddle, to ram home the message that he was hunting for souls.) But his income was not enough to enable someone with his expensive tastes to live comfortably, so he set out to enhance his earnings by betting on himself at cricket. He later estimated that he safely made £600 a year (£60,000 today) for some thirty-five years from this activity.

He was discovered by the Earl of Winchilsea as a slow bowler at Cambridge and played his first game for the MCC in 1791. He quickly showed a canny understanding of the game, anticipating any stroke a batsman might play. And he worked hard on his batting until he became one of the most prolific century scorers of the pre-Grace days. His feel for the game made him a natural captain. He was admired and respected both for his ability and his breeding, but he wasn't always liked. He was arrogant and bad-tempered and, when money was at stake, he was not averse to bending matters in his favour whenever he could.

His only rival in the early years of the century was the massively competitive George Osbaldeston, always known as the Squire. He was a superb sportsman, excelling at riding, hunting, shooting, fishing and fisticuffs. And he was no mean cricketer – a hard-hitting batsman and a ferocious fast bowler. He also had an aversion to sporting parsons and anyone with a title. In 1810 the Squire challenged Beauclerk to a single-wicket match between himself and his paid player William Lambert (one of the biggest stars in England at the time) and Beauclerk and whoever he should choose (it was T. C. Howard). The purse was to be 50 guineas.

On the morning of the match, Osbaldeston was taken ill. He asked for a postponement. Beauclerk refused: 'Play or pay.' The Squire went

George Osbaldeston MP, always known as the Squire,
one of the most competitive sportsmen of his day

in for three balls, scored one run and retired sick. But Lambert scored 56 in the first innings and 24 in the second. And playing alone, he bowled Lord Frederick and Howard out for 24 in the first innings and 42 in the second – giving victory to the Squire's cause by 15 runs.

Lambert's major weapon had been Beauclerk's temper. He bowled him wide ball after wide ball, for which at that time there was no penalty. When he finally delivered a straight ball, Lord Frederick was so apoplectic that he missed it and was bowled. Beauclerk was determined this should never happen again, and the concept of the wide was written into the Laws the following year.

It was a humiliating defeat that Beauclerk was not to forget. His revenge came through another facet of the early nineteenth-century game – corruption. After each match the nobility would repair to the Star and Garter, while the players headed for the Green Man and Still in Oxford Street. There the stars, in a manner we can recognize today, would eat, drink, gamble and be merry in a style which was hard to sustain even on the money they were being paid – five guineas for a win and three for a loss. Those that had lost were particularly vulnerable to the overtures of the 'legs' – bookies' runners so called because of the black legs they gathered from running through the mud at Newmarket.

The first historian of cricket, the Reverend James Pycroft, put it bluntly in 1851: 'The constant habit of betting will take the honesty out of any man.' He extracted a confession from one of the major players of the time, William Fennex, who had pioneered coming down the wicket to attack spin bowling:

Matches were bought and matches were sold, and gentlemen who meant honestly lost large sums of money, till the rogues beat themselves at last. They over-did it; they spoilt their own trade . . .

Fennex continued: 'One match up the country I did sell – a match made by Mr Osbaldeston at Nottingham.' At this point, Pycroft lobs in his own bombshell. He had received information which indicated that players on the Nottingham side had also agreed to throw the match for money. 'The match was sold for Nottingham too . . .'

True or not, it conjures up quite a spectacle. Two sides using all their cunning and skill to avoid winning. Squire Osbaldeston did not play in the match himself – he left matters to Lambert. But Beauclerk was on the field. Not averse to sharp practice himself, on this occasion he did everything he could to win – so much so, according to Pycroft, that 'he broke a finger trying to stop a designed and wilful overthrow' and had to bat one-handed in the second innings.

Despite their best efforts, Nottingham failed and won the match, much to the annoyance of Lord Frederick. He couldn't lay a finger on Osbaldeston himself – the code of honour among gentlemen meant any accusation would have led to a duel, and the Squire was one of the best shots in the country. But he managed to find someone to dish the dirt on Lambert who, despite his prowess, never played at Lord's again.

Beauclerk gained his revenge some time later. The Squire had always boasted that he could beat any man in England at single-wicket because of his extraordinarily fast bowling. But a new man called George Brown had emerged, playing for Brighton, who appeared to bowl even faster. The Squire was goaded into challenging him and duly lost, much to the amusement not only of his enemies but his supporters too. 'He was so angry,' Pycroft reports, 'that he went to the Pavilion and scratched his name off the list of members.' When he later asked to be reinstated, Lord Frederick gave him short shrift.

By this time, the MCC was beginning to be seen as the arbiter of the rules of the game. Disputes would be referred to the club, often to Lord Frederick personally, because he was regarded as the expert on the 'Laws'. But the club still had no formal authority. And it was about to face one of its biggest tests.

The round-arm revolt

There was a growing feeling among professionals that there was an imbalance in the game. Batsmen, through improved technique, had the advantage. Centuries were becoming almost commonplace. Bowlers were too restricted. The gentlemen amateurs of the MCC were none too concerned, because most of them preferred batting they employed bowlers to give them practice with the bat, but no batsmen to give them practice with the ball. But they made some small concessions. In 1798, they increased the overall size of the stumps to 24 inches by 7. In 1819, they increased the height by 2 inches. Four years later, they added another inch to both height and width, making the wicket 27 inches by 8. (Today, it is 28 inches by 9.)

But for some bowlers, this was not enough. Sometime around 1806, a wealthy landowner from Kent called John Willes decided to follow Tom Walker's example. He started bowling 'round-arm' in country matches in Kent. Instead of bowling underarm, he would bring his

straight arm sideways round his body. In a famous game at Penenden
Heath near Maidstone in July 1807 between 23 of Kent and 13 of All
England, for 1000 guineas, his action caused a sensation. The *Morning
Herald* reported that it 'fully proved an obstacle against getting runs
in comparison to what might have been got by the straight-forward
bowling. This bowling met with great opposition.' The MCC felt
constrained to issue a new ruling in 1816 specifically banning the
innovation. 'Rule 10' clearly states: 'If the arm is extended straight
from the body . . . the umpire shall call no ball.' But introducing a rule
was one thing; enforcing it was another.

Willes continued to bowl round-arm in country games, occasionally
causing riots, and other bowlers began to adopt the new style. Umpires
turned a blind eye if both sides agreed to it. The MCC were helpless.
Eventually, in 1822, a match was arranged at Lord's between Kent
and the MCC in which Willes's action was finally to be tested at the
headquarters of cricket. Willes bowled with his usual straight arm and
the umpire immediately called no ball. Willes stormed off the pitch in
disgust, climbed onto his horse and rode away. He never played in an
important match again, although he did take up coaching – with great
success.

The showdown changed nothing. Round-arm continued to flourish
away from Lord's. Between 1822 and 1827, Sussex became the pre-
eminent team in the country, largely on the strength of its two round-
arm bowlers, William Lillywhite and Jem Broadbridge. But opposition
continued from the conservatives in the MCC, particularly the
increasingly powerful banker William Ward, who bought the lease of
the headquarters ground in 1825 when the cunning old entrepreneur
Thomas Lord, perhaps ready for retirement, threatened to develop it
for housing.

By 1827, the supporters of round-arm had found a potent ally
within the citadel of the MCC. George Knight, the favourite nephew
of novelist Jane Austen, was a round-arm bowler of reasonable proficiency. He started a persuasive campaign to change the law. It was
agreed that there should be three experimental games between Sussex
and England (in other words the MCC), in which Lillywhite and

William Lillywhite, a pioneering round-arm bowler
and a founder member of the All England XI

Broadbridge would be able to use the new style but the England bowlers would not.

The first match took place in Sheffield – a sign of the game's growing popularity in the North – where Sussex triumphed by seven wickets. A second match at Lord's was closer, but Sussex still won by three wickets. For the final game in Brighton, Knight was allowed to bowl round-arm as well. Maybe as a result, England came out on top by just 24 runs (but still, presumably, forfeited the prize money).

The MCC old guard continued to resist change, but their defences were beginning to crumble. In 1828, they agreed to Knight's proposal that round-arm bowling should be allowed provided the hand stayed below the elbow. This new rule proved almost impossible to enforce and in 1835 it was modified again to allow straight-arm bowling provided the hand did not go above the shoulder. Not for the first or the last time, the MCC was following developments rather than leading them.

Old Clarke

Over the next few years, there were further developments in which the MCC played no part. One was the spread of protective pads and gloves. Old diehards scorned such wimpishness, as did the public schools who firmly believed, as Sir Derek Birley said, that muscular Christianity was protection enough. Another was the formation of the first true county clubs: Sussex in 1839, Nottinghamshire in 1841, Kent in 1842 and Surrey in 1845.

Nor were the MCC involved in another innovation that was to have a major impact on the status of the game: taking first-class cricket to all those parts of the country that had not seen it before. That task fell to a portly, middle-aged, one-eyed bricklayer-turned-publican from Nottingham called William Clarke.

Clarke was born in 1798 and made his debut for a Nottingham XI at the age of 17. Over the next thirty years he became a legend at the

William Clark, the one-eyed bricklayer from Nottingham
who founded the All England XI

Nottingham Old Club, missing only two recorded games and captaining the side for many years. During all that time he played at Lord's only once, for the North in their first historic victory over the South in 1836.

His second wife was Mary Chapman, a widow who ran the Trent Bridge Inn near King's Meadows in Nottingham. A true entrepreneur, Clarke bought the adjoining land, enclosed it and turned it into a high-quality cricket ground. Soon the Nottingham team forsook their traditional home, the unenclosed and therefore free Forest Ground, and moved to Trent Bridge, where Clarke charged spectators sixpence a match.

In 1844, he travelled south again to play for the North against the MCC at Lord's and for England against Kent at Canterbury. He repeated the trip the following year. Clarke seems to have been struck by the eagerness of the crowd and their willingness to part with good money to see top players perform. The following year, at the age of 47, he left the Trent Bridge Inn and his ground in the care of his stepson and moved to London to make his fortune.

For the first half of the summer, he worked at Lord's as a practice bowler for members. But when the MCC season finished early in August (to allow members to travel to the country for the start of the grouse season on the 'Glorious Twelfth'), he put together an All England XI and took them on a tour of the North. They played 22 of Sheffield, 18 of Manchester and 18 of Yorkshire. The tour was a great success.

Many teams had called themselves 'England' before, but Clarke's squad really were the best players in the land. They were all professionals, except for two famous but impecunious amateurs, Alfred Mynn and Nicholas Felix. The pros were paid between £4 and £6 a match, the going MCC rate, while Mynn and Felix received an equivalent amount in 'expenses'. Clarke, of course, made considerably more.

The following summer, Old Clarke, as he had become known, worked at Lord's again, taking time off to annihilate the Gentlemen in the annual match against the Players (he and his fellow practice bowler William Lillywhite took all twenty wickets between them). Then he took the All England XI on a more protracted tour. Over two months they played in Manchester, Liverpool, Leeds, York, Stockton, Sheffield, Birmingham, Newcastle and Stourbridge.

The All England XI of 1847: many teams had called themselves England before but Old Clarke's team really were the best players in the land

The following year, the All England XI went full-time, playing seventeen matches over the summer. They were always in demand. By 1851, they were playing thirty-four matches in a season. Not surprisingly, the MCC saw them as a threat, an assault on their authority (even though Clarke always made his players available for the North v. South and Gentlemen v. Players games). But the more open-minded saw the benefits: by taking first-class cricket to places where it had never been seen before, Clarke was turning the sport into the national summer game; and he was providing regular employment for professionals, allowing them to make steady money while they still could.

Members of Clarke's team were treated almost like rock stars. Their entertainment was planned months in advance. When they arrived at the rail or coach station, they would be mobbed by crowds of admirers. Thousands would attend the match. And afterwards there'd be more fun and games – banquets, balls, fêtes and fireworks. But then, as often as not, they'd have to board a train or a stagecoach to travel through the night to the location of the next match. It may have been fun, but it was also gruelling.

After a while the strain – and the disproportionate amount of money Clarke was making – began to tell. In 1852 two of his former players, John Wisden (who was known as 'The Little Marvel' and once took all ten wickets in an innings, all of them clean bowled) and Jemmy Dean, both of Sussex, started a rival circus called the United All England XI. Four years later, having taken a wicket just two months before with the last ball he ever bowled, Clarke died at the age of 57. His team was taken over by his Nottingham colleague George Parr, who happened also to be a business partner of John Wisden (whose company went on to found the cricketers' almanack which bears his name, although there's no evidence that he ever had much to do with it). They agreed that the two teams should not only coexist but play an annual game together at Lord's, with the proceeds going to the new Cricketers' Fund Friendly Society.

John Wisden, the 'Little Marvel', who founded the
cricketer's almanac which bears his name

Chaos and confusion

As the nineteenth century moved into its second half, cricket was in a muddle. No one quite knew how it was going to develop.

The MCC was widely regarded as the arbiter of 'the Laws' except, formally, by itself. 'We make these rules for our own matches,' they persistently said. 'If anyone else wants to follow them, that's fine. It's their choice.' It was the natural home of gentlemanly amateurism, yet it employed professionals to bowl at its members and play in its matches. Most of those matches were against second-rank sides – the Royal Artillery, Eton, the emerging county clubs – and lacked the big-name professionals who would pull in the crowds. Its major role was hosting the big 'society' games each year – Oxford v. Cambridge, Eton v. Harrow, Gentlemen v. Players and North v. South.

Then there were the travelling professional 'Elevens', as they became known. In the years following William Clarke's death many new teams competed for audiences with his old team and that of John Wisden. Many didn't last very long – there weren't enough high-quality players to sustain them – but one that was to stick around for quite a while and have a considerable influence was the United South of England XI.

The county clubs were also growing in importance. The earliest four were joined later in the century by Yorkshire, Hampshire, Middlesex, Lancashire, Worcestershire, Derbyshire, Gloucestershire, Somerset, Essex and Leicestershire. Warwickshire and Glamorgan arrived in the 1880s. These were not representative teams in any official sense, they were just clubs founded by important local cricketers. Some, such as Notts, were fiercely professional; others such as Surrey had a more amateur feel. Birth and residency qualifications were vague, to say the least: Roger Iddison, long-serving captain of Yorkshire, also played regularly for Lancashire between 1865 and 1870. The clubs chose who they would play – there was no league as such – and for years the 'County Champion' side was chosen by the press.

Finally, there was the emergence of international cricket. Bizarrely, the very first international game had taken place in Hoboken, New

Jersey, in 1844 between teams calling themselves USA and Canada, for $1000. The first English touring side was invited to Canada and the USA in 1859 by the Montreal Club. The side was made up equally of players from the original two Elevens and was captained by George Parr, Clarke's successor at All England. But the most important development was the start of regular visits to – and later from – Australia. The first visit was in 1861 2 when the proprietors of the Café de Paris in Melbourne, having failed to persuade Charles Dickens to embark on a lecture tour for which they would do the catering, invited an English cricket team instead. Two years later the Melbourne Cricket Club asked George Parr to put together another touring team. Nearly all the side were professionals, but they did take along one amateur: a 22-year-old medical student from Bristol called E. M. Grace. The professionals were paid £250 plus expenses for the eight-month tour, whereas Grace the amateur received a straight £500 in expenses. It was a precedent his more famous brother was to follow enthusiastically.

None of these sides were representative in any formal sense. They were simply put together by whoever was invited by the hosts to do so. It would be some time before any more meaningful structure would be put in place.

In the meantime, the MCC was once more forced to make a rule change. Since round-arm had been legalized in 1835, bowlers' arms had been creeping ever higher. In the main, no one minded and umpires simply didn't bother to enforce the below-the-shoulder rule. But in August 1862 an All England bowler called Edgar Willsher, who'd been bowling the same way for many years, was suddenly no-balled six consecutive times in a match against Surrey. Infuriated, he flung down the ball and stalked off the field, taking his professional colleagues with him. The match only continued when the offending umpire was replaced. As far as we know, Willsher was never no-balled again. But there is slightly more to this story than might at first appear. The umpire who caused the row was John Lillywhite, a close personal friend and business partner of Edgar Willsher (they were later to work together as Secretary and Treasurer of the United South of England XI). Could the whole episode have been a stunt to force the MCC to change the rules? We don't know, but if it was, it was highly successful.

In 1862, a campaign was launched by the powerful *Sporting Life* to replace the MCC with an elected 'Cricket Parliament'. Letter after letter accused the club of being locked in time, with no idea of how to shape the future of a fast-changing game. So dozy were the Committee, it was pointed out, that four years earlier they had failed even to bid for the freehold of Lord's when it came up for auction. (It was bought by a speculator for £7000; he sold it back to the MCC six years later for £18,313 6s 8d.) When the Parliament idea was formally put to the MCC, the steely reply came that 'without dictating to the contrary or desiring anybody, if otherwise inclined, to follow blindly in their steps, the Committee do not see any reason to depart from the course they have pursued' since 1787. Nonetheless, a few months later, the same committee voted to allow overarm bowling.

In that same year, 1864, a young batsman just three days past his sixteenth birthday scored 50 for South Wales against the MCC in his first innings at Lord's. His name was to dominate cricket for the next thirty-five years.

Grace and favour

William Gilbert Grace was born in July 1848 at Downend near Bristol, one of five boys and four girls. His father was a local GP who adored cricket – he laid down a pitch in the family orchard so that his sons could practise. His daughters (and the family dogs) looked after the fielding. What was unusual at the time was that their mother was equally committed. Not only did she keep a beady eye on the boys' stroke development and bowling actions, she also actively promoted their careers. When W. G.'s older brother E. M. was just seventeen, she wrote to George Parr suggesting he was now ready to play in that year's All England XI. (Parr did not take up the offer, but four years later he asked E. M. to join his Australian touring party.) In the same letter, she added that W. G., then just ten, was an even better prospect on account of his superior back play. She was to become known in cricket circles as a knowledgeable and opinionated observer of the game. She was the first and for many years the only woman to have her death recorded in the pages of *Wisden*.

All five sons were talented cricketers. Two of them went on to become strong club players, while the other three all played for England. W. G.'s sporting abilities were almost supernatural. Two years after his debut at Lord's, he scored 224 not out for England against Surrey at

W. G. Grace at 25: in a remarkable seven day period,
he scored 839 runs in three innings

the Oval aged just 18 and then raced off to Crystal Palace for the National Olympian Association meeting, where he won the 440 yards hurdles (he continued competing successfully at athletics until 1870). By his twenty-first birthday, he'd become a major box-office draw, helped by his distinctive and highly marketable beard. But his very success faced him with a dilemma.

Gilbert, as he was known to his family, had not been to a major public school or university, the normal background for a top-class amateur (he was rather half-heartedly studying medicine). He needed to make a living from cricket. So he characteristically decided he could have it both ways. He accepted membership of the MCC (and with it amateur status), proudly donned the club cap but also went off to 'organize' matches for the United South of England XI for a handsome fee. Naturally, he also played in them – ensuring vast crowds – but took his wages in the form of lavish 'expenses'.

This decision arguably had a profound effect on the future of cricket. It gave huge support to the MCC and the amateur ethos they idealized. At the same time, it shifted the focus onto the county teams – W. G. was already captain of Gloucestershire and would remain so for the next thirty years. While he was able to make a considerable fortune from the United South and the professional game throughout the 1870s, his decision ultimately contributed to their demise.

So what made W. G. such a crowd-puller? Leaving aside his formidable personality and marketing skills, he was an astonishing cricketer. Between 1866 and 1880, he topped the first-class batting averages twelve times. He remained at or near the top for the next twenty years, into his 50s. During that time, according to *Wisden*, he scored nearly 55,000 runs at an average of just under 40. He also took 2,809 wickets for just 18 runs apiece. In one extraordinary seven-day period he notched up 839 runs – 344 for MCC against Kent, 177 for Gloucestershire against Notts and 318 not out for Gloucestershire against Yorkshire.

He could play every stroke in the book – forward and back, on and off, attacking and defensive. He rarely took risks but looked for every run that he could. He always played to win, pushing the rules to their limit (and sometimes beyond). On one occasion, he'd run three runs before the fielder's throw ended up entangled in his shirt; he ran three more before allowing a fielder to retrieve it – he wouldn't touch it himself for fear of being given out for handling the ball. During a vital stage of the England–Australia match of 1882, the young Australian batsman S. P. Jones had completed a run. Grace started carrying the ball towards the bowler. According to *Wisden*, Jones, 'thinking wrongly but very naturally that the ball was dead, went out of his ground' to repair the wicket. Grace whipped off the bails and appealed for a run-out. The umpire had no choice. 'I'm sorry to say the gentleman is out,' he said. According to the much-respected Australian captain Joe Darling, he added: 'It's not cricket.'

This gamesmanship only added to his popularity, and Grace knew it. The best-loved W. G. story concerns an occasion when he was bowled first ball. He calmly picked up the bails and replaced them. When the umpire objected, he simply said: 'Don't be silly. They've come to see me bat, not you umpire.'

He did everything he could to exploit and profit from his popularity. When he played for the United South of England XI, his organizing fee and expenses would add up to more than the fees paid to the rest of the team put together. His 'expenses' when playing for Gloucestershire and the MCC were often a subject of controversy, but his reputation kept him immune from disciplinary action. On foreign tours he was ruthless. He was first invited to put together a team to visit Australia in 1872 by the Melbourne Cricket Club. He proposed a fee of £1500, around £70,000 in today's money. That was a bit rich for the Australians, but W. G. held his ground. He knew the tour would be worthless without him. When the Melbourne club came back and agreed to his proposal, he then demanded that they also pay for his new wife to accompany him.

He didn't travel to Australia again until the winter of 1891–2. The Earl of Sheffield (after whom the Sheffield Shield was called) asked the last of the great player managers, Arthur Shrewsbury, to put together a team to tour Australia. Shrewsbury warned against taking amateurs, because on a previous tour their 'expenses' had proved to be twice the fees of the professionals. But he agreed they could take W. G., because he would be a massive attraction. He was, but the indulgence still cost Lord Sheffield a lot of money. He lost £2000 on the tour, partly because Grace had taken his wife and family with him and insisted that they be paid as well. Shrewsbury's comment afterwards was reflective: 'If he hadn't taken Grace out Lord Sheffield would have been £3000 better off . . . and also had a better team. I told him what wine would be drunk by the amateurs. Grace himself would drink enough to swim a ship.'

Grace finally stood down from the English captaincy – and the team – in 1899. That same year he fell out badly with Gloucestershire, resigned as captain and never played for them again. He went on playing at various levels until the year before his death in 1915.

When he'd played his first match at Lord's, cricket had been in a state of confusion. The MCC was under threat, there were no Test matches, no County Championship, sheep were used to mow the outfield at most grounds and there were no boundaries. By the time he played his last first-class game in 1908, the modern national and international game was taking shape.

Home

By the 1880s, cricketing focus had switched firmly from the itinerant professional 'Elevens' to the county sides. But the organization of the county game was still completely haphazard. Each county decided for themselves who they would or would not play, there was no formal competition and the County Champion each year was still chosen by the press – on highly dubious grounds, leading to much resentment.

One subject of frequent disputes had been resolved: how did a player qualify to play for his county? As we've seen, players frequently played for two or more counties in a season. In 1873, representatives of some of the leading counties got together at the Oval under the chairmanship of the remarkable Surrey Secretary Charles W. Alcock – he was also Secretary of the new Football Association – to resolve the issue. They decided each player should be qualified either by birth or two years' residence, with disputes being referred to the MCC. More important, perhaps, they resolved that no player could play for more than one county in the same season. Roger Iddison's habit of scampering across the Pennines as the whim (or the pay-cheque) took him was finally outlawed.

By 1882, the county secretaries had at least agreed to meet regularly. And in 1888, led by the fiercely autocratic Lord Harris, captain of Kent, they set up a County Cricket Council, which in turn set up a subcommittee to try to work out a way of classifying the counties. It proposed a scheme with three divisions of eight counties each – effectively first class, second class and minor – with promotion and relegation. When the full council met in 1890 to make a decision, there was such a level of dissent – especially from the so-called second-class counties – that in the end the council voted to abolish itself.

A smaller group of counties did, however, come up with a points system for county matches. It was eccentric in its simplicity: one point for a win, minus one for a loss and nothing for a draw. Four years later, the MCC was finally asked to arbitrate on the issue of classification. It too chose to keep things simple: 'Cricketing counties shall be considered as belonging to the first class or not,' it decreed. There would be no other classification. Naturally, the MCC would decide who was in and who was out, not on results but on the basis of playing an agreed number of three-day games at home and away. Fifteen counties were declared to be first class. This system, cumbersome though it was, was to last for 100 years, during which time just three new counties were allowed into the elite. None left. The MCC also endorsed the points system. It was hardly a proper league – counties still decided for themselves who they should play – but the County Championship was at last now official.

And away

Over the same period, international cricket was slowly coming of age. The first game to be called a Test match took place in Melbourne in March 1877, when James Lillywhite's professional touring team was defeated by a combined Melbourne and Sydney XI. While an undoubted shock to the English system, the defeat was played down back home. The English team was, after all, professional; Grace wasn't there; and anyway they comfortably won a second Test held a fortnight later. But, for Australians, the world had changed. England was vulnerable.

The following year, the first Australian side to visit England proved

immensely popular (and the tour immensely profitable). Sadly, no Test
match had been arranged but the tourists did play a strong MCC side
on a rain-sodden pitch at Lord's. They won by nine wickets after less

The first ever Australian touring team: in 1878, they beat
a strong MCC team at Lords by nine wickets

than five hours' play. This time Grace was there but you might not
have noticed: he scored 4 in the first innings and 0 in the second. *Punch*
commented:

> The Australians came down like a wolf on the fold,
> The Marylebone cracks for a trifle were bowled,
> Our Grace before dinner was very soon done,
> And our Grace after dinner did not get a run.

That winter, on a tour marred by a nasty riot against the English in
Sydney, a largely amateur English side was thrashed in the only Test
match. When the next Australian side came to England, in 1880,
memories of that riot made it hard to arrange fixtures. But the ever
astute Charles Alcock, in a bid to confirm the Oval as a major ground,

arranged a late Test match there in September. This time Grace scored a century and England won by five wickets. But in Australia, over the winter of 1881–2, an English side lost a four-match Test series 2–0. That meant that out of eight Tests played, Australia had won four and England only two. But seven out of that eight had been in Australia.

There were high expectations for the Australian side which arrived in England the following summer. They didn't disappoint. In the build-up to the only Test match at the end of August, they notched up twenty-four victories and only four defeats. The scene was set for the most famous Test match of all time. On a wet and difficult Oval wicket, the Australians were bowled out for just 63. The 20,000 English spectators were jubilant. But in reply England managed just 101. On the second day, after more rain, the Australians managed to put together 122 for the second innings – setting England just 85 to win. Conditions were difficult, but they pushed ahead to 51 for 3 – just 34 more needed with much of the best batting to come. The game slowed right down. Runs came slowly, but so did wickets. At 66 for 5, victory still seemed assured. Then, in a scenario all too familiar to every English cricket follower, panic set in. England was all out for 77 and Australia had beaten England on home soil for the very first time.

What immortalized the game was the wry obituary published in the *Sporting Times* the following day:

In Affectionate Remembrance

of

ENGLISH CRICKET

Which died at the Oval

on

29th August, 1882,

Deeply lamented by a large circle of sorrowing

friends and acquaintances.

R.I.P.

NB: the body will be cremated and the

ashes taken to Australia.

That winter a weakened English side visited Australia led by the Hon. Ivo Bligh, who was jokily heard to remark that he had come 'to recover the Ashes'. After a sociable game at the home of an Australian bigwig, Sir William Clarke, a group of ladies burned something, put the ashes in a little urn and presented it to dashing young Ivo. Cricket lovers like to think the something was a stump or a bail, but the daughter of one of the ladies, the Clarke children's music teacher Florence Morphy, later said it was her veil. Bligh obviously enjoyed the joke because a year later he married Florence. He also laid firm claim to the urn by beating Australia 2–1 in the Test series. He went on to become the Earl of Darnley. When he died in 1927, he left the urn to the MCC. It remains the most hotly contested trophy in world cricket.

Over the next twenty years, the fortunes of England and Australia would ebb and flow, though England had a slight edge, with 27 victories to Australia's 19. These games were still fairly informal affairs: the touring sides played as much for profit as national honour and in England the team for each Test match was chosen by the authorities of the ground on which it was to be played, which led to inconsistency and some highly dubious decisions. By 1898, it was clear this mess had to be sorted out. The following year the first five-match Test series was set to be played against Australia and a level of consistency was vital.

The MCC set up the Board of Control, which included representatives of all the first-class clubs, which in turn appointed a team of three selectors who would first appoint and then work with the captain to pick the team. Five years later, the MCC finally took control of English touring sides, starting with the team to visit Australia in 1903–04. For the next seventy years, all English touring sides were called the MCC rather than England. In 1909, the Imperial Cricket Conference (ICC) was formed to organize Test series between the three recognized Test-match countries – England, Australia and South Africa. Over the years, others would join the ICC: India, the West Indies, New Zealand, Pakistan, Sri Lanka, Zimbabwe and Bangladesh. The pattern was set.

Not again!

It's the cry that goes up from every cricket lover whenever England's batting collapses in a Test match, or we fail to take that last frustrating tail-end wicket that would have secured victory. Why can't we play the game we invented? The answer is we can. Sometimes. Unfortunately – or fortunately, if you really love the game – the other countries that we gave it to can also play the game, and often rather better than us.

Is there any endemic reason why we muddle along at our national summer game while others excel? Yes, there probably is. And it's called the class system.

The game as we play it today was developed almost entirely by the 'players' – the working-class professionals who were so skilful that they were paid to play day in and day out. They were the ones who came up with pitching the ball on a length, the straight bat, the forward defensive, getting your foot to the pitch of the ball, round-arm and then overarm bowling. There were exceptions, of course: Old Etonian B. J. T. Bosanquet invented the googly and Indian prince K. S. Ranjitsinhji was the first to play a leg glance. But in the main it was the hard-working professionals, many from the Hambledon Club, who made the game the sophisticated activity it is today.

But how the game was run was quite another matter. This was the prerogative of the upper classes, the gentlemen amateurs. It wasn't so much that they wrote the rules – which they did, but more often than not in response to what the players were already doing on the pitch. It was their influence over how the game was administered that really had an impact.

Football was an urban game right from the start. Cricket was not. It's no accident that the county emerged as the basis for first-class teams. The early aristocratic patrons who called their makeshift professional teams the Men of Kent or the Gamesters of Surrey were landowners whose wealth was based in the countryside. The gentlemen amateurs produced by the public schools and universities (only Oxford and Cambridge at this stage) largely had similar rural ties. Those that

Googlies and Chinamen

The 'googly' – a ball from a right-arm leg spinner which turns the other way – was invented in 1897 by Old Etonian B. J. T. Bosanquet, father of the legendary ITN newsreader Reginald Bosanquet. He said he developed it while playing a game called 'Twisti-Twosti', which involved bouncing a tennis ball on a table so that your opponent sitting opposite couldn't catch it. 'It wasn't unfair,' Bosanquet said of his creation, 'just immoral.' A 'Chinaman' is the name for an unorthodox left-arm spin delivery which breaks from off to leg for a right-handed batsman. The name is believed to have come from a Test match at Old Trafford in 1933. West Indian Ellis Edgar ('Puss') Achong, the first cricketer of Chinese descent to play Test cricket, used this delivery as a variation on his normal orthodox left-arm spin to have English batsman Walter Robins stumped. As he walked past the umpire Robins muttered, 'Fancy being done by a bloody Chinaman.' Such balls have been called Chinamen ever since.

didn't were still members of the 'county set'. So the 'county' system was the ideal format for the gentlemen to enjoy their cricket before they had to knuckle down and earn a bit of money (if they needed to). But it wasn't necessarily good for English cricket.

When the MCC finally decided that counties would be 'first-class or not', they threw a dangerous die. They named fifteen first-class counties. Everyone knew right at the start that this was too many. There wasn't time in the season for them all to play each other sensibly. And there weren't enough people who had the leisure to watch them play. But the proprieties of genteel life would brook no revision.

The result is that England has far too much 'first-class cricket'. The quality of each side is inevitably diluted. Australia, New Zealand, South Africa and the West Indies all have much smaller first-class leagues – six to eight teams. So the step up from county to Test match cricket for English players is always greater. If someone fails, there's a bigger pool to choose from. Which is why we don't always have the stable teams of the kind the Aussies and others so often produce.

But change is in the air. Given what's happening elsewhere in the world, it seems unlikely that the traditional English set-up can survive for much longer. Who knows, that might have a significant impact on the way we play the game.

At least we know it was our idea in the first place. So we should celebrate those assiduous professionals who created the sport we love, and the lordly patrons who made it possible for them to do so. Let's leave the last word to our old friend, the Rev. Reynell Cotton and his Hambledon Cricket Song:

> Then fill up your glass! – He's the best who drinks most;
> Here's the Hambledon Club! – Who refuses the toast?
> Let us join in the praise of the Bat and the Wicket,
> And sing in full Chorus the Patrons of Cricket.

The language of cricket

Cricket has contributed many phrases to the English language. If you are in control and forging ahead, you are said to be 'on the front foot'. On the other hand, if things are going badly and you're on the defensive, you are said to be 'on the back foot'. Which is perhaps surprising given that many batsmen today play as aggressively off the back foot as the front. If you do everything very carefully and according to the rules, you're said to be 'playing a straight bat'. If you make a mistake, you can be 'caught out', while if you simply don't know what to do, you are 'stumped'. If things aren't going well, you're on a 'sticky wicket', whereas if everything has gone wrong, you've been 'hit for six'. The corporate world has developed a horrible piece of jargon – bcop – which stands for 'by close of play'. How can the most elegant of games be treated that way? It's just 'not cricket'.

4.
GOLF

THE ROMANTIC VERSION of the origins of golf goes something like this. Many centuries ago, shepherds in the ancient Kingdom of Fife, on Scotland's east coast, used their crooks to knock pebbles around courses laid out by nature. Rabbit runs provided the fairways, spots where sheep had worn the grass away in an attempt to get out of the biting wind provided the bunkers, and rabbit warrens provided the holes. It's an appealing image, and it may even have some truth to it, but we have no way of knowing. Those shepherds have left no record of their activities.

What we can say is that using a club to knock a ball about is an idea which has cropped up in many different countries at many different times. The Romans had a popular game called *paganica* (derived from their word for 'country dweller') which involved using a bent stick as a club to knock a ball made of leather and stuffed with feathers (just like an early Scottish golf ball) across country. It is likely that legionaries played this game across the English countryside and the marches of Scotland during the long Roman occupation. Was this what inspired the Scots to develop the sport which has become so popular around the world?

Or was it taken to Scotland from somewhere else?

Origins

Most scholars believe that the word *golf* is derived from an old Teutonic word meaning 'club'. From the same root comes the German word *kolbe*, the Flemish word *chole*, the Dutch word *kolf* and the English word *club*. Golf, it is suggested, is a Celtic version of the same word. There's no suggestion that any of these words derived from any of the others, just that they all come from same root.

One of the earliest possible depictions of the game of golf,
from a fourteenth-century manuscript book of prayers

But *kolf* does sound awfully familiar, doesn't it? It is the word for the club used in the Dutch game *kolven* and has led many to speculate that this is where golf comes from. But *kolven*, which is still played in Holland today, is a very different game. It is played on a smooth surface in a walled space or covered court, often attached to an inn. There are two posts at either end of the court, which can be anything from 40 to 130 feet apart. The idea is to use a club which has a large straight brass face to hit a ball, about the same size as a cricket ball, from one end of the court to hit the post at the other end. Ideally the ball should rebound from that post to make it easier to hit the post at the other end. The side that manages to hit both posts in the lowest number of strokes wins the point.

So not exactly like golf. On the other hand, there are a number of Dutch paintings from the seventeenth century which appear to show *kolven* being played on ice. So could there have been an early outdoor version of the game that was the forerunner of golf? The paintings certainly cannot prove that. For a start, the earliest of them is dated 1625, almost two hundred years after we know that golf was already popular in Scotland. Then there is the ice. *Kolven* is usually played on a smooth surface so it could well be adaptable to ice. Golf is not. There is a story of someone playing at Wimbledon Park when the lake beside the eighteenth hole was frozen over. He mis-hit his drive and it landed on the ice. The ball ran the entire length of the lake, some 600 yards, before coming to a stop when it reached the far edge. Golf on ice would be an even more frustrating game than golf on land.

Another contender as an ancestor of golf is the Belgian game of *chole*, a word which, as we've seen, came from the same Teutonic root. This is indeed a cross-country game like golf, but it works on different principles. There is only one ball. The two sides start by agreeing on a target, such as a church door, some distance away. They then put in a bid for how many strokes they think it will take them to reach it. The side with the lowest bid starts. They are allowed three strokes before their opponents have a single stroke in which they can *dechole* – either hitting the ball back away from the target or into any hazard they can find from where it will be difficult to play. In a way it is a cross between hockey, which has a single ball and involves attack and defence, and golf, with its cross-country element and the counting of strokes.

It is quite possible that there were elements of cross-fertilization among all of these games. Certainly there was a good deal of trade between Scotland and the Low Countries. But there is one final

*The intriguing depiction of golf from a Flemish book of hours
from the early sixteenth century, known as the 'Golf Book'*

intriguing image we should consider, which is found in the so-called 'Golf Book' in the British Museum. It is a book of hours produced in Bruges early in the sixteenth century under the direction of the miniaturist Simon Bening. It depicts three players (and a fourth man who is not playing) who appear to be at the end of a three-ball hole. They have golf-like clubs, the balls are the right size and there is a hole which they are obviously trying to play into. It's not *kolven* (even though there appears to be a fence around the 'green') because the ball is small and there is a hole. It's not *chole* because there are three balls. Is it a precursor of golf? Or is it a derivative of golf?

Because by this time golf had been widely played in Scotland for quite some time.

The royal and ancient game

In 1457, King James II of Scotland, also known as 'James of the Fiery Face', issued a famous decree declaring 'that the futeball and golfe be utterly cryed downe and not to be used'. The purpose, as with so many similar decrees, was to ensure that the people were not distracted by such games from archery practice, which was vital for the defence of the realm against 'our auld enimies of England'. A similar decree was issued by James III in 1471 and by James IV in 1491. He ordained 'That in na place of the realme there be usit Fute-ball, Golfe, and uther sik unprofitabill sportis'. These ordinances prove two things: first, that golf was popular enough to be a real threat; and second, that such bans weren't very effective. Why else would you have to repeat them every twenty years?

Just eleven years after the last of these edicts, James IV signed a treaty of 'perpetual peace' with the 'auld enimie' on the altar of Glasgow Cathedral and agreed to marry the daughter of Henry VII. Perhaps he felt this made it all right for him to play the game of golf with the Earl of Bothwell in 1503, which his accounts suggest he lost at a cost of 42 shillings (though it has to be said that similar bans on games such as tennis never stopped the kings of England from enjoying a game if they felt like it). Either way, it is significant because it is the first game of golf for which we have the names of the players.

For almost the next two centuries, there seems always to have been a monarch playing golf. James V of Scotland was a regular player and so was his ill-fated daughter, Mary Queen of Scots. One of the charges brought against her was that she was seen playing golf and pall mall

Mary Queen of Scots: playing golf days after the murder
of her husband was seen as a sign of complicity

(another stick-and-ball game) in the fields beside Seton within days of the murder of her estranged husband Lord Darnley in 1567. Their son, James VI of Scotland, took his golf clubs with him when he travelled to London to become James I of England in 1603. He in turn encouraged his sons Henry and Charles to play. We know this from a story in an old Oxford manuscript. Young Prince Henry was playing at golf – 'a play not unlike Palemaille' – with his strict tutor chatting to someone beside him. Henry asked him to move away and, thinking that he'd done so, began to raise his club. 'Beware that you hit not Master Newton,' cried one of his courtiers. Henry, stopping in mid swing, replied: 'Had I done so, I had but paid my debts.'

Henry died of typhoid when he was 18, and his younger brother became Charles I. He had played golf in his childhood and was actually playing on the links at Leith, just outside Edinburgh, in 1641

Charles I was playing golf on the links at Leith when
he first received news of the Irish rebellion

when he first received news of the Irish rebellion which was to be the beginning of his end. What he did next is disputed. Did he carry on playing regardless, in the manner of Francis Drake? In which case he was a frivolous dilettante who didn't realize the danger the rebellion posed. Or did he abandon the game immediately? In which case, of course, he panicked. Sir Walter Simpson, the Victorian author who favours the latter option, offers a golfer's explanation: that the King 'acted on this occasion with his usual cunning – that at the time he was being beaten, and that he hurried away to save his half-crown rather than his crown'.

The people's game

The connection with Leith raises an important point about golf. It was certainly royal (and ancient), but it was also popular. There were no golf courses at this time. The game was played on open, common ground which was entirely natural – it was tended only by rabbits. The citizens of Edinburgh certainly made full use of the links at Leith, especially on a Sunday, which did not always go down well with the kirk. In 1592 and again in 1593, the town council issued proclamations against this sacrilege. The later one declared that 'dyvers inhabitants of this burgh repaires upon the Sabboth day, to the toun of Leyth, and in tyme of sermonis are sene vagant athort the streets, drinking in tavernis, or otherwayes at Golf, aircherie, or other pasttymes upoun the Links, thairby profaning the Sabboth day'. In the early seventeenth century, as Puritanism stalked the land, there are records throughout Scotland of the convictions of many a poor golfer who fell foul of such decrees.

The *Statistical Account of Scotland*, a treasure trove of Scottish lore compiled by Sir John Sinclair from parish reports at the end of the eighteenth century, paints a more benign picture of golfing activity on the links in these early days: 'The greatest and wisest of the land were to be seen on the Links of Leith mingling freely with the humblest mechanics in pursuit of their common and beloved amusement. All distinctions of rank were levelled by the joyous spirit of the game. Lords of Session and cobblers, knights, baronets, and tailors might be seen earnestly contesting for the palm of superior dexterity, and vehemently but good-humouredly discussing moot points of the game, as they arose in the course of play.'

The great Scottish novelist Tobias Smollett, who was also a doctor, reflected on the same phenomenon when writing about the racecourse at Leith: 'Hard by, in the fields called the Links, the citizens of Edinburgh divert themselves at a game called golf . . . Of this diversion the Scotch are so fond, that, when the weather will permit, you may see a multitude of all ranks . . . mingled together in their shirts, and following the balls with the utmost eagerness. Among others, I was shown one particular set of golfers, the youngest of whom was turned four-score. They were all gentlemen of independent fortunes, who had amused themselves with this pastime for the best part of a century, without having ever felt the least alarm from sickness or disgust; and they never went to bed without having each the best part of a gallon of claret in his belly. Such uninterrupted exercise, co-operating with the keen air of the sea, must, without all doubt, keep the appetite always on edge, and steel the constitution against all the common attacks of distemper.'

A good example of the egalitarian nature of golf is to be found in a story about the Duke of York, the younger brother of Charles II, who later briefly became James II. He spent two years in Edinburgh, 1681 and 1682, as the King's Lord High Commissioner. Two English noblemen in his entourage had a good-humoured dispute with him about the origins of the game, which they claimed had begun in London. It was agreed that they should resolve the matter by a match on Leith links in which they would play against the Duke and any Scottish partner he chose. After taking advice, James decided on a poor shoemaker called John Patersone, the local champion at the time. The Duke and the cobbler won easily and James immediately gave Patersone half of the very large stake that had been wagered on the result. He used it to build a house in Canongate, one of the finest streets in Edinburgh. The Duke designed a coat of arms to be placed on the house with a crest consisting of a hand holding a golf club and the motto 'Far and Sure'. Below was a Latin inscription about the match above the words 'I hate no person', an anagram of John Patersone. Sadly the house

The house in Canongate which John Patersone built with his winnings from the match he played with James, Duke of York

was demolished in 1960. All that remains is a commemorative plaque.

The Links at Leith were also the scene of the first game of golf to be reported in the press. It was 'a solemn match at golf' played in 1724 between Alexander Elphinstone, younger son of Lord Balmerino, and Captain John Porteous of the Edinburgh City Guard. What aroused all the interest was the very high stake of 20 guineas. Among the large crowd who watched were the Duke of Hamilton and the Earl of Morton. Elphinstone won, but what made the match famous was what happened to the players later.

In 1729, Elphinstone fought and killed one Lieutenant Swift in a duel on the golf links. He was indicted before the High Court but was never tried and died peacefully but prematurely in his bed three years later. In 1736, Porteous was in charge of the City Guard at the execution of a popular smuggler called Andrew Wilson. The crowd became first restless, then riotous and Porteous ordered his men to open fire, killing six people. He was tried for murder, found guilty and sentenced to death. Fearing he would be reprieved by the London Government, a Scottish mob broke into the jail where Porteous was being held, dragged him out and brutally lynched him.

The first clubs

Before the mid-eighteenth century, there were no golf competitions as we know them, just private matches like that between Elphinstone and Porteous. No one kept score of the total number of strokes played; what mattered was getting your ball in the hole in fewer than your opponent. The winner was the person who won most holes. The rules, such as they were, were agreed between the players. There was no set number of holes. The Links at Leith, for instance, had just five. The players might decide to play the holes three or four times to make up the match.

Then, in 1744, 'several Gentlemen of Honour, skilfull in the ancient and healthful exercise of Golf', petitioned the City of Edinburgh to provide a Silver Club as the prize for an annual competition to be held on the Links of Leith. The competition was to be open to 'as many Noblemen or Gentlemen or other Golfers, from any part of Great Britain or Ireland' as wished to enter. The winner would be declared 'the Captain of Golf' and be the sole judge of all golfing disputes for the following year. He was also required to add a piece of gold or silver to the trophy. To regulate how the competition was to be played, the

The Silver Club awarded in the first ever annual competition run by the Honourable Company of Edinburgh Golfers

'Gentlemen of Honour' produced the first written code of rules for golf – just thirteen of them.

In the end, only ten local people entered the competition, probably the same 'Gentlemen of Honour' who had proposed the idea in the first place. The Silver Club was won by John Rattray, an Edinburgh surgeon 'for skill renowned'. For the next nineteen years the competition theoretically remained open to all, but the reality was that only local people entered. In 1764 the previous winners – the Captains of Golf – successfully petitioned the City for authority 'to admit such Noblemen and Gentlemen as they approve to be Members of the

Company of Golfers'. Henceforth, only members would be allowed to compete for the Silver Club. They had founded the 'Company of Gentlemen Golfers', later renamed 'The Honourable Company of Edinburgh Golfers', Scotland's first golf club.

In 1754, the golfers of St Andrews went through a very similar process. They subscribed for a Silver Club to be presented to the winner of an open competition. They adopted the Honourable Company's code of rules almost verbatim, with just one small change dictated by the difference in the terrain. Just as in Edinburgh, the reality was that only local people entered. In 1773, they too formed a club, which they called initially the Society of St Andrews. It is now, of course, known as The Royal and Ancient Golf Club of St Andrews. They restricted competitors for their Silver Club to their own members and members of the Honourable Company.

In 1766, the first golf club outside Scotland was formed. Or not, depending on which version of the story you believe. When James I came to London in 1603, he brought many members of his Scottish court with him to his residence at Greenwich Palace. Many would have been golfers and it's widely believed that they started playing on Blackheath, the higher land behind the palace. What is now the Royal Blackheath Golf Club claims to be the oldest in the world with a tentative starting date of 1608, but there is no concrete evidence to back up this claim. It does have a metal stamp and coat button which carries the date of 1745, which suggests there might have been some kind of organized society by then. The club certainly dates back to 1766, when one Henry Foot donated a Silver Driver to be played for in an annual competition, just like the two early Scottish clubs.

Over the next few years a number of other clubs were formed in Scotland (it was a while before any followed Blackheath in England). At this time nearly all these clubs played on what we would now call public courses. There were no private clubs and no clubhouses. Instead, members used to meet at selected local hostelries. The Leith golfers met at Luckie Clephan's, the St Andrews' men at Bailie Glass's, while the members of Blackheath met first at 'the Chocolate House' and later at the Green Man. The golfers of North Berwick solved the problem by having two marquees in which to lunch on meeting days, with the members vying with each other to provide the most sumptuous dish.

Nearly all these early clubs insisted on uniforms when playing, often rather elaborate affairs. In 1784, the St Andrews club decreed that members should wear a red coat with a dark blue velvet cape, with white plain buttons and a silver club and ball embroidered on each side. The Aberdeen Golf Club had a red jacket for playing and a blue jacket for dining. Wearing the uniform was generally obligatory. The record book of the Honourable Company for 16 November 1776 records that: 'This day Lieutenant James Dalrymple of the 43rd Regiment, being convicted of playing five different times without his uniform [his golf uniform, that is] was fined only in Six pints, having confessed the heinousness of his crime.'

The rise of the Royal and Ancient

For a hundred years or so after the Edinburgh Golfers first began competing for their Silver Club in 1744, every new club laid down its own code of rules. They followed the same general principles first adopted by the Honourable Company but they were all slightly different. Some of the discrepancies were based on local conditions, but there were also differences of opinion on some issues. From time to time they revised their rules as matters arose.

That said, there's no doubt that for the first fifty years of its existence the Honourable Company was the most prestigious club and a major influence on legislative matters. But in the early nineteenth century that began to change. The major reason was the deterioration of the Links at Leith. The lease of the course to the club also lapsed. In 1831, the Honourable Company found themselves with no clubhouse and no course to play on. Five years later they managed to re-establish themselves at Musselburgh, a little further down the coast, but they had to share the course there with the Royal Musselburgh Club and the general public. They didn't build a new clubhouse of their own until 1866.

Many members of the Honourable Company were also members of the Royal and Ancient and it's hardly surprising that during this troubled period a lot of them chose to play their golf at St Andrews. Inevitably, the prestige of the Edinburgh club declined while the reputation of St Andrews grew. By mid-century its supremacy on matters regulatory was confirmed. When the Prestwick Golf Club was formed in 1851, its first meeting voted explicitly to adopt the St Andrews Rules of Play. By 1889, even the highly independent Royal Blackheath Club was happy to record that 'The rules of the game of golf agreed to by the Blackheath Club are the Rules of Golf promulgated by the Royal and Ancient Golf Club of St Andrews in 1888.' Around the same time, the Honourable Company – about to move into its new course at Muirfield – also agreed to accept the leadership of the Royal and Ancient.

The position was formalized a few years later when, under pressure from clubs throughout Scotland and England, the St Andrews club agreed in 1897 to form a committee of fifteen of its members to be called the Rules of Golf Committee. They were given the power to consider proposals about the rules and questions of interpretation and were to be the final authority. Decisions were to be taken by majority vote but only became effective if they were endorsed by a two-thirds majority of members at a general meeting of the club. This established the Royal and Ancient as the ruling body of golf, accepted as such by golfers all over the world. Almost. But we'll come to that later.

There was one completely accidental consequence of the Royal and Ancient assuming this dominant position. In the first half of the nineteenth century, there was no standard number of holes for a golf course. Leith had five, while Montrose had twenty-five. What con-stituted a round varied from place to place. At St Andrews there were twelve holes, laid out in a line along the shore. A round consisted of playing out to the farthest hole, turning round and coming back again. The mathematically proficient will realize that meant a round of twenty-two holes. In 1764, the club decided that they should knock the first four holes into two, which meant two less on the way out and two less on the way home. Thus was born the idea of the eighteen-hole golf course.

The beginning of the Open

In the first half of the nineteenth century, the only organized contests in golf were club competitions. The only way players from different clubs could compete with each other was through private matches, often arranged for considerable sums of money. These became more interesting in the 1830s with the emergence of the first professional players.

The first of the great professionals was Allan Robertson of St

Allan Robertson, the first ever golf professional, whose canny skill dominated the sport until his death in 1859

Andrews, who came from a long line of ball-makers. His father David before him had been much in demand as a player and a teacher but he was always referred to as a senior caddie: in his day the concept of the 'professional' didn't exist. That had changed by his son's time. Most clubs had players who were recognized as professionals who could be asked for lessons or to make up a foursome. They could also be backed in matches against other professionals. Robertson became known as an almost unbeatable player, but he rarely confirmed his victory before the seventeenth hole. He said this was because he didn't want to hurt the pride of his opponents. Others suspected it was because he didn't want to move the odds against him too far. Two of Allan's most famous matches involved the Dunn brothers from Musselburgh. In 1843 he beat Willie Dunn in a match of twenty rounds – 360 holes – by two rounds and one to play. In 1849, he and his partner Tom Morris, also from St Andrews, beat Willie and Jamie Dunn in a match played over three courses – St Andrews, Musselburgh and North Berwick – for a prize of £400.

But the days of the great private matches were numbered. In 1857 the Prestwick Club, then just six years old, wrote to a number of other leading clubs suggesting a tournament between representatives of each club. The idea was taken up with some enthusiasm. A championship competition was held that summer at St Andrews between eleven clubs, each one fielding two players. It was won by Royal Blackheath. For the next year the rules were changed to make it a competition between individuals, open only to amateurs. It was won by the 20-year-old Robert Chambers, who was to become a respected author and publisher of, among other things, *Chambers Encyclopaedia*. The individual competition was repeated the following year.

Then, in 1860, the Prestwick Club decided to inaugurate a similar competition for professionals. Allan Robertson had died the previous year and no one was quite sure who the leading professional now was. The prize was to be a Challenge Belt of red morocco, ornamented with silver plates, which cost the considerable sum of 30 guineas. The rules said the trophy would become the personal property of anyone who won it three times in succession. The first championship attracted just eight entries and was won by Willie Park from Musselburgh, with Tom Morris of St Andrews the runner-up.

The following year the Prestwick Club took an extraordinarily

'Colonel Bogey'

One of the problems facing golf in the nineteenth century was how to work out someone's handicap. Even when the simple idea of giving each player a handicap of so many strokes became popular, there were still problems because clubs worked out 'scratch' according to the ability of their best players – and standards varied enormously from club to club. In 1890, Hugh Rotherham of Coventry Golf Club came up with the idea of inviting competitors to play a match under handicap against a hypothetical opponent who played perfect golf at every hole. This would be called the ground score. The idea spread fast. One of those it reached was Dr Thomas Browne, RN, of the Great Yarmouth Club. At the time a music hall song was becoming popular which had the refrain:

Hush! Hush! Hush!
Here comes the bogey man!

A friend to whom Dr Browne was explaining the new golf idea remarked that this imaginary opponent must be a real bogey man. The Doctor loved the idea and at Great Yarmouth and elsewhere the 'ground score' became the 'bogey score'. In 1892 Dr Browne did a tour of south-coast courses and introduced the idea of the bogey man to Captain Seely-Vidal, the honorary secretary of the United Services Club at Gosport, who was persuaded to work out a bogey score for his club. But he pointed out that every member of his club, even a hypothetical opponent, had to have a rank. He and Browne agreed that such a consistent player must be at least a Colonel, and so 'Colonel Bogey' was born.

More than twenty years later, bandmaster Lieutenant F. J. Ricketts was inspired by a military man on a golf course who, instead of yelling 'Fore' to announce he was about to play, whistled a characteristic two-note phrase. They became the unmistakeable opening two notes of the march he called 'Colonel Bogey', one of the biggest-selling pieces of military music of all time.

The story doesn't end there. The original Colonel Bogey didn't have the advantage of modern clubs or the new rubber-cored ball introduced around 1902. In the twentieth century, his score became a little over-generous and was gradually replaced by par. On many courses the bogey score became one over par on most holes. That's how the modern use of the term came into being.

far-sighted decision. Golf had always had an egalitarian air to it and this was about to be reinforced. At a time when other sports were beginning to tie themselves in knots about the relationship between amateurs and professionals, Prestwick resolved that the Challenge Belt 'on all future occasions until it be otherwise resolved, shall be open to all the world'. The Open was born.

'Old Tom' Morris, with his son young Tom. They both won the Open four times, but young Tom won four years in succession

Teething pains

The Open almost didn't survive, and might have gone the way of the early amateur championship, which lasted only till 1859, but for the interest aroused by the rivalry between the players who had come first and second in the first year. Between them Willie Park and Tom Morris won seven of the first eight competitions – Morris notched up four to Park's three. Then the world changed. The ninth Open was won by Morris's son, 'young' Tom, who at the time was just seventeen. He went on to win the next three championships, by considerable margins. He is the only person ever to have won the Open four times in a row.

His third victory proved pivotal. It meant the Challenge Belt became his property. A new trophy had to be found. The Prestwick Club, which had never intended to be the sole manager of the championship, persuaded the Royal and Ancient and the Honourable Company to join in subscribing for the new trophy, the silver claret jug which is still awarded every year. In return, it was agreed that the championship should rotate between Prestwick, St Andrews and Musselburgh. This changed the fortunes of the event. The first tournament at St Andrews attracted a record field of twenty-six entries, ensuring the future of the competition.

Young Tom was not so lucky. After his fourth victory, he seemed to lose his touch. Three years later, his young wife and first child both died in childbirth. He never recovered from the shock. On Christmas Day 1875, he was found dead in bed. He was just twenty-four.

Expansion

For the first half of the nineteenth century, golf remained a largely Scottish affair. But gradually that began to change. In 1818 the isolation of the London Scots at Blackheath was relieved by the founding of what became the Old Manchester Golf Club. It was more than forty years before the third English club, the first by the sea, was started: the North Devon (later Royal North Devon) at Westward Ho! After that, new English clubs came thick and fast, including such famous courses as the Royal Liverpool at Hoylake and the Royal St George's at Sandwich in Kent.

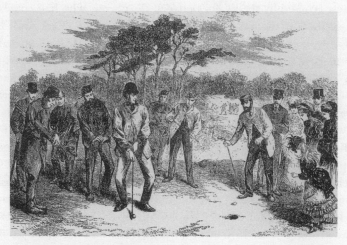

The first inter-club match to be played at Blackheath,
between Blackheath and London Scottish in 1870

In 1885, the Royal Liverpool revived the idea of an annual Amateur Championship, to be played in England and Scotland in alternate years. The Royal Liverpool also produced two of the great amateur champions of the early years. John Ball won the first of eight championships in 1888. Two years later he demonstrated the increasing strength of English golf by becoming the first Englishman and the first amateur to win the Open, breaking the vice-like grip the Scottish professionals had held on the championship until then. They were never to regain it. Two years later the second great Royal Liverpool amateur champion, Harold Hilton, achieved the same feat (he was to do so again a few years later). Just to rub Scottish noses in it a little more, the First English professional won two years later, in 1894, in the first Open to be played in England, at Sandwich.

Just a year earlier, the first Ladies' Championship had been held at the Lytham and St Anne's Club. We know that women played golf from very early on – Mary Queen of Scots is the first we know of by name in 1567. In the last years of the seventeenth century, a story was told about Dame Margaret Ross, believed to be the model for the fearsome Lady Ashton in Sir Walter Scott's novel *The Bride of Lammermoor*. She supposedly had the power to turn herself into a golf ball to frustrate her political enemies: when they were making even an easy putt, she would force herself a fraction of an inch out of line in order to miss the hole. But the man who brought this tale to the attention of the editor of the Badminton Library of Sports and Pastimes book on golf, one Colonel Fergusson, said he didn't believe the tradition: 'To act in this way she must, I should say, have retained a certain amount of sense, and sensation. If so, fancy her feelings when teed and sent hissing through the air with a *skelp* of a cleek . . . or still worse, being hacked to pieces in a bunker with a sand-iron laid in with strong arms and lost temper.'

And it wasn't only gentlewomen who played golf. A century or so later, in 1792, the *Statistical Account of Scotland*, almost certainly speaking of the fisherwomen of Musselburgh, reports that:

As the women do the work of men, their manners are masculine, and their strength and activity is equal to their work. Their amusements are of the masculine kind. On holidays they frequently play at golf, and on Shrove Tuesday there is a standing match at football between the married and the unmarried women, in which the former are always victors.

The first formal ladies' club was set up at St Andrews in 1867, the North Devon club at Westward Ho! followed the next year, then Musselburgh and Wimbledon in 1872, Carnoustie in 1873 and Pau in France – a club formed exclusively by British exiles – in 1874. In 1895, the women golfers of America followed the example of their British counterparts and founded the US Ladies' Championship – just a month after the US Open was first played. Golf was beginning to take off in America.

A depiction of the new Ladies Golf Club at Westward Ho! in Devon,
founded in 1868 and the first in England

Westward Ho!

The spread of golf in America was something of a stop-start affair. The earliest apparent mention is a Dutch ordinance forbidding the playing of golf in the street of what is now Albany, the capital of New York State, in 1659. But it would appear the game referred to is *kolven* rather than golf as we know it. In 1779, an advertisement appeared in Rivington's *Royal Gazette* in New York for golf clubs and balls. But it was aimed at Scottish officers serving with the British garrison in New York during the War of Independence. The earliest mentions of Americans playing golf are found in advertisements in the fashionable Southern cities of Charleston, South Carolina, and Savannah, Georgia, in the late eighteenth century. But after the declaration of war by the US against Britain in 1812, the game appears to have lost popularity quite dramatically. Certainly an article reprinted from the *Philadelphia Times* of 24 February 1889 in the Badminton Library book

suggests limited understanding of the game. The hapless author seems
to believe that the game is actually a race:

At the beginning of play each player places his ball at the edge of a hole which
has been designated as the starting point. When the word has been given to
start he bats his ball as accurately as possible towards the next hole, which
may be either 100 or 500 yards distant. As soon as it in the air he runs forward
in the direction which the ball has taken, and his servant, who is called a
'caddy', runs after him with all the other nine tools in his arms. If the player is
expert or lucky he bats his ball so that it falls within a few feet, or inches even,
of the next hole in the circle. His purpose is to put the ball in that next hole,
spoon it out and drive it forward before his opponent can accomplish the
same end.

The first modern club in America was the Oakhurst Golf Club,
formed in White Sulphur Springs, West Virginia, in 1884. It was
followed in 1888 by the St Andrews Golf Club of Yonkers, New York,
which was started by one Robert Lockhart, an immigrant linen
merchant who had learned his golf at Musselburgh. Then in 1891 the
Shinnecock Hills Golf Club of Long Island was founded by Samuel L.
Parrish, who had learned about golf while on holiday in Europe. He
brought in the now quite elderly Willie Dunn to design his course.

By 1895, there were enough clubs to justify the start of both the US
Amateur Championship and the US Open Championship. But the
standard was low. Followers of the modern game may be surprised to
learn that the first sixteen US Opens were won by British professionals,
the bulk of them Scottish. In 1900 a tour by the great British champion
Harry Vardon, during which he won the US Open, attracted large
crowds and started something of a golfing boom. The first inkling of
what that might lead to came in 1904, when the American Walter J.
Travis came to Sandwich and carried off the British Amateur
Championship.

For a while, the British professionals continued to hold sway in
America. But it wasn't to last. In 1911, John McDermott became the
first American to win the US Open, repeating the feat in 1912. But

these were years without a major British contingent. A bigger shock came in 1913, when the two leading British golfers of the day, Harry Vardon and Ted Ray, were beaten in a play-off by an unknown 20-year-old called Francis Ouimet. Since that time, only four British players have managed to win, and only one has been successful since the championship started again after World War II – Tony Jacklin in 1969. In the last few years, the American monopoly has been challenged, but the challenge has come from South Africa, Australia, New Zealand and Argentina rather than Britain.

The British have fared better in their own Open, but not much. The Americans had a ten-year winning streak between 1924 and 1933, and since 1946, they've won twenty-eight championships against eight for the British. Australia has also won eight, South Africa six and Spain three. The change in the game is evident from the prize money. When a money prize was first offered in 1864, Tom Morris Sr won £6. Richard Burton, the winner of the last tournament before World War II, won £100. In 1946, Sam Snead of America won £150. Tony Jacklin's victory won him £4,250. In 2008, Pádraig Harrington of Ireland pocketed £750,000. How things change.

The same has been true of the Ryder Cup, the biennial competition initially between the US and Britain. In the fifty years from the first tournament in 1927, the British team won just three times. From 1979, to make it more of a competition, it was agreed that America's opponents would come from the whole of Europe. That has changed things. Of the fourteen matches held since then, Europe has won seven to America's six, with one halved. In the Walker Cup, the equivalent for amateurs, the US leads 33 to 7; in the Curtis cup, for women, the US leads 25 to 6.

The dominance of America is reflected in the way the sport is now run. The Royal and Ancient (R&A) is recognized as the ruling body of golf everywhere except the United States and Mexico, who give allegiance to the United States Golf Association (USGA). Only in 1951 did the R&A and the USGA actually agree, for the first time, a universal set of rules for golf. Since that time the two bodies have worked together to update the rules as and when necessary, for the benefit of the millions worldwide who now play the game invented somewhere on the coast of Scotland way back when.

5.
SAILING OR YACHT RACING

Setting sail

IT WAS THE Dutch who started it. The word *yacht* comes from the Dutch *jaghte*, which derives from the verb *jagen* meaning to hunt or pursue. A *jaghtschip* was a swift, lightly built vessel originally used for warfare or perhaps hunting pirates. Over time, Holland being a great trading nation, they came to be used for commerce and government business as well. But the major contribution the Dutch made, probably early in the seventeenth century, was to introduce the idea of using such vessels purely for pleasure. It became fashionable for Dutch gentlefolk to own highly decorated *jaghts* in which they cruised the waterways of their homeland. They enjoyed getting together for aquatic parades and were even known to stage mock sea battles on special occasions. But they didn't race their yachts.

The use of sails goes back almost to the beginning of history. The ancient Egyptians had sailing ships, as did the Chinese from an early date, and the Greeks, and the Romans. It is inconceivable that none of these ships ever raced each other. They must have done. But that wasn't what these ships were for – they were working vessels. Many rulers also had vessels of state which they may have used for pleasure. Cleopatra watched the Battle of Actium from hers. Athelstan, the Saxon King of England, was given a 'vessel with purple sails' by the King of Norway in AD 925. Elizabeth I had one built for her at Cowes, inexplicably called *Rat of Wight*.

The merry monarch and Mary

But it was that inveterate gamester Charles II who introduced the idea of keeping yachts at least in part for racing. He must have spent time on yachts when living in exile in Holland before the Restoration. He was still in the country at Breda when he was proclaimed King at Westminster on 8 May 1660. The Prince of Orange immediately offered him a splendid yacht for his personal use on the first part of his journey from Breda to The Hague. She was said to be 'beautifully carved and gilded at her stern' and possessed a large cabin. A contemporary account detailed what happened next:

The King found his yacht so convenient and comfortable, that he remarked, while discoursing with the Deputies, that he might order one of the same style, so soon as he should arrive in England, to use on the River Thames. Mr Van Vlooswyck, burgermaster of Amsterdam, and one of the Deputies of the province of Holland, taking occasion to do a considerable service to his fatherland, said to the King that lately a yacht had been built in Amsterdam which was almost the same size, and at least as handsome, and he took the liberty of presenting it to his Majesty.

Safely back in his kingdom, Charles called his new yacht *Mary*. She was 52 feet long, had eight guns and required a crew of thirty. Charles clearly took every opportunity he could to make use of her. Samuel Pepys, who of course worked for the Navy Board and thus had an interest in matters nautical, made this entry in his diary on 15 August 1660, less than three months after the King had arrived back in London: 'I found the King gone this morning by five of the clock to see a Dutch pleasure boat below bridge, where he dines, and my Lord with him. The King do tire all his people that are about him with early rising since he came.' So pleased was Charles with his new toy that within a few weeks he had asked shipbuilder Peter Pett to build him another, even better one.

Charles was not alone in building a new pleasure craft. His brother

Charles II's yacht Mary: *the Merry Monarch was
one of the first people to race a yacht*

the Duke of York, later James II, had asked Pett's younger brother Christopher to build one for him. The two yachts were launched a few months later and called *Katherine* and *Anne* after the wives of their respective owners. What happened next was probably inevitable, given Charles's nature. John Evelyn, Pepys's friend and fellow-diarist, recorded the story:

October 1st, 1661. I had sailed this morning with his Majesty in one of the yachts, or pleasure boats ... being very excellent sailing vessels. It was on a wager between his other new pleasure boat, built frigate-like, and one of the Duke of York's; the wager one hundred pounds sterling; the race from Greenwich to Gravesend and back. The King lost in going, the wind being contrary, but saved stakes in returning. There were diverse noble persons and Lords on board, his Majesty some times steering himself.

This may well have been the first ever yacht race. It is certainly the first of which we have any account. During his reign, Charles was to build many more yachts – at one point he is said to have had a fleet of fifteen, which caused Pepys to throw up his hands at the extravagance. Many other wealthy noblemen and courtiers built themselves yachts. They became quite the thing. We have only a few records of races, but we can be sure that in this era of high-roller gambling there will have been many. Some of the most interesting we do know about concern Sir William Petty.

Petty was a self-made Renaissance man. The son of a Hampshire clothier, he went to sea at 14 as a cabin boy but broke his leg in an accident and was put ashore in Normandy. Undeterred, he applied, in Latin, to a Jesuit college in Caen to hone his mathematical skills,

Sir William Petty, doctor, political economist, co-founder
of the Royal Society and inventor of the catamaran

supporting himself by teaching English. He returned to England and a brief and uneventful naval career, then when the Civil War broke out returned to the continent to study in Holland and Paris, where he was private secretary to Thomas Hobbes and met Descartes. He returned to England in 1646, studied medicine at Oxford, qualified as a doctor and became Professor of Anatomy. On the side he conducted medical experiments and built up a private medical practice, achieving fame for resuscitating the corpse of Anne Greene, which had been cut down from the gallows and was intended for dissection. In 1652 he went to Ireland as physician general to Cromwell's army and stayed on to survey the lands forfeited by insurgents and distribute them among Cromwell's supporters. He ended up with more than 18,000 acres of his own. He became an Irish MP and was also a pioneering political economist. He is credited by many with the concept of laissez-faire economics. His theories influenced both Adam Smith and Karl Marx. None of that is relevant here. But his fascination with naval architecture – echoes of the cabin boy – most certainly is.

Samuel Pepys records the launch in September 1662 of a new vessel designed by Petty which the King named *The Experiment*. Quite reasonably so, because it was what we would now call a catamaran. Pepys described it as having 'two bottoms'. It was so experimental that the recently formed Royal Society, of which Petty was one of the twelve founding members, set up a committee 'to consider and report the Structure and Sailing of Sir William Petty's double-bottomed ship'. The committee decided to hold a trial and offered a flag to any ship that could outsail Sir William's vessel. This was the first open sailing match ever held. It took place in Dublin, where *The Experiment* was based, on 12 January 1663. Only three ships took up the challenge but the committee rated them as 'the prime ones this place does afford'. In tricky conditions Sir William's invention beat them all with ease.

Six months later, Pepys reports that Petty's invention 'hath this month won a wager of £50 in sailing between Dublin and Holyhead with the pacquett-boat, the best ship or vessel the King hath there; and he [Petty] offers to lay with any vessel in the world'. This was almost certainly the first ever ocean-going yacht race. Pepys's comments about the two vessels' return to Dublin are revealing:

In their coming back from Holyhead they started together, and this vessel [*The Experiment*] come to Dublin by five at night, and the pacquett-boat not before eight the next morning; and when they come they did believe this vessel had been drowned, or at least behind, not thinking she could have lived in that sea. Strange things are told of this vessel.

Sir William Petty built several more 'double-bottomed' ships, not all of which were quite so successful, but no one else followed his example. Speed was all very well, but these yachting pioneers also wanted ostentatious decorations and comfort. So they stuck to more traditional designs.

The first yacht clubs

With the death of Charles II in 1685, the fashion for yachting faded but it did not disappear. William and Mary had a yacht but they used it mainly for transport. George I and George II also had yachts which they used for frequent return trips to their native Germany. But there were a number of private enthusiasts and in 1720 the idea of a yacht club appears for the first time. It was called the 'Water Club of the Harbour of Cork' in Ireland and initially had twenty-five members. They would meet once a fortnight and sail out to sea to carry out manoeuvres under the direction of their 'Admiral'. But there is no record of them racing. The club lasted until 1765 but was then reformed in the nineteenth century as, eventually, the Royal Cork Yacht Club.

In 1749, the young Prince of Wales, later to be George III, donated a silver cup for a yacht race from Greenwich to the Nore – the sandbank at the mouth of the Thames where the river meets the North Sea – and back. It was the first open cup race in British waters that we know about. The winner, *Princess Augusta*, owned by a lawyer called George Bellas, was greeted by quite a sight when she reached the finishing line: 'The Prince of Wales, with five or six attendants in his Chinese Barge and the rowers in Chinese habits, drove gently before for some time and a crowd of boats about him, the people frequently huzzaing, at which he pulled off his hat. It was almost perfect calm and not the least damage happened, though the river seemed overspread with sailing yachts, galleys, and small boats.'

The enthusiasm for the event suggests that racing was fairly common on this part of the river at this time. But it probably consisted

Yachts of the 'Water Club of the Harbour of Cork',
the world's first sailing club

mainly of private matches. Twenty years or so later, matters were becoming more organized. We know from William Hickey's memoirs that in the early 1770s he and his friends had formed an informal sailing club which 'dined together once a week at the Swan Tavern, Chelsea'. They resolved to have an annual race for a silver cup to be held on the anniversary of the club's establishment. The first such race was held in 1774 and ended 'at dining at Smith's Tea Gardens and finishing the night at Vauxhall . . .' The following year, the event won royal patronage. On 6 July 1775 the *Public Advertiser* announced that a silver cup had been donated by the Duke of Cumberland, younger brother of the reigning monarch George III, 'to be sailed for on Tuesday, the 11th instant, from Westminster Bridge to Putney Bridge and back, by Pleasure Sailing Boats, from two to five tons burthen, and constantly lying above London Bridge'. As a result, the club took the name the 'Cumberland Sailing Society' or the 'Cumberland Fleet'.

It was the first yacht club actively to organize racing. The Duke of Cumberland gave a cup every year from 1775 to 1782 and the proprietor of Vauxhall Pleasure Gardens donated annual cups from 1786 to 1812. After the first year, the usual course was from Blackfriars Bridge to Putney Bridge and back. In 1781 a special cup worth fifty guineas was offered in a race open to 'all gentlemen proprietors of pleasure sailing boats, within the British dominions'. According to newspaper reports, thousands thronged the banks of the river to watch the contest. Open or not, it was still won by Thomas Taylor, the Commodore of the club, in his appropriately named yacht *Cumberland*.

These races were often robust affairs. The 1786 race was won by a yacht called *Prince of Wales*, but not without incident. According to the *Morning Chronicle*, 'There was an attempt of foul play against the *Prince of Wales* ... by other boats, but she got clear by a liberal use of hand-pikes.' In 1795 *The Times* reported that *Mercury* was in the lead when she somehow got foul of the *Vixen*, whose captain immediately drew his cutlass and set about *Mercury*'s rigging and 'fairly well dismantled her'. In the meantime, the third-placed *Mermaid* sailed happily through to win the race.

The language of sailing

Sailing has given the English language a host of words and expressions, some obvious, some less so. Among the obvious are phrases such as 'plain sailing', 'sailing close to the wind' and 'taking the wind out of someone's sails'. We talk about people being 'on the rocks' or maybe even 'out of their depth'. More happily, someone can be 'riding the crest of a wave'.

Most people think they know the origin of the word 'posh': in the days of the Raj, the wealthy would ensure their cabin avoided the heat of the sun by booking their accommodation '**p**ort-**o**ut-**s**tarboard-**h**ome' (although there is no hard evidence that this is where the word came from). But what about 'making both ends meet'? To save money when a rope broke, sailors would take the two ends and splice them together – though obviously you needed to 'know the ropes' to be able to do that. And, finally, 'taking the gilt off the gingerbread'. In the Middle Ages gingerbread cakes were often decorated with gold leaf to be sold at fairs. In the seventeenth and eighteenth centuries, the sterns of warships were adorned with gilt carvings which became known as 'gingerbread work'. After a while the combination of salt water and rough weather would combine to 'take the gilt off the gingerbread'.

From 1782, the Cumberland Fleet also held regular races downriver in the Thames estuary. And they also frequently indulged in the practice known as 'Admiral sailing', which involved manoeuvring in formation according to signals hoisted by the Commodore in his flagship, accompanied by much gunfire. It was a kind of nautical dancing which required skill and seamanship.

Cowes: the start of the week

By the beginning of the nineteenth century such activity was also taking place in the Solent, with the yachtsmen involved meeting for dinner in Cowes on the Isle of Wight, which had become a fashionable resort. It was probably inevitable that they would eventually organize themselves into a more formal association. On 1 June 1815, a group of them – including two marquesses, three earls, four viscounts, four barons and five baronets – met at the Thatched House Tavern in St James's Street in London and agreed to form what they originally called 'The Yacht Club'. It was the first time those two words had ever been used together. At the start it seems to have been a fairly modest affair, but in 1817 the Prince Regent let it be known that he would like to join. As a result, the club became much grander. When the Prince succeeded to the throne in 1820 as George IV, it became the Royal Yacht Club.

At first its formal activities were restricted to 'Admiral sailing', but this didn't stop some of its members from arranging private races. In 1815, Joseph Weld matched his yacht *Charlotte* against Thomas Assheton-Smith's *Elizabeth* for 500 guineas. The contest attracted a lot of attention. The *Hampshire Telegraph* declared: 'A match made on Monday last for 500 guineas is as likely to afford as much sport as any race that was ever contested by the highest-mettled coursers at Newmarket. Both yachts are of beautiful model and construction, and of celerity as quick sailors, and each gentleman confident of his vessel's superiority.' There were to be two races over two days, with a deciding third in reserve if honours were even. In the end only one was needed.

Elizabeth lost her masthead and *Charlotte*, well in the lead, had to turn around and go back to tow her into port.

Many similar races for wagers took place over the next few years, including the first 'round the island' race in 1824. Bu it wasn't until 1826 that the Royal Yacht Club finally decided to hold an annual regatta, with racing and accompanying social events. An advertisement

A 'sailing match' on Old Father Thames, from
Pierce Egan's Book of Sports

in the *Southampton Town and Country Herald* announced that 'The Annual Regatta Ball will take place at the Hotel, East Cowes, on Thursday, 10th August, and a splendid display of fireworks on the same night at the Parade, West Cowes.' The pattern of Cowes Week is pretty much the same today, even though the racing is radically different.

In 1833, the new King William IV decided that the club was 'an institution of such national utility' that it should henceforth be known as the Royal Yacht Squadron, with himself, naturally, as its head. A few years earlier the Cumberland Fleet had gone through a similar, though rather more acrimonious, name change. A row over a race had led a number of key members to start a rival club called the Thames

Yacht Club. The rump, who had short-sightedly changed their name to His Majesty's Coronation Sailing Society, lasted a few sad years before members voted to disband themselves and join what had by then become the Royal Thames Yacht Club.

Around this time, the nature of yachting began to change. Until then racing had been dominated by very large yachts owned by a small group of very wealthy men. In future there would be more emphasis on smaller yachts, and various methods of handicapping were introduced to allow them to compete with larger yachts on level terms. Against strong opposition from traditionalists, the King's Cup at Cowes adopted a handicapping system. The King himself insisted on it. But there were no set rules. Arrangements had to be agreed before every race or challenge and varied from club to club. And from the 1830s the number of yacht clubs began to grow rapidly. And not just in Britain.

America

The Dutch settlers in New York in the seventeenth century – it was New Amsterdam until 1667– almost certainly had yachts. But, as with their compatriots back home in the Netherlands, there is no evidence that they ever raced them. It wasn't until the nineteenth century that racing really got under way, led by the Stevens brothers, John and Edwin, from Hoboken, just across the Hudson from New York. The older brother John was particularly prolific, building many yachts which competed successfully up and down the East Coast. In 1844, he played host in the saloon of his schooner *Gimcrack* to the first meeting of the New York Yacht Club, which came to have the same influence in America as the Royal Yacht Squadron had in Britain. John Stevens was its first Commodore.

In 1851, Stevens headed a syndicate which commissioned a new schooner from the innovative designer George Steers. The plan was to take her to England at the time of the Great Exhibition to show off what American design could achieve. Appropriately, the yacht was called simply *America*. Via the British Ambassador, the Royal Yacht

Squadron (RYS) were informed and invited Stevens and his friends to be the guests of the Squadron at Cowes. Stevens was delighted to accept and said that he and his co-owners would 'take with a good grace the sound thrashing we are likely to get by venturing our long-shore craft on your rough waters'.

America was sailed across the Atlantic to Le Havre, where she was made ready for her appearance at Cowes. In late July, she set sail for the Solent. On the journey her owners committed a tactical error. They were met by the English yacht *Lavrock* and challenged to an informal match. Despite being heavily laden with French wine for future entertaining, *America* won easily. By the time she anchored off Cowes, word was out that she was very fast. She attracted a huge amount of interest. The *Illustrated London News* reported that 'As a model, she is artistic, although rather a violation of the established ideas of naval architecture.' Lord Alfred Paget, owner of one of the yachts which was to race against her, remarked that 'if she's right, then we must all be wrong'. Meanwhile, Stevens posted several challenges at the RYS clubhouse for anyone who wanted a private match against *America*. The first was for schooners for fun, the last for any yacht for £10,000 (more than half a million pounds in today's money). There were no takers.

The Royal Yacht Squadron had already announced a special 'Round the Island' race to take place during the Cowes Week Regatta for a £100 cup which would be open to yachts 'of all nations'. It was designed to accommodate the New Yorkers. There were eighteen entries, including of course *America*, though only fifteen eventually took part. They were the yachts of many of the most prominent sailing men of the day. The race took place on 22 August, in an extraordinary atmosphere. Queen Victoria was among the spectators. Here's a contemporary account:

In the memory of man Cowes never presented such an appearance as upon this day. There must have been at least a hundred yachts lying at anchor in the Roads; the beach was crowded from Egypt to the piers, the esplanade in front of the Club thronged with ladies and gentlemen, and with the people inland, who came over in shoals with wives, sons and daughters for the day.

Booths were erected all along the quay and the roadstead was alive with boats, while from the sea and shore rose an incessant buzz of voices, mingled with the splashing of oars, the flapping of sails, and the hissing of steam, from the excursion vessels preparing to accompany the race ... It was with the greatest difficulty the little town gave space enough to the multitudes that came from all quarters to witness an event so novel and so interesting, and the hotels were quite inadequate to meet the demand of their guests.

The yachts set sail at 10 a.m. and *America* was the last to get away. By the first marker, Normans Buoy, only three minutes separated the first nine yachts. *America* was lying fifth, behind *Volante*, *Freak*, *Aurora* and *Gipsy Queen*. Then the wind freshened and *America* forged ahead. A little later disaster struck as her rivals were short-tacking down the coast. *Freak* fouled *Volante*, which meant two of the most fancied English yachts were out of the race. Then *Arrow* went aground at Mill Bay and *Alarm* had to go to her rescue. When *America* rounded the Needles at 5.47 p.m., her nearest rival, *Aurora*, was several miles behind her. This was the moment when the famous and quite possibly apocryphal signal was sent. The Queen had been told *America* was in the lead. Who is second, she asked. The reply came back: 'Ma'am, there is no second.'

In fact, as *America* tacked back up the Solent, the wind died down almost completely. It took her nearly three hours to reach the finishing line at Cowes, by which time the much smaller and more nimble *Aurora* was hot on her tail. *America* crossed the line at 8.37 p.m., with *Aurora* just eight minutes behind her. Two more yachts came in an hour or so later, with a fifth being recorded as finishing at 1.20 a.m., after the victory dinner and the fireworks were over. No one stayed up to note what time the others reached home.

A week later, *America* raced again in a private match. Robert Stephenson of 'Rocket' fame had finally come forward to accept Stevens's challenge, but only for £100. In the end, *America* beat his yacht *Titania* quite easily. Two days later *America* was sold for $25,000 and her owners went back to New York with the cup. They considered melting it down to produce a souvenir for each syndicate member, which as many have pointed out might have saved some people a lot of

The victorious yacht America, *who gave her name*
to sailing's most prestigious trophy

money over the years. But in 1857, the cup was renamed the America's
Cup (after the yacht, not the country) and given to the New York
Yacht Club as 'a perpetual Challenge Cup for friendly competition
between foreign nations'. It was to remain in New York for 132 years,
perhaps the longest winning streak in the history of sport.

There's a curious postscript to this story. The America's Cup lists
every yacht that took part in that original race except for the *Aurora*. Is
that where the story of there being no second comes from?

After America

In the second half of the nineteenth century, yacht racing grew
fast. There were a number of developments. One was the growth of a
ding-dong battle between the rule-makers, who were trying to work out
a fair system of handicapping, and yacht designers. Every time the
rules were adapted to counter yachts that were seen as 'rule-cheaters',
the designers would come up with another way of ensuring the large
boats of their wealthier clients still had an unfair advantage. In 1875,
out of exasperation, a group of yachtsmen founded the Yacht Racing
Association to control the designers and ensure fair competition. But

some of the older clubs such as the RYS and the Royal Thames declined to recognize the new body because they said it favoured yachts designed purely for racing, putting their members who liked cruising *and* racing at a disadvantage. The stand-off was resolved through the Prince of Wales, who became President of the YRA in 1881 and Commodore of the RYS in 1882. But the YRA still found it hard to come up with rules that pleased all parties.

A second phenomenon was an explosion of yacht clubs all over Britain. Yacht racing also became increasingly international. The glamorous races of the day might make yachting appear to have been a largely Anglo-American affair, but it was also becoming popular throughout Europe and the Empire. In 1906, a number of European countries got together to form the International Yacht Racing Union to work out how to 'rate' yachts for international competition. America, however, remained aloof and kept to its own rules.

Another trend grew out of the growing popularity of the sport. Yachts became smaller. Only the very rich could afford the kind of vessels that sailed against *America* – and the professional crews required to sail them. The more yacht clubs there were, the more demand there was for yachts that amateurs, people on more modest incomes, could afford. They were called raters. Under the complex and ever-changing formulae for measuring the size of yachts, those of the wealthy would often rate 20 or 30. But at the other end of the scale, you could have half or one raters.

The move to smaller craft led to other developments. The idea of 'one-design' classes was introduced from America. These were yachts which were mass-produced and identical. Once again, the traditionalists threw up their arms. Yachts were meant to be individual, reflecting the wishes of their owner. The more progressive Americans argued that if everyone was in the same boat, the contest would be decided by the skill of the sailor. The other revolution, which was really to open up yachting in the twentieth century, was the introduction and explosive growth of dinghy sailing. Suddenly everyone (almost) could try sailing a boat, even children. This emancipation, fuelled by new materials, new designs and new ideas such as windsurfing, would define competitive sailing into the twenty-first century. The classes included in the Olympics, for instance, which have featured sailing consistently since 1900, now change for almost every games.

The late nineteenth century also saw the start of ocean racing. In 1866, three American schooners raced across the Atlantic for an enormous wager of £18,000. It was won by the newspaper magnate James Gordon Bennett with *Henrietta*. Four years later his schooner *Dauntless* raced east to west across the Atlantic against the British schooner *Cambria*, who was on her way to challenge for the America's Cup. This time Gordon Bennett lost. The first ocean race to become a regular fixture, from New York (now Newport) to Bermuda, began in 1906. The Bermuda Race now alternates with the Fastnet Race, in which competitors start at Ryde on the Isle of Wight, go around the Fastnet Rock off south-west Ireland and finish near Plymouth. It began in 1925. The third major regular ocean event is the Sydney–Hobart Race, started in 1945, which always begins on Boxing Day. Of course, there are now also regular round-the-world races.

America's Cup no longer

But the most prestigious race of all remains the America's Cup. For more than 100 years most, but not all, of the challenges to the New York Yacht Club came from Britain. They all failed, but one came very close. In 1934, T. O. M. Sopwith's 'J' Class yacht *Endeavour* won the first two races, halfway to the winning tally of four. He then lost the third race. In the fourth, Sopwith believed he had been forced off course illegally by the defender *Rainbow* but failed to raise his protest flag immediately as required under the New York Yacht Club rules. As a result the race officials refused to hear his complaint after he had lost the race, which led one American newspaper to come up with the headline:

BRITAIN RULES THE WAVES
BUT AMERICA WAIVES THE RULES

The incident appears to have had a disastrous effect on Sopwith. He threw away the next race when well in the lead and thereafter appeared to abandon the will to win. *Rainbow* retained the Cup. Sopwith tried again three years later but was easily beaten by a superior yacht.

The last British challenge was in 1964. Contenders now have to compete for the right to challenge and Britain has not been successful for the last forty-odd years. But others have fared better. In 1983, *Australia II* from the Royal Perth Yacht Club finally wrested the Cup away from New York. The Americans won it back four years later through the San Diego Yacht Club, but they lost it again to New Zealand in 1995. In 2003 New Zealand in turn lost it to a yacht from land-locked Switzerland. That must have caused the odd hiccup over the pink gins at the Royal Yacht Squadron's castle in Cowes.

But all is not lost. Britain remains a powerful force in world sailing. In the twenty-first century, Britain has been the most successful team in the sailing events at the Olympics. And sailing in turn is one of Britain's leading Olympic disciplines.

6.
FOOTBALL
(SOCCER)

IN 1801, JOSEPH Strutt decided that the sport of football was on its last legs. 'It was formerly much in vogue among the common people of England,' he writes, 'though of late years it seems to have fallen into disrepute, and is but little practised.' He makes it clear he has no regrets: 'When the exercise becomes exceeding violent, the players kick each other's shins without the least ceremony, and some of them are overthrown at the hazard of their limbs.'

Go forward two hundred years. FIFA, the international governing body of football, estimated that, at the start of the twenty first century, 250 million people worldwide were actively playing football; 1.3 billion said they were 'interested' in the sport. Almost half the world's population – more than 3.2 billion people – watched at least part of the 2010 World Cup in South Africa.

Quite a change. How did it happen?

Origins

We don't know where or when the idea of kicking a ball about originated, but certainly footballing skills of a kind were being practised in China in the second and third centuries BC. There is strong evidence that a football-like game with teams, rules, competitions and stadiums was popular in China in the first millennium AD, reaching its zenith during the eighth and ninth centuries. At the centre of the game was a

'ball wall", which has a hole in it of a regulated size above head height.
This was the 'goal'. The game was particularly popular at the royal court.
A different and rather more refied game call *kemari* seems to have been
played in Japan around the same time, which involved trying to pass a
ball around without it touching the ground. It was not competitive.

Japanese woodcut entitled 'Life at the Chiyoda Palace'
showing Samurai warriors watching a game of kemari

Ancient Greece had a game called *episkyros*, which was played at the
great athletic-poetic-dramatic festivals of the classical era. The Romans
had a version called *harpastum*, which remained popular for 700 or 800
years. It was played by two teams on a rectangular field marked with
boundary lines; the aim was to carry your ball over your opponents'
line. Harpastum was popular in Gaul and it is highly likely the Romans
introduced it into Britain. It involved the use of hands as much as feet
but, as we shall see, that doesn't mean it wasn't a precursor of football.

There is also circumstantial evidence that football was played in
Britain before the Norman Conquest. Legend has it that the annual
Shrove Tuesday match at Derby was first played to celebrate a victory
over the Romans in the third century, while similar games at Chester
and Kingston-upon-Thames are both said to have first been played
with the severed head of a captured Dane. The Welsh chronicler

Nennius, probably writing early in the ninth century, described boys quarrelling during a game of ball. But the first clear evidence of what is almost certainly a game of football comes just over a hundred years after the Battle of Hastings.

Folk football

Around 1175, the monk William Fitzstephen wrote a lively account of life in his native London, in which he described what happens in the afternoon every Shrove Tuesday:

All the youth of the city go to a flat patch of ground just outside the city for the famous game of ball. The students of every faculty have their own ball, and those who are engaged in the various trades of the city also have their own ball. The older men – the fathers and men of substance – come on horseback to watch the competitions of the younger men. In their own way the older men participate in the sporting activities of their juniors. They appear to get excited at witnessing such vigorous exercise and by taking part in the pleasures of unrestrained youth.

Shrove Tuesday was the traditional day for an annual football match in many parts of the country. Rules, such as they were, varied from place to place but the overall pattern was chaotically similar. The most famous game took place in Derby between two parishes, St Peter's and All Saints. The 'goals' were a considerable distance from each other. Upwards of a thousand men might take part, and many more thousands would travel to the city to watch. Stephen Glover's *History, Gazetteer, and Directory of the County of Derby*, published in 1829, described what went on:

The game commences in the market-place, where the partisans of each parish are drawn up on each side, and about noon a large ball is tossed up in the midst of them. This is seized upon by some of the strongest and most active men of each party. The rest of the players immediately close in upon them and a solid mass is formed. It then becomes the object of each party to impel the course of the crowd towards their particular goal. The struggle to obtain the ball, which is carried in the arms of those who have possessed themselves of it, is then violent, and the motion of the human tide heaving to and fro, without the least regard to consequences, is tremendous. Broken shins, broken heads, torn coats and lost hats are among the minor accidents of this fearful contest, and it frequently happens that persons fall in consequence of the intensity of the pressure, fainting and bleeding beneath the feet of the surrounding mob.

Glover adds that a visiting Frenchman remarked that if this is what the English call playing, 'it would be impossible to say what they would call fighting'. A similar, marginally gentler version of the game is still played on Shrove Tuesday every year in Ashbourne in Derbyshire.

In this kind of folk football, the 'goals' could be bushes, posts, houses, church porches or any other fixed object. They could be a few score yards apart or several miles – in Ashbourne the distance is three miles.

A reconstruction of what a medieval folk football
game might have looked like.

The starting point was generally midway between the two. There was rarely any limit on the numbers on each side and the contest could take place through city streets and squares, over fields and hedges, and through streams and rivers. Glover notes that 'it is certainly curious to see two or three hundred men up to their chins in the [River] Derwent continually ducking each other'.

But we can presume that football wasn't only played on high days and holidays. In 1602, Richard Carew, the High Sheriff of Cornwall, wrote an account of the Cornish game of 'hurling'. From what he writes, this had little to do with the modern game of hurling, which involves hockey-like sticks, but was simply the local name for the game which elsewhere was called football. The interesting point is that he draws a distinction between two different types of 'hurling'. One, which he calls 'hurling over country', sounds very similar to Shrovetide folk football. Two or three parishes challenge two or three other parishes. The goals are trees or buildings which can be seen or are well known, three or four miles apart. Then:

That company which can catch or carry the ball by force or slight to the place assigned gaineth the victory ... The hurlers take their way over hilles, dales, hedges, ditches, yea, and thorow briars, mires, plashes and rivers whatsoever, so as you shall sometimes see twenty or thirty lie tugging together in the water, scrambling and scratching for the ball.

The other game is called 'hurling to goales'. An agreed number of players – 'fifteen, twenty or thirty ... more or less' – are chosen for each side. They pair off against an opponent, embrace and move apart, 'every of which couple are especially to watch one another during the play'. Man-to-man marking. Then:

... they pitch two bushes in the ground some eight or ten feet asunder, and directly against them ten or twelve score paces off other twain in like distance which they term goales, where some indifferent person throweth up a ball the which whomsoever can catch and carry through the adversaries' goals hath won the game.

There were many other rules including, intriguingly, a ban on passing forward. It's clear that this is a much more containable and organized game and is likely to have involved a lot more tactical thinking. This is a game you could play every day, or at least every Sunday.

The alert reader will have noticed something quite interesting. These games are all about catching and carrying the ball. There's very little mention of – or scope for – kicking it. In other words, we're looking at prototype rugby, not soccer. There is even a well-known account of a game of football at Scone in Perthshire where 'no person was allowed to kick the ball'. So why is the game generally called football?

Montague Shearman, in his 1904 *History of Football* for the Badminton Library, suggests the name refers to the size and nature of the ball – it was big enough and bouncy enough to be kicked. There is some support for this theory in an 1823 description of the East Anglian version of the game which, confusingly, is called camp-ball. In most respects it is like Carew's 'hurling to goales', with the ball being caught and passed among players by hand. The difference is that the ball is usually said to be 'the size of a cricket ball'. But later, the author says that 'Sometimes a large football was used; the game was then called "kicking camp"; and if played with the shoes on, "savage camp".' A disturbing thought.

There were some versions of the ancient game where kicking played an important role. In 1471, poor Henry VI vanished for ever. Before long Henry came to be held in such reverence that it was thought he could work miracles. One case involved William Bartram of Caunton, near Newark, who 'was kicked during a game, and suffered long and scarce endurable pain, but suddenly recovered the blessing of health when he had seen the glorious King Henry in a dream'. The chronicler describes how he got his injury:

The game at which they had met for common recreation is called by some the foot-ball game. It is one in which young men, in country sport, propel a huge ball not by throwing it in the air but by striking it and rolling it along the ground, and that not with their hands but with their feet. A game, I say, abominable enough, and, in my judgement at least, more common, un-dignified, and worthless than any other kind of game, rarely ending but with some loss, accident or disadvantage to the players themselves. What then? The boundaries had been marked and the game had started, and, when they were striving manfully, kicking in opposite directions, and our hero had thrown himself into the midst of the fray, one of his fellows, whose name I know not, came up against him from in front and kicked him by mis-adventure, missing his aim at the ball.

What is apparent is that from at least the thirteenth to the nineteenth century, there were lots of different versions of the 'foot-ball game' being played all over the country. These were local games played according to local customs. Kicking featured more in some than in others, but interestingly there's no evidence that handling the ball was banned in any of them. What they all had in common, as poor William Bartram knew, was that they were rough and ready. The violence in his case appears to have been accidental. In many other versions, it appears to have been an integral part of the game. Certainly its numerous critics over the centuries thought it to be so.

Proclamations and prohibitions

Early in the sixteenth century, Sir Thomas Elyot railed against 'foote-balle wherein is nothing but beastlie furie and exstreme violence whereof procedeth hurte, and consequently rancour and malice do remain with them that be wounded, wherefore it is to be put in per-petual silence'. In 1576, in Ruislip, a grand jury condemned a large group of tradesmen for playing football because 'there was amongst them a great affray likely to result in homicides and serious accidents'. Five years later in South Mimms the sad case of Roger Ludforde was brought before the Coroner's Court: '... Roger Ludforde ran towards the ball with the intention to kick it, whereupon Nicholas Martyn with the fore-part of his right arm and Richard Turvey with the fore-part of his left arm struck Roger Ludforde on the fore-part of the body under the breast, giving him a mortal blow and concussion of which he died within a quarter of an hour, and that Nicholas and Richard in this manner feloniously slew the said Roger'.

Two years later, the Puritan pamphleteer Philip Stubbs, condemning ungodly games being played on a Sunday, declared:

... as concerning football playing I protest unto you that it may rather be called a friendlie kinde of fyghte than a play or recreation – a bloody and murthering practice than a felowly sport or pastime. For dooth not everyone lye in waight for his adversarie, to overthrow him or picke [pitch] him on his nose, though it be on hard stones ... So that by this means sometimes their necks are broken, sometimes their backs, sometimes their legs, sometimes their armes, sometimes their noses gush out with blood, sometimes their eyes start out, and sometimes hurte in one place, sometimes in another ...

It's quite clear Stubbs knows what he's talking about. He has the excessive zeal of the reformed. He's either played or watched a lot of football. He goes on to show that he is well aware of all the dirty tricks that can be played:

... they have the sleights to meet one betwixt the two [an echo of Roger Ludforde's fate], to dash him against the hart with their elbowes, to butt him under the short ribs with their griped fists, and with their knees to catch him on the hip and pick him on his neck, with a hundred such murthering devices. And hereof groweth envy, rancour, and malice, and sometimes brawling, murther, homicide, and great effusion of blood, as experience daily teacheth.

But if experience was teaching on a daily basis that the game could cause serious injuries, why were people still playing it? The answer is that they were enjoying it. Indeed, there seems to have been robust resistance to all attempts to ban football – of which there were many. The first came in 1314, when Edward II issued a proclamation banning the game as likely to lead to a breach of the peace: 'Forasmuch as there is great noise in the city caused by hustling over large balls ...

from which many evils might arise which God forbid: we command and forbid on behalf of the King, on pain of imprisonment, such game to be used in the city in future.' The fact that similar proclamations were issued every few years for the next three centuries by Edward's successors suggests that they were never very successful. Football was a national game and people liked playing it.

The reasons for the regular attempts to ban the game were first and foremost to do with its unruly nature: it was a threat to people and to

Etching from around 1820 showing a
chaotic street football scene

property. The burghers of Manchester became particularly exercised about having their windows broken regularly by 'lewd and disordered persons' playing football in the street. In medieval times, it was also seen, along with many other sports, as a distraction from the important task of practising archery, which was vital for the defence of the realm. Later, by the time of the Commonwealth and Oliver Cromwell (ironically enough a noted footballer at Cambridge), its major crime was that it was played on a Sunday, the only day that most ordinary people had any spare time.

Football valiantly resisted all attempts to ban it up until the time of

Cromwell. But from that point on, it began to decline. This was partly the lasting impact of Puritanism, partly the effect of land enclosures reducing the availability of space to play the game and partly the impact of increasingly effective law enforcement. Growing industrialization and urbanization also caused widespread social disruption, which eroded many folk traditions. And the growing towns and cities also became more and more strict about what could happen in the streets. The emerging mercantile middle class didn't want disruption and broken windows; their byword was discipline.

Which is why by the time Joseph Strutt was writing his book in 1801, football may well have been 'but little practised'. But he had overlooked one place where surprisingly the game was flourishing. And from where it would eventually emerge greatly enhanced.

The public schools

Richard Mulcaster was a man ahead of his time. In the late sixteenth and early seventeenth centuries, first as headmaster of Merchant Taylors' School then as High Master of St Paul's, he was a leading figure in education. As a man of the Renaissance, he believed the job of the teacher was to develop the whole person. Thus, as well as the study of the classics, he thought that time should be set aside for music, drama and athletic activity, possibly including football:

. . . the Footeball play, which could not possibly have grown to this greatness, that it is now at, nor have been so much used, as it is in all places, if it had not had great helpes, both to health and strength. And to me the abuse of it is a sufficient argument that it hath a right use: which . . . will both helpe, strength, and comfort nature, though as it is now commonly used, with thronging of a rude multitude, with bursting of shinnes, and breaking of legges, it be neither civil, neither worthy the name of any traine to health.

Mulcaster suggested reforms which would bring out the health benefits of the game: the introduction of a referee, smaller numbers on each side, each player to have a set position and 'not meeting with their bodies so boisterously to try their strength; nor shouldring or shuffling one another so barbarously . . .' It was to be nearly 250 years before such an idea re-emerged in British attitudes to education.

This is not to say that football was unknown at major institutes of learning. We know it was being played at Oxford because it was banned, for the first of many times, as early as 1555. Cambridge too had its problems. We have a vivid account of a game in 1579 between 'certayn schollers of Cambridge and divers of Chesterton', a nearby village. Unbeknownst to the 'schollers', the villagers had hidden staves in the church porch. On a signal, they pulled them out and laid into the unfortunate undergraduates, who then had to swim across a river to escape. A witness added: 'And Longe Johan, servaunt to Mr Brakyn, did folowe one Edward Wylton, Scholler of Clarehall, with a javelyn; and if this deponent had not rescued hym, he beleaveth he would have runne the said Wylton thorough.' No wonder the Vice-Chancellor shortly afterwards banned students from playing anyone from outside their own college. But Cambridge would come back into its own in the regeneration of football in the nineteenth century.

At the beginning of that century, Britain's public schools were in a bad way. They were originally foundations endowed by wealthy benefactors for the education of poor boys. A 'public' school was one where the headmaster was a salaried employee appointed by a board of trustees; 'private' schools were owned by their headmasters. The public schools always let in a number of fee-paying pupils, but in the early days these were in a minority. That changed in the eighteenth century, as the private tutors on which upper-class families had previously relied fell out of favour. As the fee-paying boys became a majority, the nature of the schools changed. The boys were now socially superior to the masters, and they didn't like being told what to do by people they regarded as little more than servants. Anarchy beckoned. Each school was a tinderbox waiting to ignite.

And that's exactly what happened on at least twenty-two occasions between 1728 and 1832. At Eton in 1768, the prefects rebelled because the headmaster wouldn't recognize their right to punish junior boys.

At Harrow, two revolts happened because the boys wanted a say in the appointment of the headmaster. The 1808 Winchester rebellion arose because the headmaster tried to make a saint's day a school day without consulting the pupils. The 1828 Winchester revolt broke out because the boys didn't approve of the prefects the head had appointed.

Rebellion was not too strong a word for many of these uprisings. Militia with fixed bayonets were needed to put down the 1818 revolt at Winchester. During an incident twenty-five years earlier, the boys armed themselves with guns, swords and bludgeons, and ransacked the school shop to stockpile food for a siege. At Rugby in 1797, the rebels used explosives to blow the door off the headmaster's classroom, broke all his windows, started a fire with desks, benches and the room's wainscoting and burned all his books. The rebellion was only quelled when soldiers arrived on site with drawn swords.

The uneasy compromise reached in most schools was that the teachers stuck to teaching and the boys – and in particular the prefects

A game of football at Winchester College around 1840:
it looks like a giant rugby scrum

– imposed what discipline there was and ran their own leisure time. It was the perfect environment for the anarchic and aggressive game of old-style football. Which is why, even as it declined in the outside

world, football thrived in the public schools. Even when it was supposedly banned. At Shrewsbury, the long-serving headmaster Samuel
Butler condemned football as 'fit only for butcher boys ... more fit for
farm boys and labourers than young gentlemen'. He formally banned
it but the boys took absolutely no notice and continued playing. The
game was equally popular at other schools.

Each school had its own unique rules, largely defined by the space in
which the game was played. At Charterhouse, for instance, the game
was played in the cloisters of the old Carthusian monastery in London,
before the school moved to the country in 1872. This made running
with the ball in hand, which inevitably involved 'collaring' or tackling
to the ground, rather inadvisable. Old paving slabs are unforgiving.
Hence emphasis was put on kicking and a 'dribbling' game was developed. But the game was still robust because scrimmaging was
allowed, in which 'shins would be kicked black and blue; jackets and
other articles of clothing almost torn into shreds; and Fags [junior boys
who had the dangerous task of defence] trampled under foot'.

Other schools which favoured the 'dribbling' game (passing at
this stage was hardly known) included Westminster, Eton, Harrow,
Winchester and Shrewsbury. All of them allowed catching and holding
the ball, but most prohibited running with it in hand. The one exception among the established schools was Rugby, where the old tradition
of catching and running with the ball which characterized much of folk
football was encouraged. (Why this was so will be dealt with in more
detail in the chapter on rugby.) Rugby School's distinctive approach
was adopted by some of the newer schools, most notably Marlborough
and Cheltenham.

Rugby was also notable for being in the forefront of the reform
movement which began to sweep the public schools from around 1830
onwards. Pressure for reform was coming in part from the emerging
middle classes, rich from the profits of industrialization. They saw
the public schools as a channel for social advancement. But the old
informal education the schools used to offer, which may have been fine
for indolent aristocrats, wasn't much use if you were going to have to
work for a living. The new breed of parents wanted something more

modern, more disciplined and more rigorous. Something which would equip their sons to be doctors, lawyers and civil servants, and enable them to run the country and the Empire. They were supported by a new breed of headmaster anxious to do away with the damaging practices of the past and improve moral and academic standards.

Foremost among these was Dr Thomas Arnold, who became Headmaster of Rugby in 1828. He proceeded to revive the school through an emphasis on 'godliness and good learning' which was designed to turn out Christian gentlemen with a strict sense of morality, a broad cultural knowledge and a strong belief in social responsibility. To impose discipline he recruited the senior boys, who had long had a powerful influence, as his partners. He made them prefects directly responsible to him. He applied the new sense of discipline to all aspects of school life, including sports. While Arnold himself never saw games as being that important, many of his contemporaries and followers did. The idea grew that disciplined team sports developed 'character' and instilled courage, teamwork, selflessness and toughness, the very qualities needed to administer the Empire. Muscular Christianity was born.

One of its core ideas was that the team was more important than the individual. That implied that the team had something at stake – it had to be competing. Competition in turn required rules. Which is why, starting in the 1840s, schools began to codify rules for football. The earliest we know of are from Rugby, from 1846. Predictably, they allowed running with the ball in hand as well as kicking an opponent's legs below the knee, with the humane proviso that he should not be held still while his shins were being hacked to pieces. Around the same time, Eton and Harrow each settled on eleven as the best size for a team and Eton introduced Mulcaster's old idea of a referee.

That same year, two former pupils at Shrewsbury, J. C. Thring and H. de Winton, tried to set up a football club at Cambridge with some Old Etonians. It collapsed almost immediately because they couldn't agree on a common set of rules. Two years later, another group representing Eton, Harrow, Rugby, Winchester and Shrewsbury tried again. This time they came up with agreed rules – but no copy of them

survives. The nearest we have is a set from the mid-1850s. Not surprisingly, given the preponderance of dribbling men over running
men, they allow catching and stopping the ball with the hand but not
running with it. They also outlaw holding, tripping and hacking.

The quest for a common set of rules now quickened pace. In 1857 a
football club was established in Sheffield, followed by a second the next
year, whose rules essentially favoured the dribbling game but allowed a
bit more physical contact. In 1862, our old friend J. C. Thring, who
was by this time an assistant master at Uppingham School, issued rules
for what he called the 'Simplest Game' – just ten short paragraphs.
They have rudimentary rules for kicking off, goal kicks, throw-ins and
offside. They ban running with the ball, hacking and tripping, but
allow stopping the ball with your hands and placing it at your feet.
A year later, a new group of nine Cambridge men, representing
Shrewsbury, Eton, Harrow, Rugby, Marlborough and Westminster,
met to update the Cambridge rules. Before they could do so, however,
an even more important meeting took place in London.

The Football Association

The Freemasons' Tavern used to stand in Great Queen Street in
London's Covent Garden, on the site of what are now the Connaught
Rooms beside the grandiose Freemasons' Hall. It was a popular dining
place for much of the nineteenth century and was remarkable for
two reasons. It was there, in 1807, that the Royal Geological Society
was founded. And it was there, on 26 October 1863, that a meeting
took place which was to lead directly to the creation of the biggest
international sport the world has ever known: soccer. (Incidentally, the
unassuming Freemasons Arms just across the road has plaques com-
memorating both occasions, but they are almost certainly inaccurate.)

At the 1863 meeting were fourteen people representing a motley
collection of London clubs, mainly founded by former public school
boys. The clubs were Forest (based in Epping Forest), N. N. (standing
for No Names) from Kilburn, Barnes (mainly rowers), War Office,

Crusaders, Perceval House Blackheath, Crystal Palace, Blackheath, Kensington School, Surbiton and Blackheath School. They were a self-selected group. No one was invited from the public schools (although there was an 'observer' from Charterhouse) or from Cambridge. There was no one there from the Sheffield clubs. The group's first action was to form the Football Association (FA), 'with the object of establishing a definite set of rules for the regulation of the game'.

The balance of power within the group was clear from the outset. The Blackheath club and the two Blackheath schools (both 'crammers') were dominated by old boys from Rugby and favoured the running and hacking game. The rest were dribblers. But there does appear to have been a genuine attempt to compromise. The first draft of the FA rules included running with the ball and tripping and hacking. Everything was up for negotiation. But the reality is that there was no room for compromise. Either you have running with the ball (what we now call rugby) or you don't (what we now call soccer). Negotiations went on for several weeks. They included, according to Montague Shearman, a crucial joint conference with the Cambridge committee mentioned above. The Cambridge rules were published on 20 November and they banned running with the ball and tripping and hacking. On 24 November, a proposal that 'the rules of Cambridge University embrace the true principles of the game' was carried in the face of opposition from the supporters of running with the ball. The momentum was with the dribblers. F. W. Campbell of Blackheath was outraged. Condemning the attack on hacking, he said '. . . it savours far more of the feelings of those who like their pipes and grog or schnapps more than the manly game of football'. Matters came to a head on 1 December. Campbell realized that he was outnumbered. He and his supporters withdrew from the Association.

What happened to Campbell and his hackers will be recounted in the chapter on rugby. The Football Association published its 'Laws' on 8 December. This moment has been seen as the start of the modern game, but many of the elements the Laws contained would seem strange today. Running with the ball and hacking were proscribed, of course, but making a 'fair catch' to claim a free kick was allowed. If the ball went into touch or over the goal line, the first person to reach it won the throw-in or kick. There were no markings on the pitch, there was no net or crossbar on the goal and sides changed ends every time a goal was scored. Most important, the offside rule forbade any kind of forward passing. So the normal style of play would involve giving the ball to your best 'dribbler' and 'backing him up' en masse while he

'The Association Game': founded by public schoolboys,
but quickly reclaimed by the working classes

charged down the field. The forwards played in no set positions and only one full back was left behind to support the goalkeeper. If the dribbler was tackled and lost the ball, the other side would do the same thing in the opposite direction.

The irony is that the public schools, which had done so much to bring the Laws about, chose in the main to ignore them. Harrow, for instance, said it was quite happy with the rules it already had. And most of the newer public schools – more were opening every year – decided that rugby was the more manly and character-defining game. Even many of the 'dribbling' teams, such as the Sheffield clubs, pre-ferred to stick to their own variations of the rules. It was to take the FA several years to establish the 'definite set of rules for the regulation of the game' that it sought. And certainly its founders could have had no conception of how their sport was going to develop.

Establishing authority

First came some pretty swift rule changes. Within a couple of years, the first revision did away with the idea of a 'fair catch' leading to a free kick. Shortly afterwards, stopping the ball with your hands was banned – in future, only the goalkeeper would be allowed to handle the ball. The thinking was that if this game was to be called football, let's make it all about the feet. In 1866, a tape was introduced between the goal-posts – the ball had to go under it to count as a score. (Fixed crossbars were to be permitted in 1875 and made compulsory in 1882.)

That same year a change was made to the offside rule which was to have major implications for the way the game was played. The original rules had banned any kind of forward passing, just as in rugby. The new law, which was in line with the rule in use at Westminster and Charterhouse schools, said that a player was onside as long as there were three opponents between him and the goal. This removed the last bar to the adoption of a universal code by all players in the South, but in the North, Sheffield continued to play by its own rules, which stated that a player was onside provided the goalkeeper at least was between him and the goal, until 1877.

In 1870, Charles W. Alcock became the Honorary Secretary of the FA. He'd been on the Committee since 1866 so would have been well aware of the need to attract more clubs – at the beginning of 1868, only twenty-eight were affiliated. In July 1871, he proposed that 'a Challenge Cup should be established ... for which all clubs belonging to the Association should be invited to compete'. This was the start of the FA Cup, probably the most emotive competition in British sport. He took the idea from his old school, Harrow, where the 'houses' played in a knockout competition each year to see which would be 'Cock House'. The idea seems obvious to us today but at the time it was revolutionary – the FA Cup was the first ever organized competition between football clubs. Fifty clubs were eligible the first year, 1872, but only fifteen entered. The Cup was won by a largely Old Harrovian side called the Wanderers, who beat the Royal Engineers at the Oval in front of a crowd of nearly 2000. The silver trophy was duly presented to

C.W. Alcock, founder of the FA Cup and organizer
of the first soccer international

the Wanderers' Captain, one C. W. Alcock. Football was indeed a small world in those days.

Alcock had also begun to explore the idea of international football. In 1867, the Queen's Park Football Club had been founded in Glasgow. Late in 1870, Alcock proposed that the Association select teams of English and Scottish players to compete against each other at the Oval in November. Queen's Park immediately joined the FA and the match duly took place, with the English winning 1–0. That first 'Scottish' side consisted of ex-public schoolboys who played their football in London or Oxford. Only one was a member of Queen's Park. But it was a start. After three more similar informal games, the first ever formal international match was played in Glasgow on 30 November 1872 in front of a crowd of 4000. The match was a 0–0 draw, but it was still enormously significant. This time the Scottish side all played for Queen's Park, perhaps because it was the only club in Scotland playing according to Association rules at the time. But as a

The Queen's Park Football Club from Glasgow:
they pioneered the passing game

result of this game many more Scottish clubs were to join over the next year or two, leading to the formation of the Scottish FA in 1873.

The game was also important for another reason. 'The strong point with the home club', reported the *Glasgow Herald*, 'was that they played excellently well together.' The Queen's Park team had used the changes to the offside rule to develop a short passing game which replaced the old style of dribbling forward play. They were not alone. The Royal Engineers claimed that they were 'the first to introduce the "combination" style of play', while the Sheffield teams, with their unique offside rule, had also developed a passing game. G. O. Smith, a renowned amateur player and commentator on the game, wrote in the Badminton Library edition of 1888 that: '. . . the introduction of a combination of passing tactics, to the discouragement of brilliant dribbling by individual players . . . so far revolutionized the game that we may fairly say there have been two ages of Association football, the dribbling and the passing'.

The revolution led to major tactical changes. First, the early passing teams like the Scottish in 1872 played with two full backs rather than just one to support the goalkeeper. Then they introduced half-backs on

either flank, then the crucial position of centre half. The game changed
for the forwards, too. Instead of running as a pack, they began to maintain their set positions on the field. 'In the modern game . . .' wrote
G. O. Smith, 'each player keeps to his own allotted place in the field
and plays not for himself but for the whole forward field.'

But there was resistance from the Southern ex-public school clubs.
For them, dribbling remained the thing. They had learned this individual skill from early in their youth and it was a major part of the
attraction of the game. 'To see players guide and steer a ball through
a circle of opposing legs, turning and twisting as occasion requires, is a
sight not to be forgotten', wrote one. And for a while, it worked. The

The Hon. A.F. Kinnaird, who played in
nine of the first eleven FA Cup Finals

Wanderers won five of the first six FA cups, and the Old Etonians, Old
Carthusians and Oxford University won most of the rest of the first
eleven finals. One man, the Hon. A. F. Kinnaird, played in nine of
these games, first for the Wanderers, then for the Old Etonians. He was
a big red-bearded man of great flamboyance. There is a story of an FA
official visiting his mother. 'I'm afraid that one of these days, Arthur
will come home with a broken leg,' said Lady Kinnaird. 'Never fear,
madam,' said the official. 'It will not be his own.'

In 1882, Kinnaird and his Old Etonians were in for a surprise. Their opponents in the final were Blackburn Rovers, the first team from the North ever to have got so far. Kinnaird's team won, but the following year they were in for even more of a shock. They were facing another team in the final not just from the North but from the same town, Blackburn Olympic. The two teams could not have been more different.

Olympic consisted of three weavers, a spinner, a cotton machine operative, an iron worker, a plumber, a clerk, a dental assistant and a publican. They had spent five days training on Blackpool sands, funded by a whip-round in the local mills and foundries, living on a diet of kippers and porridge, beer and oysters. They arrived in London two days early to recover from the journey. By contrast, the Etonians turned up at the last moment. All but one of them had played in a final

---

Women's football

One of the pioneers of women's football was Nettie Honeyball (a name you couldn't invent). She founded the British Ladies' Football Club in 1894. She was quite clear about her reasons. 'I founded the association ... with the fixed resolve of proving to the world that women are not the "ornamental and useless" creatures men have pictured. I must confess, my convictions on all matters where the sexes are so widely divided are all on the side of emancipation, and I look forward to the time when ladies may sit in Parliament and have a voice in the direction of affairs, especially those which concern them most.' Nettie and her team-mates clearly scared the hell out of the FA. In 1902 – after the death of Queen Victoria – the FA Council issued instructions to affiliated associations not to allow matches against 'lady teams'. In 1921, they passed the following resolution: 'Complaints having been made as to football being played by women, the council feel impelled to express their strong opinion that the game of football is quite unsuitable for females and ought not to be encouraged.' They banned women from playing on their members' pitches – a ban that was reiterated in 1946. It wasn't finally lifted until 1971.

before and they regarded training as not only unnecessary but also ungentlemanly. After all, they were going to go on and run the country and the Empire (one would become Lord High Commissioner of the Church of Scotland, another a Professor of Latin, a third the leading commercial lawyer in British India).

Blackburn Olympic won 2–1 in extra time. No Southern amateur team was ever to win the FA Cup again. What had happened?

The return of working-class football

By the time the Football Association had been formed, industrialization had transformed the landscape of Britain. There had been a mass exodus from the countryside to the new manufacturing towns of the North and the Midlands. A mature industrial working class was beginning to emerge, living back-to-back in smoke-filled towns close to the factories and mills where they worked. Slowly, their conditions were beginning to improve. Starting around 1850, the idea of finishing work at lunchtime on a Saturday began to spread, first among textile workers and then among other trades. Progress wasn't uniform – Liverpool workers didn't enjoy free Saturday afternoons until after 1870 – but it was steady. And from the 1850s, real wages began to rise. For the first time, working men found themselves with time on their hands and a bit of money to spend. What should they do with it?

There were plenty of people who thought they had answers to that question, including ex-public schoolboys with a sense of social responsibility who were keen to enhance the lives of working people. Many were clergymen who had chosen to work in the industrial towns. They valued the idea of the muscular Christianity that had imbued their own education, so they went out to save souls with a Bible in one hand and a football in the other. As free Saturday afternoons became more common, they started football clubs. By the 1880s, 83 of the 344 clubs in Birmingham had church connections; in Liverpool it was 24 out of 112. Many famous clubs started this way. The Villa Cross Wesleyan Chapel in Birmingham spawned Aston Villa in 1874. Birmingham

City started at Trinity Church in 1875. Bolton Wanderers grew from Christ Church in Bolton. Everton began as part of St Domingo's Church Sunday School in 1878; fourteen years later, after a row over rent, the club chairman and three first-team players split to form a separate club called Liverpool FC. St Andrew's Sunday School in West Kensington in London started what became Fulham. On 15 March 1877, the headmaster of St Luke's Church School in Blakenhall in the Black Country wrote this entry in his logbook: 'Let boys out earlier on Friday afternoon and they had a Football Match.' That was the start of Wolverhampton Wanderers. Both Burnley and Swindon had religious beginnings. Young men from St Mary's Church in Southampton began a club in 1885 which changed its name to Southampton in 1897 (which is why the team is still known as 'the Saints').

The public school belief in organized sport also spread to the state education system. Old boys of Blackburn Grammar School formed Blackburn Rovers in 1875, while ten years later former pupils of Wyggeston School in Leicester started the club that became Leicester City. In London a year later the boys of Droop Street School started Queen's Park Rangers. Both Sunderland and Northampton grew out of local teachers' associations.

Then there were the factory football clubs. Some were encouraged or even started by enlightened management (occasionally with public school connections); others were founded by the workers themselves. One of the earliest was founded in 1863 by workmen from the North Staffordshire Railway, possibly with the help of ex-public schoolboys employed as teachers nearby; their club became Stoke City. Railway workers from the great junction at Crewe already had a cricket club which met at the Alexandra Hotel; in 1877 they started a football club and naturally called it Crewe Alexandra. Workers from a cycle company in Coventry founded Singers FC in 1883, which became Coventry City, while Millwall began life at the local Morton's factory. Not far away in the East End the owner of the Thames Ironworks, educated at Harrow and Oxford, helped his workers start a football club in 1895. In 1900, it became West Ham United.

Two of the most famous clubs in British football started at the workplace. Men who worked for the Lancashire and Yorkshire Railway Company in 1878 started a club they called Newton Heath; twelve years later it changed its name to Manchester United. Further south, workers at the munitions factory in Woolwich formed a team which at first was called Royal Arsenal, then Woolwich Arsenal and finally just Arsenal

Cricket was a much better-established sport in the second half of the nineteenth century, but cricketers often wondered what they should do in the winter. In 1867 members of the Sheffield Wednesday Cricket Club, keen to play together during the darker months, started their own football club. In 1881, the Preston Cricket Club founded an associated football club which became Preston North End, while in London a year later the Hotspur Cricket Club started Tottenham Hotspur FC. Even the county clubs became involved. Derbyshire spawned Derby County in 1884 and Yorkshire started Sheffield United in 1889.

These famous clubs were, of course, just the tip of a rapidly expanding social phenomenon. From the 1860s onwards, the number of working-class football clubs in the North and the Midlands simply exploded. After the 1072 international match, the same thing happened in Scotland. The successful clubs that we still recognize emerged from the general mass for a number of different reasons. Inspired leadership in some cases, inspired players in others, who in turn attracted other gifted footballers. Another reason was the support of local business leaders, which was often financial. This was important because, by around 1880, something new was beginning to emerge among the better Northern clubs.

Professionalism

In 1879, the footballing world was shocked when a small cotton workers' club from Lancashire called Darwen drew an FA Cup quarter-final with the mighty Old Etonians, not just once but twice. The Etonians went on to win the third tie but this was not how things were meant to be. It transpired that two of Darwen's players, Fergus Suter and James Love, were Scottish. The story was that they had originally gone to Darwen on tour with Partick Thistle and had so impressed their hosts that they had been persuaded to stay on, perhaps by the offer of a soft job in a local cotton mill and a perk in their boots after each game.

This was not an isolated case. Quite a number of the Lancashire teams fielded recently arrived Scottish players. Scotland had pioneered the new passing game and was producing excellent players (after the draw in the first Scotland–England international, the Scots won nine out of the next eleven encounters). On the other hand, employment prospects in booming Lancashire were much better. Enterprising Scottish players could easily be attracted south by the offer of a good job and some inviting 'expenses' for each game. Some clubs even openly advertised in Glasgow newspapers. The Blackburn Rovers team which caused such a stir by reaching the FA Cup final against the Old Etonians in 1882 had no fewer than four Scotsmen in its team.

Football was becoming a business. The introduction of free Saturday afternoons meant that not only did people want to play football, a very much larger number wanted to watch it. The good clubs started to attract large crowds. It was a small and inevitable step for the clubs to start charging an entrance fee. Writing for the Badminton Library a few years later in 1888, Montague Shearman said: 'No words of ours can adequately describe the present popularity which, though great in the metropolis, is infinitely greater in the large provincial towns ... it is no rare thing in the north and midlands for 10,000 people to pay money to watch an ordinary club match, or for half as many again to assemble for a "Cup Tie".'

To start with, the clubs reinvested the money they were making in better equipment, better stadiums and better facilities for spectators (although they remained pretty basic). Why not also invest in better players? By the late 1870s, secret inducements to players were commonplace. To the Southern gentlemen amateurs of the Football Association, such a notion was anathema. It undermined the very reason why they had tried to unify their beloved sport just fifteen years

earlier. But reality was against them. Some clubs were fined, some
players were banned, but most Southerners simply averted their eyes.
This couldn't go on for long.

The crunch came in January 1884, after a drawn cup tie between
Preston North End and Upton Park which was watched by 12,000
people. The London club lodged a protest that Preston had openly

*Darwen FC from Lancashire, a workers' club who caused a shock by
drawing twice with the mighty Old Etonians in the FA Cup*

used professionals. Preston were duly disqualified but for once they
did not protest innocence. The robust response from its powerful and
influential founder, William Sudell, a cotton manufacturer, was that
everyone knew that professionalism was rife and it wasn't doing the
game any harm at all. The FA's initial response was to suspend
two more clubs, Burnley and Great Lever, but Sudell was in no mood
to back down. In October, he convened a meeting of twenty-
six Lancashire clubs together with Sunderland and Aston Villa, and
proposed setting up a rival 'British Football Association' which would
recognize the reality of professionals. The ever astute C. W. Alcock
saw the danger of a fatal rift and a couple of weeks later proposed a
motion to a subcommittee of the FA meeting in Manchester: 'That it is

expedient to legalize professionalism under stringent conditions, but that no paid player shall take part in Association Cup Competitions.'

That didn't quite resolve the issue. Alcock's proposal was rejected at two successive Special General Meetings of the FA. But in July 1885, a third meeting finally accepted the inevitable and legalized professionalism, albeit under strict rules of residency remarkably similar to those of cricket (Alcock, of course, was also Secretary of Surrey County Cricket Club). The new rule allowed professionals 'to compete in all Cups, County and Inter-Association matches', but expressly forbade them from serving 'on any Association Committee or representing his own or any other club at any meeting of the Football Association'. It was one thing to let these bounders play the game, but they damn well weren't going to run it.

Nonetheless, Alcock's far-sighted pragmatism had avoided a schism and preserved a solid base from which football could expand. There were still diehards within the FA who proclaimed that it was 'degrading for respectable men to play with professionals'. Alcock put them firmly in their place. 'Professionals are a necessity to the growth of the game,' he said, 'and I object to the idea that they are the utter outcasts some people represent them to be. Furthermore, I object to the argument that it is immoral to work for a living, and I cannot see why a man should not, with that object, labour at football as at cricket.'

As we shall see elsewhere, rugby failed to recognize this reality and as a result remained for many years a 'pure' but marginalized sport.

The coming of the League

The diehards had predicted many appalling consequences that they believed would flow from accepting professionals, but they failed to foresee the most important, which would have a massive impact on football around the world. Professionalism meant that clubs could hire the players they wanted, but they also had to pay for them. As things stood in 1885, it was cup ties that attracted the biggest crowds and therefore generated the most revenue. Other matches were more or less meaningless 'friendlies'. If a club was knocked out of the FA Cup in the early stages, it still had to go on paying its professionals for the rest of the season. How could it avoid going bankrupt?

In March 1888, William McGregor, the powerful and influential boss of Aston Villa, attempted to address this pressing issue. He sent a letter to some of the major clubs in the English FA. 'Every year it is becoming more and more difficult for football clubs of any standing to meet their friendly engagements, or even arrange friendly matches,' he wrote. 'The consequence is that at the last moment, through cup-tie interference, clubs are compelled to take on teams who will not attract the public. I beg to tender the following suggestion as a means of getting over the difficulty. That ten or twelve of the most prominent clubs in England combine to arrange home and home [*sic*] fixtures each season.' He proposed a 'friendly conference' at Anderton's Hotel in Fleet Street in London on the eve of the Cup Final between Preston North End and West Bromwich Albion.

It quickly became clear that none of the Southern clubs nor any of the major amateur clubs were interested. McGregor called another meeting in Manchester which formally decided to establish the Football League. Its twelve founder members were Aston Villa, Accrington, Blackburn Rovers, Bolton Wanderers, Burnley, Derby County, Everton, Notts County, Preston North End, Stoke City, West Bromwich Albion and Wolverhampton Wanderers. Six were from Lancashire, six from the Midlands. It says something about the enduring nature of football that all but one — poor Accrington, who went out of business in 1896 – are still playing league football and six (at the time of writing) are in the Premiership.

The world's first football league kicked off on 8 September 1888, even though the points system – two for a win and one for a draw – wasn't finalized till 21 November. The first champions were Preston North End, who went the whole season without losing a match. A league was founded in Ireland in 1890 and the Scottish League began the following year. That same season the English League expanded to fourteen clubs, then in 1892 a Second Division was started with another fourteen clubs. But they were still all from the

North or the Midlands. Arsenal finally made it into the league in 1893, but the other clubs in the South had to form their own Southern League in 1894 to have access to organized competition.

The dominance of the North and the Midlands was so strong that it wasn't until 1901 that a Southern professional side – Tottenham Hotspur – managed to win the FA Cup. The winning Spurs side contained one Irishman, two Welshmen, five Scots and three Northerners. By 1905, the Football League had expanded to include forty clubs in two divisions and gradually the South was beginning to break through. Luton Town followed Arsenal in 1897, Bristol City in 1901, Chelsea and Clapton Orient in 1905, Fulham in 1907 and Tottenham Hotspur in 1908.

The speed at which football developed after the formation of the FA in 1863 was astonishing. It had been a motley collection of diverse games played according to different rules by a handful of public schoolboys. Fifty years later, as a result of massive industrial and social change and the development of a comprehensive railway network to

'Saving a High Shot': an illustration from the
Badminton Library *book on football, 1887*

transport fans to matches, it had become a major form of mass entertainment and a thriving business. More than 120,000 people attended
the 1913 Cup Final. But what was even more remarkable was that this
expansion was not limited to the British Isles.

Conquering the world . . .

The original name of the hugely successful Italian club AC Milan,
nemesis of many an English team of European hopefuls, was the Milan
Cricket and Football Club. It was founded in 1899 by one Alfred
Edwards and a group of British and Swiss businessmen. In their honour, its current name is still AC Milan and not, as it should be in
Italian, AC Milano. The name under which the leading Uruguayan
side Penarol started life was the Central Uruguayan Railway Cricket
Club. It was founded by four British workmen who were employed, not
surprisingly, by the Uruguayan railways.

This was not unusual. Wherever the British went in the second half
of the nineteenth century – and they went pretty well everywhere –
they set up clubs so that they could continue to play the sports they had
enjoyed at their public school and university. These might include
cricket, athletics, rugby and, nearly always, football. The founders
might be merchants or entrepreneurs; they might be financiers exporting British capital to wherever it was needed; they might be factory
managers exporting British manufacturing skills; or they might be engineers – the British built almost all of the South American rail network,
for instance.

At the time, of course, Britain was the most modern and successful
country in the world, and it was much admired. When British expats started a sporting club, often the local elite wanted to join. They
also took to sending their children to the schools the British had
founded for their own offspring, complete with English teachers and
an English curriculum which, of course, included English sports. The
rich of Europe and South America also liked the idea of sending their
children to England to finish off their education at public schools and

universities. They came back full of enthusiasm for English sports and keen to continue to play them.

Cricket took hold among a minority in a few places, most notably the Netherlands. Rugby prospered in south-west France and Argentina. But football took off almost everywhere. The appeal was the same as it was to the English working class. The rules were simple. It was flexible – you could play it almost anywhere. It was cheap – all you needed was a ball and something to mark out the goals. You weren't as likely to get injured as you might be at rugby. And, above all, it was skilful and exciting.

Throughout Europe and South America, the elite took it up first, followed by the middle class. Then, at different rates in different countries, it was adopted by the working class. The pace may have varied but the pattern of development remained much the same as it had been in England. Clubs were formed, followed by a knockout cup competition, local and national leagues and professionalism.

The process began in Northern Europe – in the Low Countries and Scandinavia. They were urbanized, industrialized, had a strong and literate working class and a transport system that made inter-city travel possible: perfect conditions for football to take off. The first football club on the Continent was founded in Denmark in 1876. That same country formed the first continental football association in 1889. Holland, Belgium and Sweden followed soon after. Switzerland started its own FA in 1895 followed by a league in 1898. The first game in Austria took place in November 1894 between the Vienna Cricket Club and a team made up of the Scottish gardeners of the Rothschild family. Czechoslovakia and Hungary weren't far behind. In 1904, the captain of an amateur English touring side praised their Hungarian opponents for taking defeat in a thoroughly sporting manner and for being 'ready to take a few hints from a team with a far greater experience of the game'. Half a century later, that attitude would come back to haunt the English.

Greece, where the British had a strong commercial presence, took to football early, followed by the Balkans and Romania. The first football club in Spain was founded in 1889 in remote Andalusia by British mining technicians brought in to work the rich copper deposits. In the Basque country on the north-west coast, Athletic Bilbao was started by locals who had studied in England, together with British residents working in mining and shipbuilding; while in the north-east, FC Barcelona was founded by an anglophile Swiss and originally included a number of Britons in its team. The Swiss, generally in partnership with British expats, also had a major and long-lasting influence on the spread of football in Italy. In the 1909 national championship – the first in 1898 had been won by the Genoa Cricket Club – the Torino team had seven Swiss players, Genoa had five, Milan had four and Juventus had three. The winners that year, Pro Vercelli from a small town in Piedmont, had nine Swiss footballers out of eleven.

The first two football clubs in France were started in 1891, one by Paris-based Scots, the other by Paris-based Englishmen. But football remained a minority sport for quite some time, behind cycling and rugby. The same was true to an extent in Germany, where the first enduring clubs were founded in Hamburg and Berlin in the 1880s. Football was actively opposed by the adherents of the widespread nationalist form of gymnastics called *Turnen*. One of them wrote an outspoken polemic against the game in 1898 which carried the subtitle of 'The English Disease'. In Russia, several clubs were started in St Petersburg by British residents in the 1890s, while in Moscow the Lancastrian manager of a textile factory started a club for his workers (to distract them from drinking vodka) called OKS Moskva. It became a dominant force in Moscow football until the Revolution, when the factory was taken over by the Soviet Electrical Trade Union and the team renamed Moscow Dynamo.

By the early years of the twentieth century, football was popular right across Europe. The same was true in South America. The earliest players of the game on that continent were English sailors. The first game played under FA rules took place in 1867 in Buenos Aires, where around 40,000 Britons were living and working. By 1891, the city had its own league, administered by a Scottish schoolteacher called Alexander Watson Hutton. Similar stories could be told about Uruguay, Brazil, Chile, Paraguay, Bolivia and, slightly later,

Venezuela and Colombia. As ever, the game started among the educated elite but it quickly became an obsession among the working class. Britain's economic foothold in South America came to an end with World War I, but by that time the legacy of football was firmly established.

... but not the whole world

Here's a conundrum. Throughout Europe and South America, football became the dominant winter team sport. But it failed to take off in the same way in the one place it might have been expected to: the British Empire. Football was played in Australia, New Zealand, the Caribbean, South Africa and the subcontinent, as it was in the USA and Canada, but it never became as popular in these places as it did in the rest of the world. It is not always easy to see why.

Take Australia. In the 1850s, Melbourne was a thriving city with an established industrialized working class – very similar to the conditions which led to the take-off of football in Britain. There was a tradition of folk football and the elite played various games based on the traditions of English public schools. Such was the enthusiasm for football, in fact, that Melbourne came up with its own set of rules. Australian Rules were laid down in 1859, four years before the FA agreed its own code in London (just how this happened will be explained in the chapter on rugby). The game immediately became popular, at least in Victoria and South Australia. That's one cogent reason why the Australians never embraced soccer fully – they had their own game. But this obsessively sporting nation did subsequently embrace both forms of Britain's other major winter sport, rugby union and rugby league. So why not soccer?

New Zealand was largely settled after both soccer and rugby had been codified, so it had a clear choice. Many of the settlers were Scottish, fervent devotees of Association football, and from 1880 onwards they did form clubs and leagues. But gradually it became clear that rugby union was going to dominate the country in winter. Perhaps this was because of a determination to be able to compete with the old country. New Zealand was not large enough to sustain a professional soccer infrastructure that could compete with that of Britain. It stood a much better chance against the divided, amateur players of rugby.

In South Africa, the story is different again. Initially, football was popular among working-class white settlers and the country's FA was founded as early as 1880. But the elite always preferred rugby, as did the school system, and gradually the alternative game became more popular. The fact that soccer was taken up enthusiastically by black South Africans from early on was an important contributing factor. (In the rest of Africa, soccer didn't really take hold until after large-scale urbanization took place following World War II. Then it spread like wildfire, as a look at the roster of most Premiership clubs in England now clearly indicates.)

In India, football is massively popular. Some would say that at local level it's as popular as, if not even more popular, than cricket. But as an outsider, you wouldn't know it. The British in India always played football and the Indians began to take it up enthusiastically around the 1880s. For a while, the game prospered. India qualified for the Olympics regularly until 1960, they won the Asian Games in 1951 and 1962 and were invited to play in the World Cup in 1950 – they couldn't in the end because they still played in bare feet. But in recent years they've been unable to qualify for the World Cup or even the Asian Cup. In the Asian ratings for 2004 India, a nation of more than one billion people, was ranked 28, below the Maldives with a population of 318,000. The reasons are complex but have to do with the size of the country, regional conflicts and, above all, incompetent officialdom. There are no local coaching structures and, it seems, the main interest of the people who run the game at all levels is staying in office rather than developing the sport. According to FIFA, Pakistan has nearly three million footballers but its national team also remains extremely weak.

That would never be a problem in the highly organized sporting world of the USA. In many ways, America in the late nineteenth century would seem a perfect breeding ground for football. It had a vibrant urban industrialized economy with a working class which had more often than not recently arrived from countries with a passion for football. So why didn't soccer take off more strongly? The stock answer is that America developed its own style of football, the gridiron game. But this was developed out of rugby by the elite in the Ivy League universities of the north-east. Even today you cannot be a professional football player unless you are a graduate (although footballing scholarships ensure that anyone with talent can go through the system, regardless of academic ability). So why didn't the working class stick with the people's game? Of course soccer has continued to be played in the US, but perhaps the reason it has always been a minority sport has to do with the identity crisis that inevitably besets an almost entirely immigrant country. Just as Hispanic immigrants from Catholic countries in recent years have embraced evangelicalism, America's folk religion, so the newly arrived workers of the late eighteenth century may have wanted to prove their new national credentials by adopting American football. Canada followed, but they had another reason. In large parts of the country the ground is too frozen to play football for much of the winter. So they developed ice hockey.

The world bites back

In 1902, the Dutch Football Association wrote to the English FA to suggest setting up a body to regulate international football. After sounding out the other home nations, the FA eventually replied that it would set up a meeting in London at some unspecified time in the future. The following year Robert Guérin, head of one of the three organizations which regulated football in France, came to London to try to hurry things along. He reported that his talks with the FA President, the formidable Lord Kinnaird, were like 'slicing water with a knife'. In May 1904, the exasperated Guérin convened a meeting in Paris. Representatives of seven countries attended: Belgium, Denmark, France, Holland, Spain, Sweden and Switzerland. Britain did not. The meeting agreed to set up FIFA, the Fédération Internationale de

Football Association, the body which still governs international football today.

The FA's aloofness was a portent for the future. England did join FIFA two years later, followed eventually by the other home nations, but the attitude remained wary: football was a British game and we knew how to look after it better than these inexperienced foreigners. What lay behind this attitude was the simple fact that Britain was indeed the dominant force in European football before 1914. English and Scottish sides toured Europe frequently, almost always triumphantly. When football was first included in the Olympic Games in 1900, albeit in the most chaotic way, the winners were Upton Park FC, amateurs from East London. In the much better organized games of 1908, England won the Gold Medal by beating Denmark in the final, a result repeated exactly in 1912. (In the 1904 games in St Louis only two football teams took part – Canada beat the US.)

During the interwar years, England and the other home nations withdrew from FIFA on two occasions: first in 1920 because of a reluctance to play Germany and Austria; second in 1928, because of a row over amateurism. They did not rejoin until after World War II. The prevailing attitude was summed up by a Football League official called Charles Sutcliffe:

I don't care a brass farthing about the improvement of the game in France, Belgium, Austria or Germany. The FIFA does not appeal to me. An organisation where such football associations as those of Uruguay and Paraguay, Brazil and Egypt, Bohemia and Pan-Russia, are co-equal with England, Scotland, Wales and Ireland seems to me to be a case of magnifying the midgets. If Central Europe or any other district want to govern football let them confine their power and authority to themselves and we can look after our own affairs.

England did not withdraw from European football altogether. Between 1918 and 1939, the national team played 45 internationals in Europe, winning 34, drawing four and losing seven. The first defeat came in Madrid in 1929, when England lost to Spain 4–3. But such

losses were seen as minor aberrations. There was a consummate belief
that the professional superiority of British teams was such that it did
not need to be tested in the international arena. Hence the response of
the FA to an invitation from Uruguay to take part in the first World
Cup finals in 1930:

> Dear Sir,
> The letter of the 10th ultimo from the Associación Uruguay de Football
> inviting a representative Team of the Football Association to visit
> Uruguay in July and August next to play in the Worlds Championship
> in Montevideo has been considered by our international committee.
>
> I am instructed to express regret at our inability to accept the
> invitation.
> F. J. Wall, sec.

England did not in fact take part in the World Cup until 1950, when
they received a well-deserved comeuppance: they were defeated by the
United States. But that was not the first indication the FA had that
British dominance had become a myth. In November 1945 Moscow
Dynamo, the team founded by a Lancastrian factory manager, came
on a short tour of Britain. Large crowds watched them draw 3–3 with
Chelsea, win 10–1 against Cardiff and 4–3 against Arsenal and draw
2–2 with Glasgow Rangers. The real shock was not so much the results
but the skill the Russians displayed. It was a revelation – the first of
many. One player-turned-journalist summed it up: '... the foreigner
has stepped ahead of us in his style of play ... We exported the goods
and lost the knack of making them.'

That lesson was driven home yet again in November 1953, when
England was thrashed 6–3 by Hungary at Wembley, the first defeat for
the national side on home soil. In the World Cup the following year,
England were knocked out by Uruguay (one of Charles Sutcliffe's
midgets). It was clear that English football needed to come to terms
with what was happening in Europe and South America. But when the
European Cup was founded in 1956, the Football League advised the
champions Chelsea not to enter because it might interfere with their

domestic schedule. Thankfully, the following year Matt Busby told the League what to do with their advice and began Manchester United's illustrious career in Europe.

It was perhaps a turning point. Better coaching and tactical innovations improved English football immeasurably over the next few years, culminating in the unforgettable victory in the 1966 World Cup. At least, English supporters have never forgotten it, which is just as well. Only that memory keeps hope alive. Back in 1863, England gave the world the beautiful game. Now they're just another team.

Football speak

The beautiful game has contributed a number of not-so-beautiful phrases to the language of its inventors. If you want to start something, you might say 'to kick off'. Alternatively, you might want 'to get the ball rolling'. The dynamics of the game have led to the discussion of an idea being described as 'kicking it around'. If you decide in the end that you don't like it, you can 'kick it into touch'. In the corporate world, football seems to loom large. Employees are often encouraged 'to give it your best shot'. They might be warned about 'moving the goalposts'. They certainly will not be wanted 'to score an own goal'. On the domestic front, everyone knows about the dangers of 'playing away from home'. Much better 'to keep a clean sheet'. Football has a lot to answer for.

7.
RUGBY
(AND RUGBY LEAGUE, AUSTRALIAN RULES AND AMERICAN FOOTBALL)

THERE IS A plaque on a wall at Rugby School which reads: 'This stone commemorates the exploit of William Webb Ellis, who with a fine disregard for the rules of football as played in his time first took the ball in his arms and ran with it, thus originating the distinctive feature of the Rugby game. A.D. 1823.' It's the source of one of the best-known stories of British sport, so well known that the Rugby World Cup today is called the William Webb Ellis Trophy. (Or Bill, to the Australians.)

But is the story true? Much debate has raged among sports historians. More will be added here in just a moment. But first, a word of warning. If you are a rugby enthusiast and have turned straight to this chapter, stop right there. For the full story, you need to read the early

The plaque at Rugby School, which enshrines
the story of William Webb Ellis

part of the chapter on football (as in Association football) first, because both games come from the same root. Take it up to the point in 1863 when Mr F. W. Campbell of the Blackheath Club storms out of the meeting that led to the creation of the Football Association.

For at least 600 years before that momentous meeting, various forms of folk football had been played throughout Britain. The rules, such as they were, varied in every town and, most likely, every village. In some places kicking was seen as central to the game, in others it was carrying the ball. The one thing they had in common was extreme violence: everything was fair bar murder and manslaughter. In the big annual games that took place on particular festivals, most commonly on Shrove Tuesday, and involved hundreds and even thousands of players, carrying was almost of necessity the optimum way of moving the ball. Here's a description of the great game which took place every year at the Cross of Scone in Scotland. At two o'clock on Shrove Tuesday the married men and bachelors would assemble on opposite sides of the Cross. A ball would be thrown up and play would continue till sunset:

The game was this: he who at any time got the ball into his hands, run with it till overtaken by one of the opposite party; and then, if he could shake himself loose from those on the opposite side who seized him, he run on; if not, he threw the ball from him, unless it was wrested from him by the other party, but no person was allowed to kick it . . In the course of the play there was usually some violence between the parties; but it is a proverb in this part of the country that 'All is fair at the ball of Scone.'

In the later stages of football's pre-history, more organized games with restricted numbers in each team and a restricted playing area developed, and some argue that these tended to feature the kicking game more. But it's clear that both kicking and carrying were wide-spread. By the late eighteenth century, society was becoming less tolerant of the violence involved in these games and – more signifi-cantly – the damage that was being done to property. Great efforts were made to ban such disruptions to orderly life.

Except in the public schools. In the early nineteenth century, these institutions – Eton, Harrow, Charterhouse, Westminster, Winchester and Rugby – all had their own versions of football. They were entirely controlled by the pupils – masters didn't get involved and in some cases were actively opposed to such games. There were no written rules. But as the century progressed and the educational reforms led by Dr Thomas Arnold at Rugby took hold, the games became more

A drawing from the Illustrated London News, *1871: players were "giving and receiving . . . the wickedest punishment without the slightest anger"*

formalized. The first written rules were compiled at Rugby in 1845. The other schools followed soon after. At this time, there were no inter-school football matches, so it didn't matter that each school had its own regulations. But as team games came to be seen as a desirable activity, former pupils wanted to continue to play when they arrived at univer-sity (then just Oxford and Cambridge) or went to work. The need arose for a unified code. That is what the meetings of 1863 were all about and that is when the rift opened between those, the majority, who favoured the dribbling game and those who backed the carrying game, developed exclusively at Rugby. So how did the Rugby game start?

Legend or myth?

Which brings us back to William Webb Ellis. The stone plaque at Rugby School was erected by the Old Rugbeian Society in 1900. Normally such plaques celebrate a well-established and accepted story. Not in this case. This was the first unequivocal statement ever made claiming that Ellis had indeed originated 'the distinctive feature of the Rugby game'. The plaque grew out of a report by a subcommittee of Old Rugbeians set up in 1895 to respond to claims made by Montague

The only known picture of William Webb Ellis:
he never mentioned rugby during his life

Shearman in his book on football for the *Badminton Library of Sports and Pastimes*, published in 1888. Shearman's theory was that the rules of football at each public school differed largely because of the location where the game was played. He goes on:

One school alone seems to have owned almost from its foundation a wide open grass playground of ample dimensions, and that school was Rugby; hence it happens, as we should have expected, that at Rugby school alone do we find that the original game survived almost in its primitive shape ...

the 'Rugby game' was originally played at Rugby school alone, while other schools adopted more or less modified forms of the kicking game.

The Old Rugbeians really didn't like their game being called 'primitive', so they set up the subcommittee to investigate. They gathered evidence from a wide range of former pupils at the school. This established that in fact Rugby did not have a playground of any kind until 1749, when it moved to its present location, and that its playground was not really of 'ample dimensions' until 1816–17. And it came up with a rather different version of how the 'Rugby game' began:

... (1) in 1820 the form of football in vogue at Rugby was something approximating more closely to Association than to what is known as Rugby football today; (2) that at some date between 1820 and 1830 the innovation was introduced of running with the ball; (3) that this was in all probability done in the latter half of 1823 by Mr Webb Ellis ... To this we would add that the innovation was regarded as of doubtful legality for some time, and only

'Football at Rugby', a sketch published
in the Graphic *magazine, 1870*

gradually became accepted as part of the game, but obtained a customary status between 1830 and 1840, and was duly legalized first . . . in 1841–2.

The subcommittee only had one source for the Webb Ellis story: an article from 1880 in the school magazine *Meteor* by an antiquarian called Matthew Bloxam. His father had been a teacher at the school and he and his five brothers had all been pupils – he himself was there from 1813 to 1820. This is how he remembers football in his time:

Few and simple were the rules of the game: touch on the sides of the ground was marked out, and no one was allowed to run with the ball in his grasp towards the opposite goal. It was football not handball, plenty of hacking but little struggling . . .

In the latter half-year of 1823, some fifty-seven years ago, originated, though without premeditation, that change in one of the rules which more than any other has since distinguished the Rugby School game from the Association rules.

A boy of the name of Ellis – William Webb Ellis – a town boy and a foundationer . . . whilst playing Bigside at football in that half-year, caught the ball in his arms. [*At this point he explains that the normal thing to do was to step back a few paces and kick the ball. The opposing side weren't allowed to proceed beyond the point where the ball had been caught until it was kicked.*] Ellis, for the first time, disregarded this rule, and on catching the ball, instead of retiring backwards, rushed forwards with the ball in his hands towards the opposite goal, with what result as to the game I know not, neither do I know how this infringement of a well known rule was followed up, or when it became, as it is now, a standing rule.

The first problem is that Bloxam left the school in 1820, three years before the incident is said to have taken place. So his story is hearsay, possibly deriving from his younger brother, who was still at the school in 1823. Further problems arise from some of the other witnesses who gave evidence to the committee.

The oldest was Thomas Harris, who was at the school from 1819 to 1828. He said he remembered William Webb Ellis perfectly – 'He was an admirable cricketer, but was generally regarded as inclined to take

Matthew Bloxam, on whose sole testimony
the William Webb Ellis story is based

unfair advantages at football. I should not quote him in any way as an authority' – but he could not confirm Bloxam's story. This seems odd because, if the incident was as shocking as it has been made out to be, it surely would have been the gossip of the school. Everyone would have known about it, including junior boys such as Harris. What's more, he goes on to say that when he was a junior 'the cry of "Hack him over" was always raised against any player who was seen running with the ball in his hands' – which suggests the practice was not uncommon even before the supposed date of the Webb Ellis incident.

Another doubt arises from the evidence of Thomas Hughes, the author of *Tom Brown's Schooldays*, who was at the school from 1834 to 1842. During that time, running with the ball became more and more popular but he accepts that might not have been the case in the early 1820s: 'I don't doubt Matt Bloxam was right that "running in" was not known in his day. The "Webb Ellis" tradition had not survived to my day.' Which again is odd. When Hughes was at the school, the rules of the game were still being passed on orally. If the Webb Ellis incident had been so shocking, wouldn't that story have been passed on as well?

But the biggest difficulty is that as far as we know, throughout his life, William Webb Ellis himself never once mentioned the story. He died in 1872, a year after the Rugby Football Union was formed, so he's likely to have known that the old school game had become a mainstream sport. But he never once claimed any credit for having had a hand in developing it. In his article, Bloxam said that Ellis 'had plenty of assurance, and was ambitious of being thought something of'. Wouldn't such a man have said something if he believed he had single-handedly invented a new sport?

So what happened? Jenny Macrory, long-serving librarian and archivist at Rugby School, has pointed out that football was not an entrenched tradition at Rugby. It only became popular early in the nineteenth century and that was when a code of play began to emerge. The accepted idea was that new practices could be incorporated if they helped the game. What may have happened is that sometime in the early 1820s boys began running with the ball in hand as an experiment. One of them may have been William Webb Ellis, and this action may have so annoyed Bloxam Minimus that he went bleating on about it to his older brother. Fifty-seven years later, the memory may have re-emerged as an interesting story to put into an article. It is highly unlikely that a single act could have made so much difference. But it's a good story.

In later editions of his book, Montague Shearman reported on the findings of the subcommittee and graciously accepted them. He added, a little waspishly: '. . . the truth appears to be that in the first half of the nineteenth century Rugby School, having then an ample playground, developed a game of football which in its essential features resembled the "primitive game" . . .'

1863 and all that

There is no doubt that Rugby School did develop a unique form of football in the first half of the nineteenth century. Many others had run with the ball in hand throughout history – and were still doing so in the famous folk games played nearby at Ashbourne and Derby – but Rugby's game had elements found nowhere else. For instance the H-shaped goals and the manner of scoring a goal. In *Tom Brown's Schooldays*, set in the 1830s, Thomas Hughes describes the goals as:

... a sort of gigantic gallows of two poles eighteen feet high, fixed upright in the ground some fourteen feet apart, with a cross bar running from one to the other at the height of ten feet or thereabouts ... the match is for the best of three goals ... it won't do just to kick the ball through these posts – it must go over the cross bar; any height'll do, so long as it's between the posts.

An early version of the oval ball also seems to have been in use at the school by the 1830s. The suggestion is that the shape derived from the pigs' bladders originally used to make the ball (they were covered with four leather panels). As running with the ball became more popular, the shape was judged to be more practical than a round ball and it was refined, becoming narrower and more pointed.

The notion of a 'try' was also introduced early on. The idea was that if you could touch the ball down behind your opponent's goal line, you earned a 'try at goal' – a free chance to kick a goal between the posts. At this point, though, you scored nothing from a try – it just gave you the opportunity to score a goal. The offside rule was also developed in the 1830s – no forward passing – and it was enshrined in the first written set of rules for any football game, which were devised at Rugby in 1845.

Interestingly, it wasn't any of these unique features that became the major bones of contention at the early meetings of the Football Association in 1863. The sticking point was hacking – deliberately kicking opponents on the shins. When F. W. Campbell led the rugby supporters out of the fateful FA meeting in December, he declared that the rules they had adopted, which banned hacking, would 'emasculate' football. 'I think that if you do away with it,' he said later, 'you will do away with all the courage and pluck of the game, and I will be bound to bring over a lot of Frenchmen who would beat you with a week's practice.'

Ironically, within three years Campbell's own club Blackheath and
its great ally Richmond had agreed not to allow hacking when they
played each other. Richmond unilaterally issued a set of guidelines
against unnecessary hacking and firmly stated that they would not play
against any club which did not agree to abide by them. Their action
was a good example of what was happening in rugby in the 1860s. The
growing number of clubs were all developing their own nuanced

An early Rugby game, dating from around 1879, eight years
after the Rugby Football Union was established

version of the game. There was clearly a need for a unified code. But
no one seemed to be in a rush to draw one up. In the end, two curious
catalysts brought matters to a head.

The first was a letter to *The Times* on 23 November 1870 from
'A Surgeon', who wrote that he had recently treated a number of boys
from Rugby for injuries caused by hacking: 'One boy with his collar
bone broken, another with a severe injury to his groin, a third with a
severe injury to his ankle, a fourth with a severe injury to his knee, and
two others sent home on crutches.' He went on to say he was not a milk-
sop but 'I do protest against a system which results in injury more or less

felt for life, because it is a practice easily remedied.' Despite instant denials from boys and old boys, saying there hadn't been that many injuries and anyway they weren't all caused by hacking, the impact on public opinion among those who cared about such matters was powerful. If rugby was to progress as a sport, the hacking issue needed to be sorted out. And that required an authoritative national body.

The other motivator, strangely enough, was the England v. Scotland soccer international – the first ever – which had taken place at the Oval four days before the surgeon's letter was published. What upset the Rugby world was that soccer was hardly played in Scotland – at that time there was only one club playing according to Association rules – whereas there was a strong rugby tradition north of the border. The jokes started flowing. Of the almost entirely London-based 'Scottish' soccer team, one player was said to have qualified because he'd once crossed the border to shoot grouse, while another was included because of his known fondness for single malts. What was required was a proper rugby international between real representative sides. But for that, again, you needed a national body (or two).

On 4 December 1870, the secretaries of Richmond and Blackheath rugby clubs, both Old Rugbeians, wrote to *The Times* suggesting 'that some code of rules should be adopted by all clubs who profess to play the Rugby game'. They asked secretaries of all clubs who approved of this idea to get in touch with them.

Enter the RFU

On 26 January 1871, thirty-two men representing twenty-one clubs met at the Pall Mall Restaurant on the corner of Pall Mall East and Cockspur Street. There should have been twenty-two clubs, but the man from the Wasps never made it. The official story was that an administrative hitch meant that he turned up at the wrong venue at the wrong time on the wrong day. The unofficial story, much more widely believed, was that he went to the wrong pub and became so drunk that he was unable to find his way to the right one.

The thirty-two who did make it worked quickly. Within two hours, they had agreed to form the Rugby Football Union, elected a committee (mostly made up of Old Rugbeians) and set up a subcommittee to draft a new set of rules. These were formally adopted by a special general meeting called on 24 June. There were fifty-nine laws, most of them reflecting the rules then being followed at Rugby School. But

The Pall Mall restaurant in Cockspur Street, where the RFU
was started: the man from Wasps never made it

there were four significant differences. The offside laws were clarified; a 'knock-on' led to a scrum; when a ball went into touch it would be returned into play from the point where it crossed the touch line; and, most important of all, 'hacking', 'hacking over' and 'tripping' were finally abolished.

There was a good deal of reluctance to accept this last innovation. Rugby School itself continued to allow hacking until 1881. And a number of clubs continued to celebrate the grand old tradition until almost that time by allowing five minutes of 'glorious hacking' at the end of a game. Being former public schoolboys, they called this assault on each other's shins a 'Hallelujah'. The no hacking rule was imposed on the first ever rugby international, the long-awaited contest between England and Scotland held on 27 March at Raeburn Place in Edinburgh, even though it had not by that time been formally ratified. It caused a great deal of frustration – one of the players called hacking 'an instinctive action' – but the umpire H. H. Almond would not relent.

It was not the only controversy to arise from the game. Scotland won by a goal and a try to a try, but the English players complained vociferously about the legality of the try which had led to the Scottish goal. Almond found in favour of the Scots and later remarked: 'When an umpire is in doubt, I think he is justified in deciding against the side which makes the most noise. They are probably in the wrong.'

The Scottish formed their own union in 1873, followed by the Irish in 1879 (there had been separate North and South unions earlier) and the Welsh in 1881. England played Ireland for the first time in 1875 at the Oval. During the 1870s the game spread across England and into Wales – the first Welsh club was Neath in 1871. By 1880, every major town in South Wales could boast its own rugby club. In 1881, England played Wales for the first time, winning by seven goals, a drop goal and six tries to nil.

In the North of England, rugby blossomed. Some of the earliest clubs, such as Manchester and Liverpool, remained socially exclusive, dominated by former public schoolboys. But elsewhere, especially in Yorkshire, the impetus came from the newly emerging middle class – industrialists, businessmen and entrepreneurs. In many cases, they actively encouraged working-class participation. Soon the clubs began to command intense loyalty from the local community and with it large crowds – this was a time of large-scale population growth, increased leisure time and increased income, up a third on average between 1850 and 1875.

In 1876 and again in 1881, proposals were put forward for a Challenge Cup open to all, along the lines of the hugely successful FA Cup. But the establishment at the RFU, while admitting that the idea would attract interest, were not at all keen. If a cup really took off, it

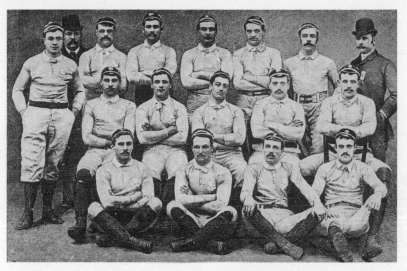

*The Yorkshire rugby team, which won seven out of
the first eight county championships*

would begin to attract all manner of evils, such as betting. But they
couldn't stop local county unions from setting up their own competitions. In 1877, Yorkshire started its own knockout cup, which
quickly became known as 'T'owd Tin Pot'. It was an instant hit. In
1881, 15,000 watched a quarter-final tie between Wakefield Trinity
and Dewsbury, far more than watched internationals in the South.
This growing divide was to have all too predictable implications.

The game evolves

So what did rugby look like in 1871, after the RFU was founded? Not
easily recognizable by today's spectators, is the short answer. There
were twenty players on each side, and most of them, generally fourteen, were forwards. The abolition of hacking, previously the normal
way of breaking up a scrum, gave a central role to the scrummage. It
must have been a strange sight. Upwards of twenty-eight men, standing

bolt upright – Arthur Budd, later President of the RFU, said that 'to put one's head down in a scrummage was regarded as an act of high treason' – pushing against each other, with the ball nowhere to be seen, for sometimes several minutes. To the connoisseur, this was the very apex of the game. 'I have often in the old days heard spectators cheer vociferously over the prolonged equipoise of a well-balanced scrummage,' wrote Budd. To the less informed spectator, it must have seemed rather dull. When one of the few backs got hold of the ball, he was expected to run until he was tackled, when there would be another scrum. Passing was seen as the height of cowardice.

Not surprisingly, this situation did not persist for long. From 1875, clubs began moving to fifteen-a-side, and from 1877 that was the norm. The usual formation was two full backs, one three-quarter back, two half-backs and ten forwards. In 1878 a new rule was introduced which required a player to release the ball as soon as he was tackled. The aim was to do away with wrestling matches, which could go on for minutes, and thus make the game faster. It also encouraged the forwards to dribble the ball rather than always pick it up. It was further agreed that if no goals had been scored, the result could be settled by the number of tries achieved. This encouraged running with the ball.

Blackheath were by now experimenting with the revolutionary idea of using feet to control the ball in a scrum and get it out where you wanted it. Hitherto feet had only been used to drive the ball out of the scrum to the opposing half-backs. Further innovation was led by Harry Vassall of Oxford University, who trained his forwards to play a more open game and use short passes to move the ball. He also encouraged his backs to use longer passes as a standard form of attack.

In 1881, another change occurred which now seems blindingly obvious but which at the time was revolutionary. In a North v South match, according to Arthur Budd, the first ever pass from a half-back to a three-quarter was made by Payne of Broughton to Teddy Bartram, who went on to score. It was the first time half-backs had been seen as a link between the forwards and the three-quarters. Vassall's Oxford team immediately adopted the innovation, with great success. Around the same time, the Thornes team which beat

Wakefield Trinity in the Yorkshire Cup final in 1882 became the first side to assign its forwards fixed positions rather than scrumming down in the order in which they arrived.

In 1886, the new running game was expanded further. Some of the hospital sides and Cardiff experimented with having four three-quarters. The Welsh international side took on the idea in 1887, but it didn't become the norm till the 1893–4 season. So the format was now the familiar eight forwards, two half-backs, four three-quarters and a full back. Other changes included the introduction of neutral umpires in 1881 (previously, disputes had been settled between captains or, if necessary, by the umpires appointed by each side). In 1885, referees were introduced and given whistles while the umpires were gradually replaced by touch judges with flags. In 1886, a points system, which had long been in use at Cheltenham College, was adopted. Initially it was three points for a goal and one for a try, which was discounted if it resulted in a goal. By 1893 it had been changed to the more familiar

The Calcutta Cup

The Calcutta Football Club was a short-lived affair but it left a lasting legacy. When the club ceased to exist in 1877 because of a lack of members, the Secretary, G. A. James Rothney, wrote to the Rugby Football Union to say that: 'I proposed at a meeting of the last few remaining members of the club held on Tuesday last . . . as the best means of doing some lasting good for the cause of Rugby Football and as a slight memento of the Calcutta Club, that the funds remaining to the credit of the club should be devoted to the purpose of a Challenge Cup and presented to the Rugby Football Union to be competed for annually.' He offered the RFU the choice of having a cup made in India or taking the money and buying a cup in Britain. Wisely, they chose the former. The cup is of the finest Indian chased work made from silver melted down from the rupees withdrawn from the bank when the club closed its account. It is competed for annually by England and Scotland in rugby's oldest international fixture.

three points for a try, two for a conversion, three for a penalty and four
for a drop goal.

The modern game was beginning to emerge. But there were troubles
ahead.

The schism

In the 1892–3 season, 27,654 people watched a third-round Yorkshire
Cup tie between Leeds and Halifax at Headingley. The divide between
North and South was growing – such crowds were unknown in London
and the Home Counties. The quality of rugby was higher in the North
as well. Yorkshire won seven of the first eight County Championships.
The other one was won by Lancashire. The Northern clubs were
taking in large amounts of gate money and they were under immense
pressure from their loyal supporters to get results. That meant attracting the best players they could.

Professionalism will always raise its head when there are large numbers of people willing to pay to watch a sport and some of the skilful
players they are paying to watch need extra money, on the simple
grounds that they don't have any. Neither of these was true in London
but they were in the North. Many working-class players could not
afford to travel to away fixtures, so their clubs started paying their
expenses. Hull paid half the cost from 1874 and the full cost from 1879.
Clubs also started making 'broken-time' payments for loss of earnings.
Wakefield did this openly from 1881. And there were other ways of
attracting good players. Just as Scottish footballers had been persuaded
to move south to Lancashire by the promise of a good job if they joined
a particular club, so Welsh rugby players were travelling north-east to
Yorkshire for the same reason.

It was an issue which divided all sports. In 1885 the Football
Association, under the benign leadership of C. W. Alcock, had avoided
a split by legalizing professionalism. Other sports took a very different
view. Rowing issued rules which banned anyone who 'has ever been
employed in or about boats, or in manual labour ... [or] a mechanic,

artisan or labourer'. In other words, if you're so lowly you have to get your hands dirty working for a living, don't come and mess up our sport. The RFU took a less extreme view but still brought forward rules on professionalism that stated that not only was money for playing illegal, so was any kind of 'broken-time' payment. The RFU also awarded itself a veto over any player transferring from one club to another. Future President Arthur Budd declared that 'no mercy but iron rigour shall be dealt out'.

Between 1888 and 1893, there were numerous accusations, investigations and suspensions. The England captain Dickie Lockwood, who came from Heckmondwike, was subjected to a three-day inquisition

David (left) and Evan James, two Welsh international half-backs
who were suspended for 'professionalism'

about where his income came from. In March 1893, two Welsh international half-backs, David and Evan James, were suspended for 'professionalism' while playing for Broughton Rangers. The club, on the other hand, wasn't penalized. Six months later, two Yorkshire committee members proposed 'That players be allowed compensation for bona fide loss of time'. This was vital for the Northern clubs because since 1892 they'd been playing in highly successful leagues which required regular fixtures, often in working time. Against them, the President and Secretary of the RFU proposed the amendment 'That this meeting, believing that the above principle is contrary to the true interest of the Game and its spirit, declines to sanction the same.' The amendment was carried by 282 votes to 136; 120 of the majority figure were proxy votes. The Yorkshire contingent later claimed that instead of Oxford and Cambridge being given a single vote as members of the Union, each college had been given its own vote.

The following year, four Northern clubs were suspended. Towards the end of the year, the Yorkshire clubs declared that the RFU position was 'not a reasonable and just interpretation and cannot be accepted by us'. In January 1895, eighteen clubs (with four apologies for absence) proposed 'a mutual protection society' called the Northern Union. Not surprisingly, the RFU vetoed it. To rub salt in the wounds, the RFU then reissued its penal code on professionalism. On 29 August, twenty-two Yorkshire and Lancashire clubs met at the George Hotel in Huddersfield to form the Northern Rugby Football Union on the basis of 'payment for bona-fide broken-time only'. They then resigned from the RFU.

What happened to the Northern Union (which was renamed the Rugby Football League in 1922) will be looked at later. For Rugby Union, the impact of the schism was profound. At first, the number of defections looked to be limited. But as Northern clubs realized they had lost their strongest fixtures and their largest gates, more and more began to switch to the Northern Union. Before the split, 132 clubs had entered the Yorkshire Cup competition; by 1901, the figure had dropped to just eleven. In 1893, there were 481 clubs in the RFU. Ten years later, that figure had been halved to 244.

One arguably positive impact was to make the Home Nations championship more exciting. Before the schism, there was always a danger that it would be dominated by England. But many of the best English players had come from the North and were now playing what became rugby league. In the fifteen years up to the split, England had won 23 matches and lost 9 in the Home Nations championship. In the next fifteen years, it won 12 and lost 29. Wales suffered too. Rugby was a largely working-class sport in the hills and valleys of South Wales, which made many of the best players vulnerable to the predatory recruitment agents of the Northern Union. Scotland, on the other hand, was safe, because the game there remained a largely middle-class affair. The net result was that the championship became unpredictable, highly competitive and very watchable.

Intercontinental rugby

For the last quarter of the nineteenth century, the rugby season in Britain was dominated by the Home Nations championship, as it still is today (the Home Nations became the Five Nations in 1910, with the addition of the French, and the Six Nations in 2000, when Italy were finally allowed to join). But over the same period good rugby was being played all around the world, as developments early in the twentieth century would make abundantly and, for the home teams, rather embarrassingly clear.

The very first unified set of rules for a football code was written in 1858, five years before the Football Association came into being and codified the laws of soccer. They were drafted in Melbourne for a game which came to be called Australian Rules (see page 222) by a man called Tom Wills, who had been educated at Rugby. He regarded the Rugby School game as too violent and 'unsuitable for grown men engaged in making a living', so he invented his own game, which quickly became hugely popular in Victoria and spread to South Australia and Tasmania. In Sydney, however, it was rugby which caught on, especially at the university. By 1874, there were fourteen clubs in the city which came together to form the Southern Rugby Union, which became the New South Wales Rugby Union in 1892. The Australian Rugby Union wasn't formed until 1949.

The first rugby game recorded in New Zealand took place in Auckland in 1870 between a local team and sailors from the visiting HMS *Rosario*. Later that year Charles Monro, the son of the Speaker of the House of Representatives, who had just completed his education at rugby-playing Sherborne School, persuaded his local football club to try the game. The team liked it and adopted it, setting a trend across the country. New Zealand was growing fast at this time and rugby quickly became the new nation's sporting passion. From the start, it was a socially inclusive game enjoyed by all classes, including native New Zealanders. The New Zealand RFU came into existence in 1892.

A form of the 'carrying game' had been played in South Africa as early as 1862. It was based on the game as played at Winchester and was called 'Gog's football' after the only legible part of the signature of the man who introduced it, Canon G. Ogilvie. The clubs which played it switched over to rugby union in 1878. The first non-white club was formed in Cape Town in 1882 and the following year the first Afrikaans-speaking club was started in Stellenbosch. The South African Rugby Football Board was set up in Kimberley in 1889.

In Europe, the game was played in Germany in the 1860s, but it was in France and Italy that it was to become popular – and later Romania. A game was recorded at McGill University in Montreal, Canada, in 1865; and there was rugby in Ceylon (now Sri Lanka) and India in the 1870s, although it was only played by British expats and never really took off. But it did certainly catch on in Fiji, where the first game was played in 1884. Rugby reached South America quite early via British-run cricket clubs in Uruguay and Argentina; by 1886, Hispanic names were appearing on the team lists as the game took hold.

The first British touring side visited Australia and New Zealand in 1888. It was a speculative affair designed to make a profit, exactly like the cricket tours of that time. Indeed, it was tacked on to the end of one and shared some of the same players. The side played 53 matches, including 18 under Australian Rules. Unsurprisingly, they lost more games than they won under Rules, but they were victorious in all their rugby games in Australia. In New Zealand, however, they lost to both Taranaki and Auckland. It was a portent of things to come. Later that year a Maori team visited Britain and attracted a great deal of atten-tion. They played an astonishing 107 matches and won 49, including an international against Ireland.

There were various British tours to South Africa and Australia over the next sixteen years, most reasonably successful. Then in 1904 a British side travelled to Australia and New Zealand. They comfortably won all fourteen of their games in Australia, but it was a different story in New Zealand. Out of five games, they lost two – including the only international – and won two. They also lost an informal game against the Maoris. This was no longer a portent, it was a warning.

In 1905, an All Black side came to Britain. It was the beginning of a torment which has afflicted British rugby ever since. By the time they came to play Wales, they had won all 27 of their matches, including internationals against England and Ireland. They had scored 801 points; their opponents had managed just 22. Rugby was taken very seriously in New Zealand. The team trained harder than anyone in Britain, and they were innovative. They reduced their pack to seven men, playing 2-3-2. The two wing forwards stood off, protecting their half-backs. Everything was designed to deliver quick ball. A wing forward put the ball into the scrum, it was rapidly channelled to the scrum half, who then set in motion a back division which included a five-eighths option – Jimmy Hunter, who created that position, scored 42 tries during the tour. They had developed new skills at passing the ball just before they were tackled and expected their forwards to be as quick as their backs. It sounds all too familiar.

The key men in the team were Captain David Gallaher and Vice-captain Billy Stead. Such was their command of the new style of play that they wrote one of the classic books of rugby literature: *The Complete Rugby Footballer on the New Zealand System*. They also managed to com-pletely sideline the tour coach Jimmy Duncan. But he found other interests to enliven his travels, recalling later 'the numbers of young ladies and old widows who were desirous of taking me into partnership as a sleeping partner only'.

The All Blacks were a sensation. 45,000 people watched them beat England by five tries to nil. 43,000 turned out for the game against Wales. But the Welsh, having watched the tactical tide overwhelm the rest of the country, had come prepared. In a complicated pre-planned tactical manoeuvre, they managed to score a try. But the All Blacks fought back. Late in the second half their oversized three-quarter Bob Deans was brought down on the Welsh line. To the fury of the tourists, the referee decided that the ball had not gone over. This decision is disputed by every New Zealand rugby supporter to this day.

The following year, the South African Springboks toured Britain. They weren't quite in the same class as the All Blacks, but still only lost to Scotland and Cardiff. In 1912, they came back to defeat all four home nations. In 1908, it was the turn of the Australian Wallabies. They played 31 matches and won 25, losing just 5. They beat England but lost to Wales (they didn't play Scotland or Ireland). All these tours aroused great interest and healthy gate receipts which enabled the RFU to go ahead with William Williams's proposal to develop a former market garden in rural Twickenham as the venue for England games. 'Billy Williams's cabbage patch' was about to become not just the best-known ground in the world but also the spiritual home of Rugby Union. The sport was beginning to recover from the schism. The way forward was set.

Full circle

On 26 January 1995, just three days short of the centenary of the meeting at the George Hotel in Huddersfield which led to the formation of the Northern Union, the International Rugby Board voted to accept open professionalism. It was a decision which by this time had become inevitable.

The introduction of the Rugby World Cup in 1987 had confirmed rugby as a major world sport. Television and the enormous popularity of the (then) Five Nations championship – long gone were the days when you could buy a ticket on the day – meant that it also involved large amounts of money. The old amateur principle had long ceased to be a reality. Star players were not paid a salary, but were provided with cars and given all kinds of other perks. Australia and New Zealand argued that it was time to take hypocrisy out of the game and recognize what was happening. Though England was reluctant, it had no choice but to accept the majority decision.

But was it 100 years too late? Who knows what might have happened if rugby had followed the example of Association football and accepted professionalism back in the early days. Certainly rugby could never be as simple and accessible as soccer (we're talking about the rules here rather than the tactics), but it's proved that it can draw the crowds. A united England would have been a powerful force, as it was before 1895; and so would a united Australia, where since their own schism in 1907 they have had three codes. But might some of the atmosphere and spirit of the game have been lost along the way? We will never know.

The transition to professionalism was not easy in Britain. There was fierce financial competition for the best players and a consequent demand for new sources of income, which led to a cap on total salary bills in 1999. British clubs chose to stay out of the Heineken Cup for the first season of its existence in 1995–96, but joined once they realized it was going to be the major cauldron of club competition in Europe. One of the oldest English clubs, Richmond, went bankrupt after three years of the professional game (though it has now restarted as an amateur concern).

But there have also been silver linings. The first four World Cups were all won by southern hemisphere teams. In 2003, Martin Johnson's England side finally broke that monopoly and, against all expectations, came close to repeating the feat in 2007.

Rugby remains an unpredictable game, and perhaps that's how it should be.

Rugby League

When the Northern Rugby Football Union was established at the meeting in Huddersfield in 1895, it was absolutely adamant that it was not in favour of professionalism. All it wanted was 'payment for bona-fide broken-time only'. Within nine days, it held the first fixtures of the Northern Rugby Football League, a temporary arrangement which involved the twenty-two founding clubs playing each other at home and away. But it seems, as the establishment at the RFU had always argued, that once you set foot on the slippery slope, there was no going back. In 1898, the Northern Union accepted full professionalism, but perversely said that you could only be paid as a professional if you had another job. The unemployed and full-time players were excluded. This bizarre rule was abolished in 1905, but even today most rugby league players still have another job.

Over the next ten years, the Northern Union (NU) tried multiple permutations of competitions to find the most productive format. By 1905, it had settled on a league championship, split into two divisions with a final-four play-off to decide the overall champions. It had also set up the Challenge Cup, which became a major draw and culminated eventually in a final at Wembley. And it had created a County Cup and separate Yorkshire and Lancashire Cups. So in any one season, a club could aspire to win four different trophies.

More significantly, it had changed the nature of the game. As a commercial operation, the NU had realized it needed to make the game as exciting as possible. With valuable professional players, they also wanted to make it safer. The *Wakefield Express* had carried out a survey of rugby injuries in Yorkshire between 1890 and 1893 – before the schism. It reported 71 deaths, 208 broken limbs and 158 other injuries. Something had to be done.

What the NU did was to cut the size of the team to thirteen – it was the wing forwards who went. The line-out was abolished and replaced with a scrum ten yards in. And the battle for possession when a player was tackled was done away with: from 1906, a tackled player got back on his feet, placed the ball on the ground and played it back to a team-mate. (Theoretically, he could play it in any direction.) The result was a much faster game, with fewer scrums and a lot more excitement. These changes formed the basis of the modern game, though the precise rules have been fiddled with constantly over the last one hundred years.

For the first few years, what was to become Rugby League was confined to the North of England. Perversely, the all-conquering All Blacks rugby union tour of 1905 was to change all that. Some of the New Zealanders were impressed by the crowds that the professional game was attracting. On the way home, one of them, George William Smith, met up with an Australian entrepreneur called James J. Giltinan to discuss the possibility of starting professional rugby in Australasia. They soon heard that another New Zealander, Albert Baskerville, was trying to recruit a professional team in New Zealand to tour England, where he was in touch with the Northern Union. Smith and Baskerville decided to join forces.

At exactly this time, tension between middle-class amateurs and working-class players who wanted compensation for loss of earnings was coming to a head in Sydney. The particular case at issue involved a player called Alick Burdon who had broken his arm playing for New South Wales and been denied any compensation for his time off work. Early in August 1907, Burdon, Giltinan and the great Australian Test cricketer Victor Trumper attended a meeting in Sydney which set up the New South Wales Rugby Football League to establish professional rugby in Australia. Trumper was there because the rugby players wanted to share the profits of international tours in the same way that Australian Test cricketers did.

That same month, Smith and Baskerville's professional New Zealand side arrived in Sydney on its way to England. Giltinan had arranged for them to play three matches against the first ever professional Australian side. The games, which were played under rugby union rules because the Northern Union's regulations were not available in Australia, were a great success and provided the fledgling Australian professional game with much-needed funds. The press, most of whom supported the amateur game, accused the New Zealanders of greed and dubbed them the 'All Golds'. The team was undeterred. They duly recruited the best Australian player, Herbert 'Dally' Messenger, to their cause and set sail for England.

When they arrived on British soil, most of the All Golds side had never even seen a game played under Northern Union rules, let alone played in one. After a week's intensive training in Leeds, they won their first eight matches before losing to Wigan 8–12 in front of a crowd of 30,000. Overall, they won 19 out of 35, with two matches drawn. They lost narrowly to Wales but, following an all too familiar script, they won the Test series against Great Britain by 2 matches to 1. On their way back to New Zealand they stopped off to play a match in Brisbane and help establish professional rugby in Queensland. The tour had been such a success that a number of the players were immediately offered considerable sums to return to England to play for Northern clubs.

By 1908, the path of what was to become rugby league was largely set. Despite various attempts to break out into the rest of the country, the game in Britain remains confined to its Northern fastness. In Australia, rugby league predominates in New South Wales and Queensland, while Australian Rules is the major football game in Victoria, South Australia and Tasmania. Rugby union is a close second in each area, but annoyingly that doesn't seem to stop the national team from being immensely successful internationally. In New Zealand, the early exodus of good players to the rich pastures of Northern England left the amateur game dominant, and that hasn't changed. France established the professional game in the early 1930s and it continues to this day, but it has rarely had much of an international impact.

Australia, on the other hand, has won every Rugby League World Cup since 1975 and hadn't lost an international tournament or series of any kind for twenty-seven years until they were defeated by New Zealand in the final of the 2005 Tri-Nations Series at Elland Road in Leeds. And this from a country which is also a major force in rugby union and has its very own, highly popular version of the game.

Australian Rules

Thomas Wentworth Wills was born in the town of Geelong, one hundred miles from Melbourne, but educated at Rugby School in England, where he excelled at both cricket and football. When he returned in 1857 to Melbourne, a city expanding at a rapid rate on the back of the 1850s gold rush, he suggested to his fellow members of the Melbourne Cricket Club that they form a football club to keep themselves fit during the winter.

Various forms of folk football were almost certainly being played in Melbourne at that time, but as in Britain there was no unified code of rules. So Wills and his team-mates set up a committee to devise one. Wills was against adopting the rules he had played under at Rugby on the grounds that they were 'unsuitable for grown men engaged in making a living'. They were also a bit too rough for the dry conditions of Australia. So the committee also looked at the rules of other English public schools, notably Winchester, Eton and Harrow. It is said that Wills was further influenced by an Aboriginal game called 'Marn Grook', which is recorded as early as 1841 (Wills is believed to have played with Aboriginal children when growing up on his father's property in the country). The committee may also have taken elements from Gaelic football, which was widely played by Irish immigrants at the time.

The rules were finally agreed on 17 May 1859. They were the first formal football code to be established in the world – it was another four years before the rules of soccer were agreed by the Football Association in London in 1863. They are also one of the few sets of rules in sport which were invented rather than created by a process of evolution. Aussie Rules is often called a compromise between rugby and soccer, but actually it's quite different from either.

At the start there were twenty players on each side (later reduced to eighteen). There is no offside rule, so from the kick-off players are positioned all across the oval field (generally larger than a rugby pitch) in opposing pairs. There are echoes here of the game of 'hurling to goales' described by Richard Carew in Cornwall in 1602 (see page 161). Players are allowed to run with the ball in hand but, from 1866, they have had to touch it to the ground or bounce it every fifteen metres – not easy with an oval ball. No scrimmaging is permitted, nor is throwing or passing: to move the ball to a team-mate, a player must kick it or hold it in one hand and punch it with the clenched fist of his other hand.

If a player is tackled in possession, he has to drop the ball immediately and, as soon as he has done so, the tackler has to release him.

One of the most spectacular features of the game is the 'high mark'. A player can win a 'mark' or free kick if he manages to catch the ball directly from the kick of a player who is at least fifteen metres away from him. He can then take an unhindered kick – at goal if he is in range – from anywhere behind the point at which he caught it. Often three or four players will be trying to out-leap each other to catch a high mark, sometimes trying to ride on the back or shoulder of an opponent. Goals are scored by kicking the ball at any height between the goalposts, which are seven yards apart. On either side of each goal post, again seven yards away, are two further posts called behind posts. If a ball misses the main goal but goes between a goal post and a behind post, something called a 'behind' is scored. Goals are worth six points, a behind just one. Play is started by the 'field umpire' bouncing the ball in the middle of the pitch with players leaping to try to knock it down to a team-mate. A match consists of four twenty-minute quarters.

The aim of the founding committee was to produce a game which was as fast and exciting as possible, and in this many Australians and most observers would say they succeeded. The early chronicler of the game for the *Badminton Library of Sports and Pastimes*, writing in the late 1890s, said it would not be incautious to agree 'that there is no football game which appears to a crowd of spectators so quick, so picturesque, and so interesting'. Certainly the game quickly became immensely popular. In the 1890s, it was normal for more than 10 per cent of Melbourne's population of around half a million to be watching a match on a Saturday afternoon. It's also interesting that, from the start, around a third of the spectators have been female.

The *Badminton Library* author was clearly taken with the game. But he still couldn't resist gently teasing the Australians of Victoria for their fanatical devotion to their invention:

Whether rightly or wrongly, the Australian footballer who has toiled in uniform for a few seasons, or the old stager who has 'barracked', as it is locally called, for the club of his district during half a dozen winters, will agree in declaring that the game of football, as evolved under the guidance of Providence in Australia, is the crowning mercy vouchsafed to the human race.

Nonetheless, its devotees found it hard to spread their enthusiasm for Aussie Rules beyond its initial heartland. In 1877 the Victorian Football Association (VFA) was formed for the 'promotion and extension of football throughout the colony'. South Australia and Tasmania adopted the new game and outposts were established in Western Australia and even in rugby-mad New Zealand. But New South Wales and Queensland remained resistant, preferring rugby union (joined later by rugby league).

In 1896, the leading eight clubs of the VFA split off to form the Victorian Football League (VFL), which quickly became openly professional. By the 1920s, the VFL had established itself as the major competition for Aussie Rules. It expanded to include twelve clubs, but they were still all within Victoria. It wasn't until the 1980s that teams in New South Wales, Queensland, Western Australia and South Australia began to play in the league, which as a result was renamed in 1990 as the Australian Football League. But it is still largely focused on Melbourne.

Within its heartland, Aussie Rules remains immensely popular. It is the most popular spectator sport in Australia – 121,696 fans were at the Melbourne Cricket Ground to see Carlton defeat Collingwood in the VFL Grand Final in 1970. In 2005, the average attendance at league games was 36,791 – over 2000 more than the average attendance at an English Premiership soccer game. And the game remains the most-watched sport on Australian television. For its fans, perhaps, a 'crowning mercy' indeed.

American football

Can we really argue that American football, still a complete mystery to many people in Britain, actually has British origins? Yes, we can, with only a little bit of dodging and weaving. Here's the evidence, from the official website of the National Football League (NFL), the governing body of the sport:

1869: Rutgers and Princeton [East Coast universities] played a college soccer football game, the first ever, November 6. The game used modified London Football Association rules. During the next seven years, rugby gained favor with the major eastern schools over soccer, and modern [American] football began to develop from rugby.

The authoritative *Encyclopaedia Britannica*, originally British but based in America since 1901, is equally definitive:

Gridiron [American] football evolved from English rugby and soccer (Association football); it differs from soccer chiefly in allowing players to touch, throw, and carry the ball with their hands, and it differs from rugby in allowing each side to control the ball in alternating possessions.

So how did it all happen? Just as soccer and rugby emerged from the English public schools, so American football stems entirely from the elite East Coast universities. That match between Rutgers and Princeton on 6 November 1869, just six years after the rules of soccer were laid down by the new Football Association in London, was the very first intercollegiate football game. Columbia, Cornell, Yale and several other colleges in the north-east quickly adopted the soccer-style game and, in 1873, they got together in New York City to form the Intercollegiate Football Association. Conspicuous by its absence from this gathering was Harvard, which preferred to play by its own rules, a mixture of soccer and rugby known as the 'Boston Game'.

In 1874, Harvard agreed to play two matches against McGill University of Montreal in Canada. The first was played under the 'Boston Game' rules, but the second was played under the new rugby union code, which the Canadians had reputedly learned from British soldiers. The Harvard men immediately decided they preferred the rugby game to their own. The following year, they agreed to play the first ever football game against their traditional rivals, Yale. The two universities agreed a slightly bizarre compromise between Yale's favoured American version of the soccer game and Harvard's preferred rugby code. Both the Yale team and spectators from other East Coast colleges seem to have been converted to the benefits of the rugby game. The following year representatives of Harvard, Yale, Princeton and Columbia agreed to form a new Intercollegiate Football Association based on the rules of rugby. The 1876 Harvard–Yale match was played under the rugby union code.

Writing the section on the 'American Game' for the *Badminton Library* sixteen years later, the renowned 'Father of American Football', Walter Camp, suggests that this 1876 Harvard–Yale game was a turning point: 'From this match dates the real introduction of Rugby Football into the catalogue of American sports; and although the present rules, as they appear in the Intercollegiate Association code, differ in many respects from those of the English, their foundation was the same.'

For a brief moment, rugby union was the intercollegiate game of America. But it was not to last. Unhampered by tradition, the Americans began to improvise. Walter Camp, a Yale man who was a dominant figure on the rules committee for three decades from 1878 and a key instigator of the changes, put it like this:

... while the Englishman had a school where the traditions of what was allowed and what was forbidden in football were as fixed and unalterable as the laws of the Medes and Persians, the American player had nothing but the *lex scripta* [written law] to guide him, and no old player to whom to refer disputed points, or from whom to obtain information. The result in the case of the American was that the first year of Rugby Union was simply full of questions as to interpretations of the code.

Led by Camp, the Americans began to reinterpret the rules. They replaced rugby's scrummage with their own scrimmage, which allowed the attacking side to keep possession of the ball. When tackled, the ball carrier is allowed to snap the ball back to one of his team-mates (echoes of rugby league), now almost always the quarterback. To prevent one side from defensively hanging on to possession (which happened in the early days), the system of 'downs' was introduced. Today, a side has four 'downs' to advance the ball ten yards, or they have to give up possession. This generally (but not always) means they'll kick on the fourth down if they haven't gained the required territory. As late as 1906, the forward pass was legalized, which gave the quarterback the power to control the attacking game. It also became legal for players to run 'interference' to protect the runner with the ball.

In marketing terms, Camp and his fellow reformers got it absolutely right. Attendance at the Intercollegiate Football Association championship game rose from 5000 in 1876 to 40,000 in 1893. Later, college games were to draw as many as 120,000 spectators. College football dominated the sport until the 1950s and is still a huge draw today. Given the numbers involved, it was impossible for professionalism not to creep in. The very first professional player was the wonderfully named Pudge Heffelfinger, a former Yale man who was paid $500 to play one match for the Allegheny Athletic Association (AAA) against the Pittsburgh Athletic Club in 1892. He delivered on his contract, scoring the only touchdown to give the AAA victory by 4–0 (scoring was a bit different then).

The professional game itself didn't really begin until the 1920s, when the NFL was formed. Initially it was seen as a rather cheap alternative to the purity of the college game. But the arrival of television in the 1950s changed all that. While college football was nervous of television at first, the NFL embraced it and went on to make professional football the most-watched sport in America, and on the night of the Super Bowl quite possibly the world.

And they still occasionally have a brief game of rugby at half-time.

8.
ROWING

WHEN CHARLES II returned to London to claim his throne in 1660, there was only one bridge across the Thames. If you wanted to cross the river anywhere else – or if you simply wanted to travel up or down – you hailed a ferry. There were steps all along the river (some still survive) which acted as aquatic taxi ranks where 'watermen' hung about waiting for a fare. There were at least 10,000 of them operating on the river.

They were heavily regulated by the Watermen's Company. They had to serve a seven-year apprenticeship before they could have the freedom of the river and they were carefully monitored. This strict system had been introduced by an Act of Parliament in 1555 which set up the company to prevent 'mischances' which had been occurring to the nobility and the common people 'by reason of the rude, ignorant and unskilful number of watermen ... which do work at their own hands ... and do for the most part of their time use dicing and carding and other unlawful games, to the great and evil example of other such like ... practising robberies and felonies and other detestable facts, and yet do repair again to their former trade of rowing ...' Clearly, something had had to be done.

Yet the regulated watermen of the Restoration still liked a bit of fun and were not averse to some extra income. This was an age when few gentlemen could resist a wager on anything. Imagine two noblemen or rich merchants setting off in their brightly coloured boats, rowed by their private boatmen in colourful livery, from the same steps heading

A romantic picture of a Thames waterman, around 1825. The reality, especially in the seventeenth and eighteenth centuries, was rather more down to earth.

for the same destination. Of course they'd have a bet on who would get there first – and there would be a bonus in it for the waterman or crew who did. Or you're a gentleman who comes across a particularly swift ferryman. You mention him to an acquaintance. He wagers that he is not as fast as a man he knows. A match is arranged. Again, the winning waterman is also paid a reward.

By the 1660s, such matches were common and, if the watermen had a reputation, very popular, attracting sizeable crowds. Samuel Pepys records one in his diary on a spring day in 1661. He was looking forward to it, 'But upon the start, the wager boats fell foul one of another, till at last one of them gives over, pretending foul play, and so the other row away alone, and all our sport lost.' Such matches were purely private affairs, although they attracted crowds and no doubt a good deal of side-betting. It wasn't until the next century that the first organized race was established – by a comedian.

Thomas Doggett was born in Castle Street in Dublin in 1670 and became involved in acting at an early age. He made his name at 21

playing Deputy Nincompoop in Thomas D'Urfey's *Love for Money*. It
was the first of a long line of successes that led a critic in 1708 to
describe him as 'the only Comick Original now Extant'. But his talents
went beyond acting. He also successfully became involved in management, first at the Haymarket Theatre and then at Drury Lane. He
wasn't so good at getting on with his partners but they eventually paid
him off with a handsome sum which enabled him to retire – almost. He
couldn't resist returning to the stage from time to time. His new wealth
also enabled him to found the event for which he is now best known.

During his time in London, Doggett had always used ferries
regularly, to take him from his home in the City to the West End
theatres and to reach the theatres on the South Bank. One of his
favourite haunts was the Swan Tavern at London Bridge, from where
he liked to watch wherry races ('wherry' was the name given to a
ferryman's boat). The story goes that one evening he wanted a ferryman to row him home. It was a rough night with a strong tide and no
one came forward. Eventually a young man agreed to take on the job.
On the journey, Doggett discovered that the youth had only just

The coat and badge still awarded to the winner of
the race set up by Thomas Doggett in 1716

finished his apprenticeship. There and then he decided to set up a race for young watermen who had just gained the freedom of the river. The prize was to be a coat and badge and £10 in cash.

The first race took place on 1 August 1715 between the Old Swan Stairs at London Bridge and the White Swan Inn in Chelsea. It was part of the celebrations to mark the second anniversary of the accession of George I (much approved of by Doggett, who was a staunch Whig). It was a great success and established the race as an annual event. Doggett was able to watch several of his races – and afterwards 'repair to the White Swan to drink a cool tankard and shake the hand of the winner' before his death in 1721. In his will he left a bequest which modestly decreed that the race should be run every year 'for ever'. So far, it has been. It is one of the oldest annual sporting events in the world. But it was certainly not the first time that rowers had ever raced.

Origins

Rowing is almost as old as humankind. The instinct of ancient man, when faced with a body of water that needed to be crossed, is likely to have been to find something which floats – a log maybe – and then use whatever means were available to propel it, probably the hands at first. From there to dugout canoes and then primitive boats were not huge steps. The first rowing vessels of which we have evidence were from Egypt, as far back as 3000 BC. These were already elaborate vessels, with high stems and sterns, sails, and as many as twenty-five oars on each side. They were stylish, beautiful and, when needed, fast. There is some evidence that they may occasionally have been used for recreation, but it is not conclusive.

The Egyptians passed on their knowledge to the Phoenicians, the great seafaring merchants of the ancient world, and the Greeks. The trireme, with three rows of oars banked on top of each other, was efficient, beautiful and to this day the fastest rowing boat ever built. But it was purely a weapon – its only purpose was to ram enemy ships with its reinforced underwater prow. On 20 September 480 BC, 271 nimble Greek craft defeated more than 800 ships of the Persian invaders at Salamis, thus preserving the fledgling democracy in Athens and beginning the growth of the Athenian Empire. The Romans inherited the idea of rowing –and they knew about rowing races. In the fifth book of

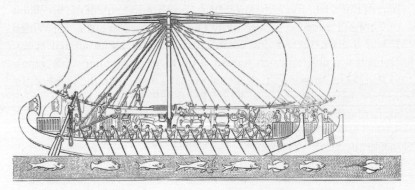

The fleet of the Egyptian Queen: there is evidence of
rowing on the Nile as early as 3000 BC

the *Aeneid*, Virgil describes a race that Aeneas organizes between four of his warships for the funeral games for his father. Quite exciting it was too, though the intervention of the gods in the final stages might well contravene modern regulations.

The Vikings were heavily reliant on their swift, oar-powered longships. These were cleverly designed vessels that didn't need harbours because they could be beached and could also navigate waters shallow enough to allow them to travel far inland, as both Paris and York discovered to their cost. The Venetians too had powerful warships driven by the muscle and sweat of rowers. The last oar-powered battle was at Lepanto in the Gulf of Corinth in 1571, when the Venetians defeated the Turks to put the Christian world firmly in control of the trade routes of the Adriatic.

But Venice, being Venice, also developed stylish craft for the transportation of people – and produce – through its elegant waterways. Because of the narrowness of many of the passages and the amount of traffic on the water, they developed a style of boat in which the oarsman – the gondolier – faced forwards and pushed rather than facing backwards and pulling. Even so, they could still race. Competitive rowing in Venice can be traced back at least as far as 1274. From then on regular events were held – generally many times a year – which involved celebratory parades of finely decorated boats and a series of races between different categories of gondola and other craft. Such a festival was called a *regata*.

From professional to amateur

The diarist William Hickey makes the first mention of a regatta in Britain in 1768. It took place in Walton-upon-Thames and seems to have been mainly an aquatic entertainment, a parade of colourfully liveried barges in front of a party on the riverbank. There is no mention of any racing. Another regatta is recorded off Ranelagh Pleasure Gardens in Chelsea in 1775. This time there was racing – but only as part of a bigger celebration. The crowd is said to have numbered some 200,000. Throughout the eighteenth century, one-off matches for money between watermen had continued to proliferate. A number of new races had been set up by various benefactors similar to the one for Doggett's Coat and Badge, but none had the same longevity. The first race for eight-oared boats was recorded by *The Annual Register*, the precursor of *The Times*, in 1778 between two crews called Chatham and Invincible (which suggests there may have been a naval connection). It was for 60 guineas and there was a good deal of side-betting.

Such events were immensely popular. Writing at the beginning of the nineteenth century, in his *Sports and Pastimes of the People of England*, Joseph Strutt noted that: 'When a rowing-match takes place near London, if the weather be fine, it is astonishing to see what crowds of people assemble themselves upon the banks of the Thames as spectators, and the river itself is nearly covered with wherries, pleasure boats, and barges, decorated with flags and streamers, and sometimes accompanied with bands of music.' It was inevitable that such a popular activity would be copied for pleasure by people who were not professional watermen. It is believed that the first amateur clubs on the Thames were called the Star and the Arrow, probably for scullers (single oarsmen), but we know little about them except that they were absorbed around 1820 by Leander, the oldest surviving amateur club, which was founded somewhere between 1815 and 1818.

Also among the first amateur rowers, almost certainly, were the pupils of Eton. Longboats were recorded at the college as far back as 1760. By 1793, there are reports of six boats taking part in celebrations for the King's birthday on 4 June. Three or four years later a boy wrote to his mother that 'There are four eight-oared boats and two sixes this year. I have heard it said that the Collegers intend manning another six.' Westminster was not far behind. In 1817, Eton challenged Westminster to a race, but the authorities were not in favour and prohibited the idea.

Not surprisingly, young men from Eton and Westminster took their love of rowing with them to the universities. Towards the end of the eighteenth century, Oxford undergraduates would row down the river

An early 'bumping' race: each boat tries to 'bump' the boat
which starts a length ahead of them

in fours or sixes to Iffley or Nuneham, play quoits or ninepins and dine on eel or perch from the river. On the way back, they would often race against each other. But the first organized races between college eights didn't take place at Oxford until around 1815. These were so-called bumping races. The river at Oxford is not wide enough to take more than two boats racing side by side, so the tradition grew up of boats starting one behind another. Over the four days of 'Eights Week', the aim was to catch the boat in front and 'bump' your prow against its stern. Both boats then stopped racing and pulled over to the bank. The next day, they would start in reverse order. Similar races began in Cambridge a little later, in 1827. (The tradition continues to this day.) It was clearly not going to be long before the two centres of learning took each other on. The first challenge came from Oxford in 1829.

The Boat Race

The annual race between Oxford and Cambridge is known throughout the world simply as 'The Boat Race'. There have been times when those watching the race on television might have been forgiven for wondering why they were doing so. All too often it was clear within two minutes who was going to win; the next eighteen minutes then became a rather dull procession. Those watching from the towpath had an even tougher time: two minutes of flashing blades and then they were out of sight.

So what was – and is – all the fuss about? The answer can only be tradition. The race was founded, strangely, by an old Harrovian cricketer. Charles Wordsworth was the son of the Master of Trinity, Cambridge. As an undergraduate at Christ Church in Oxford, he was a stalwart of the University Cricket XI and founded the University Cricket Match in 1827, the first established competition between Oxford and Cambridge. He had also taken up rowing and after the success of the first university cricket match, he used his contacts at Cambridge to suggest a similar rowing event. It took place at Henley in 1829. It was reported in the press that the race was for £500 a side, though this was denied by some (especially to parents). There was certainly a lot of side-betting. After a restart necessitated by a collision – 'fouling' was all part of the fun at the time – Oxford won by several lengths. A curious but true fact is that the entire Oxford crew went on to become clergymen.

It was seven years before Oxford and Cambridge could agree on where and when to race each other again. This time they rowed in London, from Westminster to Putney. It was the first race between

*The Oxford crew which won the first university boat race at Henley
in 1829: every single one became a clergyman*

dark blues and light blues. Oxford had worn dark blue stripes in 1829, but Cambridge had worn pink. The second time around, Cambridge at first had no colours, so a couple of their supporters were sent off to the nearest haberdashers. One of them was an Old Etonian and suggested 'Eton ribbon [light blue] for luck'. Light blue it was. Cambridge won the race easily and have stuck with that colour ever since.

By 1845, the crowds watching the race were becoming too large for Westminster, so it was moved upriver to the current course from Putney to Mortlake. By mid-century, it had become a major date in the London calendar. Like the Derby, it was particularly popular among cockneys, most of whom presumably had no connection with either university. Contemporary reports suggest the day was almost like a public holiday with seemingly every Londoner wearing light blue or dark blue. The river was packed with crowded steamers, barges and launches, the towpath was filled to bursting point and the adventurous and the reckless were hanging off every part of every bridge. In the days before football, it was one of the most popular sporting events of the year.

And of course it was free. This was an amateur event. But it's important, in the light of what was to come, to understand what that meant in the first half of the nineteenth century. Well-known contemporary oarsman W. B. 'Guts' Woodgate declared that at that time the words 'gentleman' and 'amateur' were interchangeable. If a gentleman chose to compete for a wager or for stake money, this didn't make him any less an amateur. Clear evidence of this came in 1831, when Oxford agreed to race Leander at Henley for £200 a side. Both boats were coxed by hired watermen, the only time an Oxford eight has ever been steered by a professional. Leander won by two lengths. Curiously, all memory of this race seems to have been repressed until it came to light, by accident, some fifty years later.

Not to be outdone, Cambridge challenged Leander to a match in 1837 (another year when the two universities could not agree where to meet). Rather against the odds, Cambridge won. Leander immediately asked for a rematch. The resulting race in 1838 between Westminster and Putney reveals a lot about the nature of rowing in those days, and in particular the tendency to 'fouling' (even though both sides had agreed to a no fouling rule). Each boat was steered by a professional waterman: Paddy Noulton, boatman to Westminster School, looked after Cambridge, while Leander used their regular cox, Jim Parish. The two were arch rivals and determined to take every advantage they could.

Cambridge fell behind at first, but then started to gain ground. They then found themselves being squeezed up against a moored barge by Leander. Noulton, their cox, was all for following watermen's practice and breaking their opponents' rudder, but the Cambridge captain, William Baliol Brett, insisted on giving way. First point to Parish.

Cambridge were outmanoeuvred again on their next challenge and again yielded. When this happened a third time, Brett had had enough. 'Finding all hopes of being allowed to pass useless,' he wrote in an angry exchange of letters, 'and convinced that you were sanctioning your steerer's conduct, we told [Noulton] to run into you, and there broke your oar, etc.' The mind boggles at what the 'etc.' might have included.

Cambridge then asked the umpire whether the race was 'fair or foul'. The umpire replied 'foul', so Cambridge put up their oars 'to claim the match'. But Leander were having none of it. They took on a new oar and headed off. When they were 200 yards away, Cambridge decided to set off in pursuit. They caught their opponents in less than half a mile but were again denied any way of passing. Exasperated, they rammed Leander as they passed through Putney Bridge. Not surprisingly, the umpire abandoned the race.

The story hints at why rowing was so popular at this time. Still mourning the prohibition of blood sports such as cock fighting and bear baiting, the people of London wanted their sports to be red-blooded. And, in the spirit of competition, the gentlemen amateurs of the time seemed quite willing to let the gentlemanly side slip a bit.

From amateur to professional

In 1830, Henry C. Wingfield, of whom little is known, set up an annual single sculling race 'between gentlemen' on the tideway in London. Like Thomas Doggett, he decreed it should last 'for ever'. The Wingfield Sculls is the only amateur race that is called a national championship and it continues to this day. It was from the start a sweepstake – all the entry fees were put into the pot – and the winner took all. Until, that is, the debate about amateurism (see below) took over.

But at the start the innovation seems to have sparked an idea among some of those who were eligible to take part. If amateurs could have a national championship, why couldn't the much more skilled professionals? Gentlemen from the Lyon's Subscription Room, one of the select amateur venues of the time, decided in September 1831 to set up the first professional sculling championship of England. It was the start of a forty-year bonanza of professional rowing in England – and ultimately around the world.

It worked a bit like the World Heavyweight Championship in boxing. It wasn't an annual event – it took place whenever anyone could raise enough money from serious betting men and lovers of rowing to challenge the incumbent. The sums involved were considerable, so championship races were rare. In the forty-five years from 1831 to 1876, when the championship first went abroad, there were just twenty-two contests. The first nine competitors for the championship (1831 to 1857) were all watermen from the Thames.

The Championship was reserved for the very best scullers. But there was plenty of racing to be had by lesser men. These were generally private matches. The norm was for an aspiring sculler to place an advertisement in the sporting press 'throwing down the gauntlet' against a named opponent for a relatively modest stake of around £20 a side. He would then invite his supporters to come to a particular hostelry to put up the money and 'make the match'. By mid-century, such races were taking place on the Thames almost every evening in the summer. They attracted good crowds and frequently a large amount of betting. But it would be wrong to suppose that these modest professionals could make much of a living. In 1843, a group of amateur oarsmen set up an event called the Thames Regatta, which was to run on and off and under various names until 1876. *The Times* reported that they were satisfied with their first attempt because '. . . it earned a good deal of money to be diffused amongst a class of person to whom very little is a great deal of help, viz the watermen of the Thames'.

But it wasn't only on the Thames that watermen were trying to supplement their income.

On the Tyne

A year before the first Thames Regatta, Robert Coombes, one of the leading professionals of the day who was to go on to win the sculling championship three times, took a Thames four up to Newcastle to challenge a boat stroked by local hero Harry Clasper. It began an intense rivalry between watermen from the two rivers which was to last for thirty years.

In the first half of the nineteenth century, most of the rivers of Britain were hustling, bustling places with their own watermen. But only the Tyne could rival the Thames as a centre for professional rowing. The sporting newspaper *Bell's Life* described Newcastle in 1859 as '... pre-eminently a sporting town, possessing men of wealth who are devoted to the support of all kinds of athletic amusements, and more especially rowing'. The oarsmen of the Tyne had a fierce local pride and a determination to prove that they were second to none – especially the men from the Thames. The large crowds that supported them were equally partisan and much more knowledgeable than might be suggested by the copious drinking and gambling in which they indulged. They had a real rapport with their heroes.

So when Robert Coombes brought his four up to the Tyne and had the audacity to defeat Harry Clasper's boat, it was seen as a real challenge. Clasper was convinced he had only lost because his boat was too heavy and slow. So he set about designing a new one. Like several of the Tyne watermen, Harry Clasper was a boatbuilder as well as an oarsman. He had no education – he was illiterate – but he had a clear eye and a strong instinct. He is believed to be the first person to come up with the idea of a keelless boat, in which the frame is put inside the boat so the bottom surface is completely smooth and therefore much faster. It was a four, which he took down to the second Thames Regatta in 1844. On the first day, he won easily, but he lost the next race because of steering problems. The following year, he won the first of many clear victories, much to the delight of his many Geordie supporters.

The young Harry Clasper sculling on the Tyne:
he probably built the boat himself

Clasper became a massive hero on Tyneside. In October 1845, when he was due to row in Liverpool, the Newcastle and Darlington railway put on a special excursion train to transport all his supporters across the country. The following year, when he was racing against Robert Newell on the Tyne, the same company provided five special trains to follow the race along the river on the line of the Newcastle and Carlisle railway.

One reason for professional rowing's popularity was that it was, to say the least, lively. The 1837 rules for the Durham Regatta stated: 'In the case of skiffs fouling, all jostling is allowable which can be accomplished with the sculls in the rowlocks, and the rower on his seat.' Things often went further. Consider this newspaper report of a race in which Harry Clasper was competing at Durham against four amateur scullers – the only time he was ever allowed to race against non-professionals. His opponents were so in awe of him that they drew lots to see which of them should sacrifice his chances to take Clasper out:

Robinson endeavoured to pull right into Clasper's boat, but missing it the oars became entangled, when the former jumped out of his boat and tried to pull the latter out of his. Clasper, seeing that all chance of winning the race was gone, and that his boat was likely to be capsized in the struggle, hit Robinson on the head with his fist, and was just on the point of striking him with his oar when he found that his boat was fast filling with water and going down bow foremost, and to save himself he had to jump out and swim to shore. On arriving at Bow Corner, Bone placed his boat right across the river for the purpose of fouling Newby. Succeeding in his object, both boats became entangled and immediately afterwards Newby's boat upset and, in tumbling out, its occupant seized hold of Bone's boat and upset it ... The race was ultimately won by Craggs.

Such fun and games aside, Harry Clasper and some of his fellow Tyneside professionals had a big impact on both amateur and professional rowing through their technical innovations. It's yet another example of the major developments in a sport coming from the professionals rather than the 'administrators'. When Clasper started, there was no such thing as a racing craft, just working boats designed to carry people or cargo. One of the first changes was the introduction of

A Foul: 'all jostling is allowable which can be accomplished with
the sculls in the rowlocks, and the rower on his seat'

outriggers, the V-shaped struts that go out from the side of the boat to hold the oars. They enabled boats to become much narrower, lighter and therefore faster. Clasper didn't invent the outrigger – credit for that goes to various other Tyneside boatbuilders – but he was the first to make them reliable enough to be trusted by rowers. He first fitted them onto a four in 1845, the same year a Cambridge student called J. W. Conant used them on his sculling boat at Henley. The following year both Oxford and Cambridge used them in the Boat Race. They have been standard ever since.

Clasper's idea for a keelless boat was developed further by another Tyneside boatbuilder called Matt Taylor. In 1854 he built a keelless four for the Royal Chester Rowing Club. They took it to Henley in 1855 and, even though observers said they could hardly row it, they still won the Steward's Challenge Cup easily. The following year, the club won both the Challenge Cup and the Ladies Plate in a keelless eight built by Taylor. The following year Oxford won the Boat Race in another of his boats.

Despite his reputation, Harry Clasper never felt he was a good enough sculler to challenge for the national championship. But his pupil Robert Chambers did. In 1859, he became the first man of the Tyne to become champion. He went on to retain the title four times. Tyneside being Tyneside, his defeat of the hated Thames men was immediately celebrated in song by music hall entertainer George Ridley:

> O, ye Cockneys all,
> Ye mun think't very funny,
> For Bob he gans and licks ye all,
> An collars all your money.

Harry Clasper lived just long enough to see another Tynesider, James Renforth, win the championship in 1868. When he died of 'congestion of the brain' in 1870, he was hailed as the 'father and teacher of modern aquatics'. It was reported that 130,000 people attended his funeral, when he was laid to rest in a magnificent carved tomb. The

Newcastle Daily Chronicle said he was 'but a lowly artisan at best', but 'He took his tools, and his strong arm and honest heart, and hewed himself a pathway to fame and a sepulchre kings might envy.'

The move towards elitism

While the watermen of the Thames and the Tyne were battling for supremacy, amateur rowing was beginning to move in a very different direction. The Henley Royal Regatta had been founded in 1839. It was initially a speculative venture by the local town authorities, who thought it would be both entertaining and beneficial for the town's businesses and inhabitants. But it was quickly taken over by the rowing establishment and became an elegant and important part of the social season. This elevated status was to be a critical factor in amateur rowing's self-image.

One reason why Henley was important was that it gave the leading clubs a chance to compete against crews from the universities. But they did not always see eye to eye. In the early days, as we've seen, the universities were not averse to competing for money. But by the time Henley began they were beginning to change. In 1839, a man from the Dolphin Club wrote to the press because he was concerned about rowing a Leander man for a wager. Was this allowable? The Leander man had no doubt: 'Public interest in the river as well as the spirit of rowing would soon cease if all contests were for honour only.' But oarsmen from Oxford and Cambridge wrote in to disagree. The Leander man's response was petulant: 'Your correspondents of last week would lead us to infer that he who rows for money is no gentleman, while some may consider that he who makes a public match without some stake is no small fool.'

The first published laws of boat racing were drawn up by representatives of Oxford and Cambridge and the leading London clubs in 1847. They were adopted by Henley Regatta the following year. But they failed to address the issue which was to bedevil British rowing for the next one hundred years or more. What is an amateur? It was not just the question of rowing for money – in the end that was fairly easy to resolve, no doubt much to the annoyance of the Leander man. There was also the much more controversial problem of status.

The year before, the organizers of the Lancaster Regatta had sought advice from the sporting journal *Bell's Life* on whether they were right to admit a crew of tradesmen. The response was careful: 'On the London river many members of the most distinguished amateur clubs are engaged in trade. This does not include journeymen or mechanics, whose crews are called "landsmen" to distinguish them from gentle-

Rowing as the early amateurs wanted to see it: gentlemen
competing only with other gentlemen

men amateurs and professional watermen. If the oarsmen in question are master tradesmen, the decision should stand; if journeymen or mechanics, they should be defaulted.'

This was very different from eleven years earlier, when the same newspaper had defined an amateur simply as anyone who rowed and was not a waterman or otherwise engaged in rowing for a living. What had changed? The real influence – and it became stronger over the next thirty years – was coming from the universities and the public schools. They were an amalgam of the old landed gentry and the enterprising and socially ambitious middle class who were emerging from the Industrial Revolution. This latter group was paying good money to send their sons to the new public schools and the universities so that they could qualify as gentlemen. They didn't want that threatened. In short, they were snobs.

The landed gentry and nobility, on the other hand, had supreme confidence in their social superiority. They felt under no threat. Remember the noble Duke who was quite happy to play in a cricket team captained by his gardener. But the new middle class knew that, in the main, they had made their money in trade. Now they wanted to distinguish themselves from those who could still be called tradesmen and in particular from those who still worked with their hands. There was some suggestion that it would be unfair to pit poor innocent gentlemen against brawny labourers because the latter would be much stronger. But in a sport which depended a good deal on skill, that was patently nonsense.

In 1866, Edwin Brickwood, a double winner of the Diamond Sculls at Henley and Rowing Editor of *The Field*, lamented that 'several so-called gentlemen amateur clubs contain members who are really and truly tradesmen in the literal sense of the term – though perhaps not working mechanics – but who, by reason of belonging to the clubs in question, are eligible to compete with amateurs who are gentlemen by birth, profession or education'. He suggested that the term 'amateur' should be restricted to officers in the military or civil service, members of the clerical, medical or legal professions, members of the universities, the public schools and members of any club 'not composed of tradesmen or working mechanics' which would be allowed by the stewards of Henley.

In 1874, a Northern regatta disqualified a crew from the Bolton and Ringley club *after* they had won their event because they were found to be artisans. Bolton replied as follows: 'If any gentlemen would kindly give us a true definition of what an amateur is, we should feel greatly obliged, as we have always been under the impression that if a person did anything for pleasure and not for money, that person was an amateur, but if he should do anything for money, or in any shape for his living, he loses his title to be an amateur.'

There was no authority to answer their query. To try to sort the matter out, representatives of some of the leading rowing organizations met in Putney on 10 April 1878. They included Oxford and Cambridge and the Thames, Leander, Kingston and London rowing clubs. They adopted Brickwood's definition of what an amateur should be; and they concluded by saying an amateur 'must not have competed in any competition for either a stake, or money, or entrance fee, or with or against a professional for any prize; nor have ever taught, pursued or assisted in the pursuit of athletic exercises of any kind as a means of livelihood, nor have ever been employed in or about boats, or in manual labour; nor be a mechanic, artisan or labourer'.

Just three months later four American crews rowed at Henley. Columbia College became the first overseas crew to win a trophy. But the real shock was that a crew called the 'sho-wae-cae-mette' four turned out to be lumberjacks. This focused the minds of the Henley stewards on who should and should not be allowed to row. They did some research. They discovered, for instance, that all amateur prizes in France were for cash. They decided that all foreign crews had to apply for entry early so that they could be thoroughly checked. Such crews were also required to make a declaration in front of a Notary Public

The Henley Royal Regatta as it used to be:
the upper-middle class at leisure

about the profession of each and every crew member. The stewards then produced their own set of regulations. They accepted the Putney rules for what an amateur should not be, but they didn't spell out what he (and at this time it always was a he) should be. Their critics were quick to point out that this allowed in foreigners, which perhaps was the point.

The ARA and the not so ARA

In 1882, the need for an overall authority to regulate rowing led to the formation of the Amateur Rowing Association (ARA). Its initial brief was to select crews to ward off the threat from foreign opponents and generally to maintain the standards of British rowing. It did not get around to the question of defining an amateur until 1884. Then, in essence, it followed the Henley rules, rather meanly adding to the final clause, which said that no one was an amateur 'who is or has been, by trade or employment for wages, a mechanic, artisan or labourer', the words 'or anyone engaged in menial duty'.

They also added a further clause, to the effect that no one could be an amateur who 'was a member of a boat or rowing club containing anyone liable to disqualification under the above rules'. Guilt by association, in other words. This would have ruled out members of many clubs up and down the country. The Secretary of Tewkesbury Regatta remarked that the customs and practices of many clubs would 'shock the delicate feelings of the lavender-gloved amateur; but if rowing is to be encouraged, we must not be too thin-skinned'. The clause was quietly dropped within two years.

Many clubs and many oarsmen remained unhappy at the ARA's definition. Their views were best expressed by Dr Frederick Furnivall, a Cambridge graduate and leading light of the 'muscular Christianity' movement who taught at the London Working Men's College. He believed the 'manual labour' clause undermined the values he had learned at Cambridge: 'We feel that for a University to send its earnest intellectual men into an East-end or other settlement to live with and help working men in their studies and sports, while it sends its rowing men into the ARA to say to these working men, "You're labourers; your work renders you unfit to associate and row with us", is a facing-both-ways, an inconsistency and contradiction which loyal sons of the University ought to avoid.'

In 1890, Furnivall and a number of like-minded Cambridge-educated clergymen, along with the philanthropist Quintin Hogg who founded the Regent Street Polytechnic, started a rival organization they called the National Amateur Rowing Association (NARA). Its rules excluded true professionals but definitely did not exclude menial or manual workers, artisans or tradesmen. Many members of ARA-affiliated clubs sympathized with the NARA stand and negotiations took place. But the hardliners of the ARA would not budge. In 1893 they did concede that ARA and NARA people could row together in private matches, but not in regattas. In the end the NARA attracted around a third of the clubs in Britain, while the ARA had most of the rest (some stayed aloof from both). The split was to last for another sixty years.

Foreigners

Organized rowing, once it had taken its first rudimentary strokes at Oxford and Cambridge and on the tideway in London in the early nineteenth century, spread around the globe with astonishing speed. This was a time when Britain was beginning to dominate the world. The Empire was spreading across the globe and trade links reached into almost every corner of every country. And wherever the British went, they took their sports with them. The first recognizable rowing club outside Britain was formed in Barcelona in 1821. The English Rowing Club was formed in Hamburg in 1830 (the first German club followed six years later). The first American and Hungarian clubs began in 1834, the first Australian club a year later and the first French club a year after that. There was a regatta in Rio de Janeiro in 1840.

The Harvard–Yale race was first held in 1852, the first intercollegiate sporting event in the USA. Organized rowing began in Belgium in 1860 and a club called the English Crew was started in Prague the same year. It was followed by clubs in South Africa and New Zealand in 1861, the same year that rowing started in Switzerland. It spread to Vienna, Turin and Trieste in 1863. What happened next was both predictable and fair. Those to whom the British had given the sport were determined to come to Britain to demonstrate how well they'd learned it.

Professional rowing felt the impact first. By the mid-1870s, new bridges and steamers had almost driven watermen from the Thames and the Tyne. As a result, professional rowing was dying. British rowers had seen off the first challengers for the national sculling championship from Australia and America in the 1860s, but in 1876 Edward Trickett of Sydney beat Joseph Sadler from Putney over the traditional tideway course. *The Advertiser* in Melbourne declared that the victory 'will have done more to make these colonies known throughout the old world than all the lectures given and statistics published during the last twenty years'. That's how much it meant to the Australians.

The championship – now known as the world championship –

Ernest Barry after beating H. Pearce of Australia in a £500 match:
still popular enough to need a police escort.

didn't return to Britain for some thirty-six years. In the intervening years, it switched constantly from Australians to Canadians to New Zealanders. When Ernest Barry finally brought the championship back to the Thames in 1912, the magic had gone. Fouling was out of fashion, the crowds had disappeared and, without the cheering, a rowing race was a pretty desultory affair. Professionals found amateur clubs reluctant to take them on as coaches and many had to go abroad to make a living. By the 1930s, professional rowing in Britain was effectively dead.

Amateur rowing, on the other hand, was thriving around the world. In 1892, the leading European nations had got together to form the Fédération Internationale des Sociétés d'Aviron, or FISA, for the express purpose of starting a European Championship. The first was held on Lake Orta in Italy in September 1893. In true British fashion, the ARA declined to join for fear of compromising the purity of its amateur principles. Britain would take no part in the European Championships until 1950.

The Olympics were another matter. Baron Pierre de Coubertin, the French aristocrat who organized the first modern games in Athens in 1896, was a serious anglophile who had spent time at Henley. He was an admirer of the way that the British upper classes, through their universities and public schools, put such stress on athleticism. The ARA, despite its qualms about possibly compromising its amateur principles (which Coubertin admired) could hardly resist an invitation to take

---

Fair play?

Henley is the only place to have held the Olympic rowing regatta twice. The first time was in 1908. That year the Henley Committee decided that no foreign crews should be allowed to compete in the Royal Regatta because it might allow them to familiarize themselves with the course and thereby gain an unfair advantage. In the event, Britain won all four Olympic gold medals. All the winners had been practising on the Olympic course for many weeks.

part. No rowing took place in Athens because of bad weather and Britain took little part in the games of 1900 and 1904. But the British swept the board in the 1908 Games, when the rowing was held at Henley, and did well in the 1912 Olympiad in Stockholm. After that, the performance of British crews was little more than average until the achievements of Steve Redgrave, Matthew Pinsent and their triumphant successes between 1984 and 2008.

Reunited at last

While world rowing was growing all around them, the Amateur Rowing Association and the stewards of Henley (who remained independent) stuck rigidly to what they saw as their principled stand on amateurism. Not that it was always easy to work out exactly what their stand was. In 1895, the ARA concluded that an ironmonger, a tailor and a printer's apprentice were not eligible, but a booking clerk at Henley railway station was.

The Henley stewards excelled themselves in 1920 when they refused the entry of Jack Kelly Sr, a building contractor who constructed much

Jack Kelly, triple Olympic champion and
father of Princess Grace of Monaco

of modern Philadelphia and was the father of the film star Grace Kelly, partly on the grounds that he had once been an apprentice bricklayer. (It was also in part because he was a member of the Vesper Club, which Henley had banned fifteen years earlier because it had used a public subscription to raise travel money for their crew.) Shortly afterwards, Kelly won gold medals in both the single and double sculls in the Olympic Games. He never forgot the slight but got his own back by coaching his son to two wins in the Diamond Sculls in 1947 and 1949. In 1981, his daughter, as Princess Grace of Monaco, was invited to Henley to give the prizes.

There was more nonsense to come. The Australian sculler Bob Pearce, the 1928 Olympic champion, was banned from Henley because he was a carpenter. But when he reapplied as a Canadian in 1931, when he was working for Lord Dewar as a whisky salesman, he was allowed in and duly won the Diamond Sculls. The final *reductio ad absurdum* came in 1936 when Henley banned the Australian Olympic eight from Sydney on the grounds that they were policemen and therefore could not possibly be amateurs. Even the ARA realized after this that things could not go on as they were. In 1937, they agreed to talks with the NARA.

At the opening session Charles Tugwell, the NARA Secretary, made this delicate point: 'No other branch of athletic sport throughout the world has found it necessary to legislate specifically against the working class and to exclude that class from taking part in its sport on the grounds that that class has a physical advantage.' This wasn't, of course, the real reason why the ARA had excluded manual workers, but this was a diplomatic negotiation. In the end, the ARA agreed to expunge all social-exclusion clauses from its rules. Sanity had finally prevailed.

Largely for administrative reasons, the two governing bodies continued to exist side by side. After the interruption of World War II, they both joined FISA in 1947, in time for the London Olympics in 1948, when the rowing once again was held at Henley. In 1950, Britain took part in the European Championships for the first time and discovered

that its infatuation with a distorted kind of elitism had set British
rowing back a long way. In 1956 the two organizations finally amalga-
mated and British rowing took its first faltering steps back into the real
world.

9.

BASEBALL

SURELY SOME MISTAKE, you might think. And in one sense you'd be right. Britain cannot claim to have developed baseball into the major sport it is today. The modern game is definitely American. But the origin of the sport is another matter. It has been the subject of obsessive debate among baseball fans since the 1870s, which has involved national pride, arm-twisting, deception and even murder. It led to the construction of a shrine to celebrate the birth of America's national pastime – in the wrong place, on the wrong date and in honour of the wrong man. It's a highly entertaining story. And one in which Britain plays a major part.

Opening pitch

The first recognized baseball reporter was English-born Henry Chadwick, who started writing about the game in New York in the 1850s. He became such an expert on the game and promoted it so assiduously that he was called the 'father of baseball'. In 1860, he wrote the introduction to the game's first ever annual guide in which he said that baseball was of 'English origin' and 'derived from the game of rounders', which he had played as a child in Devon before his family had emigrated to America when he was thirteen. At the time the game was in its infancy and had not acquired the iconic status it was to achieve later. For many years Chadwick's statement went unchallenged.

The first to cast doubt on Chadwick's view was another journalist called William M. Rankin. In a widely syndicated article in 1886, he argued that there were major differences between baseball as it was by that time being widely played all across America, and the English game of rounders. He dismissed the theory that the one had its origins in the other. 'It is like Mr Darwin's theory of the origin of man,' he wrote, 'it lacks the necessary connecting links to carry out the idea. The game of

An early depiction of what looks like baseball: from
Children's Amusements, *published 1820*

baseball seems to have sprung up, just as any game has.' He didn't suggest how that might have happened.

Two years later one of the best-known players of the day decided to join in the argument. In his book *Base-ball: How to Become a Player*, John Montgomery Ward set out to prove that baseball was an all-American invention. He accused Chadwick and his followers of a snobbish belief that 'everything good and beautiful in the world had to be of English origin'. He compared baseball and rounders in detail and concluded that there was no reason to believe one was descended from the other. Instead, he proclaimed, 'I believe it [baseball] to be the fruit of the inventive genius of an American boy.' He argued that baseball had probably evolved from the early American game of 'cat-ball' and concluded: 'In the field of outdoor sports the American boy is easily capable of devising his own amusements, and until some proof is adduced that base-ball is not his invention I protest against this systematic effort to rob him of his dues.'

Ward's fame ensured that his proclamation received wide publicity. It also drew a swift response from Henry Chadwick. 'To say that there is no similarity between [rounders] and our American game of base ball,' he wrote, 'or to attempt to make the latter a distinctive game of strictly American origin, as Mr Ward does in his otherwise ably written book on base ball, is not in accordance with historical facts, to say the least.' He didn't think it worthwhile to go into those historical facts. 'There is no need of presenting any arguments in the case, as the connection between rounders and baseball is too plain to be mistaken.'

In October 1888, Ward and a number of other professional base-ball players embarked on a six-month Around the World baseball tour to promote the sport. It was organized by another towering figure who looms large in this story: Albert Spalding, a former star pitcher, one-time owner of the Chicago White Socks and co-founder of the massively successful sports goods company. The tour visited Hawaii, New Zealand, Australia, Ceylon, Egypt, Italy, France and England (where inevitably a number of spectators commented that the game looked just like rounders). The players and their wives travelled first class, largely at Spalding's expense. When they returned to New York, a grand banquet was held in their honour at Delmonico's restaurant attended by such figures as Mark Twain and Teddy Roosevelt. One of the key speakers was former National League president Abraham Mills, who declared that 'patriotism and research alike vindicate the claim that [baseball] is American in its origins'. According to reports, the diners responded with cries of 'No rounders! No rounders!'

After this outburst, the debate seems to have quietened down. For a while.

The Special Commission

In 1903, America was feeling confident. Victory in the war against Spain had generated a proud nationalism, and baseball was seen very much as a symbol of the nation. Henry Chadwick chose this time to take up his pen once again. Now nearly eighty, he did so in his role as editor of Spalding's annual baseball guide. It was perhaps a deliberately provocative move. Spalding had originally gone along with his old friend Chadwick's rounders theory, but after the world tour he had switched sides. Now he was being challenged in one of his own publications.

He embarked on a campaign of speeches and articles in which he attempted to prove that baseball was indeed an entirely American

Boys playing baseball on Boston Common:
from The Book of Sports, *1832*

game. 'I have been fed on this kind of "Rounders pap" for upward of forty years,' he wrote, 'and I refuse to swallow any more of it without some substantial proof sauce with it.' He took up John Ward's suggestion that baseball may have stemmed from the early American 'cat-ball' games (which, ironically, originally came from England).

One-old-cat had developed into two-, three- and four-old-cat, which featured a four-base infield. This, argued Spalding, had evolved into the American game of town ball, which had in turn spawned base ball.

The battle between Chadwick and Spalding generated a huge amount of coverage in the baseball-obsessed sporting press. In response, Spalding decided to set up a 'Special Base Ball Commission' to decide the game's origins 'once and for all'. Under the chairmanship of former National League President Abraham Mills, the fiery speaker from Delmonico's fifteen years earlier, the commission included two other former National League presidents, one of whom was also a US Senator, a second US Senator and two famous retired players. But it was Spalding who was in charge and he didn't make much of a secret of what he was looking for. This is an extract from a letter he wrote to the Massachusetts baseball veteran John Lowell:

I have become weary of listening to my friend Chadwick's talk about base ball having been handed down from the old English game of 'Rounders', and am trying to convince myself and others that the American game of base ball is purely of American origin, and I want to get all the facts I can to support that theory. My patriotism naturally makes me desirous of establishing it as of American origin, if possible, and as the same spirit will probably prompt you, I would like your ideas about it.

The tale of two Abners

On the morning of 3 April 1905, Abner Graves was sitting in his room at the Thuma Hotel in Akron, Ohio, reading the local newspaper, the *Beacon Journal*. He was a 71-year-old mining engineer on a business trip from his home in Denver, Colorado. Turning the pages, he came across a story written by Albert Spalding headed 'The Origin of the Game of Base Ball' which outlined the controversy and called upon anyone who was interested to send whatever evidence they had to the commission's secretary. Graves went straight to his typewriter and wrote a letter to the editor of the *Beacon Journal* with a copy for the commission secretary James Sullivan.

He did not beat about the bush. 'The American game of "Base Ball" was invented by Abner Doubleday of Cooperstown, New York, either the spring prior, or following the "Log Cabin & Hard Cider" campaign of General Harrison for President, said Abner Doubleday being then a boy pupil of "Green's Select School" in Cooperstown, and the same, who as General Doubleday won honor at the Battle of Gettysburg in the Civil War.'

He went on to describe the rather muddled game of 'town ball' that the boys of Cooperstown used to play in those days. Up to fifty boys

Early engraving of boys playing baseball:
from Mary's Book of Sports, *1832*

might be involved at any one time and painful collisions were common. Doubleday came up with 'a plan of improvement'. It involved equal sides of eleven players each, who all had set positions when fielding. It had four bases, marked by flat stones, which is why he chose to call it 'Base Ball'. A runner could rest free by putting his foot on the stone without fear of being put out, while the next on his side took the bat. If he could eventually reach home base he scored. But if anyone fielding the ball managed to throw it at him and hit him, he was out. 'Baseball,' Graves concluded, 'is undoubtedly a pure American game, and its birthplace Cooperstown, New York, and Abner Doubleday entitled to first honor of its invention.' Thus was born what Stephen Jay Gould has called the 'creation myth' of baseball.

Graves's letter eventually found its way to Albert Spalding. He wrote to Graves in November making it quite clear that he was excited by the story. He said that if it could be verified, 'I feel quite certain it will have great weight with the commission in deciding when, and where and how the American national game originated.' Graves replied that he was 'at a loss' about how he could verify his story because most of his contemporaries were dead or feeble-minded. But he expanded his story a little by describing how Doubleday, who he thought was sixteen or seventeen at the time, had interrupted him and his friends while they were playing marbles to explain his idea in detail, even drawing a diagram of the bases in the dirt with a stick.

In March 1908, the special commission published its report. They had amassed a mountain of evidence but chose to ignore nearly all of it in favour of Graves's letter. The report was written by Mills based on analysis of the evidence put together by the secretary James Sullivan, who was an employee of Spalding. There is little doubt that Spalding was the driving force behind it. He couldn't resist having a Civil War hero as the inventor of his beloved game. Abner Doubleday had not only taken charge of I Corps on the first day of the Battle of Gettysburg, he had also been in charge of firing the first shots at the rebel forces in Fort Sumter in the encounter which had begun the war. The report concluded that, without a doubt, Abner Doubleday had invented baseball in the spring of 1839 in Cooperstown, New York.

No one seemed concerned that there was no evidence to corroborate Graves's recollection. Indeed, the final report tampered with it. Graves had said that a runner could be put out by being hit with the ball thrown by a fielder. The commission said Doubleday had introduced the innovation that the runner had to be put out at a base, which was the case in 1908. Graves had also said that he couldn't be sure whether Doubleday had introduced his invention in 1839, 1840 or 1841. The commission decided, seemingly arbitrarily, on 1839.

That was that. Baseball was officially American. There were a

*Abner Doubleday, the civil war general wrongly
hailed as the inventor of baseball*

couple of dissenting voices, but they weren't widely heard. In 1909,
Will Irwin wrote a series of articles for *Collier's* magazine in which he
proved that baseball predated 1839. William Rankin, Chadwick's first
opponent, pointed out that official records showed Doubleday had
enrolled at West Point in 1838 and had not taken any leave of absence
in 1839 or 1840. There was no evidence that he had ever been to
Cooperstown. Rankin instead suggested that baseball had been
founded by Alexander Joy Cartwright of the Knickerbocker Club in
New York around 1845. Henry Chadwick himself, now very old and
far from well, wrote to Abraham Mills the day the report was
published. 'I want to say to you', he said, 'that it is a masterly piece of
special pleading, which lets my dear old friend Albert escape a bad
defeat ... I was so sure of my case that I failed to present detailed
evidence. The fact is, the whole matter was a joke between Albert and
myself, for the fun of the thing.'

Enshrining the myth

But for most Americans, the matter was now decided. Within a year or two, the story of Abner Doubleday's invention began appearing in children's history books. Cooperstown, delighted to be named as the birthplace of a national institution, renamed the cow pasture where baseball's creator was said to have played 'The Doubleday Field' and turned it into an exhibition ground for Major League matches. In 1935 an old baseball believed to have belonged to Abner Graves was found in a place called Fly Creek. Might it have been handled by Doubleday himself? Could it even be the original base ball? The town bought it and decided to build a museum to house it. Possible exhibits were sent to Cooperstown from all over America.

The baseball authorities began to plan for the centenary of the game

THE THROWER.   THE STRIKER.

THE CATCHER.   BASE TENDER.

Uniformed players of the Massachusetts
variety of baseball, 1859

in 1939. It was decided to site the Baseball Hall of Fame in Cooperstown alongside the museum. It was ceremonially opened on 12 June
1939, accompanied by a pageant featuring historical highlights of the
game and an all-star contest featuring leading players of the day on
the original Doubleday Field. President Franklin D. Roosevelt sent a
message saying 'we should all be grateful to Abner Doubleday. Little
did he or the group that was with him at Cooperstown, N.Y., in 1839,
realize the boon they were giving the nation in devising baseball.' The
US government issued a special postage stamp to mark the occasion.

Just before the celebrations took place, a man called Robert W.
Henderson threw a bit of a curve ball into the proceedings. He worked
for the New York Public Library and was also the curator of the library
of the New York Racquet and Tennis Club, where he had put together
a formidable collection of books on ball games. He published an article
in the *Bulletin of the New York Public Library* which proved conclusively
that the Doubleday story was a myth. His most powerful evidence was
an extract from a volume called *The Book of Sports* by Robin Carver,
published in Boston in 1834, which outlined the rules of a game called
'Base or Goal Ball' and included a diagram of the diamond-shaped
infield. Even more damning, these rules and the diagram were an
exact copy of some rules printed in a book called *The Boy's Own Book*
by William Clarke, published in London in 1828, where they were
described as the rules of a game called 'rounders'. Henderson also
pointed out that Abner Doubleday had written extensively about his
life and had never once even mentioned baseball.

The baseball establishment and the press did not let this inconven-
ient truth get in the way of the celebrations. The general public went
on believing the Doubleday story, and many still do to this day. But
grudgingly, over time, those who care about such things have come to
accept Henderson's refutation. The National Baseball Hall of Fame
and Museum is still in Cooperstown, but it now exhibits that 'original'
ball over the caption 'Doubleday didn't invent baseball, baseball
invented Doubleday.' So how did it all happen?

It's easy to see why the fiercely patriotic Albert Spalding wanted to
believe that the game was invented by a Civil War hero and why he

Abner Graves relished the publicity he received
for telling the Abner Doubleday story

was keen to persuade his commission to take the same view. But what of Abner Graves? Did he just make it up? It has emerged that Graves had a history of mental instability and he was certainly prone to exaggeration. As he grew older, he was always happy to talk about his recollections and every time he did so, he embellished them a little more. He also, tragically, grew more and more irrational. In 1924, he came to believe that his second wife Minnie was trying to poison him. In the middle of a blazing row, he pulled out a gun and shot her four times, leaving her fatally wounded. At his trial for murder he was judged to be insane and committed to an asylum, where he died two years later at the age of ninety-two.

But some elements of Graves's story ring true. It has emerged that a cousin of the Civil War general, also called Abner Doubleday, did live in Cooperstown at the relevant time. It is also now known that organized baseball was being played in New York and maybe elsewhere by this time. This has led one historian to speculate. Could it be that an older boy from Cooperstown, perhaps the other Abner Doubleday, had either seen or heard about this new game? Armed with this superior knowledge, and faced with Abner Graves and a group of marble-playing seven-year-olds, he may have wanted to

Southpaws and curveballs

To the British, 'southpaw' is purely a boxing term, meaning someone who is left-handed and therefore leads with their right. But its origins probably lie in baseball. In America, most baseball 'diamonds' are laid out so that the pitcher throws from east to west to ensure that the batter doesn't have to look into the sun. A right-handed pitcher's arm is always to the north. But a left-hander's arm is to the south. In the nineteenth century, American sporting journalists – always wonderfully creative with their slang – dubbed such a person a 'southpaw'. Soon the term was being applied to left-handed fighters as well.

Other baseball phrases have become widely used in Britain, including 'out of left field' and 'curveball'; most common of all, perhaps, is 'stepping up to the plate', much beloved of footballers and other sportsmen.

impress by sharing the new idea and possibly even claiming it as his own. Boys have been known to tell such tall tales. Sixty-five years later the old Abner Graves, remembering this incident and understandably confusing the spotty youth involved with the famous general – how many people do you know called Abner Doubleday? – fired off his letter to the *Beacon Journal*. He could not have foreseen the consequences.

Finally, the truth

So, it's settled. Baseball is derived from the old English game of rounders. Not necessarily. The problem is that the 1828 English book from which the 1834 American rules of baseball were taken was the first ever use of the word 'rounders' in print. Rounders seems to have been a new name for an old English game that was originally called . . . base ball.

Robert Henderson knew some of these references. Others have been rediscovered since his time. In *Northanger Abbey*, published posthumously in 1818 but written around the turn of the century, Jane Austen wrote of her heroine that '. . . it was not very wonderful that Catherine, who had by nature nothing heroic about her, should prefer cricket, base ball, riding on horseback, and running about the country at the age of fourteen, to books'. A few years earlier, in 1796, a comprehensive German book on children's games included seven pages on the rules of *das englische base-ball* – English base ball – which were the most detailed until the Knickerbocker Club rules of 1845. Half a century earlier, in a letter published in a later collection, the well-connected author Mary Lepel, Lady Hervey, wrote about the behaviour of the family of the Prince of Wales: 'In the winter, in a large room, they divert themselves at base-ball, a play all who are, or have been, schoolboys are well acquainted with. The ladies, as well as gentlemen, join in this amusement.'

The earliest and perhaps the most charming reference comes in a children's book called *A Little Pretty Pocket Book*. It was published in 1744,

The earliest mention of baseball in print: from
A Little Pretty Pocket Book of 1744

though we only have a later edition. It contains a woodcut entitled 'Base-Ball' which features three young men on a field with three bases marked by posts. One is about to throw the ball, another is waiting to hit it – not with a bat but with the palm of his hand, while the third appears to be fielding. Then in 2009, after the first edition of this book came out, a hand-written diary was discovered in a shed near Guildford belonging to a well-known Surrey lawyer and antiquarian called William Bray. On Easter Monday, 31 March 1755, he describes going to 'play at Base Ball' with a group of friends, both male and female. It is the earliest manuscript reference to the game that we have. The conclusion seems clear. In England from at least the early eighteenth century there was a popular children's game called base ball, which had probably evolved from earlier medieval games such as stool-ball and tut-ball. At some point it was taken by English immigrants to America, where Henderson suggests it was known from 1762. In England in the early nineteenth century it seems to have changed its name, at least in some parts of the country, to round-ers. In America it grew in popularity, retaining its original name of base ball. We now know it was being played in an organized fashion in New York in 1823. In 1845, the Knickerbocker Club produced a new set of rules which were then developed over the next fifty years into what is now America's summer pastime. Clearly derived from an old English children's game. Henry Chadwick can rest easy in his grave.

10.
LAWN TENNIS
(AND ASSORTED GAMES)

A summer interlude

ONE SUMMER'S DAY in the early 1870s, the young Lord Lansdowne, later to be Governor General of Canada, Viceroy of India and Foreign Secretary, received a visitor at his house in Berkeley Square.

A young Captain of Artillery, Major Wingfield, presented himself and said he had invented a new game and would like to demonstrate it to me and my friends on the lawn in front of my house. He said it required four players. Being interested, I consented and asked him to tea the following day. To make up the four I invited Walter Long and Arthur Balfour [the future Prime Minister] to join us.

The next afternoon we four played the first game on my lawn, over a net about two feet wide hung on sloping posts kept erect with strings attached to pegs. We found it good exercise and quite interesting, even with the crooked racquets and plain uncovered balls of that day.

That summer we four used to meet three or four times a week, and the more we played the more we enjoyed it. The inventor called the game by a Greek name – Sphairistike – a name no one could possibly remember. One day Walter Long said, 'Look here, if you want your game to catch on you must find a more reasonable name for it.' To this we all agreed, but were at a loss for a suitable name. 'Why not call the game Lawn Tennis,' said Arthur. We all agreed this would do, and the name was adopted by the inventor.

If this story is true – and there is no reason to doubt it except that it is a memory reported at fourth hand – lawn tennis was given its name by a future Prime Minister. What is beyond doubt is that what was to become one of the most popular and most widely played of all sports was introduced to the world by Major Walter Wingfield. But, as he himself made abundantly clear, it was a modern development of a truly ancient game.

First service

The origins of tennis are shrouded in mystery. Just how shrouded can be seen from the earliest known mention of the game. There was a young monk in Paris around the middle of the twelfth century who had such a bad memory that he couldn't learn anything. One day, the devil appeared to him and offered him a magic stone. If you hold this in your hand, he said, you will know everything. The novice became a

An early picture from France of what we would
now call a Real Tennis court

brilliant student – but shortly afterwards he was struck down by illness and seemingly died. Demons snatched his soul and took it down to hell. There, in a valley filled with sulphurous vapours, were two teams of devils. 'And those standing at one end hit the poor soul after the fashion of the game at ball, and those at the other end caught it in mid-air with their hands.' The devils' hands were as sharp as iron nails, inflicting unimaginable pain. We know this because the young monk survived to become the Abbot of Morimond. He told his story, presumably a dream, to a fellow abbot who told it to Caesarius of Heisterbach, who put it in his *Dialogus Miraculorum*. What is significant is that everyone involved was clearly familiar with this 'game at ball'.

This story may be one reason why it's often thought that tennis was invented by French monks. Young novices, it's suggested, with time on their hands and little other means of distraction, used to bat a ball between them in their cloisters, sometimes over a piece of rope or string. They used their hands – the French name is *jeu de paume*, game of the palm. References in ancient documents tell us that such activity certainly did take place. But there's no way that we can know for sure that this is how the game began.

It's just as likely that it began as a game of hand ball played by ordinary people in parks and other open spaces. Even today, variations of the ancient game are played in towns in France, Italy, the Basque country and elsewhere. But in the Middle Ages such activity was much less likely to be written about. There is evidence that by the middle of the thirteenth century the game was being played in market squares in towns in Picardy and in Flanders. And we know that before the end of the century, it had become popular at the French court. By 1292, there were thirteen makers of tennis balls in Paris.

As the game developed, so did the instruments with which it was played. First the playing hand was covered with a strong glove. Then someone worked out that you could gain more power if you put strings across the glove. Then, to deliver more leverage, a form of the glove was put on to a handle. To begin with, this seems to have been a wooden bat, perhaps with some parchment covering the head. But sometime around the beginning of the sixteenth century, the stringed racket came into use. Balls were made of animal hair or wool refuse covered in sheepskin. (In England, human hair was sometimes used: in *Much Ado About Nothing*, Shakespeare has Don Pedro ask: 'Hath any man seen him at the barber's?' Claudio replies: 'No, but the barber's man hath been seen with him; and the old ornament of his cheek hath already stuffed tennis-balls.') As rackets came into vogue, balls became harder.

What's in a name?

Where does the word 'tennis' come from? Over the years, numerous theories have been put forward, many of them delightfully fanciful. One suggests a Latin origin – the verb *tenere*, meaning to catch – because James I in his *Basilikon Doron*, the manual he wrote for his son, refers to 'playing at the caitche or tennise'. Suggested German derivations include *tanz*, presumably because the ball dances; and *tenne*, a threshing floor, because it might have been used as a court. More exotic is the notion that it came from the Egyptian town Tinnis, known to French archaeologists as 'la ville de Tennis', which was renowned for its fine linen. The suggestion is that early tennis balls were stuffed with cloth and that it might have come from this town, which was visited by French crusaders before it sank into the sea in 1226. Why you would use fine linen to stuff a tennis ball is not explained.

The most likely theory, annoyingly, is that it comes from the French word *tenez*, meaning 'take this', which players may have called out before they served. This was first suggested by John Minsheu, an English lexicographer, in 1617, when he wrote: '*tenez*, i.e. *hould*, which word the Frenchmen, the onely tennis-players, use to speake when they strike the ball at tennis'. This derivation was later accepted by Dr Johnson in his dictionary. The only problem, as the *Oxford English Dictionary* points out, is that 'no mention of this call has yet been found in French'. And why would the English aristocracy, who at the time would all have spoken fluent French, adopt this word rather than the French name for the game, *jeu de paume*. The question remains unanswered.

The first medieval picture to show the roofed gallery of a traditional
tennis court, based on monastery cloisters

The method of scoring used in the modern game – 15, 30, 40, game – existed from very early on. We have a reference to it from 1435. But its origins are far from clear. The Italian priest Antonio Scaino de Salo, who wrote the first book on tennis in 1555, put forward a vastly complicated theory and then admitted he had made it up. The French scholar Jean Gosselin in 1570 suggested another idea: a physical sextant, the sixth part of a circle, consisted of 60 degrees; each degree was made up of 60 minutes, each minute of 60 seconds. As with time. So 60 was a special number in the medieval era. It made up a whole, so the four points which made a game in tennis were worth 15 each. Gosselin too had no evidence but it sounds more plausible than the alternatives. Deuce is easier. When both players reached 40 (for some reason every authority just accepts that as a contraction of 45), the French said '*à deux*', meaning you had to play advantage and game. The English simply corrupted that to deuce. 'Love', however, is trickier (as we all know). The most amusing explanation is that it is a corruption of the French word 'l'oeuf' meaning egg, in the same way that a nought in cricket was called a 'duck's egg', quickly abbreviated to duck. There's no evidence but it's a nice thought.

Jeu des rois

We know that tennis was played from early on by the French royal family because, in 1316, Louis X – known as the Quarrelsome – met his end because of it. He played an energetic game in the Forest of Vincennes and immediately afterwards drank a beaker of cold water or cold wine, depending on which version of the story you follow, lay down to rest and caught a chill from which he died.

Fifty years later, Charles V was playing tennis on a primitive court within the Palace of the Louvre. Over the next few decades, courts were to evolve into the complex structure we call a real tennis court today. Their complexity and the cost of building them might have made this form of tennis the exclusive preserve of the rich. But we know that ordinary people were still playing the game in the street – and maybe on courts – because in 1365 Charles issued an ordinance forbidding them to do so. Like many an English monarch after him, he was concerned that such frivolous entertainments were distracting his subjects from the important matter of archery practice.

For the next three hundred years, French monarchs appear to have played tennis whenever and wherever they could. And the people seem to have followed their example. Courts sprang up everywhere. The rules were first codified by a Master Professional (such people existed by then and had their own Corporation) called Forbet in 1592. A visitor to France in 1596 reported that there were at least 250 well-appointed courts in Paris and that 7000 people made their living from the game. This was out of a city population of 300,000. Two years later an English traveller, Sir Robert Dallington, reported that there were sixty courts in Orléans alone. 'Of this I am sure,' he wrote, 'that if there were in other places the like proportion, ye should have two Tennis Courts, for every one Church through France.' He concluded that there were probably more tennis players in France than ale-drinkers, which seemed to disturb him.

During the eighteenth century, interest in tennis began to wane. By 1783, there were only fifty-four courts left in the whole of France, just thirteen of them in Paris. The final irony came in Versailles in 1789. Under intense political pressure, Louis XVI had been forced to call a meeting of the Estates General – the First Estate (the Clergy), the Second Estate (the Nobility) and the Third Estate (the Commons). In an act of defiance, the Third Estate, supported by many of the clergy and a number of radical nobles, declared themselves to be the National Assembly, representing 'the People'. To stop them convening, the King ordered the closure of the Salle des États where they were due to meet. The Assembly moved instead to the King's tennis court, where they took an oath that they would not disband until they had given France a constitution. The artist David recorded the event in a painting called *The Tennis Court Oath*. It was an early step on the road to the revolution which was to cost the King his head.

The game of kings

The English in the Middle Ages seem to have been almost as keen on tennis as the French. The game was probably first played in Britain in the thirteenth century. We know it was popular by the fourteenth century because of the frequent attempts made to ban it. Edward III issued an edict against it in 1365 (the same year Charles V was prohibiting it in France). Richard II tried again in 1389 and Henry IV in 1410. As ever, the idea was to encourage people to spend their leisure time practising archery. Such laws did not, of course, apply to the upper classes. In the sixteenth century, the nobility and anyone with an income of more than £100 a year could keep a tennis court on their property. Everyone else had to apply for a licence and there were heavy fines for transgressors.

We know from a number of sources that the French Dauphin sent a set of tennis balls to Henry V as a present in 1414 and we have accounts for the supply of balls to every subsequent king from Henry VI onwards. The Tudors were particularly fond of the game. Henry VII played at courts in Woodstock, Wycombe, Westminster, Sheen and Windsor. There was an interesting moment when he entertained Philip,

Archduke of Austria and King of Castile, in 1506. He arranged a tennis match between Philip and the Marquess of Dorset. Philip used a racket and, even though rackets were at that time at a primitive stage, this gave him such an advantage that he gave the Marquess 15 points in each game.

The young Henry VIII was particularly fond of sports and especially tennis. The Venetian ambassador at the time painted a fetching portrait of him around 1519: 'His Majesty is twenty-nine years old and extremely handsome; nature could not have done more for him; he is much handsomer than any other sovereign in Christendom; a great deal handsomer than the King of France; very fair, and his whole frame admirably proportioned ... He is extremely fond of tennis, at which game it is the prettiest thing in the world to see him play, his fair skin glowing through a shirt of the finest texture.'

It may have been a pretty sight, but that does not mean that Henry always won. A contemporary writing around the same time said that 'the Kynge thys tyme was moche entysed to playe at tennes and at dice, which appetite, certayn craftie persones about hym perceyuynge, brought in Frenchmen and Lombardes, to make wagers with hym, and so he lost moch money'. It was Henry who built the tennis court at Hampton Court which is still in use today. He built four more at the Palace of Whitehall.

While tennis continued to flourish among the ruling classes, it remained theoretically illegal for the bulk of the population. In 1555–6, some former licences were revoked in an 'Acte to make voyde dyvers Lycences of Houses wherein unlawful Games bee used'. But the regulations don't seem to have been too effective. In 1558, the year Elizabeth I came to the throne, a distinguished Frenchman called Maître Etienne Perlin reported that in England 'you may commonly see artisans, such as hatters and joiners, playing at tennis for a crown, which is not often seen elsewhere, particularly on a working day'. Which may be why there were so many attempts to ban it.

Elizabeth loved watching tennis, and James I thought it was a suitable game for his son and heir Henry to play. It is said it may have contributed to Henry's death at the age of eighteen, but his younger brother Charles still took it up equally enthusiastically. He continued playing as King all through the Civil War. Oliver Cromwell inevitably banned the game but the future Charles II played throughout his exile in France and immediately rebuilt the court at Hampton Court after the Restoration in 1660. He also constructed new courts at Windsor

James, Duke of York, playing tennis in 1641,
a year before the start of the Civil War

and his beloved Newmarket. But towards the end of the seventeenth century, the game began to lose popularity. James II never had time to play it and William and Mary were not interested (even though the court at Hampton Court was rebuilt again and still bears William's monogram).

In the eighteenth century, not much tennis was played. In 1737, the famous tennis court in James Street off the Haymarket began to turn away from tennis to become a place of entertainment, first as Punch's Theatre and then as the New Theatre. There was a brief revival in the middle of the century because the Prince of Wales – Poor Fred – was fond of the game. But, in yet another example of tennis being an often mortal diversion for royalty, it may have killed him. Horace Walpole writes in 1751 that 'he had had a blow upon his stomach in the summer by a fall, from which he had often felt great pains ... he was dead! An imposthume [abscess] had broken, which, on his body being opened, the physicians were of opinion had not been occasioned by the fall, but from a blow of a tennis-ball three years before.'

In the eighteenth century there was a modest revival of what we now call real tennis. A new court was built in Brighton in 1836 and another at Lord's Cricket Ground in 1839, which was to become the head-quarters of the game. There was renewed interest at Oxford and Cambridge and in the second half of the century new courts were built in some of the grandest private houses. By now this kind of tennis had definitely become a minority sport purely for the wealthy. It was soon to be completely overshadowed by a new variation on its theme. But before that could happen, another new game raged briefly through Victorian middle-class society, only to fade away almost as quickly as it had come.

The crookey craze

Sometime in the 1830s, a game was developed in Ireland which involved mallets, large balls, six hoops and a peg. It was called 'crookey'. It reached the mainland early in the 1850s where it was rather mis-leadingly renamed 'croquet' – it had nothing to do with France. It was an instant hit. Before long no rectory, vicarage or country house was complete without its croquet lawn.

The success of croquet was made possible by a new development: the manufacturing and marketing by Alexander Shanks of Arbroath and Thomas Green of Leeds of the 'garden mowing machine'. The manicured lawn required by the game – and which gave it a lot of its elegant appeal – would have been hard to achieve if grass still had to be cut by scythe. The other reason for the game's instant popularity was that it was the first outdoor sport which could be played on equal terms by women and men.

The language of croquet

Over the years, there have been two different ways of ending a croquet match. In Victorian times, the winning player had to drive his or her ball through two hoops which crossed each other at right angles, forming a dome from which a bell was suspended. The winning ball thus rang the bell. Croquet lovers swear, a little improbably, that this is the origin of the phrase to 'ring a bell', meaning to recall a distant and vague memory. They are perhaps on firmer ground with the modern way of ending a match, by which the winner has to strike his or her ball against a coloured peg in the middle of the lawn. This is called 'pegging out'. That is why, it is claimed, when you finally come to the end of the game of life, you are sometimes said to 'peg out'.

For a decade and a half, croquet spread throughout Britain and the Empire. As a sport, it was initially wonderfully shambolic. The basic rules varied according to whose set you had bought and almost every household introduced variations of its own. It wasn't until 1866 that a man called Walter Whitmore first attempted to write a coherent set of common rules. (They were superseded by the Conference Laws of 1870.) Two years later, Whitmore was one of a group of people who formed the All England Croquet Club and subsequently rented some land on which to play near Wimbledon railway station.

This codification of the game was to prove a complete disaster. For most Sunday afternoon players, the game suddenly became far too scientific. Here's an example: most casual players over the years have delighted in the practice of putting their ball beside someone else's, putting their foot firmly on their own ball and then knocking their opponent as far away as possible. That move was actually made illegal in 1870. The game was just no fun any more. There was also a growing demand for a summer garden sport which was a little more energetic. But what could you do with your old croquet lawn?

Enter Major Walter Clopton Wingfield.

'Sticky' and the Major

Wingfield came from one of the oldest families in England, which could trace its origins back to well before the Norman Conquest. He was born in 1833 in the house of his grandfather, the vicar of Ruabon in the North Wales county of Denbighshire. As a young man, he was commissioned into the prestigious 1st Dragoon Guards. He served in India, where he married Alice Cleveland, the daughter of his general, and saw action in the China campaign of 1860 and the capture of Peking. He returned to England in 1861 and joined the

Major Walter Clopton Wingfield, Welsh-born eccentric
and inventor of the game of Lawn Tennis

Montgomeryshire Yeomanry, where he was eventually made a major, and became a member of the Honourable Corps of Gentlemen-at-Arms, the ceremonial bodyguards of the monarch. He moved with his family to London in 1867.

There is no evidence to suggest that the Major was ever particularly

good at sports, but he liked inventing things. By his own account, he began work on his new game in the spring of 1873. His encounters with Lord Lansdowne and friends probably took place in the summer of that year. His idea was to produce a set which contained everything required to play the game. He sourced the thin grey balls, made of the new substance called vulcanized rubber (see box on page 284) in Germany. The bats came from Jeffries and Mallings, who supplied players of both real tennis and rackets. He spent the winter writing a booklet containing full instructions.

On 23 February 1874 he was awarded a provisional patent for his invention. It contained the essence of the modern game but differed in a number of ways. The court had an hourglass shape, the net being narrower than the baseline. The net itself had 'wings'. One side of the net was for serving and had a central serving crease. The other side was for receiving and looked more like a modern court. Only the server could score. If he lost the point, his opponent took over serving. Wingfield adopted the 'rackets' system of scoring, which was 15 points (known as 'aces') for a game.

Armed with his patent, Wingfield went to the press, with spectacular results. The following paragraph appeared in the London *Court Journal*, compulsory reading for the upper class, on 7 March:

We hear of a new and interesting game coming out, which is likely to attract public notice, now blasé with croquet and on the *qui vive* for novelty. It has been patented under the name of 'Sphairistike or lawn tennis'. It has been tested at several country houses, and has been found full of healthy excitement, besides being capable of much scientific play. The game is in a box not much larger than a double gun case, and contains, besides balls and bats, a portable court, which can be erected on any ordinary lawn, and is ornamental as well as useful.

On the same day the *Army and Navy Gazette*, read by the military throughout the Empire, reported: 'A new game has just been patented by Major Wingfield, late 1st Dragoon Guards, which, if we mistake not, will become a national pastime.' They said it could be seen 'how

admirably the game is suited … to the barrack yard and parade
ground' and recommended it 'to relieve the monotony of barrack life'.
A few days later *The Field*, read not just all over Britain but also

*The cover of Major Wingfield's booklet of rules,
first published in February 1874*

throughout the colonies and the United States, reprinted large parts of
the Major's booklet in its 'Pastimes' section. This was edited under the
nom de plume of 'Cavendish' by one Henry Jones, who happened to
be the cousin of Walter Whitmore and a co-founder of the All England
Croquet Club.

The effect was electric. Sphairistike, which was quickly shortened to
'Sticky', swept the country within weeks and the English-speaking
world within months. The Prince of Wales bought a set, as did most of
the crowned heads of Europe. More than a thousand sets of the
Major's game were sold and other manufacturers quickly started to
produce their own copies. The croquet lawns of Britain had been
transformed. And the idea began to spread around the world. We
know that by August, 'Sticky' was being played at Nahant, a small sea-
side resort just ten miles outside Boston. Devotees of the old traditional
game started calling it 'real' tennis to differentiate it from the new
upstart.

But the Major's success did not come without a price.

New balls, please

In February 1839, so the story goes, Charles Goodyear walked into his local general store in Woburn, Massachusetts. In his hand he had a rather messy-looking rubber concoction. He was excited. He wanted to show off his latest formula for mixing gum and sulphur, which he was convinced was going to work. His neighbours standing around the stove chuckled. Not again, they thought. They had heard it all before.

Goodyear was obsessed with rubber. Born in 1800, he had been a partner in his father's hardware business, but a bad investment decision had tipped the company into bankruptcy in 1830. Out of work, Charles decided that his future lay in rubber. There had been a 'rubber fever' in the early 1830s, but it had fizzled out. The apparent wonder product was found to freeze and break in cold weather and melt and stick to everything when it was hot. Goodyear was convinced that he could find a way of stabilizing the gum. Years of experimentation had put him in and out of debtors' prison and driven his family into poverty – the local farmers in Woburn gave his children milk and let them dig half-grown potatoes for food.

But he remained convinced that he could solve the problem. Faced with resigned and quizzical looks in the store, he became agitated. His latest sample flew from his hand and landed on the pot-bellied stove. Distraught, he went to scrape it off. He found that instead of melting, which he'd expected, it had charred like leather. And around the edges was a dry, springy rim. After so many years of experimenting, Goodyear understood immediately the significance of what had happened. He had solved the problem of making this substance weatherproof. He had invented vulcanized rubber.

He never made any money out of his invention. A hopeless business-man, he died in 1860 more than $200,000 in debt. The Goodyear Tire and Rubber Company, today the largest rubber business in the world, was founded thirty-eight years after his death and named after him. But what he did had a huge effect. Not only did it make possible the growth of the automobile industry, it also gave the world a ball that would bounce on grass.

By accident, he had enabled a brand new sport to spring from the shadow of one of the oldest games known to man.

Jealousy and chaos

The huge popularity of 'Sticky' provoked copious correspondence in *The Field*. The letters can be split into two types. The first disputed Wingfield's claim to have invented lawn tennis. One said that the game had been played at Ancrum, the house of Sir William Scott in Roxburghshire, as early as 1864. The future Bishop of Bath and Wells, Lord Arthur Hervey, claimed to have played outdoor tennis on the lawn of his rectory in Suffolk. Another correspondent said a similar game was popular in Leyton, Essex, in the late 1860s. They may all have had some kind of point, but the fact remains that none of them had tried to spread the word about their version of the game. The rapid growth of interest in lawn tennis was entirely due to the efforts of Major Wingfield.

A more serious claim, some thought, came from a solicitor from Leamington called Harry Gem. He wrote to say that he and his Spanish-born friend Augurio Perera had invented a game fifteen years earlier when they both lived in Birmingham. They had called it *pelota* – the Basque name for a ball game – and had played it on Señor Perera's lawn. Both men had moved with their families to Leamington Spa in 1872, and there they had founded a club to play the game on the lawn of a local hotel. It seems to have been a small affair – the only other known players were a pair of local doctors – but many have claimed since that it was the first lawn tennis club. But it was only renamed the Leamington Lawn Tennis Club in 1874 after the Major's game had been widely publicized.

The interesting thing about Gem's letter is that it made no attack on

The much-loved hour-glass shape of Major Wingfield's court
as illustrated in the first edition of his rules

Walter Wingfield and no claim to have been the inventor of the new sport. Gem wanted to take part in the debate which was the subject of the second type of correspondence in *The Field*: had the Major got the rules right? Even Wingfield himself didn't seem to be sure: he issued revised rules in August 1874 and a further set in November of that year. Many others put forward their own ideas. John H. Hale, a cricketer who had been captain of Sussex and yet another co-founder of the All England Croquet Club, came up with his own version of the game which he named (and marketed) after his house as Germains Lawn Tennis. The major difference from 'Sticky' was that it used a rectangular court.

There was a danger that the new sport would be swamped in confusion. In December, the Secretary of the MCC wrote to *The Field* pointing out that as recently as 1872 the club's Tennis and Rackets Subcommittee had revised the rules of real tennis. Perhaps they could do the same for lawn tennis? There was general agreement and a meeting was scheduled for Lord's in March the following year. (There was an intriguing footnote to these plans. A member of the subcommittee let it be known he had developed a better ball. He had found Wingfield's uncovered rubber version difficult to control, especially in wet weather. He had asked his wife to cover one in white flannel and it had been a great improvement. Tennis balls have been so covered ever since.)

At the Lord's meeting, both Wingfield and Hale laid out their courts and demonstrated their versions of the game. Many others had their say, although some were conspicuous by their absence – Harry Gem did not attend. The subcommittee adjourned to consider its view and reported two months later. It made some changes, most notably pushing the server back to the baseline and requiring him or her to serve into the two areas of the court on either side of the centre line between the net and the service line. But they kept Major Wingfield's hourglass-shaped court.

This was enough for the Major. Shortly afterwards, he wrote a letter to *The Field* effectively removing himself from future discussion of tennis. He said he was indebted to the Lord's committee for its trouble: 'I write this letter simply because I felt it necessary, on account of the daily letters I receive asking me what I think of the new rules, to state that I think their labours have been most successful and that they have made the game at once simple and excellent.' He notes that they have adopted his patented hourglass court, which he says is used by them 'with my full sanction and approval'.

That was the last comment he ever made on the game he had invented. His interest had been in the idea; once the important questions had been answered, he wanted to move on. Many years later, after his death, he came under attack as being an impostor and a money-grubbing cheat. There is no evidence for that. He never tried to enforce his patent against the many other companies who copied his idea (including Hale) and he did not renew the patent when it came up in 1877. He made (and sought) very little money from his invention. His subsequent life was filled with tragedy. His wife went mad and all three of his much-loved sons died at a young age. But he remained cheerful and in his way productive: he invented a new bicycle and devised a pipe tobacco mixture – the 'Wingfield' – which is still on sale. He died in 1912. His grave in Kensal Green Cemetery in north-west London was hidden from view by grass and vines for many years but is now maintained by the Wimbledon Lawn Tennis Museum.

His hourglass court, however, did not last for long.

Wimbledon

On 25 February 1875 Henry Jones of the All England Croquet Club, otherwise known as 'Cavendish' of *The Field*, proposed a motion that a court should be set aside at Wimbledon for lawn tennis. The new game was a great success and in November 1876 it was decided to change the name of the club to the All England Croquet and Lawn Tennis Club. On 2 June 1877 John Walsh, another co-founder and editor of *The Field* who was then club secretary, proposed holding a national lawn tennis championship, open to all amateurs. The plan was to hold it just five weeks later, starting on 9 July. In the meantime, a sub-committee was set up to revise the rules yet again.

Much of what they came up with has survived the test of time. They changed the size of the court to 26 yards by 9 yards, finally getting rid of Major Wingfield's hourglass shape. They adopted the old tennis scoring method of 15, 30, 40, advantage, game. And they allowed one fault in the service. Over the next few years the club, initially in conjunction with the MCC, made adjustments to the height of the net and the weight and size of balls. Apart from that, the shape of the modern game was set. The only major changes since then have been the introduction of open championships – in other words professional-ism – in 1968; and the tiebreak in 1971.

Back in 1877, there were twenty-two entries for the first cham-pionship. The players wore white flannel shirts and trousers, often with a cap, a tie and a schoolboy belt round their waist. A majority of con-testants were real tennis players and they were confident their ability to 'cut' the ball heavily would bring victory. But, in the end, two hundred spectators paid a shilling to watch Old Harrovian rackets player

Spencer Gore beat W. C. Marshall 6–1, 6–2, 6–4 in the final. His tactic was to put his opponent on the defensive and rush right up to the net and volley away the return. Often he'd lean right over the net to hit the ball, which was legal at the time. The net was three feet three inches high at the centre, but five feet high at the posts, which made passing shots difficult. He had outmanoeuvred the real tennis players.

The next year's championship had an All Comers' Round, the winner of which then met the reigning champion in the Challenge Round (this system lasted until 1921). The challenger turned out to be Patrick Hadow, a coffee planter on holiday from Ceylon who had been persuaded to try his hand at this new game. Spencer Gore once again adopted the tactics which had been so successful the year before. At first, Hadow's attempts to pass him failed because of the height of the net at the posts. Out of desperation, he invented an entirely new stroke. 'I was told the lob had not been introduced before,' he wrote years later, 'certainly I had never tried it before. It was natural enough, though, with a tall, long-legged and long-armed man sprawling all over the net, ready to reach over at the ball before it had even reached the net.' Hadow won 7–5, 6–1, 9–7.

Hadow's innovation put an early stop to those players planning to emulate Gore's volleying tactics. For the next three years, rackets players dominated with seemingly interminable baseline rallies (or 'rests', as they were called then). One such rally, not at Wimbledon, was counted at 81 strokes. There began to be real concern that the game, like croquet before it, would bore itself to death. But help was at hand in the shape of twins from the alleged cradle of lawn tennis, Leamington Spa.

The game evolves

Spencer Gore, the first Wimbledon champion, later said that what lawn tennis was waiting for in those early days was the arrival of a completely new race, a generation of young players who had grown up with the game. That generation arrived in 1881 in the shape of William and

Ernest Renshaw. They played something very close to the modern game. They perfected the overhead service, which had first been tried unsuccessfully in 1878 but was now becoming more common. They turned it into what their contemporaries called a real 'hammer' and were widely criticized by their opponents for resorting to 'nothing but brute force and ignorance'. They also invented the smash, which for years was called the 'Renshaw Smash'. And they changed the nature of the game by volleying not from right up by the net but from near the service line, which meant they could cover the whole court.

They made an immediate impact. In 1881, William sailed through the All Comers' Round. In the Challenge Round he faced the two-time

*Early stars of lawn tennis: William Renshaw is on the extreme
right, his brother Ernest is seated left*

champion, the Rev. J. T. Hartley, a supreme baseline player. Renshaw won 6–0, 6–1, 6–1 in just 37 minutes, the shortest final ever. It was a revolution and a revelation. Over the next seven years, William won the championship six more times and his brother won it once (when William was suffering from the first recorded case of tennis elbow).

In 1879, an Irish championship began in Dublin which for a while

enjoyed almost as much prestige as Wimbledon. It also set a precedent
by including a ladies' championship. That same year, the Oxford University Club inaugurated a national doubles championship. In 1884,
Wimbledon took over the doubles championship – inevitably won by
the Renshaw twins – and started a ladies' tournament, which was won
that first year by Miss Maud Watson, a parson's daughter. She won
again the next year. But there was a female version of the Renshaws
waiting in the wings.

Miss Lottie Dod

The nature of early sport was such that there have not been many
opportunities in this book to write about women. Tennis is the exception. And the most exceptional of early women tennis players was Miss
Lottie Dod. She first appeared at the age of 15 in 1887, when she won
the final with the loss of just two games. She repeated her victory the

Lottie Dod won her first Wimbledon title aged fifteen,
for the loss of just two games

next year, then chose not to compete in the next two championships. She did, however, at the age of eighteen, contribute a chapter to the *Badminton Library* book on tennis in 1890. It shows her to be every bit as feisty as any modern ladies' champion.

She begins by praising Major Wingfield's invention as 'avowedly a game for every age and every sex'. But, she goes on, for a while there was a danger that men's and ladies' tennis 'should be entirely separated'. Old newspapers confirm, she says, that at first the game was thought to be beyond both the body and the mind of women. 'It was represented, not it may be hoped by ladies, but on their behalf, that no lady could understand tennis scoring.' She quotes many proposals that women should be given every possible advantage when playing against men.

'Most of these suggestions were made through the medium of *The Field* newspaper,' she reports, 'and the editor of that journal was thus for a time made the ruler of the game, as well as an arbiter of fashion, credited with the ability to regulate not only the weight of a lady's racket, but also the length of her skirt. For a moment, in fact, he was invested with the prerogative of an irresponsible despot.' Ouch.

The matter was settled by the introduction of the Ladies' Championship in Dublin in 1879, Bath in 1881, the Northern Championship in 1882, Cheltenham in 1883 and finally Wimbledon in 1884. Women were playing under the same rules as men: '. . . there can be no doubt that healthy rivalry and keen following of a noble game is as beneficial as it is novel to ladies'. She goes on with some hard words for some of her fellow female players: 'Ladies should learn to run, and run their hardest, too, not merely stride. They would find (if they tried) that many a ball, seemingly out of reach, could be returned with ease; but instead of running hard, they go a few steps and exclaim: "Oh! I can't," and stop.'

But, she concludes, women do play under a severe disadvantage. 'Ladies' dress . . . is a matter for grave consideration; for how can they ever hope to play a sound game when their dresses impede the free movement of every limb? In many cases their very breathing is rendered difficult. A suitable dress is sorely needed, and hearty indeed would be the thanks of puzzled lady players to the individual who invented an easy and pretty costume.'

She went on to win three more Wimbledon titles. She then retired to play golf and won the ladies' championship at that game as well. She was also a hockey international and an Olympic medal-winning archer.

The game spreads

In 1888, just fourteen years after Major Wingfield had launched his new invention, the Lawn Tennis Association (LTA) was established to bring together all the new clubs which had sprung up around the nation. In return for being granted the perpetual right to hold the national championship, the All England Club relinquished its role in formulating the rules of tennis to the new LTA. The structure of British tennis was thus established. Similar initiatives were going on around the world.

As we've seen, a set of Major Wingfield's 'Sphairistike' had reached New England. By the following spring other sets had reached Newport, Rhode Island. All these sets were in private hands. But that same spring, Miss Mary Ewing Outerbridge came across a set of 'Sticky' at the British barracks in Bermuda. She managed to acquire one and took it back with her to New York. There she persuaded her brother, A. Emilius Outerbridge, who was at that time a director of the Staten Island Cricket and Baseball Club, to let her set up a court in a corner of the club's cricket ground. This caught the attention of many other clubs and the game began to spread.

In 1880, another of Mary's brothers, Eugenius H. Outerbridge, then secretary of the club, proposed to hold a 'national championships' on the club's courts. It began on 1 September and was reported by the New York papers to be a fine and elegant occasion. But they didn't mention the results. This may have been because the handsome silver cup bearing the words 'The Champion Lawn-Tennis Player of America' was won by an Englishman, O. E. Woodhouse, who happened to be in America at the time. He had reached the final of the All Comers' Round at Wimbledon earlier in the year, but it was still a shock. Further consternation was caused when Dick Sears and Dr James Dwight from Boston, who had played on that first court laid out at Nahant in 1874, found the balls being used were two-thirds of the size of the regulation English balls they normally used. After much protestation, they were knocked out early on.

To avoid such confusion in future, it was agreed that a supreme authority was needed. On 5 May 1881, a notice appeared in the journal *American Cricketer* announcing the inaugural meeting of the United States National Lawn Tennis Association in New York. That meeting adopted the rules of the All England Club and proposed that a national championships should be held at Newport at the end of August. This time the balls were to Dick Sears' liking and he won the first of his seven national titles.

From then on, tennis spread steadily around the world. The first State Championship was held in Victoria in Australia in 1881, under the auspices of the Melbourne Cricket Club. New South Wales followed four years later. The first French championship was held in 1891 and was won by an Englishman. Lawn tennis was included in the first modern Olympics held in Athens in 1896 and once again the first men's singles gold medal was won by Great Britain in the form of Irishman John Boland. In 1900, the Davis Cup was inaugurated in New England. The 'International Lawn Tennis Challenge Trophy' was donated by one of the leading American players, Dwight Davis, who promptly helped defeat the English team to win the first tournament. From the start the Davis Cup was open to challengers from any country which had an official association. That first year that included Australia, South Africa, Canada and India, but only Britain and the United States had chosen to take part. Within a couple of years Austria, Belgium, France, Germany, Holland, Norway, Sweden and Switzerland had joined the ranks of potential challengers.

Britain won the Davis Cup in 1903 and held it till 1907, when Australasia (including New Zealand) took over. It was the beginning of the end of British supremacy in tennis. That same year an Australian won the men's singles at Wimbledon for the first time. An Englishman, A. W. Gore, won for the next two years, but since 1910 only one Briton (Fred Perry from 1934 to 1936) has won the title. Britain has fared a little better in the ladies' singles, but since 1937 only three British women – Angela Mortimer, Ann Jones and Virginia Wade – have won the title.

Major Walter Wingfield would not have been too perturbed. For him, getting the idea right was what counted. His idea has not done too badly.

ASSOCIATED SPORTS (SORT OF)

Rackets

Rackets is a sporting rags-to-riches story. It began life in the debtors' prisons of London, escaped into the taverns of the town, became a professional sport with champions along the lines of prizefighting and then wheedled its way into some of the best public schools. As a result it became – and remains – an elite sport of the wealthy, played predominantly in the English-speaking world.

Rackets seems to have begun fairly early in the eighteenth century in London's two main debtors' prisons, the King's Bench and the Fleet. Gentlemen who were incarcerated until they could pay off their creditors used to amuse themselves in the prison yard with a variety of games, including skittles and 'fives', a version of handball (using the palm of the hand, as in *jeu de paume*) played against a wall. Some brought tennis rackets with them and improvised a game against any convenient wall, with or without side walls. Visitors were allowed to come and watch matches: one Major Campbell was particularly admired at the King's Bench, but then he did have plenty of time to practise. He was there for fourteen years.

Dickens's Mr Pickwick is unfortunate enough to find himself in the Fleet at one point. He describes a game being played in a court with a

Rackets grew out of the debtors' prisons of London,
but became a sport of the wealthy

front wall and one side wall, watched by idle and listless inmates from
the yard and the surrounding windows. In 1814 there were four courts
at the King's Bench and six racket masters to look after them. Clearly
the authorities did not want bankrupt gentlemen to become bored.

By the 1830s, the sporting journalist Pierce Egan reported that there
were by then several open courts outside the prisons. The 'Open Court
Championships', a professional affair, were played at the Belvedere
Tavern in Pentonville. Other venues included the Eagle Tavern in City
Road, the White Bear in Kennington, White Conduit House and the
Rosemary Branch in Peckham, salubrious one and all, no doubt.
There were also reports of courts in Bristol, Bath, Birmingham and
Belfast.

Harrow was the first school to adopt the game, probably in the
1820s. It was played in an open court in the newly enlarged schoolyard. By mid-century, covered courts were becoming popular. The
MCC built one at Lord's in 1844 and the Prince's Club opened in
1853 with several covered courts. Oxford and Cambridge both had

courts by 1855. By this time the pub courts were closing down and rackets was becoming exclusively a sport for the wealthy. It remains so today. Fourteen public schools have courts today, and there are five rackets clubs in Britain. There are eight active rackets courts in the USA. But the game's enthusiasts still manage to organize a regular world championship.

Squash

Squash evolved from rackets at Harrow School by way of another schoolboy game called fives. Rackets was originally played at Harrow in a part of the schoolyard known as 'The Corner'. It became immensely popular and in 1850 the school built two new outdoor

Squash developed at Harrow School
from the new sport of rackets

rackets courts. They still couldn't meet the demand; younger boys were forced to try and play in the much smaller stone-walled yards of their boarding houses or in village alleys. The rock-hard balls and heavy bats of rackets were difficult to use in these confined spaces so the boys, being an enterprising lot, started using a softer rubber ball and sawn-off rackets to play a slower game which they called baby rackets or soft rackets.

In 1865, the school opened a new enclosed rackets court and a number of fives courts. Fives was a handball game – essentially rackets played with a gloved hand – which came in two main varieties, Eton fives and Rugby fives, which each used a slightly different court. When the new complex opened, the rackets court (which is still in use) and the Eton fives courts were immediately popular. But the Rugby fives courts were never used for their intended purpose. Instead, the boys found them perfect for their 'baby rackets' game, which became known as squash because the ball 'squashed' when it hit the wall. They became the world's first squash courts.

Over the next fifty years or so, the game spread steadily. The first private court was built in Oxford in 1883 and other courts appeared at Lord's, Cambridge, the Royal Automobile Club and Queen's Club. But they were all slightly different and those who used them played according to different rules and even with different balls. It wasn't until 1928 that the Squash Rackets Association was formed and the rules in Britain were standardized.

By this time, squash had already travelled around the world. Indeed the first national body, the US Squash Racquets Association, had been formed in Philadelphia as early as 1904. Predictably, it used a different ball and a different-size court from the British. Other courts cropped up all around the globe, of all shapes and sizes. Professional tournaments began in America in 1914 and international competition followed in 1922. After World War II, the sport's popularity soared. The International Squash Rackets Federation was formed in 1967, though it still couldn't standardize ball type and court size among the many countries which were now playing the game. In 1992, it became the World Squash Federation and finally managed to get most nations playing by the same rules. By 1994, 15 million people were playing the sport.

Today, 130 nations play squash on some 47,000 courts. More than twenty nations have players in the top one hundred in the men's world rankings. Australia has traditionally been a major force, the Egyptians are very strong, but some of the most exciting players ever have come from Pakistan, an extraordinary feat for a country which has fewer than 400 courts. Britain, in the meantime, has not done badly. Those Harrow schoolboys were on to something.

Badminton

Badminton derives from the ancient children's game known in this country as 'battledore and shuttlecock'. It involved two players with small rackets made of parchment or stretched rows of gut trying to keep a shuttlecock in the air for as long as possible. There's evidence that this game existed in Greece 2000 years ago and spread from there to China, Japan, Thailand and India. That's significant in the light of developments in the modern game.

An early depiction of the ancient children's game
known as 'battledore and shuttlecock'

The game was called 'Poona' in India and became popular among British Army officers serving in the Raj in the middle of the nineteenth century. In the 1860s they began to bring a competitive version back

to Britain. In 1873 it was played at Badminton House, the Gloucestershire estate of the Duke of Beaufort, and it is from that event that the
sport derives its name (or so it is said; there is precious little evidence
for it).

Until 1887, the game was played under the rules that had been
haphazardly brought back from India. That year, the Bath Badminton
Club tried to standardize the regulations according to English taste.
In 1893, the Badminton Association of England published the first set
of rules and officially launched the sport at a house called Dunbar
in Portsmouth. They went on to hold the first All England Open
Badminton Championships in 1899.

The Badminton World Federation was formed in 1934 and it
became an Olympic sport in 1992. Britain is still an enthusiastic competitor but, in the modern era, dominance has moved back to the
Far East with countries such as China, Indonesia, South Korea and
Malaysia in the forefront. It's an intriguing story of sporting entrepre-
neurism. Enterprising Britons a long way from home come across an
interesting local game, bring it back to Britain, make it into a sport with
an obviously English name and then give it back to the world. Who, of
course, promptly take it over.

Table Tennis

As the popularity of lawn tennis exploded in the 1880s, the ever-
enterprising Victorian upper class tried to improvise an indoor version
of the game which could be played as an after-dinner diversion. Books
were used to form the net, balls were fashioned out of the end of cham-
pagne corks or balls of string and anything to hand, such as cigar-box
lids, were used as bats.

The popularity of this new entertainment did not go unnoticed by
the manufacturers of games. They tried all kinds of variations, including card games, a tiddlywinks version and board and dice games – the
first use of the name 'Table Tennis' was on a board and dice game
which appeared in New York in 1887. The first 'action' version was
patented in England in 1890: it included strung rackets, a 30-mm

rubber ball covered with cloth, a low wooden fence all around the table and large nets down each side, presumably to protect surrounding ornaments. A year later the well-known game company John Jaques of London introduced their 'Gossima' game, with a 50-mm cork ball, a foot-high net and bats made of parchment stretched on a frame, which made a ping-pong noise.

Neither of these games really worked. The problem was the balls – the rubber bounced too far and too fast, while the cork ones hardly bounced at all. The idea fizzled out until an English enthusiast brought some novelty celluloid balls back from America in 1900. They had just the right kind of bounce. Shortly afterwards hard bats covered with stippled rubber were introduced. John Jaques teamed up with the toy store Hamley's to reintroduce their game, this time patented as 'Gossima or Ping Pong'. Other manufacturers produced variations under such names as Whiff Whaff, Pom-Pom, Pim-Pam, Netto, Parlour Tennis and ... Table Tennis. Fairly quickly Ping Pong and Table Tennis emerged as the favoured names. They spawned two different 'Associations' which played according to different rules. To resolve the confusion, the two bodies agreed to amalgamate in 1903 to form the Table Tennis Association. But it was too late to stop the game going into a serious decline in England. The Association ceased to exist. Elsewhere, however, it was a different story. The game became popular in Eastern Europe, and via Japan it was also introduced to China and Korea.

After World War I the sport, which had been kept alive by a few enthusiasts, began a revival. The Table Tennis Association was reconstituted in 1922 and established standard rules. In 1926, the International Table Tennis Federation was established and the first World Championships were held in London. Three years later Budapest hosted the second Championships, in which the men's event was won by subsequent Wimbledon champion Fred Perry. But that was a rare British triumph. Until the 1950s, during what is known as the 'Hard Bat Era', the sport was dominated by Europeans, but most of them came from Eastern Europe.

In 1952, Hiroji Satoh of Japan became the first player to win the

World Championship using a sponge-covered bat. This new innovation made the game faster and allowed for much more use of spin. It also seems to have introduced the era of Asian domination. Table tennis became an Olympic sport in 1988. Since then, in the men's and women's singles and doubles, only one non-Asian has won a gold medal – Jan-Ove Waldner of Sweden in the men's singles in 1992. Since 1981, the Chinese have achieved a clean sweep of all World Championship gold medals five times. Nary a Brit has featured.

11.
HOCKEY
(AND MAYBE EVEN ICE HOCKEY)

MODERN HOCKEY WAS developed in the suburbs of London in the second half of the nineteenth century, but its adherents are prone to claim that it is one of the most ancient of games. One of the most fanciful fragments of evidence they produce is a painting from a tomb at Beni-Hassan in the Nile delta dating from around 2000 BC. It shows two men who appear to be about to 'bully off' at hockey. Another example is a sculpture from an ancient wall built to protect Athens in the fifth century BC. It shows young men with curved sticks who appear to be involved in some kind of game. Again, two of them seem to be engaged in a 'bully'. What those who offer this evidence fail to address is how the ancient Egyptians and the Greeks came to know of a strange

An apparent depiction of a game of hockey, minus the shorts,
found at the base of a wall in Athens in 1922

ritual invented by the Victorians and virtually abandoned just eighty years later.

Stick-and-ball games

The reality is that most societies have played some form of stick-and-ball game and there is no reason why some should not have existed in the ancient world. But to describe such games as hockey is going too far. In Britain there were traditional games which bore some resemblance to hockey which were called 'bandy-ball' in England and Wales (one of the many banned by Edward III in 1365 to prevent

What looks like a game of hockey, from an early
fourteenth century illuminated manuscript

people being distracted from archery practice), 'shinty' in Scotland and 'hurling' in Ireland. The earliest mention of the word 'hockey' comes in the Galway Statutes of 1527 which ban, among other things, the 'horlinge of the litill balle with hockie stickes or staves'. The origins of the word are not clear. It might have come from the French word *hoquet*, meaning shepherd's crook; or it might be a diminutive of the English word 'hook'. It certainly seems to relate to the stick used in the game.

The rules for these games varied from village to village. Often they resembled Shrovetide football, with one parish battling against another in pretty unrestrained combat. The first slightly more organized versions of the game emerged in the public schools. There are indications it was played at Eton in the eighteenth century. Certainly by 1832 it was well established. Writing in the *Eton College Magazine*,

Hockey, from The Book of Games, *1810: many schools played hockey then, using widely differing rules*

G. W. Lyttelton, later Lord Lyttelton, said it was an old indigenous game 'never heard of beyond the channel, and almost forgotten even in England'. He went on to describe the game:

It is a game, in which, as in poetry, mediocrity is not tolerable; indeed, a bad game at hockey is one of the most stupid sights poor mortal can see; but, on the other hand, when it is played, as at Eton, with a considerable degree of dexterity, we think it one of the most elegant and gentlemanlike exercises there is, being susceptible of very graceful attitudes, and requiring great speed of foot, and skill in not missing the blow aimed at the ball; neither is it a very dangerous game, though by no means unattended by peril; for a severe blow on the shins with so weighty a weapon as a hockey stick, is attended by very great pain.

As the youthful Lyttelton suggests, the rules for the game differed at every school which played it, depending on the equipment used and where it was played. At Mill Hill, they used one-handed sticks, a rubber ball and played in the school quadrangle. At Rossall in Scotland they played on the beach. The one thing all versions had in common was that they were robust. Cassell's *Popular Educator* of 1867 says that there were few rules and a great deal of rushing after the ball. 'It will be apparent that in the rush and struggle of this description, a fall or hard knock is exceedingly likely to occur, and Hockey is therefore not a game suited to weakly or timid players.'

The first clubs

The first hockey club was at Blackheath, made up mainly of old boys from Blackheath Proprietary School. The game they played would hardly be recognized today. They used one-handed sticks and the 'ball' was a cube of leather which was boiled frequently to keep it elastic. There were fifteen players on each side, made up of a goalkeeper, two full backs, two three-quarters, three half-backs and seven forwards. If that sounds remarkably like a rugby team, it's hardly a coincidence. Blackheath were pioneers in that sport as well. And the major feature of Blackheath or 'Union' hockey was scrimmaging – the cube made passing or dribbling impractical. Players could catch the ball and make a mark, just as in rugby. They would step back four paces and take a hit either in the air or on the ground. The pitch was 200 yards long and consisted of rough heathland. It is possible that the club first started

*Hockey around 1861: probably the Blackheath game, with one
handed sticks and scant regard for anyone's shins*

meeting in the 1840s, but the earliest formal record we have is from
1861.

A few years later a very different version of the game emerged in a
suburb south-west of London. Teddington Cricket Club played its
matches in Bushy Park, with permission from the Deputy Ranger of
this royal preserve, Sir John Barton, who was also Controller of the
Royal Mint. His son John was the club captain. His members had been
looking for a while for a game they could play in the winter to keep
themselves fit. They liked hockey but, as most of them were married
men, they didn't want to play the kind of rough and ready game
favoured by Blackheath. So they decided to devise their own version.
They had enough members to field two teams of eleven. In the autumn
of 1871 they started playing on the smooth outfield of their cricket
pitch with a cricket ball. This allowed them to develop positional play,
passing, dribbling and running off the ball.

Over the next three seasons, they refined the rules of their new
game. Whenever a problem cropped up, it was resolved by the two
team captains. If their solution had a general application, it was written

down as a rule. They weren't trying to start a new sport, they just wanted to provide themselves with an agreeable form of exercise. And initially they didn't want to play anyone else. But in 1874, Richmond Football Club heard about the game and decided to give it a try. Some Teddington members went along to help them. Then Surbiton formed a club. The three started playing matches against each other and send-

By 1899, there were two hundred hockey clubs, all playing each other in friendly matches and studiously avoiding 'ruinous' competition

ing reports to the local press. The publicity encouraged the creation of more new clubs – Upper Tooting, East Surrey, Sutton and the Strollers. In 1875 they decided to form a Hockey Association. A representative of Blackheath was invited to the meeting but, according to the press reports, he decided that the way Blackheath played 'was so totally different from the game played by the other clubs that he felt it would be totally useless for him to remain and give an opinion'. The rules agreed by the new association included a scoring circle, an offside rule, and bans on raising sticks above shoulder height, left- or back-handed play, charging, tripping, collaring, kicking or shinning.

Unfortunately the new association proved to be a little premature. Enthusiasm for the new game waned. Four of the clubs folded and Richmond and Surbiton went into hibernation. Teddington were left to develop their game by themselves. Which is how they liked it.

W. Trevenen Esq.

On 30 October 1880, a special committee meeting of the Teddington Hockey Club was convened for the sole purpose of electing W. Trevenen Esq. of 'The Palace, Hampton Court' as a member. There is no record of such a person in the Palace records, which has led some to suggest that W. Trevenen was a pseudonym for the Duke of Clarence, the elder son of the Prince of Wales (later Edward VII) and therefore second in line to the throne. To support their argument, they point out that John Barton, the club captain, was the young Duke's aide-de-camp. Also, Teddington played no matches against other clubs that season and they refused to arrange any for the following season. And an unusually large number of other new members, nine, joined around the same time. Were they equerries or bodyguards?

Others argue that in fact the Duke spent most of his time at Sandringham and that for much of the period in question he was away at sea with the Royal Navy. What we know for certain is that by the time he went up to Trinity College, Cambridge, in 1883, he already knew how to play hockey, because he asked the college to start a hockey club so he could continue to enjoy the sport. It was said that 'he was wont to wield his club with more rigour than discretion'. Trinity became the first Oxbridge college to adopt hockey (and the Teddington rules) but it was quickly followed by Clare, King's and Caius. The Duke's example also seems to have sparked interest elsewhere. New clubs were formed at Molesey, Wimbledon and Ealing and the Surbiton club was revived. It is interesting that Molesey and Wimbledon both asked Trinity for a match, but not the other Cambridge colleges. This was a time of egregious social climbing.

At the beginning of 1886, the London clubs got together with

Trinity to form the second Hockey Association. Molesey and Wimbledon agreed to draft a constitution and a new set of rules which helped to put the new sport on a firm footing. Perhaps even more important was the Duke of Clarence's agreement to become the president of the new association, a decision which gave the sport instant social recognition. (He remained president until his death in 1892 from pneumonia, at the age of 28.) Not to be outdone, Blackheath got together with some clubs in the Bristol area which played according to their 'Union' rules the following year to form the National Hockey Union. But there was no disguising the fact that the Teddington or 'Association' game was very much more sophisticated. In 1895, the Union was dissolved 'owing to the Association game gaining such favour and so many Union clubs resigning their membership and adopting the Association game'.

'Popular, but ruinous, competition'

Between 1885 and 1890, the south-west London clubs ran a league which was dominated by Molesey. But in 1892 the Hockey Association made a decision which was to have major implications for the future of British hockey. They took the view that hockey was a social game played for recreation by friends. It was not about winning or losing. Therefore they agreed to ban all leagues, cups or other forms of competition. The editor of *Hockey* roared his approval: 'Such a vital decision has undoubtedly saved hockey from disaster and being sacrificed upon the altar of popular, but ruinous, competition.'

By the turn of the century, Britain had 200 hockey clubs, all playing each other in friendly matches and studiously avoiding organized competition. The game was a relaxed affair with a premium on intelligent movement, a long way from the fast pace and highly developed skills of the modern game. Such unsporting tactics as man-to-man marking and deliberately putting an opponent offside were eschewed. 'The rules were modelled for a game to be played by gentlemen as gentlemen,' said the Hockey Association. There were home internationals each year, but they were social occasions as much about paying tribute to senior players as proper competitions. It was the honour of playing for your country which counted. After each match there was a good deal of enthusiastic dining and drinking.

Women's hockey was not far behind. A women's club was founded in Molesey in 1887, quickly followed by clubs in Wimbledon and Ealing. The women's colleges at Oxford and Cambridge took up the sport, as did a considerable number of fee-paying girls' schools. In 1894

*'Our Ladies Hockey Club' in 1899: forty years later, there
were twice as many women's clubs as men's*

a past and present Newnham College side toured Ireland, which already had a Ladies' Hockey Union. In 1895 the English followed with the All England Women's Hockey Association. The real growth came after the Great War, which had given women a greater degree of independence. By 1930 there were 1200 women's clubs, by 1939 there were 2100 – more than twice as many as the men could muster. Women's home internationals attracted huge crowds, largely made up of schoolgirls. Some 68,000 watched a women's international at

Lefties' lament

In cricket, you have natural right-handed batsmen and natural left-handed batsmen (although many of them are not left-handed in any other way). In hockey, left-handers are not allowed. The rules state quite clearly that the smooth striking face of a hockey stick must be on the left side. They also prohibit hitting the ball with the rounded back of the stick. This means that the normal hockey stroke is always from right to left. A backhand stroke is permitted, but there can be no left-handed forehand shot.

Wembley in 1976, whereas men had to make do with smaller venues and crowds which rarely exceeded 5000.

Foreigners and federations

Hockey spread first to the outposts of the Empire, carried by British soldiers who found it a pleasant way of keeping fit. The Calcutta Club was founded as early as 1885 by, among others, a member of the Teddington club. At first it was for officers only, then it spread to other ranks and finally it was taken up by native Indians. They very quickly developed extraordinary sharpness and stick skills, largely, it was thought, because they were forced to play on fast baked-mud surfaces rather than the lawns of the white men's clubs. (Indeed, the Europeans, Australians and New Zealanders only began to catch up with the Indians when they started playing on artificial grass pitches.) Expansion in Europe came rather more slowly.

The story of how international hockey developed reveals a great deal about British attitudes to sport. It is best told through hockey's history at the Olympics. The first modern games in Athens in 1896 were largely about individual sports. The French tried to introduce team sports in Paris in 1900 but the Hockey Association declined, saying quite reasonably that no one else took the sport seriously. But in 1908, the Games were held in London. Curiously hockey was included at the instigation of the French, without the HA being consulted. Officially, the hosts had to enter as Great Britain, but in order to make it more of a competition, all the home countries played, along with France and Germany. England won gold, Ireland silver and Wales and Scotland shared bronze.

In 1910, a proposal to set up a European Hockey federation foundered because the HA refused to contemplate any leagues or cups. There was no hockey in the 1912 Olympics. In 1920 in Antwerp, the only teams were England, Belgium, Denmark and France. England won easily, partly because the French failed to turn up after a blow-out dinner at which they had allegedly planned to drink the English team under the table. But the English decided they wouldn't take part again because it looked dangerously like 'pot-hunting', which was not an acceptable pastime.

During the 1920 games, the International Olympic Committee (IOC) decided that all sports to be included in the Olympics in future must have a world federation, which was a problem for hockey because there wasn't one. The French put forward a proposal but the British prevaricated. As a result, there was no hockey in the 1924 Olympics. Out of frustration, the French joined with six other European nations to form the Fédération Internationale de Hockey (FIH). The British declined to join. At the time, the Hockey Association comprised 500 men's clubs, 1000 women's clubs, numerous schools and several affiliated Empire associations. Between them, the founding members of the FIH could muster just 40 clubs. Nevertheless, the FIH was recognized by the IOC as the governing body of world hockey.

Hockey was reinstated for the Amsterdam games of 1928. The European countries entered, but so for the first time did India. Britain, not being a member of the FIH, was excluded. India won easily, as they did again in Los Angeles in 1932 and Berlin in 1936.

After World War II, Britain still controlled the rules of hockey (they had the copyright) and still had more hockey clubs than the rest of the world put together. When London was chosen as the venue for the first post-war games, the Hockey Association came under great pressure to participate. This was going to be a showcase for the nation, a celebration of victory. Hockey was a British sport and we played it better than anyone else. We had to take part. The HA ruminated. In the end, they reached a decision: 'The council considered that it was advisable for a team to take part.' But that meant Britain had to join the FIH. All four home countries could have signed up as full members and started to use their considerable influence. Instead, the HA decided merely to 'adhere' as a GB group. It was enough to qualify, but meant that the FIH had to be given token membership of the HA Rules Board. In the event, it turned out Britain no longer played better than anyone else. The Great Britain team lost to India in the final.

Things could only get worse. In Helsinki in 1952 Britain won bronze. In Melbourne in 1956 it came fourth. It was the same in Rome in 1960. In Tokyo in 1964 Britain came tenth – the team members said they were surprised at the aggressive competitiveness of the other countries. The manager said that friendly matches against the other

---

Polo

Polo was often described as 'hockey on horseback' by the English tea planters and army officers who took it up in India in the 1860s. But its origins go back very much further. There are definite historical references to it being played in Persia in the first century AD, and it may be very much older. From there it spread throughout Arabia, to Tibet (*polo* is a corruption of the Tibetan word for 'ball') and to Japan and China, where it became hugely popular. It reached India in the thirteenth century. There it was discovered by the British around 1859. The first match in England was played between the 10th Hussars and the 9th Lancers on Hounslow Heath in 1869 with eight on each side and virtually no rules. By 1875, matches in Richmond Park and Hurlingham were attracting as many as 10,000 spectators. In 1876, the ubiquitous newspaper tycoon James Gordon Bennett introduced the game to the US. The first rules were drawn up by the Hurlingham Club in London in the early 1880s.

home countries did not add up to useful training. In Mexico in 1968, Britain came twelfth.

Finally, the bubble burst. The patience of British hockey players ran out. Some of the London clubs started their own league. Others followed. The HA could only stand by and watch. Wales was the first to apply for full membership of the FIH, which was still heavily influenced by France. England and Scotland had no choice but to follow, albeit reluctantly. The no-competition rule was finally abandoned.

Did it make a difference? Maybe. Britain won bronze in Los Angeles in 1984 and gold in Seoul in 1988. We've won nothing since. Women's hockey became an Olympic sport in 1980. Britain's only medal so far has been bronze in Barcelona in 1992.

Who can say what would have happened if British hockey players had embraced competition right at the start? The sport might have attracted different sorts of players: people who were interested in winning rather than just participating. Competition would have led to leagues, which might have attracted more supporters, larger crowds, more revenue and the kind of excitement that the game generates in the subcontinent. It might also, of course, have led to pressure to allow professionalism, which is what the hockey establishment was determined to avoid. What is not in doubt is that the lack of real domestic competition severely limited Britain's chances at international level in a sport we once dominated. Whether finally allowing competition was ever going to lead to regaining that dominance was always questionable.

Ice hockey

Throughout North America, the term 'hockey' always refers to 'ice hockey'. But that doesn't mean the game actually originated on that continent. There are references to informal British stick-and-ball games – Scottish shinty, Irish hurling and English bandy-ball – being played on frozen lakes and rivers from quite early on. We also have pictures of the Dutch playing their game *kolven* on ice from 1625. There's no doubt that early immigrants took these games with them to

North America – and that's where the modern game evolved. The first recorded games of ice hockey were played in Kingston, Ontario, and Halifax, Nova Scotia – between soldiers from the British garrison.

The land around the army camps was frozen too hard for most of the winter to allow what the Americans would call field hockey, so the troops donned rudimentary skates and took to the ponds and lakes. The games were fairly chaotic affairs, played according to rules which were flexible to say the least, with as many as fifteen or twenty people on each side. A contemporary account from a British Army officer describes the whole process as 'great fun'.

The first record of a puck being used instead of a ball was in a game in Kingston in 1860. The first set of formal rules was drawn up by students at McGill University in Montreal in the late 1870s, which laid down that there should be just nine players on each side. The students also established the first recognized ice hockey team, the McGill University Hockey Club. Over the next few years the game became immensely popular throughout Canada. By the early 1890s, there were nearly one hundred teams in Montreal alone and leagues all across the land. In 1892, the British Governor General of Canada, Lord Stanley of Preston, decided there should be an annual award for the best team and donated what is now known as the Stanley Cup. Today it is still awarded annually to the champions of the National Hockey League, the major professional league in North America.

Professional ice hockey began in 1904 and is now one of the four major North American sports. The amateur game became an Olympic sport in 1920. Great Britain managed to win the gold medal in 1936, but the dominant countries have been Canada, the US and the former Soviet Union, with Sweden, Finland, Switzerland and the Czech Republic also featuring regularly. But curiously the oldest continuing rivalry in ice hockey history began in St Moritz in Switzerland in 1883 – between Oxford and Cambridge.

12.
ATHLETICS
(AND THE MODERN OLYMPICS)

THE BRITISH HAVE always liked fun and games. As far back as medieval times – and probably much earlier – no country fair or religious festival would be complete without a closing session of rustic competition. Men – and women – vied with each other at running, leaping and hurling heavy weights. There would also be dancing, wrestling and cudgelling. There would be much drinking and a good deal of gambling. The result would frequently be 'general orgies of intoxication and riot'.

Put that popular tradition in the melting pot with the landed gentry's perennial habit of gambling on anything that moves (including their own servants), the public's growing demand for mass entertainment and the increasing devotion of the public schools and universities to healthy physical activities and the unlikely result, around the middle of the nineteenth century, was the emergence in Britain of modern athletics.

How did it all come about?

Starting blocks

In 1801 Joseph Strutt wrote of foot-racing that 'It is needless ... to assert the antiquity of this pastime, because it will readily occur to every one, that occasions continually present themselves, which call forth the exertions of running even in childhood; and when more than one person are stimulated by the same object, a competition naturally takes place among them to obtain it. Originally, perhaps, foot-races had no other incitement than emulation, or at best the prospect of some small reward: but in process of time the rewards were magnified, and contests of this kind were instituted as public amusements.'

The first games that we know of predate even the ancient Greek Olympics. The Tailteann Games are thought to have been founded in County Meath in Ireland as long ago as 1829 BC. The thirty-day festival was held in honour of Queen Tailte and involved events such as foot-racing and stone-throwing and no doubt much else. The games lasted for more than 3000 years and died out around 1180, soon after the Norman invasion of Ireland.

There is evidence that the Greeks too held organized athletic games 1500 years before Christ. The ancient Olympic Games are said to have

Sixth century BC Athenian vase depicting a running race:
the post is a marker for the runners to turn back

begun at Olympia as early as the thirteenth century BC. We have clear records from 776 BC. At that time, the *stadion*, or 'sprint', was the only athletic event. We know that the winner that year was one Coroebus of Elis. Soon, middle-distance and long-distance races were added, along with long jump, discus and javelin.

The classical Olympics lasted for at least 1170 years – and more probably for 1670 years. They were finally abolished by the Roman emperor Theodosius I in AD 394. The Romans generally were luke-warm towards athletics – they preferred their games to have a bit more blood and guts. And after the fall of the Empire in the fifth century, organized athletic competition seems to have disappeared.

The Middle Ages

But running and jumping clearly didn't. In the seventh century AD, the Venerable Bede describes St Cuthbert (c. 634–87) as someone who excelled at jumping, running and wrestling. Five hundred years later another monk, Fitzstephen of Canterbury, tells us that in his native London in the reign of Henry II, open spaces were set aside for young men to practise, among other things, 'leaping, wrestling, casting of the stone and playing with the ball'. It is inconceivable that they wouldn't also have engaged in running. 'Casting of the stone' – the medieval version of the shot-put – became so popular that in 1365 Edward III issued an edict prohibiting it, for the now familiar reason that it was interfering with archery practice.

Henry V, the victor of Agincourt, was said to be such a swift runner that he could catch a wild buck in a large park 'without bow or other engine'. While Henry VIII, before he reached the portly and much-married state with which we are so familiar, was said to be outstanding at hammer-throwing, shot-putting, leaping and running. Such activities were given the seal of approval by Sir Thomas Elyot in his guidebook for the education of a gentleman called *The Boke Named the Governour*. He says 'Rennyng is bothe a good exercise and a laudable solace' and is to be included in the 'sondrye fourmes of exercise necessarye for a gentilman'.

For gentlemen at the time, such activities, as well as being a pleasant solace, also served a serious purpose. They helped prepare young men for their most serious duty, the waging of war. Aspiring knights were encouraged to add athletic achievement to their equestrian skills. In the

A farcical picture of Henry VIII throwing the
hammer in front of admiring courtiers

early fifteenth-century poem *Of Knyghthode and Batayle*, the following advice is given to young gentlemen:

> In rennynge the exercise is good also,
> To smyte first in fight, and also whenne
> To take a place our foemen will forrenne,
> And take it erst; also to serche or sture,
> Lightly to come and go, rennynge is sure.
> Rennyng is also right good at the chace,
> And for to lepe a dike is also good:
> For mightily what man may renne and lepe,
> May well devict, and safe his party kepe.

But, for the common people, running and jumping were simple amusements to be enjoyed on festive occasions. In Elizabethan times, country fairs were an essential part of the rural economy. Horses, farm animals and all the provisions needed for the coming season were traded at several hundred fairs throughout the country. Every one culminated in a boozy and boisterous round of dancing, merriment and competitive games.

These were simple affairs. Along with running, leaping and throwing the hammer were such popular activities as grinning contests, shin-kicking, sack-jumping, donkey-racing and climbing the greasy pole. Prizes were practical: cheeses, joints of meat and items of clothing. For men, the prize for a running race was generally a hat, which was not to be worn but hung at home as a trophy. One report talks of a young man who 'carried an Air of Importance in his looks' because he and his ancestors had won so many hats 'that his parlour looked like a haberdasher's shop'. For women the prize was often a smock, also known as a 'she-shirt'.

One of the oldest festivals, said to date from Saxon times, was the Cotswold Games, held in a field between Evesham and Stow-on-the-Wold on the Thursday and Friday of Whitsun week. In 1612, as Puritanism was beginning to stalk the land, a local lawyer called Robert Dover took them over and, with King James I's express approval, redesigned them as the Cotswold 'Olimpicks'. (This was the year after the publication of the King James Bible and reflects the

Robert Dover's Cotswold Olimpicks, one of many festivals
involving events like shin-kicking and sack-jumping

desire at the time to make classical achievements more accessible.) The aim was to give the games an air of romantic Hellenism and poets such as Michael Drayton and Ben Jonson were impressed enough to sing their praises. But at heart, as Dover himself made clear, they were an attempt to spread 'jollity' at a gloomy time, with a little antiquarianism masking what was in essence just another country festival.

The original games didn't long survive Dover, who died in 1641 (although they have been revived since and continue today). By then the Puritans were trying to outlaw 'all sports and publick pastimes' by banning festivals. One overzealous minister wrote that 'There would not be so many loytering idle persons, ruffians, blasphemers, swinge-bucklers, tossepots etc., etc. . . . if these dunghills and filth on commonweals were removed.' But such harsh times were not to last.

Jollity restored

When Charles II returned to London in 1660 to claim his throne, his restoration 'lighted such a fire of sporting enthusiasm as has never yet been extinguished'. As early as 10 August 1660, Samuel Pepys made this entry in his diary: 'With Mr Moor and Creed to Hide Park by coach, and saw a fine foot-race three times round the park between an Irishman and Crow, that was once my Lord Claypoole's footman'. Another entry for 30 July 1663 confirms how popular such races had become: 'The towne talk this day is of nothing but the great foot-race run this day on Banstead Downes, between Lee, the Duke of Richmond's footman, and a tyler, a famous runner. And Lee hath beat him; though the King and the Duke of York and all men almost, did bet three or four to one upon the tyler's head.'

It was fashionable at the time for gentlemen to keep 'running footmen' in their service. There was a practical purpose. If you had a house both in town and in the country, as many people of fashion did, it was useful to have a footman who could run messages between the two. On the appalling roads of the time, a footman could move much faster than a coach and travel further even than a man on horseback. If you were travelling yourself, a footman could always run ahead to make arrangements. A strong runner could always find employment. And given the propensity for gambling in the late seventeenth and eight-eenth centuries, it was inevitable that gentlemen should want to wager that their man could beat the other fellow's.

Running footmen had a practical purpose,
but were also used for racing

A fabled story is told of the Duke of Queensberry – 'Old Q' – who used to put potential footmen through their paces by dressing them in full livery and making them run up and down in front of his house. One very hot day, a candidate was running so well that Old Q, watch-ing from the balcony, made him carry on and on just so that he could admire his style. Eventually the Duke called out 'You will do for me'. 'Yes,' said the man, suffering from the heat and not happy with the prospect of working for such a master, 'and these things (pointing at the gold-laced outfit he was wearing) will do for me.' Whereupon he took off into the distance and easily outpaced those sent out to pursue him.

A good account of the sheer scale of the wagers placed on running footmen comes from the diary of Sir Erasmus Phillips, who was an undergraduate at Oxford in 1720. He wrote: 'Rode out to Woodstock; dined at the Bear (2s 6d). In the evening rode to Woodstock Park, where saw a race between Groves (Duke of Wharton's running footman) and Phillips (Mr Diston's). My namesake ran the four miles round the course in 18 min. and won the race, and thereby his master £1000, the sum he and Groves started for. On this occasion there was a most prodigious concourse of people.' Not just big money, but big crowds as well.

Some of the wagers reported over this period were bizarre. The 'Loyal Protestant' tells of a foot-race between two lame men in Newmarket Heath, in the presence of Charles II: 'At 3 of the clock in the afternoon there was race between 2 cripples, each having a wooden leg. They started fair and hobbled a good pace, which caused great admiration and laughter among the beholders; but the tallest of the

Illustration of a story from The Loyal Protestant *on a race between two lame men in front of Charles II at Newmarket*

two won by 2 or 3 yards.' A fish-hawker is said to have run seven miles from Hyde Park Corner to Brentford with 56 lb of fish on his head in just forty-five minutes. Another match was between a man on stilts and a man on foot over 120 yards. With a twenty-yard start, the man on stilts won. In 1788, a young man carrying a booted and spurred jockey on his back raced an 'elderly fat man' called Bullock (the record does not say who won).

Sometimes, the nobility made themselves the subject of wagers. In 1690, 'Mr Peregrine Bertie, son to the late Earl Lindsey, upon a wager, ran the Mall in St James's Park eleven times in less than an hour'. A hundred years or so later, Lord Paget, Lord Barrymore, Captain

A recorded race between a man on stilts and a man running:
the man on stilts had a twenty yard start . . . and won

A race between an elderly fat man and a young gentleman
carrying a jockey with whip and spurs

Grosvenor and the Hon. Mr Lamb ran a race across Kensington Gardens for a sweepstake of 100 guineas. In 1793, we hear of perhaps the very first charity walk. Colonel the Hon. Cosmo Gordon undertook to walk five miles along the Uxbridge Road in less than an hour for a bet. He completed his task easily and promptly donated his winnings to a fund for the widows and children of soldiers and sailors.

Pedestrianism

In the eighteenth century, a new kind of professional athlete began to emerge. They were called 'pedestrians'. Some were former running footmen, others just set up in business for themselves. They travelled the country taking on challenges, rather like prizefighters, on race-courses and the high road. In 1780, a professional from Penrith walked fifty miles in thirteen hours on Newcastle Racecourse. In 1785, a pedestrian called Woolfit walked forty miles a day for six consecutive days, between six in the morning and six in the evening, on the high road. In 1787 a butcher from Newgate Market called Walpole beat a well-known professional called Pope over a mile along the City Road in four and a half minutes, a worthy feat if the time is accurate. In 1788, a pedestrian called Evans attracted a large crowd to Newmarket to watch his heavily backed attempt to run ten miles within an hour. He's reported to have completed the distance in 55 minutes 18 seconds, winning £10,000 for his supporters.

Surprisingly, what captured the public imagination more than any-thing else at this time were feats of endurance against the clock. The most celebrated pedestrian in this field in the eighteenth century was a lawyer's clerk called Foster Powell. He was thirty when he performed his first feat, running fifty miles on the Bath Road in seven hours in 1764. For the next quarter of a century he travelled Britain and Europe stacking up ever more astonishing achievements. One of the greatest was walking from London to York and back, some 402 miles, in less than six days (he did it in five days and eighteen hours) for a substantial bet. Strangely, thousands lined the route to watch him. When he was

57, he repeated the feat in the same time, then two years later knocked nearly three hours of his own 'record'. His resulting fame was such that he was engaged for twelve nights at Astley's Amphitheatre 'where he exhibited his pace in a small circle'. But the final walk to York and back had taken too much out of him. He died shortly afterwards and is buried in the east corner of St Paul's Churchyard.

But even Powell's feats were eclipsed by those of Robert Barclay Allardice. He came from a Scottish landowning family and realized

*Robert Barclay Allardice, known as Captain Barclay, whose
greatest feat was to walk 1000 miles in 1000 hours*

early on that he had a talent that could make him money. At the age of 15 he won 100 guineas by walking six miles in an hour on the Croydon road. Soon afterwards he showed his skill at manipulating the market by taking on a wager for 500 guineas with 'Mr Fletcher of Ballinshoe' to walk 90 miles in 21½ hours. On the first attempt he caught a chill in training and was unable to make the appointed day, forfeiting his stake. He upped the bet to 2000 guineas. This time he had reached 67 miles when he 'incautiously' drank some brandy and became too sick to continue. He upped the stakes further to 5000 guineas and went into serious training with John Smith, an old farmer on Lord Falconberg's estate who was 'very skilful in the best mode of training in pedestrian feats'.

The date was fixed for 10 November. At midnight, six stopwatches were set and sealed into a box at the winning end (he was walking a back-and-forth measured course). Allardice set off in a flannel shirt, flannel trousers and nightcap, lambswool stockings and stout shoes. Thousands had come to watch – and to bet. At the start the odds were 2 to 1 in his favour. After 16 miles Allardice stopped to 'refresh himself' and change clothes. He looked spry and cheerful and the odds moved out to 3 or 4 to 1. By 11 in the morning he'd walked 50 miles. By the time he took a ten-minute break at 60 miles, the odds were 6 or 7 to 1 in his favour and the crowd were getting excited. He finished with one hour, 7 minutes and 56 seconds to spare. He was 5000 guineas richer, a great deal more famous and still only 21.

To prove his versatility, he shortly afterwards beat a Mr Ward over 440 yards in 56 seconds. He was the most prominent runner and walker of his day. In 1809, he performed his most famous feat. The challenge was to walk 1000 miles in 1000 hours at a rate of one mile an hour. One mile an hour may not sound very fast, but just imagine walking one mile every hour of every day and night for forty-two days. Others had tried the feat but none had got beyond thirty days.

Captain Barclay – the name he was now using for public appearances – began on 1 June. He kept to a strict routine. He walked a measured half-mile out and back from his lodgings. He breakfasted at five on a roast fowl with a pint of strong ale, lunched at twelve on beef steaks or mutton chops, dined at six on roast beef or mutton chops and supped at eleven on cold fowl. With each of these meals he drank porter and two or three glasses of wine. He was eating five to six pounds of meat a day. He rarely got more than half an hour's sleep. The daily log kept by one of his attendants talks of endless pain in his legs and feet, but also of constant good spirits. Newspapers reported regularly on his progress and spectators turned out every day to watch him. The odds fluctuated according to his appearance.

By eleven o'clock on the morning of the final day a crowd of 10,000 had gathered. By one o'clock there was barely room for him to walk. At three o'clock, cheered on by the crowd, he completed the final mile in twenty-two minutes. He promptly went to bed, slept until midnight, woke up and took some water gruel, then slept again till nine the next morning. When he got up, he appeared to be in perfect health and spent the morning strolling round Newmarket enjoying the adulation. He is reputed to have made £16,000 from his endeavours, more than half a million pounds in today's money.

Captain Barclay's exploits made athletics tremendously popular. At the time, there was no formal distinction between amateurs and professionals. Peers, army officers and gentlemen of fortune were to be seen racing each other or the clock around Newmarket, between the mileposts of the Uxbridge Road or on the sprinting track at Lord's cricket ground – always for a wager. Sometimes a gentleman pitted himself against a pedestrian. The professionals, meanwhile, developed championships for the various distances which were fought for in much the same way as the championships of the prizefighting ring, and often in front of comparable crowds. Indeed, until 1838 the sporting paper *Bell's Life* listed forthcoming pedestrian events under the heading 'The Ring'. After that time it gave pedestrianism its own heading, listing between twenty and thirty events a week.

By the middle of the century, pedestrianism had reached the peak of its popularity. Tens of thousands turned out to watch Billy Jackson (the American Deer) contest a mile match with J. Davies (the Lame Chicken) and Tom Maxfield (the North Star) on the Slough Road (Maxfield won). The industrial towns of the North became major centres. Crowds of 25,000 became common. In 1850, most of the sporting population of Liverpool, Manchester and Newcastle flocked to Aintree racecourse to watch Tommy Hayes beat Johnny Tetlow over four miles. When George Frost (the Suffolk Stag) won the ten-mile championship at the Copenhagen Grounds in Manchester in 1852, a lithograph was produced of the event which sold in its thousands.

As was so often the case, it was the professionals who were the great innovators of the sport. They were responsible for developing the first purpose-built running tracks (the earliest was a narrow two-man sprint-ing track around the pitch at Lord's). They were the first to attempt to record times accurately and keep records. And they defined the events – 110 yards, 440, 880, one mile, two miles, four, six and ten, the high jump, long jump and pole jump (as it was then called) – which were to be adopted by modern athletics.

The entry of the amateurs

It was inevitable that the popularity of pedestrianism, coupled with the growing obsession with physical activities in the post-Arnold public schools, should lead to the development of something akin to modern athletics in schools and universities. Sandhurst is reputed to have held an annual sports day for a few years early in the century, but little is known about it. Rugby School began its annual cross-country Crick Run in 1837, while regular sprint, hurdle and steeplechase races took place at Eton from 1845. But the first recognizably modern amateur athletic meeting took place at Exeter College, Oxford, in 1850.

Its origins were a little eccentric. Exeter had an annual steeplechase for horses and riders known informally as the 'College Grind'. On the evening after the 1850 race, a group of students sat sipping wine and protesting about the difficulties of riding poor-quality horses across the Oxfordshire countryside. 'Sooner than ride such a brute again,' said one whose horse had landed on his head after one jump, 'I'd run across two miles of country on foot.' 'Why not?' said the others. They agreed to set up a 'College Foot Grind'. As preparations for the steeplechase proceeded, they decided to add some 'flat' races over 100, 300 and 440 yards and a 140-yard hurdles. There was also a 'Consolation Stakes' for 'beaten horses'. It is now recognized as the first amateur meeting for 'Athletic Sports'. Exeter founded the first college athletics club – possibly the first ever athletics club – shortly afterwards.

From 1852, 'sports days' started spreading among the public schools. By the middle of the decade, other colleges at Oxford and Cambridge were following the example of Exeter, whose annual sports day had become an institution. Cambridge set up a university sports meeting open to all undergraduates in 1857. Oxford followed in 1860. It was only to be expected, given the popularity of the Oxford and Cambridge cricket match and the Boat Race, that the two universities should agree to meet each other at athletics. The first Inter-Varsity Sports took place at the Christ Church Cricket Ground in Oxford on 3 March 1864. Many date that as the beginning of modern athletics as an institution.

Amateur athletics outside schools and universities took a little longer to get going. It was given fresh impetus by the arrival on the professional pedestrian scene of Louis Bennett, a Native American widely known as Deerfoot. His matches against British 'peds' attracted big crowds and in 1861, 6000 people – including the Prince of Wales – saw him win a six-mile race at Cambridge. The Prince of Wales invited Bennett to dine with him afterwards at Trinity, an action which caused a mild scandal among some but served to greatly increase the respectability of athletics.

Shortly afterwards, the West London Rowing Club held an athletics meeting in London, partly aimed at keeping their members in training during the winter. The next year a well-known promoter of pedestrian races called William Price, spotting a trend, offered a 'handsome silver cup' to be competed for by 'amateurs only' at the Hackney Wick running track. One of the competitors was Walter Chinnery, who was to become the first amateur to run a mile in less than four and a half minutes. He recalled later that he arrived in 'a pair of side-spring patent leather boots, but Teddy Mills, the celebrated (professional) long-distance runner ... took compassion on my ignorance and lent me a pair of running shoes'. He still lost, but the event was successful enough for Price to repeat the exercise soon afterwards.

There was no club for these stray amateurs in London until a group of athletes who had run at both the Rowing Club and Hackney Wick events got together in 1863 to form the Mincing Lane Athletic Club. They held their first event at the West London Cricket Ground at Brompton in April, just weeks after the first Oxford and Cambridge meeting. Another followed soon afterwards and within months the club was flourishing, attracting a wide range of athletes from all across London.

But athletics was growing even faster in the North. An amateur club had been started in Liverpool, a stronghold of pedestrianism, in the early 1860s. It was founded by Charles Melly and John Hulley, two stalwarts of the 'muscular Christianity' movement. In June 1862, they held what they called an 'Olympian Festival' on the parade ground of the Volunteer Movement at Mount Vernon. 10,000 people 'of a highly respectable class' came to watch. The festival was repeated for the next three years and began to attract entries from all over the country. For this reason, Melly and Hulley decided to rename Liverpool Athletic Club as the 'Athletic Society of Great Britain'. This sent shock waves through the athletes of London, who naturally felt that they should be in charge of athletics in the country.

It was the start of a fifteen-year battle for control of the new sport which was to turn region against region, club against club and involve at least two very shady characters.

Athletics at war

John Graham Chambers, the Eton-educated son of a Welsh landowner, was a natural administrator. He had already rowed for Cambridge in the Boat Race before he set about reorganizing Cambridge athletics: he replaced events such as sack racing and pole jumping for distance with putting the shot and throwing the hammer. He then set about drawing up the programme for the first Oxford and Cambridge Inter-Varsity Sports. When he went down from Cambridge, his father's financial difficulties prevented him from being a sporting gentleman of leisure as he would have liked. Instead he became a journalist on the weekly newspaper *Land and Water*.

This didn't stop him from organizing things. In 1866, in response to the pretenders from Liverpool, he was the driving force behind the formation of the Amateur Athletic Club (AAC). Its express purpose was to establish a permanent ground for amateur athletic sports, but his real ambition for it was to run athletics in the same way that the MCC ran cricket and the Jockey Club ran racing. He was not deterred by the fact that their authority dated from the eighteenth century. The first step was to establish the first national championships.

They took place at the Beaufort House ground near West Brompton in London in March 1866. The timing was important. At Oxford and Cambridge, athletics was a winter sport (the summer was given over to cricket and exams). Chambers expected most of the competitors to come from the universities, so the spring was an appropriate time. Despite terrible weather – the wind ripped the canvas roof off the grandstand – the meeting was a success. Of the eleven events included in this first ever national championship, nine still feature in the Olympics. Chambers himself won the seven-mile walk. It seemed a good omen. A little later, the Liverpool club made its attempt at a national meeting at Crystal Palace, grandly called the National Olympian Association. It was an anticlimax, notable mainly for W. G. Grace winning the hurdles when he should have been fielding at the Oval. Membership of the AAC boomed. The capital's other major club, now renamed the London Athletic Club or LAC, began to see the new body as a threat.

The AAC was resolutely amateur. But what was an amateur? The club's initial definition was simple: 'An amateur is any person who has never competed in an open competition, or for public money, or for admission money, and who has never for any period of his life taught or assisted in the pursuit of athletic exercises as a means of livelihood.' But this proved too liberal for the club's largely university and public school membership. In 1867, it added the clause '. . . or is a mechanic, artisan or labourer'. In 1868, the opening words of the definition were changed to 'An amateur is any gentleman who . . .'

But while the club became exclusive, its championships remained open to everyone who was not a professional. For two years, the AAC continued to hold the meeting at the Beaufort House ground. But it was not ideal. The club shared it with a farmer. In 1868 Edward Colbeck, attempting a double in the 880 and 440 yards, collided with a sheep which stood steadfastly in his way. He broke both the poor animal's leg and the 440 yards world record with a time of 50.4 seconds, which was to stand for eleven years. It was a relief when Chambers's dream of a permanent home for athletics was made real at Lillie Bridge, near West Brompton station, in March 1869. As well as athletics, it had facilities for cricket, cycling, football, tennis, rackets, gymnastics and billiards. To pay for it, Chambers persuaded Middlesex to play their home county cricket matches there, staged the FA Cup in 1873 and organized the first amateur cycling championships and the first amateur wrestling championships.

The AAC's problem was that it never really functioned as an athletics club. It held no meetings other than the national championships and most active athletes remained loyal to the London Athletic Club. In 1870, the LAC had fallen under the control of the nefarious Waddell brothers, James and William, later described in the official history of the Amateur Athletic Association as being 'as infamous a pair as you would find in any Victorian melodrama'. Their ultimate aim was to get rid of Chambers and take control of the national championships. In 1871, they tried and failed to get support from other clubs to start a rival national association. They decided to bide their time.

The irony was that the Waddells were forced to hire the AAC's Lillie Bridge ground for their regular meetings, because it was by far the best running track on offer. By the mid-1870s, Chambers was relying on the LAC for this money to keep the ground going (Middlesex and the FA had moved on). The only other meetings now being held at Lillie Bridge were the Inter-Varsity Sports and the championships. In 1876, Chambers asked the LAC for a larger share of the gate money from its meetings. The Waddells were forced to pay up but they immediately started a subscription fund to build their own ground. It opened at Stamford Bridge, defiantly close to the AAC, in 1877.

This wasn't the only challenge the AAC faced. There was a growing feeling that the national championships should be held in the summer rather than the spring. The world of athletics had changed dramatically since the event had first been established eleven years earlier. Then most athletes were university students. By 1877 they were mainly working men, especially in the North and the Midlands, where the sport had become massively popular – even a cricket club sports day could attract crowds of 10,000. To prepare for a spring championship, the only option these men had was to train in the dark, which not surprisingly they were reluctant to do.

As a result, the 1877 championships attracted just twenty-six entries for twelve events. The Waddells led the way in urging that the meeting be switched to the summer, but Chambers would not give in. The 1878 championships were once again held in the spring. Almost the only entries were from Oxford and Cambridge. The following year, there was open warfare. Chambers again insisted on holding his championships in the spring, but this time the LAC held a rival meeting in the summer. Both failed – the spring meeting was all Oxbridge, the summer one all London. To make matters worse, the powerful clubs in the North and the Midlands – fed up with squabbling Southerners – set about forming their own associations. The fledgling sport was fragmenting.

The birth of the three As

To the rescue, a little strangely, came three young men from Oxford. The AAC's only hope of survival was the continuing support of Oxford and Cambridge. But Bernhard Wise, the young President of the University Athletic Club at Oxford, wasn't sure it was worth saving. What was the point of a so-called national championship if it was only a replay of the inter-varsity match? He consulted the mentor of Oxford athletics, a don at Hertford called Clement Jackson. Together they brought in a bright young lawyer called Montague Shearman, a former athletics club president now reading for the Bar. Together they developed a plan for a new association which would legislate for athletics and take over running the national championships. A simple idea in theory, but they still needed to reconcile the warring factions.

There followed a period of brilliant diplomacy. They squared

Cambridge by offering to make it a joint initiative. They brought the North and the Midlands on board by promising there would be no manual labour exclusion clause and the championships would rotate between London, the Midlands and the North. They persuaded the Waddells to take part, albeit reluctantly, by saying the championships would be held in the summer and include two events the Waddells were pushing. They also made it clear that everyone else would boycott any rival LAC meeting. Finally they brought it home to John Chambers that he had no option but to join them. As a consolation they assured him that the London championships would be held at Lillie Bridge.

All the interested parties met at the Randolph Hotel in Oxford on 24 April 1880. They were presented with a set of resolutions reflecting the tense weeks of preparatory negotiations and an invitation to dinner. John Chambers made a last-minute attempt to introduce the AAC's manual labour exclusion clause but was quickly told it was not acceptable. He conceded and announced that the AAC's national cups would be handed over to the new organization. With that, it was agreed that the Amateur Athletic Association should come into existence, with Wise as Vice-President, Jackson as Treasurer and Shearman as Secretary.

The AAA quickly established itself as the governing body of British athletics. It held its first championships at Lillie Bridge in July 1880. It was a miserably wet day and only 1200 attended. The following year's championships, as planned, were held in Birmingham and were a great success, attracting a crowd of 12,000 to watch, for the first time, two Americans challenge the best of British athletes. This was the start of the internationalization of athletics, with the AAA becoming the model for governing bodies throughout the Empire, in the United States and later in Europe and the rest of the world. The Secretary of the AAA was also to play a part in the next major development in athletics, the founding of the modern Olympics. But he wasn't the only British influence to be involved in that story.

The Modern Olympics

In 1875, a young French aristocrat read a book which was to have a far-reaching effect both on his life and the future of international sport. The boy was 12-year-old Baron Pierre de Coubertin. The book was *Tom Brown's Schooldays*. The result was the creation of the modern Olympics.

Coubertin was born on New Year's Day in 1863 into a conservative family which had been ennobled in 1477 by Louis XI. He grew up during a turbulent period in French history. The humiliation of defeat in the Franco-Prussian War of 1870 had left particularly bitter memories. Many French people believed they had lost because their soldiers were not physically fit enough. The Germans had their compulsory gymnastics – *Turnen* – while the French preferred to study literature.

After reading of the exploits of Tom Brown, the young Coubertin took a rather different view. Non-competitive gymnastics were all very well, he thought, for training in warfare, but competitive sports as developed in English public schools produced physical, moral and social benefits that could be used for both peace and war. This idea became his obsession.

As an aristocrat, Coubertin believed it was his duty to give something back to society. When he was 17, he joined the military academy of St Cyr. But before long he decided that military life was not for him. He later said that he had foreseen a long period of peace and couldn't face the monotony of garrison life. He also believed that education should be about developing the individual, whereas military training was about subjugating the individual to the common good.

Uncertain what to do next, in 1883 he set off on a journey through England to explore his ideas about education. His pilgrimage took him to Eton, Harrow, Oxford and Cambridge. Most important of all, he went to Rugby, the place where Tom Brown had spent his schooldays under the tutelage of the man who by this time had become Coubertin's hero: Dr Thomas Arnold.

During the first half of the nineteenth century, as we saw in Chapter Six, Arnold had revolutionized the idea of the public school. Following the example he laid down as headmaster of Rugby, public schools became institutions geared to producing young men with the moral fibre to go out and run the empire. And while Arnold himself had little interest in sport (a fact Coubertin always refused to acknowledge), his followers most certainly did.

By the time of Coubertin's visit, sport had become a major part of public school life, a vital component in 'the individual moral development of gentlemen'. Coubertin believed it promoted the qualities Arnold was so keen on instilling: 'Initiative, daring, decision, habits of self-reliance and blaming no one but oneself when one stumbles'. This emphasis on 'muscular Christianity' had also led directly to the development of such modern sports as football, rugby, rowing and athletics. Coubertin was hooked.

On his return to Paris, he tried a brief flirtation with the *Faculté de Droit* (School of Law). It didn't work. He returned to England in 1886, where he talked of having a vision while visiting the tomb of Thomas Arnold in Rugby Chapel. It inspired his '21-year campaign' to bring Arnold's legacy to France.

From that time on he decided he would devote himself to introducing *la pedagogie sportive* to France. But he didn't want it to be elitist, as it was in Britain. He wanted sport for the masses. This view was shared by the author of *Tom Brown's Schooldays*, Thomas Hughes, who went on to be a pioneer of educational projects for working men and a founder of the Christian Socialist Movement.

The following year Coubertin wrote a major article on the subject, which inspired one of the grand old men of French public life, former Prime Minister Jules Simon, to make a speech arguing that physical health required physical exercise, which he said should be 'half of pedagogy'.

Never one to miss an opportunity, Coubertin asked Simon to write the preface of his forthcoming book *L'Education Anglaise en France*. The two men also set up a high-powered committee to promote physical exercise, to which Simon's reputation attracted some major figures. They split into four groups: the hygienists, interested in physical health; the gymnasts, in favour of organized non-competitive exercise; the militarists, aiming to promote soldierly requirements; and the smallest group, led by Coubertin, who wanted competitive English games that stressed character development, liberty and social education.

For the Paris Universal Exposition of 1889 (for which the Eiffel Tower was built) the Simon committee hosted a congress on physical exercises that featured demonstrations of various sports. They were judged a great success. But just before the congress began, Coubertin received a letter from an eccentric English country doctor which was to have a major impact on his life.

The Much Wenlock Olympian Games

In 1994 Juan Antonio Samaranch, then President of the International Olympic Committee, paid a visit to the small and attractive town of Much Wenlock in Shropshire, just on the English side of the Welsh border. There he laid a wreath on the grave of William Penny Brookes, the local doctor for much of Queen Victoria's reign. He said: 'I came to pay homage to Dr Brookes, who really was the founder of the modern Olympic Games.'

Dr Brookes was born in Much Wenlock in 1809, the son of the village doctor. Following in his father's footsteps, he studied medicine in London, Padua and Paris, which was where he heard of his father's death in 1830. Quickly finishing his studies, he hurried home to Much Wenlock to take over the family practice.

He then embarked, for the next sixty-odd years, on a heady journey of community service and philanthropy. As well as maintaining his practice, he was a magistrate, a Commissioner of Roads and personally helped bring both gas and the railway to Much Wenlock. He founded the Agricultural Reading Society, a free lending library for rural workers, which quickly spawned groups known as the Art Class, the Philharmonic Class and the Botany Class (needless to say, Brookes was also a distinguished botanist). Then, in 1850, he started a new class which was to have a considerable impact on international athletics.

It was called The Olympian Class (Brookes also loved Classics) and was designed to 'promote the moral, physical and intellectual improvement of the inhabitants of the Town and neighbourhood of Wenlock and especially of the Working Classes, by the encouragement of outdoor recreation, and by the award of prizes annually at public Meetings for skill in athletic exercises and proficiency in intellectual and industrial attainments'. Brookes firmly believed that the working classes should have access to both physical exercise and education. As part of the class, Brookes staged the first Wenlock Olympian Games Meeting in October of the same year. They were a great success and quickly became an annual event.

The programme of the Wenlock Games was not quite what we expect from the Olympics today. From time to time, as well as athletic contests, there were wheelbarrow races, an old ladies race for a pound of tea and a handwriting competition for the under-7s. There were brass bands, bell-ringing, glee singing, football and cricket. But the games did have an opening procession and – most important of all – they were open to all-comers, to what Brookes describes as 'every grade of man'. He was not interested in the elitism of the gentlemen amateurs. The games flourished.

In 1858, Brookes noticed a small article about a planned revival of the Olympic Games in Athens the following year, the brainchild of a wealthy shipping financier and veteran of the Greek War of Independence named Evangelis Zappas. He was entranced. He found out more from the British Minister in Athens and sent suggestions for the Olympic programme based on his Wenlock experience. He particularly recommended a favourite of his, the medieval sport of 'tilting at the ring', in which a rider has to spear a small ring hanging from a frame with his lance. He sent ten pounds sterling, a tidy sum, to be offered as a prize for this event. The money was accepted – it turned out to be the biggest prize of the games – but the suggestion was not.

Unfortunately, the Zappas games of 1859 were a not a success. The government had persuaded Zappas to make them more of an agro-industrial exhibition with a few games added on. There were discus and javelin contests, climbing the greasy pole and three running races. The winner of the longest, nearly a mile, was awarded Brookes's ten pounds. But it was a ramshackle affair, held in a town square which offered very few facilities for spectators. There was no rush to repeat the experiment. Zappas died in 1865. There were a couple of attempts to revive his dream using money he had left in his will but there was little overall enthusiasm for the idea and it was allowed quietly to die.

But Brookes went from strength to strength. In 1860, The Olympian Class split from the Reading Society to become the Wenlock Olympian Society. Their games began to attract athletes from across the country. In 1861, Brookes helped found the Shropshire Olympian Games. In 1865, he joined Charles Melly and John Hulley of Liverpool in setting up the National Olympian Association. But they were outmanoeuvred by the AAC. After their first attempt at a national meeting at Crystal Palace in 1866, John Chambers let it be known that any athlete who appeared at a further NOA event would not be eligible for the AAC's nationwide championship. Neither the Shropshire Olympics nor the national event were able to survive this attack from the new athletic establishment.

But Brookes did not give up on his Olympic dream or the Wenlock Games. They began to attract competitors from further and further afield. He took to rewarding the victors with a laurel wreath crown and a medal inscribed with an image of Nike, the Greek goddess of victory. And they remained firmly open to all amateurs regardless of class. This approach was finally vindicated in 1880 with the establishment of the AAA and the abolition of the manual labour exclusion clause.

His other dream – reviving the Olympics – was proving harder. Throughout the 1880s, he bombarded the Greek King, the Prime Minister and the ambassador in London with his proposal for a revival of the Olympic Games in Athens. 'As a Greek,' the long-suffering ambassdor wrote to him, 'I cannot help but feel indebted to you that you continue with this idea of a revival of the Olympic Games.' But, he said, the political situation in Greece was far from stable. 'If, as we must hope, later on a more settled and satisfactory state of affairs be established . . . I have every reason to believe that such a proposal would meet with a ready and cheerful response.' Brookes wrote again every year to ask if the situation had changed. The answer was always no. The Greeks weren't really very interested in the ideas of an eccentric country doctor.

In 1889, Brookes learned about the activities of the young Pierre de Coubertin, and his belief that English-style sports were vital for the future of French education and for restoring French pride. Brookes was all in favour and invited Coubertin to visit Much Wenlock. In October 1890, Coubertin accepted the invitation.

Brookes staged a special meeting of the Wenlock Olympics for his distinguished visitor. The Baron was highly impressed. More significant still, Brookes then took Coubertin aside and harangued him at length about his ideas for a revival of the Olympic Games in Athens. He told him about the Zappas games, the London games of 1866 and showed him all his correspondence with the Greek authorities. At the time of this meeting, Coubertin was 27, Brookes was 82. Brookes effectively passed the Olympic torch to the younger man.

On his return to Paris, Coubertin wrote an article in praise of Brookes. He wrote: '. . . if the Olympic Games that modern Greece has not yet been able to revive still survive today, it is due not to a Greek but to Dr W. P. Brookes. It is he who inaugurated them 40 years ago and it is he, now 82 years of age but still alert and vigorous, who continues to organize and inspire them.' Coubertin wrote about Brookes's correspondence with King George of Greece, as a result of which the King had 'donated a magnificent cup for the competitions at Wenlock, and supported the restoration of the Olympic Games at Athens'. It was the first time Coubertin had ever mentioned such a revival.

Let the Games Begin . . .

Did the Baron take the idea of the modern Olympics from William Brooks and the Much Wenlock games? Throughout his life Coubertin never talked about where his great idea had come from, perhaps because he was reluctant to share the credit with anyone else.

As a well-educated, upper-class Frenchman, Coubertin would certainly have had a wide knowledge of the classical world. And the ancient Olympics held a strong fascination at the time. Major excavations had begun at Archaia Olympia, the site of the ancient games, in 1875. These discoveries were major news: the archaeologists involved were feted almost as Indiana Jones-type heroes.

There had also been previous attempts to bring back the games. As we've seen, Robert Dover called his festivities the 'Cotswold Olimpicks' in the seventeenth century and there were attempts to hold 'Scandinavian Olympic Games' in Sweden in the 1830s. There is no evidence that Coubertin knew about these efforts. But he certainly heard about the Zappas games on his visit to Much Wenlock.

After paying his tribute to Brooks after his trip, Coubertin was silent on the subject for two years. Then, at a prize-giving dinner at a sports festival he'd organized in Paris in 1892, he issued a ringing plea for the restoration of the Olympic Games. The idea, he recalled later, was met with 'total, absolute incomprehension'. No one took it seriously. Most people thought he was mad.

Coubertin realized he needed to prepare the ground better if the seed of his idea was ever to germinate. Over the next two years he visited the US and Britain to drum up support. Then in 1894 he organized the 'Paris International Athletic Congress', a major international meeting whose overt purpose was to discuss the vexed question of amateurism. But the real agenda was the revival of his Olympic idea.

The opening banquet was attended by 2,000 people, including 79 official delegates from 49 sporting societies in 12 different countries. Coubertin set out to 'seduce and inspire' them with lavish hospitality, exquisite decorations in the halls of the Sorbonne and a special performance of the 'Delphic Hymn to Apollo' set to music by Gabriel Fauré.

His argument was that just as the ancient Games had promoted pan-Hellenic unity – all conflict between the Greek city states traditionally ceased for the period of the Games – so the modern games would promote 'pan-human' unity. The moral basis for his games would no longer be religion but 'healthy democracy and wise and peaceful internationalism', which would promote global peace. It was a message Thomas Hughes would have heartily endorsed.

At the dazzling closing ceremony, the Congress voted unanimously for the restoration of the Olympics and accepted Coubertin's proposal that the first modern games should take place in Athens in 1896. Coubertin's vision was on its way to being realized.

It was not to be easy. Coubertin overcame many obstacles on the road to Athens, including an attempt by the Greek government to appropriate the games and make them a regular Greek fixture. But when the games finally opened on 5 April, they were a tremendous success, attracting the largest crowd yet known for a sporting event.

Coubertin may have been heavily influenced by Thomas Hughes, Thomas Arnold and William Brooks, but the credit for making the games happen should be entirely his. No other modern institution of such importance owes its existence so fully to the actions of a single person: a French visionary inspired by an idea of sport which at that time was uniquely English.

Same old story . . .

This English influence was not to last. At first the Amateur Athletic Association was heavily involved in the development of the idea. Coubertin wrote later of the importance of the executive board for the Paris conference in 1894: 'At the head, an immovable trinity: [Charles] Herbert, Secretary of the Amateur Athletic Association [London], for Great Britain and the British Empire; [William Milligan] Sloane, professor at Princeton University for the American continent; and myself, for France and continental Europe.' But perversely Charles Herbert of the AAA chose not to attend the games in Athens. Nor was there a British team. The story goes that the English were waiting to be invited, as seemed to them appropriate. In fact, they needed to apply. The result was that the few British athletes who did compete were private pleasure-seekers.

The reality was that the British, once again, weren't sure they needed the Olympics. To most international athletes of the time, the three As annual meeting was seen as the world championships. The AAA never claimed that title – it was after all committed to the Olympics – but the foreign sporting press certainly did. With good reason. Between 1881 and 1912, the Irish won at least one event at every championship. The Americans won forty-one medals over a similar period. The dominions were well represented (although not very successfully) and from 1902, continental Europe produced occasional winners.

By contrast, the second Olympics in Paris in 1900 were a sad affair. They were little more than a sideshow at an international trade fair (the ice-skaters were listed as participants in the cutlery exhibition). The French government refused to back them or allow them to be called Olympics, and the few athletes who competed in the sproadic events on the outskirts of the city generally didn't know they were taking part in the Olympics. The 1904 games were not much better. They were held in the United States as an appendage to the St Louis World Fair. Hardly anyone from outside North America bothered to go.

1908 was different. The games that year were scheduled to be held in Rome, but an eruption of Mount Vesuvius meant the funds set aside for them had to be diverted to the rebuilding of Naples. London stood in at just eighteen months' notice. The games were a success and the British, perhaps not surprisingly, comfortably headed the overall medal table. But not in athletics. Britain won eight gold medals at the brand new White City stadium, while the Americans walked off with fifteen. At their victory reception in City Hall, New York, the American team paraded a 'British lion' on a chain.

The AAA was not pleased. It set up a special Olympic committee to develop British athletes and ensure that the same thing didn't happen again at the 1912 games in Stockholm. Unfortunately, so did every other nation. Britain won just two gold medals in the athletics, against the Americans' sixteen. Finland and Sweden both won more than Britain. From that time on, the Olympics were seen as the major international championships, while the three As meeting became largely a national affair.

Since then, Britain has had many worthy Olympic champions. But no more than many other nations, and rather less than some. Once again, we had given a way to approach sport to the people of the world, and they had grasped it with open arms. But one huge contribution Britain has made to athletics has been the Paralympics. In 1948 Dr Ludwig Guttman, who was treating war veterans for spinal injuries at Stoke Mandeville hospital near Aylesbury, began using sport as rehabilitation for his patients. To coincide with the London Olympics, he set up a competition with other hospitals. The idea caught on and in 1960 he took 400 wheelchair athletes to Rome to compete in the Olympic city. From that small start the Paralympics have mushroomed into the major sporting event attracting worldwide media attention that they are today.

13.
SWIMMING

ANYONE WHO HAS ever seen a small baby put into a swimming pool knows that swimming is a natural human instinct. It must have been practised all around the world from the earliest times. We know it was highly regarded by the Egyptians and the Assyrians. The Greeks thought it was important – Plato said a man who couldn't swim was uneducated – but they didn't see it as a major sport. It was never included in the original Olympics. The Romans thought swimming was a vital element of military training, but never saw it as an organized sport. Across Europe, after the Romans, swimming disappears from view. It is one of the least recorded of all ancient sports. But most

*An Assyrian bas-relief from 880 BC of fugitives swimming: the bottom
two figures are swimming on inflated skins for buoyancy*

authorities (there aren't many) believe it was revived in its modern form by the British in the nineteenth century. In no small part because we wanted our people to smell better . . .

A toe in the water

The first English epic poem *Beowulf* has its hero involved in a swimming contest, but not one we'd recognize. It's an exhausting five-day endurance test, in which contestants have to swim in the open sea carrying swords to fight off the whales. Beowulf was eventually defeated, after being set upon by sea monsters. Naturally he killed them all, but he was so exhausted that he was washed up on the beach and therefore disqualified from the contest.

For much of the Middle Ages, ordinary people were afraid of swimming because they believed the sea and the rivers were the carriers of

'Circumvolution': one of many strange woodcuts from a treatise
on swimming by Everard Digby, published 1587

the plagues which so often beset them. But this didn't put off their leaders. We are told Edward II liked swimming; and in his 1531 treatise on the education of noble youth, *The Boke Named the Governour*, Sir Thomas Elyot praised swimming as a useful skill but one that was little practised by the nobility at that time despite its classical heritage. Elizabeth's tutor Roger Ascham agreed that swimming should be part of a proper courtly education, even though he himself preferred cock-fighting and gambling. Charles II used swimming as one of his ways of keeping fit for his hyperactive life.

In the eighteenth century, swimming went through something of a popular revival. Part of this was inspired by royalty taking to the waters in Weymouth. Bathing in the sea became quite the thing among those wealthy enough to be able to travel to the newly developed resorts. But it also fired the public's imagination. Around the turn of the century, swimming became an occasional spectacle. In 1791, *The Times* reported a swimming race in the Thames for a wager of 8 guineas, seemingly not remarkable in itself but noted because the winner drank himself to death immediately afterwards. In the next few years crowds were drawn to watch a soldier swim from Deal to Ramsgate and a sailor splash his way across Portsmouth Harbour.

The professors

The attraction of such events led to the emergence for the first time of swimming professionals, who for some reason liked to call themselves 'professors'. They were on a par with the professional athletes of the pedestrianism era. They undertook bizarre endurance tests, such as treading water for hours on end. And they organized aquatic entertainments, with stunts, 'fancy' swimming and competitive races. Such organized swimming as there was in the first half of the nineteenth century was professional. Most of the press coverage over the period was of races between well-known 'professors' for large wagers, with a good deal of side-betting. A fast swimmer could make good money.

Many of these entertainments were in the sea or in rivers. Lakes were also popular, particularly the Serpentine in London's Hyde Park. Then gradually swimming baths began to appear. The first that we have any record of was the 'Peerless Pool', an open-air bath built in Baldwin Street off City Road in north London in 1743 expressly for swimming. It seems to have been open to the public, at least to those who could afford to pay. Harrow School constructed a pool around 1810 which was known as the 'Duck Puddle'. As its name implies, it was a muddy hole filled with water, but what it lacked in comfort it made up for in length – it was 500 yards long. By the 1830s, private companies were opening baths in London as profit-making enterprises. One was the National Tepid and Cold Swimming Baths in Westminster Road in Lambeth. Another well-known complex was in Holborn. In 1828, way ahead of its time, Liverpool City Council opened the first municipal swimming pool, the St George's Baths, which took its water directly from the Mersey.

Most of these baths had professionals attached to them who gave lessons and organized events. Some became quite well known. In 1842,

*'Professor' Stevens giving a lesson in Lambeth: all the pupils
are swimming naked, normal in Victorian times*

Captain Stevens of the National Baths in Lambeth put an advertisement in the press about a forthcoming 'benefit' to be held at the Baths,
the beneficiary, of course, being himself. This became common
practice among 'professors' attached to baths or clubs whenever they
needed extra money. Captain Stevens certainly did: within a year of
the benefit, he was in a debtors' prison.

One of the best-known professionals was Frederick Beckwith, one of
Stevens's successors at Lambeth. By all accounts he was possibly a
great swimmer, but definitely a great showman. He was also shrewd.
At one point he organized a swimming match against Louis Bennett,
the wildly popular Native American pedestrian known as 'Deerfoot'.
Sadly Deerfoot was forced to forfeit, so the much-awaited event never
happened. But Beckwith, of course, took all the stake money. Even
when he was past his prime, Beckwith liked to keep his name before the
public. In 1873, he placed this advertisement in the press:

PROFESSOR BECKWITH, LAMBETH BATHS,
WESTMINSTER BRIDGE ROAD

This celebrated Ex-Champion Swimming Teacher begs to inform the nobility
and gentry that he is constantly in attendance at the above magnificent
Establishment. Beckwith wishes it be known that he has given over 300 prizes
towards furthering the interests of this art, and to prove the excellence of
his teaching, points to many celebrated swimmers brought out by him, both
amateurs and professionals. N.B. – there will shortly be a great gala on the
Thames, and races (open to the world) for all classes.

Such advertisements drew some comment from the leading swimming reporter of the day, one Robert Watson, who made it clear who
he was talking about: 'I mean the gentleman who has given about
4,999 prizes, including a stop watch, for the promotion of swimming.
Good luck to you, old man, and may you live to give another 4,999
prizes for swimming, minus that bit of string at the end of them.'

Certainly Beckwith liked to stack the odds in his favour when he
could. When he had finished racing himself, he issued challenges
involving one or more of his four children. In the 1870s, he proposed a

match in which his 14-year-old son William would race another well-known professional, J. B. Johnson, over 1000 yards with just a twenty-yard start. When Johnson was outraged at this insult to his ability,

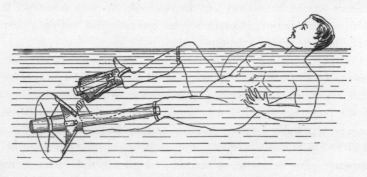

One of many curious devices designed to aid swimming in
the nineteenth century: few if any of them worked

Beckwith promptly put an advertisement in the press saying he had made a terrible mistake because of course his son couldn't win with just a twenty-yard start. So he proposed instead that Johnson should give him one hundred yards. Sadly we don't know if the race ever took place – or whether Johnson was all the time co-operating in a publicity stunt.

Beckwith went on teaching and promoting events long after most professionals had given up the game. In 1875, at a time when a woman swimming was still quite rare, his daughter Agnes staged an endurance swim from London Bridge to Greenwich. A few years later, she set a record by treading water for thirty hours in the whale tank of the Royal Aquarium at Westminster. The high point of Beckwith's career was organizing an aquatic entertainment for the royal family. He staged his last show in 1897, just a few months before his death at the age of 79. By that time most swimming was firmly in the hands of the amateurs.

The start of competition

The first clubs, often known as swimming societies, came into existence in the 1830s. There were several in London founded with the express purpose of promoting the idea of swimming among the populace. The most ambitious was the National Swimming Society, founded by John Strachan, a Dean Street wine merchant. They organized a race in the Serpentine in 1837 and another in the Thames the following year. We also know from a report in *The Times* that in their first few years, they

*The Serpentine Race between the bridges began in 1837: the Royal
Humane Society funded a boat to help 'the apparently drowned'*

had taught more than 2000 to swim in the Serpentine, the Thames and the Surrey Canal.

The Society aspired to be the national body for swimming. It had a policy of offering three silver medals to any local swimming society that applied, to be competed for by their members. In 1840, it provided a medal to the Glasgow Swimming Society for a race swum over 960 yards. That same year it gave three medals to the Oxford Swimming Society for a race of 400 yards. In the early 1840s, it seems to have changed its name to the British Swimming Society. In 1843 it organized four competitions: a race for youths under sixteen at Holborn Baths, a race for adults for three medals, the Society's annual championship and a 'fancy' swimming competition.

It is also often said to have been behind a fabled event that took place in 1844. The oft-repeated version of the story has two Native Americans – they would have been called Red Indians at the time – coming over to take part in a Society competition and soundly thrashing the shocked British swimmers. Sadly, it didn't quite happen like that. But the truth is almost as exotic.

The Flying Gull and Tobacco

In 1844, a group of Ojibwa Indians was brought to London by a former army officer called Rankin, who had fought in Canada during a recent rebellion, to stage an exhibition of their crafts and skills at the Egyptian Hall in Piccadilly. They also gave regular demonstrations of dancing, archery, horse riding (at Lord's cricket ground) and foot-running (at Vauxhall Gardens). It was also arranged for two of them to give an exhibition of swimming at Holborn Baths, whence they were conveyed by omnibus along with 'Mr Harold Kenworthy, the well-known swimmer'. *The Times* of Monday, 22 April 1844 takes up the story:

In the rear of the omnibus, in full costume and on horseback, were We-nish-ka-wea-bee (The Flying Gull) and Sah-ma (Tobacco) with Mr Green, their medical adviser, who has attended them since they have been in London, and who, on this occasion, suggested that the temperature of the water should be raised to 85 degrees.

While the two braves went off to get themselves ready and the squaws were taken off to 'an interior room' (at this time it was not generally thought proper for women to watch men swimming because most men swam in the nude), 'Mr Kenworthy went through a series of scientific feats' which seem to have excited the applause of the large crowd gathered for the event. Then the braves reappeared.

At a signal, the Indians jumped into the bath, and, on a pistol being discharged, they struck out and swam to the other end, a distance of 130 feet, in less than half a minute. The Flying Gull was the victor by seven feet. They swam back again to the starting place, where The Flying Gull was again the victor. Then they dived from one end of the bath to the other, with the rapidity of an arrow, and almost as straight a tension of limb.

They afterwards entered the lists with Mr Kenworthy, who is accounted one of the best swimmers in England, and who beat them with the greatest of ease.

Perhaps not surprising, after all the Indians' exertions. The braves were taken off to dress and join the squaws for 'wine and biscuits' before going back to the Egyptian Hall. Meanwhile the crowd was left to discuss what they had seen. What had really stunned them was the way that The Flying Gull and Tobacco swam:

Their style of swimming is totally un-European. They lash the water violently with their arms, like the sails of a windmill, and beat downwards with their feet, blowing with force, and forming grotesque antics.

They were swimming a sort of crawl, which had not been seen in Britain before. It seems to have been used for centuries throughout the Americas and the Pacific, but it was unknown in the 'civilized' world. British swimmers swam a sedate breaststroke, with their head kept well above water. They were fascinated by what they had seen, but they did not try to emulate it. There were limits, after all. It was to be another few decades before an Englishman called J. Arthur Trudgen reintroduced a basic crawl, which he had observed in South America.

Keeping the nation clean and healthy

In 1846, the Baths and Washhouses Act was passed. It was designed to promote cleanliness among the poor by encouraging local authorities to provide indoor baths, washhouses and laundries for those who didn't have them. Swimming baths were not specifically mentioned but many councils decided to build large 'plunge baths', ostensibly to provide a cheap way for more people to wash themselves. But they could also be used by people to take healthy exercise – in other words, to swim. Councils were given the further option of building open-air bathing places, which could be used for bathing or swimming. Uptake was slow, but the Act was undoubtedly the beginning of opening up swimming for the masses. It is also why swimming pools in Britain are still more often than not known as swimming baths.

Over the next twenty-odd years, swimming clubs sprouted up all over the country. In 1869, a number of them got together for a 'swimming congress' at the German Gymnasium in London, which had some very superior baths, and founded the Metropolitan Swimming Clubs Association. As an organization, it had an annoying habit of constantly changing its name, but its intentions were good: to teach people how to swim both as a safety measure and as a form of healthy exercise. Competition was not at the forefront of its thinking but it did set up the first national championship – the Men's Mile to be swum from Putney to Hammersmith. But it found it hard to expand from its original base. In the mid-1870s, it still only had six affiliated clubs. A catalyst was needed to kick-start a real expansion of swimming.

Captain Webb's feat

Matthew Webb, known as 'Captain' because he had briefly commanded the *Emerald of Liverpool*, was a merchant seaman who had undertaken exhausting swims all over the world. In the early 1870s, he read a newspaper report of the unsuccessful attempt by the well-known professional J. B. Johnson to swim the English Channel. He decided to quit his job and have a go himself. He embarked on months of careful training. The journalist Robert Watson accompanied him in a small boat and became bored with watching his 'slow, methodical, but

Captain Webb photographed in 1875, the year he became the first person to swim the Channel

perfect, breaststroke, and the magnificent sweep of his ponderous legs'. Webb was forced to abandon his first attempt not because he was in trouble but because the rough seas were threatening to swamp the boat that was accompanying him. Twelve days later, on 24 August 1875, he tried again.

At 1 p.m., a sizeable crowd watched him dive off the Admiralty Pier at Dover, wearing a red silk bathing costume. He was accompanied by a lugger full of special correspondents and kept going as he swam by imbibing 'cod-liver oil, beef tea, brandy, coffee and strong old ale'. As night fell he was passed by the *Maid of Kent*, whose passengers cheered him on with some verses of 'Rule, Britannia'. Seven miles from the French coast the tide turned and he seemed to start going backwards, but he eventually made landfall in France after nearly twenty-two hours in the water. The currents had made him swim more than forty miles. But he recovered quickly and said he felt just a strange sensation in his limbs 'similar to that after the first day of the cricket season'.

His 'superhuman' feat caused a sensation. On his triumphant return to London, even the Stock Exchange was brought to a halt. One sporting newspaper gushed: 'Among the many feats of human strength and endurance that have been recorded in the columns of *Bell's Life in*

Captain Webb being assisted into a trap
at Calais after completing his feat

London, that performed on Tuesday last – with which all of England is ringing, and of which the whole Anglo-Saxon race should be proud – stands as one of the greatest.' Webb won £125 for his swim, which was boosted by a generous testimonial. He promptly set off on a lecture tour of the country.

His achievement gave the popularity of swimming a tremendous boost and may have helped persuade the government to amend the Baths and Washhouses Act to encourage the building of municipal pools. Swimming baths and with them swimming clubs blossomed all over the country. There wasn't a single municipal pool in London in 1846; by 1914, there were 101. Liverpool, always ahead of this particular game, had nine indoor baths and four outdoor pools by 1880. The Royal Humane Society, who provided a boat to assist swimmers in difficulties in the Serpentine, estimated that 250,000 people swam in the lake in the summer of 1881.

Such was the impact of Captain Webb's swim. But despite all the public adulation, he himself did not prosper. He tried to earn a living from endurance races and water-treading stunts, but never made much money. In 1883, in desperation, he travelled with his young family to America. Against all advice, he was determined to tackle one of the most dangerous stretches of water in the world. Three miles below the Niagara Falls, the river emerges from a narrow gorge to form a

Captain Webb became a potent marketing tool: this matchbox was registered in 1876 by Collard, Kendall & Co

whirlpool a quarter of a mile wide. More than ten thousand people gathered to watch him attempt to swim through it. At 4 p.m. on 24 July, he was rowed out into the middle of the river. He dived in and was immediately caught by the current. He was pulled towards the whirlpool and then suddenly threw up his arms and went under. His body was found by fishermen some days later. He is buried in the cemetery at the edge of the falls.

Swimming goes international

As amateur swimming grew in popularity, business for the profession-als went into swift decline. Professional footballers and cricketers could draw crowds of thousands, but very few swimming pools could hold more than a couple of hundred. All that was left for the 'pro-fessors' was teaching. Even so, in keeping with the climate of the day, the sport managed to have a temporary split over the relationship between amateurs and professionals. Swimming always had a down-to-earth attitude – there was never any attempt to introduce the kind of social exclusion clauses that existed in rowing and, briefly, in athletics.

Poster for 'Professor' Frederick Cavill, who falsely
claimed to have swum the Channel

Professionals were people who swam for money, amateurs didn't. They couldn't take part in amateur races, but for most of the time there was no bar on amateurs racing against professionals provided they weren't paid to do so. The dispute, which led to some clubs breaking away briefly from the governing body, was more about whether certain individuals were professionals or not. The rift was healed in 1886 and the governing body was renamed for the final time as the Amateur Swimming Association.

Meanwhile, swimming had been developing independently in Europe, America and the Empire and in the 1890s international competition began. Swimming was one of the founding sports of the new modern Olympics in Athens in 1896, although Britain did not send a team. Britain did compete in the 1900 Olympics in Paris, with some success, then missed the 1904 Olympics in Los Angeles. In the 1908 Olympics in London, Britain was the dominant force, winning four of the available six gold medals. During those games, an international conference established the Fédération Internationale de Natation Amateur, or FINA, which became the sport's international authority. Its first General Secretary was George Hearn, an English swimming administrator, and many of its early rules and policies were taken straight from the ASA handbook. Since that time Britain has produced some fine individual swimmers, but it has never been such a strong influence again.

The other aquatic sports

Water polo was developed in Britain during the 1870s. In some parts of the country it began as a kind of water-based version of polo on horseback, with players 'riding' horses made from barrels, complete with horses' heads and fancy tails. They used double-bladed paddles both to strike the ball and for propulsion. Elsewhere it was initially called aquatic handball – some early matches were played in Bournemouth in 1876. In the end, the horses were abandoned and the handball technique took over, but the name water polo stuck. In 1881,

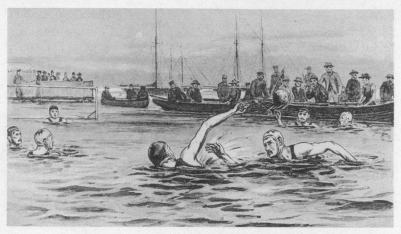

An early game of water polo: some versions involved 'horses' made from barrels, as in polo - the horses were abandoned, but the name stuck

an adapted form of the Football Association rules was adopted. This form of water polo became an Olympic sport in 1900.

A different form of the game was played in America for a brief while. It involved a partially inflated ball and allowed rugged underwater tackling, in which players were sometimes held underwater until they passed out. It was called the roughest sport on earth. Not surprisingly, its popularity dwindled and in 1935 the Americans adopted the hard ball used in the international game, which banned underwater tackling.

Diving grew as a sport as swimming pools became more widespread. Even though it has something in common with gymnastics, it is governed by FINA. It became an Olympic sport in 1904.

Strange though it may seem, **synchronized swimming** also had its origins in Victorian Britain. It was originally called 'graceful' or 'ornamental' or 'scientific' swimming and was initiated by male professional swimmers. As well as the kinds of movements we are familiar with today, it involved such novelties as eating while swimming and underwater, and even smoking while swimming and underwater. In the late 1880s it was taken up by amateurs and then around 1900 by women. It was developed further in America in the twenties and thirties under the influence of Hollywood and directors such as Busby Berkeley and became an exclusively female sport. It achieved Olympic status only in the 1980s.

14.
PUB GAMES

ALCOHOL AND SPORT have always been close bedfellows in Britain. Many sports began their formal life in pubs. Many sporting grounds and sporting teams were attached to pubs. Crowds throughout history have enjoyed a drink before, during or after a game, preferably all three. Today, large numbers of people gather in pubs to watch major sporting events on television.

Probably the most famous sporting pub was the Star and Garter tavern in Pall Mall. It was the favourite meeting place of the aristocratic sportsmen of the day. It was there that the Jockey Club, which governed horse racing for 250 years, was founded. And it was there that the early Laws of Cricket were written.

The Hambledon Club, which played such a key role in shaping the game of cricket, was initially based at a pub, the Bat and Ball on Broadhalfpenny Down in Hampshire. Its captain was the landlord. Most other early cricket grounds were attached to a pub. The Football Association was founded in a pub. And pubs run by prizefighters provided a vital information network for the illicit world of early boxing.

Inns and taverns have always played host to a variety of games. Most have not gone on to become sports and many of the most traditional were not in fact British in origin. Skittles hailed originally from third- and fourth-century Germany. Quoits are probably related to the ancient discus and may have been brought to Britain by the Romans. Backgammon and draughts are ancient games whose origins are uncertain but which are certainly not British, while dominoes originated in twelfth-century China and came to us via the Italians (hence the name). Bagatelle, popular in Victorian times, probably comes from France.

There are some British games. Shove-halfpenny dates from around the fifteenth century, when it was called 'shoffe-grote', because it was played with Edward IV groats. While cribbage is attributed by John Aubrey to the notorious gamester and poet Sir John Suckling. He is said to have developed the rules in the early seventeenth century from the old Tudor game of 'noddy' or 'noddie'. He certainly tried to turn his brainchild to his advantage. His most famous exploit involved distributing large numbers of marked packs of playing cards to the aristocracy of Britain. He then travelled the country playing cribbage with the gentry and fleecing them of some £4 million in today's money. But to no avail. He became embroiled in a plot to free the Earl of Strafford from the Tower and had to flee to Paris, where he committed suicide at the age of 32.

But three British games which began life in pubs (or, to be strictly accurate in one case, in an officers' mess) have gone on to become popular sports which have spread, slowly but surely, around the world.

Bowls (but not bowling)

The game of bowls, redolent of cream flannels, Earl Grey tea and cucumber sandwiches, has a guilty past. For much of its long existence in Britain, it was a pub game, a 'pothouse recreation'. Most bowling greens were attached to 'common drinking houses', which led Joseph Strutt to conclude that 'their play is seldom productive of much benefit, but more frequently becomes the prelude to drunkenness'. Even worse, in the seventeenth and eighteenth century, they became centres of gambling and, dare one say it, double-dealing and dishonesty.

Origins

The idea of rolling a ball along the ground towards a target goes back a very long way. The tomb of an Egyptian child buried in 5200 BC contained objects which clearly made up an early game of skittles. There were nine pieces of stone to be set up as 'pins' and a stone for a ball which first had to be rolled through an arch made of three pieces of marble. In the Italian Alps, 2000 years ago, a different game was developed which involved the underhand tossing of stones at a target; this is believed to be the origin of the game *bocce*, which is still played by people of Italian origin all around the world.

The Germans formalized the idea of bowling at pins in the third or fourth century AD, not as a game but as part of a religious ceremony – the pins were said to represent heathens and the aim was to knock them over. But the practice gradually evolved into a leisure pursuit and became popular all over Germany. Some versions had as few as three pins, others as many as seventeen. It is believed to have been the austere figure of Martin Luther who decided the optimum number was nine in the sixteenth century. German settlers took this nine-pin game with them to America. Legend has it that the modern ten-pin version was invented by a quick-witted sportsman in Connecticut in 1841 to get round a state law banning the nine-pin game because it gave rise to so much gambling.

By the Middle Ages, bowling at pins had spread throughout Continental Europe. But it never became popular in Britain. Instead, the British very early on developed the idea of the bowling green, on which wooden balls were bowled at a 'jack'. Something very similar to the modern game is depicted in a thirteenth-century manuscript. In 1299, a bowling green was laid out near the old city walls in Southampton on the south coast of England. The Southampton Old Bowling Green club have records of its continuous use from that day to this. Bowls had become so popular by 1388 that it was distracting the men of England from archery practice. It was banned by Richard II in that year and by Henry IV in 1409. But it was hard to suppress.

In the fifteenth century, bowls became fashionable among the landed gentry, played on elegant private greens in the grounds of their mansions. It was also played in alleys, which might be strips of lawn between yew hedges at a country house but could also be long narrow

(After a 14th-Century MS. in the Bodleian.)

(After a 13th-Century MS. at Windsor)

(After a 13th-Century MS.)

Bowlers of the thirteenth and fourteenth centuries, used by Joseph Strutt in
his Sports and Pastimes of the English People, *1801*

spaces between buildings or even indoors in the city. In 1455, when the young Henry VI lifted the ban on bowling in London, the city soon filled with greens and with alleys, both outdoor and indoor, which quickly became dens of gambling, drink and disorder. In 1477, Edward IV banned the game once more. In the second year of his reign, Henry VIII repeated the ban, declaring that 'the game of bowls is an evil because the alleys are in conjunction with saloons, or dissolute places, and bowling has ceased to be a sport, and rather a form of vicious gambling'.

The ban did not of course apply to Henry himself, who enjoyed both playing bowls and gambling heavily upon the outcome. He had bowling alleys built in the Palace at Whitehall. In 1541 he decreed that any nobleman or other gentleman who had an estate of more than

£100 a year could play without penalty in their own house or garden, but their servants and all other working people were restricted to playing only at Christmas, and then only in the house or the presence of their masters. Keeping an alley or place of bowling for 'gain, lucre or living' was forbidden. But the law does not seem to have been strictly

'The Devil's Bowling Green': a condemnation of bowls from
Quarles' Emblems, Divine and Moral from 1635

enforced. In 1579, the actor-turned-preacher Stephen Gosson drew a poignant picture of the perils of bowling alleys, calling them 'privy moths that eat up the credit of many idle citizens; whose gains at home are not able to weigh down their losses abroad; whose shops are so far from maintaining their play, that their wives and children cry out for bread, and go to bed supperless often in the year'.

Drake and the Hoe

On 19 July 1588, Captain Thomas Fleming risked putting his Scottish privateer into Plymouth Harbour to report that he had sighted the

Spanish Armada in the mists off Cornwall that morning. He found Sir
Francis Drake playing bowls on Plymouth Hoe. According to the story,
Drake's response was that they had plenty of time and should therefore
finish the game. He duly lost the rubber he was playing to his fellow
captain Sir John Hawkins, and then went off to defeat the Spaniards.
Experts in naval strategy say the story cannot be true because there
would have been no time to lose. But a Plymouth librarian investigat-
ing the legend found a document from 1624, just thirty-six years after
the event, which has the Duke of Braganza saying the Spanish fleet

*News of the Armada reaching Sir Francis Drake at bowls
on Plymouth Hoe: did he finish the game?*

arrived at England's shores 'while their commanders and captains were
at Bowls upon the Hoe at Plymouth'. Certainly the story hasn't done
the reputation of either bowls or Sir Francis Drake any harm over the
years.

Keen bowlers argue that Shakespeare must also have been quite a
player because of the way he uses bias as a metaphor in the 'commod-
ity speech' of the Bastard Philip Faulconbridge in *King John* (Act II,
Scene 2). That and other references prove that balls already had bias in
his day. He also suggests that bowls was played by women as well as
men. *Richard II* has the Queen conversing with a lady-in-waiting in the
Duke of York's garden at King's Langley in Hertfordshire:

QUEEN: What sport shall we devise here in this garden,
                To drive away the heavy thought of care?
FIRST LADY: Madam, we'll play at bowls.
QUEEN: 'Twill make me think the world is full of rubs,
                And that my future runs against the bias.

In 1620, James I issued licences for a number of bowling greens and alleys in London, which legalized the gambling that was already going on. The courtier and poet Sir John Suckling, a favourite of Charles I, said that he prized 'a lucky hit at Bowls above all the trophies of wit'. He was the best player at the court but, as John Aubrey reports, this still didn't stop his sisters going 'to the Peccadillo Bowling Green crying, for feare he should lose all their portions'. Charles I himself was a heavy gambler at bowls, on one occasion losing £1000 to Richard Shute, a turkey merchant, at Barking Hall in Essex. When he was confined at Caversham Park, he used to play at the inn at Collins End near Goring Heath in Oxfordshire. After his execution, the landlord put up a signboard with a likeness taken from Van Dyck and the following verse beneath it:

> Stop, traveller, stop! In yonder peaceful glade
> His favourite game the royal martyr played;
> Here, stripped of honours, children, freedom, rank
> Drank from the bowl, and bowl'd for what he drank;
> Sought in a cheerful glass his cares to drown
> And changed his guinea ere he lost his crown.

Samuel Pepys played bowls and refers to the game quite frequently: 'May 1st, 1661. Up early, and bated at Petersfield, in the room that the King lay in lately at his being there. Here very merry and played us and our wives at Bowls.' But gradually the image of bowls became seamier and seedier. Charles Cotton, poet and friend of Izaak Walton, spoke of the 'swarms of rooks which so pester Bowling Greens . . . and Bowling Alleys where any such places are to be found, some making so

PUB GAMES 371

small a spot of ground yield them more annually than fifty acres of land shall do else where about this city, and this done [by] cunning, betting, crafty matching and basely playing booty'. As the eighteenth century dawned, some of the gentry continued to play behind closed doors, but playing bowls in public became deeply unfashionable.

The Scottish revival

It was the Scots who rescued bowls. The game had reached Scotland in the sixteenth century and had never been banned (except on Sundays, by the Kirk Session of 1595) and had never fallen prey to the perils of drink and gambling that bedevilled English greens and alleys. The first club, Willow Bank, was formed in Glasgow and played originally on a green laid in Candleriggs in 1695. Over the next hundred years, nearly every town built a bowling green, to be used by people of all ranks. Most were of a quality not easily seen in England, truly level and often laid with sea-washed turf. This allowed the game to be played to a much higher level of scientific and strategic skill (as well as developing techniques that would prove useful later in the construction of putting greens). For a while bowls became the national summer game, being replaced in the winter by curling, which shared many of the same principles.

In the first half of the nineteenth century, the number of clubs grew steadily. In 1848 two hundred club representatives met in Glasgow Town Hall to look at the possibility of setting up a national body for bowls. In the end they decided this was impractical but they did set up a committee to draw up a complete Code of Laws for the sport. It was headed by William W. Mitchell, a Glasgow lawyer who had started to play bowls at the age of eleven on the green at Kilmarnock. The laws he produced have remained the basis for the sport ever since. Mitchell himself proved quite enduring. On 25 December 1879 he played for four hours on the Willow Bank green before going home for his Christmas dinner. He even wrote a poem about it:

Yet I ha'e played on Christmas Day,
Before gaun hame to dine,
An' never looked on better play
When summer days are fine.

On 12 September 1892, the Scottish Bowling Association was finally
brought into being and quickly assumed the same relationship to bowls
as the MCC has to cricket and the Royal and Ancient to golf.
Meanwhile the Scots were busy exporting their revived game to the rest
of Britain and to Canada, South Africa, Australia and New Zealand.
Indeed, the first bowling associations were set up in New South Wales
and Victoria in 1880. The England Bowling Association was not started
until 1903, under the aegis of the irrepressible W. G. Grace. The Irish
and Welsh associations followed in 1904. They all chose to adopt the
Scottish rules. Since 1904 a round-robin tournament involving all four
home nations has been played every year.

The game remains predominantly a British and Commonwealth
sport. The American Lawn Bowling Association was formed in 1915
and many towns have public bowling greens, but it is very much a

The green at the Southampton Town Bowling Club
in 1870: in continuous use since 1299

minority sport compared to ten-pin bowling. Four-yearly World Championships were started in 1966 for singles, pairs, triples and fours and a World Indoor Championship is held every year. Both are dominated by Australia, New Zealand, South Africa and the home countries. The USA has won two world titles since 1966, Israel has won one. The current world singles champion is Safuan Said from Malaysia. But for most players, the pleasure of the sport remains a little sociable competition – and the tea and cucumber sandwiches.

Snooker (and billiards)

Snooker is much the most popular of the cue sports in Britain and much of the Commonwealth and it is incontrovertibly of British origin. But it is derived from billiards and the origin of billiards is a mystery. In the sixth century BC the Scythian philosopher Anacharsis writes about watching a game similar to billiards while travelling through Greece. The Romans are said to have played a game something like it. Even China is said to have invented a game along the same lines. The truth is that we simply don't know.

The likelihood is that billiards is an indoor variant of outdoor stick-and-ball games and therefore has something in common with ancient palle malle and more modern croquet, hockey, golf and even bowls. In particular it may be connected to a medieval lawn game which involved hoops which had to be gone through and hazards which had to be circumvented. It is suggested that Louis XI of France (1461–83) was the first to put a version of this game onto an indoor table. Certainly the word *billiards*, thought to derive from the Old French word *billard*, meaning 'a curved stick, mace or cue', suggests that the game may have had its origins in France. The word *cue* comes from the French *queue*, meaning 'tail', the thin end of a mace. Originally, as contemporary pictures show, the thick end of the mace was used to strike the ball. But, over time, players discovered that the 'cue' end gave them more control.

By the middle of the sixteenth century, the game was popular in grand houses both in Britain and in France. Mary Queen of Scots, just a few months before she lost her head, complained that her *table de billiard* had been taken away. After her death, the green cloth was

An engraving of Louis XIV playing billiards: he is playing with the thick end of the mace - the queue, *or 'cue', was the thin end*

ripped from it to cover her decapitated corpse. In 1588, accounts show that the Duke of Norfolk owned a 'billiard bord covered with a greene cloth . . . three billiard sticks and eleven balls of yvery'. Spenser, Jonson and Shakespeare all mention the game. Over the next 200 years, the game spread from the mansions of the rich – the diarist John Evelyn made a point of describing the billiard table at every country house he visited – to the taverns of London and the cafés of Paris. At both ends of the social spectrum, it was a gambling game.

In the late eighteenth century, the game began to develop differently in different countries. The French favoured carom billiards, a three-ball game played on a pocketless table where players score by achieving a 'carom' or 'cannon', striking both the other two balls with their cue ball in the same shot. This is the game primarily played in France and the rest of Europe, in the Far East, in Central America and to a smaller extent in the United States. But the most popular American game is 'pool', played on a smaller table with pockets and balls which are coloured and numbered. 'English' billiards combines elements of the two. It is played with the same three balls as carom billiards – a red, a white and a white with a spot – but on a table with pockets. Initially there were two – one in the middle of either end; then four, one at each corner; then six, with a pocket added in the middle of either side. This is the game which is played in Britain and the former Empire and it is the version which concerns us here.

'English' billiards

By the early 1800s, professional billiards players had emerged in Britain. Rather like prizefighters, they accepted challenges from each other for money. Their matches were public affairs and attracted good crowds and a great deal of betting. By 1820, the sporting press and the public began to recognize one player as the champion. The first was Edwin Kentfield, known as Jonathan, from Brighton, the pre-eminent player of his day and the author of one of the first books on how to play

An idealized picture of ladies at play: in reality, the
billiard room was largely a male preserve

billiards. He was champion until 1849 when advancing age led him to decline a challenge from John Roberts Sr. Roberts beat off all challenges until 1870, when the first formal title championship match took place. The leading players met beforehand to decide the championship rules – the first formal rules of the sport. Before a large crowd which included the Prince of Wales and a number of aristocrats, Roberts lost his crown (and the £200 prize money) to the much younger William Cook. But within two months his son John Roberts Jr had won the title back.

He was to dominate the sport for much of the rest of the century. For ten years he defeated all challengers for his title. He then retired from championship play but was still acknowledged as the leading player, the king in exile, which didn't enhance the prestige of the championship. He travelled the world giving exhibitions, taking on all-comers in handicap matches and making money. The Maharajah of Jaipur paid him an annual salary of £500, a handsome sum, to be his court billiard player for one month a year. On his visits he was given a palace for his personal use, complete with one hundred servants. At home he set up a professional circus, crossing the country to play short matches on handicap and promoting week-long matches at venues such as the Horticultural Hall in Westminster, the Argyll Billiard Hall (now the London Palladium) and the Egyptian Hall in Piccadilly.

After Roberts finally retired, the circus continued. The leading players would fight for the championship but also play each other in private matches which could last as long as a fortnight in front of a different crowd each day. In the end, the players' skill effectively killed the goose that laid the golden egg. They started developing techniques which would allow them to amass huge scores. One player managed to jam the two 'object' balls – the red and the white spot – at the top of a pocket, which allowed him to score cannon after cannon after cannon. Over five unbearably tedious weeks he notched up a score of 499,165 until someone finally took pity and called the whole thing off. Despite constant rule changes to stop such practices, the public became disillusioned. By the mid-1930s, professional billiards was in terminal decline. It has never really recovered.

A symbolic blow came in 1936, when the *Daily Mail* switched its annual Gold Cup tournament from billiards to the newly emerging game of snooker. For most people, the game survives only in the form of bar billiards, a pub game introduced by a games manufacturer in the 1930s.

The rise and fall and rise again of snooker

In 1875, the young officers of the Devonshire Regiment stationed in Jubbulpore in India whiled away the long afternoons of the rainy season around the mess billiard table. Like the public sixty years later, they became bored with the standard game and looked for alternatives which were both exciting and offered more opportunities for gentle gambling. One well-known variation was 'pyramid', which started with fifteen red balls lined up as a triangle. Every time a player potted a red, his opponents had to pay him the stake money agreed per ball. Another was 'life pool', in which each player used a different coloured ball as his cue ball. All the snooker colours except black were used. Every time you potted the ball of one of your opponents, he lost a life and had to pay the agreed stake into the kitty. When he'd lost three lives he had to pay extra for a final life. Once he'd lost that, he was out. The last man left in scooped the 'pool' – hence the name of the game. A variant was 'black pool', in which you were allowed a separate go at the black after each regular ball you potted. Every time you potted the black, your opponents had to pay extra.

During that rainy season, a Devonshire subaltern called Neville Chamberlain persuaded his fellow officers to try a new variant which combined elements of all three of these games. They used the triangle of fifteen reds and all the colours (except for blue and brown, which were added later). They decided they liked the idea. One day, as they were playing their new invention, one of the men missed an easy pot. 'Why,' exclaimed Chamberlain, 'you're a regular snooker.' Bemused and no doubt a little insulted, the officer asked what on earth he meant. Chamberlain had to explain that he'd recently had a visit from a fellow officer who had trained at the Royal Military Academy at Woolwich.

His guest had told him that a brand-new cadet at Woolwich, the lowest of the low, was called a 'snooker'.

'To soothe the feelings of the culprit,' Chamberlain recalled many years later in an interview with Compton Mackenzie, 'I added that we were all, so to speak, snookers at the game so it would be very appropriate to call the game snooker. The name was adopted with enthusiasm and the game has been called snooker ever since.'

Chamberlain, who subsequently became Sir Neville and is not to be confused with the later Prime Minister, then took the game with him through various postings around the subcontinent. From 1881 to 1885 he was aide-de-camp to the commander-in-chief in Madras, spending every summer at the hill station of Ootacamund. Snooker became very popular among members of the Ooty Club, who worked out the rules in detail for the first time and posted them in the billiards room. From there it was spread all over India by officers who were introduced to the game while on leave. Word soon began to filter back to Britain. On one of his regular visits, John Roberts Jr, the dominant figure in billiards, sought out Chamberlain while he was having dinner with the Maharajah of Cooch Behar and learned the rules from him. Roberts then brought the game back to England.

It took a while to catch on. The idea of building a break was particularly slow to develop. Around 1910, the Scottish billiards champion Tom Aiken was reported to have notched up a break of 102. The first amateur competition was played in 1916, and won by an American who had taken up the game just weeks beforehand. In 1919, the rules were standardized by the new Billiards Association and Control Club (BA&CC). The first professional tournament was the Midland Professional Championship of 1921. In 1924, a billiard hall owner from Nottingham called Tom Dennis wrote to the BA&CC suggesting a national championship. The Secretary, A. Stanley Thorn, replied: 'The suggestion will receive consideration at an early date but it seems a little doubtful whether snooker as a spectacular game is sufficiently popular to warrant the successful promotion of such a competition.'

The championship was finally started in 1927. And it looked at first as though A. Stanley Thorn might have had a point. Joe Davis, who was to dominate snooker for the next forty years, won against a handful of opponents. In 1929, there were five entries. In 1930, there were six. In 1931, there were just two – Joe Davis beat Tom Dennis, the man who first thought of the idea, in Dennis's own snooker hall. But after that, the sport began to take off. The crowds increased in size. In 1936, Davis won a tumultuous world championship in which he had to take all the last ten frames to keep the title. It was after that match that the *Daily Mail* switched its allegiance.

When snooker resumed after World War II, Davis retained the world title in 1946 and then decided to follow the example of John Roberts Jr and retire from championship play. But, again like Roberts, he continued to dominate the sport for the next fifteen years. Or rather he presided over its near terminal decline. The number of professional players dwindled to just a handful and the public became bored with watching the same old faces. That in turn meant there was little incentive for talented young amateurs to turn professional. It looked as though professional snooker had reached the last black. Having finally achieved his ambition of scoring a perfect 147 break in an official competition in 1955, Joe Davis eventually retired. He had amassed a total of 682 century breaks during his career. From 1957 to 1964, the world championship lay dormant. From 1964 to 1969 it was revived but only on a challenge basis. Then, in 1969, snooker's fortune changed yet again.

The unlikely catalyst was BBC2. In order to attract people to watch its new colour broadcasts, it started the legendary snooker programme *Pot Black*. Suddenly snooker on television made sense. The players became well-known personalities. Sponsors, particularly the tobacco companies, moved in to revive the world championship as a knockout competition. New and exciting young players began to emerge. There was money to be made.

In 1977, the world championship moved to the Crucible Theatre in Sheffield for the first time and television coverage increased dramatically. The BBC found that the more live snooker it showed, the higher the audience. Today, the two-week tournament culminating on the spring bank holiday is a major national sporting event. And at the moment most, but not all, of the players competing in it are British.

But the world of snooker is changing. The TV audience in Britain is suffering a small but noticeable decline. More than twice as many people now watch the world championships in Europe, especially in Switzerland, Germany, Holland and Denmark. And the sport has exploded in popularity in the Far East, attracting huge numbers of viewers. Players from China and Hong Kong are beginning to make their mark in the world rankings. British domination may once more be under threat.

Clearing the colours

Snooker is almost certainly the only sport which has an explicit provision in its rules for those who are colour-blind. Under Section 5 (The Officials), paragraph 1 (a) (v) states that the referee shall 'tell a player the colour of a ball, if requested'. For many years the rule actually used the phrase 'colour-blind', but in these more enlightened times it does not. No provision is made for referees who might be colour-blind.

Darts

Darts as weapons have been around for centuries, but darts as a sport is barely 100 years old. The *Oxford English Dictionary* lists the first recorded use of the word as 1314: 'launces, swerdes and dartes'. Chaucer used it as a verb: 'As the wilde bole ... ydarted to the herte'. Then it crops up fairly frequently in literature. Anne Boleyn gave Henry VIII 'darts worked in the Biscayan fashion, richly ornamented', presumably for use in hunting.

There is some suggestion that the Pilgrim Fathers may have played a game called 'buttes', in which they threw shortened arrows at the butt of a wine cask marked out with concentric circles, scoring five for the centre and one for the outer ring. But there is no hard evidence and somehow it doesn't sound like a very Puritan thing to do. In late

Victorian times there seems to have been a parlour game called 'dart and target'. A contemporary book gives instructions on how to make your own set: 'The dart is a straight piece of stick, with a pin stuck in one end, and a paper guide at the other.' It suggests using soft wood for the dartboard, again painted in concentric circles like an archery target.

But the game didn't start appearing in pubs, its natural habitat, until the 1890s. The design of the dartboard varied from region to region – there are still a handful of local variations in use even today. What has become the standard board, with doubles and trebles, is sometimes attributed to a 44-year-old carpenter from Bury in Lancashire called Brian Gamlin. He's said to have started the design in 1896, but died before he could patent it. But others dispute the claim, saying it evolved over time and was the work of many hands. The evidence is inconclusive.

Indeed, for a relatively young sport, the history of darts is about as murky as the smoke-filled rooms in which it was generally played. For instance, there is an oft-repeated story which says that in 1908, at a time when games of chance were banned in licensed premises, a Leeds publican called William 'Bigfoot' Annakin was brought before the magistrates' court accused of allowing darts to be played on his premises. He asked for a dartboard to be set up in court and threw three twenties. He then challenged anyone in court to do the same. A court official only managed to get one dart on the board. Annakin then threw three more twenties, which was enough to persuade the magistrates that darts was a game of skill. But the reality may not have been quite so dramatic. In the 1980s, Annakin's grandson said in an interview that his grandfather was not a publican but a steelworker – and also the best darts player in the area. When the landlord of the Adelphi Inn was summonsed for allowing a game of chance in his pub, he asked Annakin to go with him to court to prove it was a game of skill. He did this by accurately hitting numbers nominated by the magistrates. But we don't even know for sure if that's true, because the court records for the period are lost.

Competition in the early years of the twentieth century was very

The earliest known photograph of a
darts team, dating from 1901

much a local affair, either confined to 'in-house' leagues or matches
between pubs close to each other. The first brewery leagues were not
started until after World War I. By 1924 the sport had become popular
enough for a governing body, the National Darts Association, to be
set up to standardize the rules. Over the winter of 1927–28, the first
major knockout tournament was held in the London area, sponsored
by the *News of the World*. It attracted around 1000 entries and was won
by Sammy Stone, a Boer War veteran and father of nine. During the
1930s there was a darts boom and the *News of the World* competition
spread to cover most of the country. In the 1938–39 season, the total
number of entrants was more than 280,000.

During World War II, darts became massively popular among
servicemen. It was played by all ranks, in the officers' mess and the
humblest billet. Prisoners of war made their own darts and dartboards.
Darts were standard issue in the NAAFI sports pack given to servicemen. American soldiers stationed in England liked the game and took
it back to the United States. At home, the *News of the World* sponsored
a foursome of professional darts players to travel the country giving
exhibitions to raise money for the Red Cross.

From this sort of charity work, two figures emerged to become major
post-war stars. Jim Pike and Joe Hitchcock became so well known that
they separately travelled the country giving exhibitions and performing
trick shots in music halls. There was a huge clamour for them to meet

each other for a showdown match. Between 1946 and 1948, they met in three epic confrontations attended by large paying audiences and broadcast live by BBC Radio. Hitchcock won on all three occasions.

The *News of the World* tournament was revived for the 1947–8 season, this time on a national basis. Another Sunday newspaper, *The People*, brought back the National Team Championships it had started just before the war. This was a boom time for darts. Ex-servicemen continued to play, and with TV and cars being rare, the game became a popular form of entertainment for both men and women. Brewers sponsored leagues, companies ran leagues for their employees and hospitals and charities joined in. It was claimed at one point that ten million people in Britain were playing the game at least occasionally. The real figure was probably closer to six million, but that still represented an extraordinary phenomenon.

In the 1950s and 1960s, with the growth of television, the sport's popularity declined. It was still widely played, but sponsors such as *The People* withdrew. A new governing body, the National Darts Association of Great Britain, set up county leagues and just managed to keep the major competitions going on gate money alone. But in the 1970s, a second darts boom began. New split-screen television technology made the sport popular among TV viewers, which in turn attracted new sponsors. In 1973, the British Darts Organization was set up to run the professional game. It began to introduce new competitions, culminating in the World Professional Darts Championship in 1978, which became a major television event in Britain and around the world.

Part of the appeal for the television audience was the character of the players. Some, such as Eric Bristow and Jocky Wilson, became household names. All of them were larger than life, sometimes heroic, on occasions tragic. One player was reputed to need to drink ten pints of beer during a match. He never did so on camera, he never appeared drunk and it didn't seem to affect his game. He wasn't thin, mind.

Then there was the commentary. At its highest level, darts is a mite repetitive. It relies on the skill and eloquence of the commentator to keep the interest going. The legendary Sid Waddell, voted Sports Commentator of the Year in 2002 by his peers, has always kept the game firmly in perspective. 'When Alexander of Macedonia was 33 he cried salt tears because there were no more worlds to conquer,' he once famously said. 'Bristow is only 27!'

By the 1990s, the sport had heeded Waddell's aspirations and become international, at least in terms of its audience. In 1993, a group of sixteen leading professionals broke away from the BDO to form what is now the Professional Darts Corporation, which has taken darts in a new direction. Alexander-like, it is building a 'world circuit' of darts based around new competitions such as the Las Vegas (where else?) Desert Classic, which began in 2002. Despite such international aspirations, the vast majority of the players are still British. But watch out, the Dutch – the Dutch? – are on the march.

15.
THE ONES THAT GOT AWAY

BRITAIN DEVELOPED THE concept of sport: games which can be played according to agreed and supervised rules anywhere in the world. Britain has also been responsible for developing many of the world's most popular individual sports, and for providing the basis on which others were built, such as baseball and American football. But there are some sports – a few major, some minor – for which Britain cannot take credit. Some are obvious – martial arts, for instance, clearly originated in the Far East; the great Gaelic sports evidently came from Ireland; and we were never going to be at the forefront of winter sports (though we had much more influence than we might have expected). Others are less so.

So can we generalize about the sports Britain did invent, and the ones that we didn't? To an extent, we can. You can put the word 'play' in front of the majority of the sports we invented. You can play cricket, you can play soccer, you can play rugby (and American football), hockey, golf, tennis, baseball, bowls, snooker and darts. OK, there are exceptions – you don't play boxing, swimming, sailing, athletics, rowing or horse racing. But you can play the horses. And therein lies a clue. All the British sports that you can't put 'play' in front of began life as major gambling activities. The British have always liked gaming as well as games.

The only sport the British didn't invent that you can put 'play' in front of is basketball, which is a bit of a special case. We didn't need an indoor winter game because the ground outside was frozen. Most of the rest are sports that are disciplines rather than games, such as gymnastics, equestrianism (think dressage), weightlifting, shooting, fencing and wrestling. The British are not very good at disciplines.

Some of the others we could have invented. They just got away.

Motor racing

The biggest of these sports, at least in terms of worldwide television audiences, is motor racing. The first patent for the manufacture of a motor vehicle was taken out by Karl Benz in Germany in January 1886. He was followed a few months later by his compatriot Gottlieb Daimler. But the first ever race of any kind between motor vehicles took place in France just eight years later.

It was a reliability trial designed to show the doubters that motor cars really could travel faster than horses without exploding. Twenty-one contestants set off from Paris to make the 80-mile journey to Rouen in less than eight and a half hours. Halfway along they stopped for lunch in Mantes – this was France, after all – then continued to Rouen. The first vehicle to arrive was a steam tractor which had completed the route in six hours and forty-eight minutes, at an average speed of 11 mph. Peugeots came second and third. All the nineteen cars that finished had solid wheels.

The first proper race took place the following year from Paris to Bordeaux and back, a total of 745 miles. The winner had an average speed of 14.9 mph. That same year the Automobile Club de France (ACF) was formed. In 1896 there were twelve races in all, including the first international event from Paris to Amsterdam and back. Manufacturers were beginning to realize that such events, which were beginning to attract a lot of attention, were a powerful tool for promoting their massively expensive wares. They were starting to produce cars specifically for racing. Drivers were becoming sporting stars. That year racing also started in Italy and America.

There were no enclosed tracks at this time, so all races followed the town-to-town format. In 1903, the ACF organized an ambitious race from Paris to Madrid, to be run on open, public roads. Two hundred and thirty cars entered, some of which were quite fast. It was a disaster waiting to happen. The French pioneer Marcel Renault was killed when his car overturned while he was duelling with another French driver. There were three other fatalities in the early stages. The French and Spanish governments combined to bring the race to a halt when it reached Bordeaux. They even insisted that the racing cars be towed back to Paris by horse. It was the end of town-to-town racing.

A couple of years earlier, the American newspaper magnate James Gordon Bennett, who was based in Paris, had started his own race because he felt the French were dominating the fledgling sport. It was

One of the casualties of the Paris–Madrid race of 1903: four people were killed during the first stage, causing the race to be abandoned

for national teams who were allowed three entries each. A more controlled affair than the Paris to Madrid debacle, the Bennett Trophy now became the most important race of the year. This annoyed the French because, even though their automobile industry was immensely strong, they were still only allowed three entries. In 1906, the ACF came up with an alternative.

Their idea was to close off a circuit of sixty-four miles of country roads near the town of Le Mans. They put up forty miles of palisades to keep spectators back and built grandstands, a timekeeper's box, a leaders' board and a rudimentary pit area in the small town of

Montfort. It was to be a massive affair – six laps of the track a day for two days, a total of 769 miles. They wanted it to be the greatest prize in motor sport. So naturally they named it the Grand Prix.

There were thirty-four entries, twenty-five from France, the rest from Germany and Italy. There was no British involvement. The drivers set off at ninety-second intervals, starting at six in the morning. It soon became apparent that the ACF had spent far too little on the roads. They were essentially dusty tracks which the ACF had tried to cover in tar. But in the heat of a June day, the tar melted and spun up into the faces of the drivers, getting under their goggles and causing horrendous inflammation. There were innumerable punctures. The race became an appalling endurance test.

After two days of drama, a Renault driven by Hungarian-born Ferenc Szisz emerged as the clear winner. He had completed the twelve laps in 12 hours, 14 minutes and 7 seconds, at an average speed of 62.8 mph. Louis Renault is said to have broken down in tears, overcome by the emotion of victory but also perhaps by the memory of his dead brother. No one at the event could have had any clue about the scale of the phenomenon they had just set in motion.

The second Grand Prix the following year was held near Dieppe. There were twenty-four French entries and fourteen others from six different countries, including one from Britain and one from the United States. The race was won by Italian Felice Nazzaro in a Fiat. The next year's race, also in Dieppe, attracted even more entries. There were forty-eight starters, including three Austins from Britain. This time it was the turn of the Germans. Mercedes took the first three places. The French were distraught. During that same year, the legendary Brooklands banked circuit just outside London opened for the first time. It was to stay in business until 1939.

There were no Grands Prix for the next three years. The 1912 race was also held at Dieppe. French honour was restored through the victory of Georges Boillot in a Peugeot. Boillot won again in 1913 near Amiens. The final Grand Prix to be held before World War I took place a few days after Archduke Franz Ferdinand had been shot in Sarajevo. It came down to a straight battle between France and

Germany. In the end, after Boillot broke down on the final lap, the first three places all went to Mercedes. The French had held six Grands Prix up to this time. The Americans had held five. No other country had held any.

Grand Prix racing began again in France in 1921. The following year Italy held its first Grand Prix at Monza, while 1923 saw the first British driver to win a Grand Prix, the elegant Sir Henry Segrave. The

The Motor

The National Motor Journal.

VOL. XLIII. No. 1,125.   TUESDAY, JULY 10, 1923.   FOURPENCE.

ENGLAND WINS THE GRAND PRIX.

Sweeping Success of Sunbeams in Most Thrilling Contest Ever Run.

It Was Anyone's Race from Start to Finish.

Sunbeams were First, Second and Fourth. Bugatti Third.

The first English victory in a Grand Prix, in France in 1923:
the victorious driver was Sir Henry Segrave

first British Grand Prix was held at Brooklands in 1926. There were five races in 1927, nine in 1929 and eighteen in 1934. Formula One racing began in 1946 and the World Drivers Championship started in 1950 – the first race to count was the British Grand Prix at Silverstone.

Britain started late in motor racing but since World War II it has been a major force. It has produced more than twice as many world champions as any other country – a total of nine, with the nearest rival being Brazil with three. In the constructors' championship, which started in 1926, Britain has won thirty-three times to Italy's twenty-one. France on the other hand has produced only one world champion, who admittedly won four times, and has carried off the constructors' trophy just three times. Maybe it doesn't always pay to be in the vanguard.

Motorcycle racing

Motorcycle racing developed hand in hand with motor car racing. Many of the nineteenth-century French road races had a separate class for motorbikes. The sport reached America in 1903. The following year, the Fédération Internationale de Motorcyclisme was set up to administer international racing between five nations: Austria, Denmark, France, Germany and Britain. Britain's major contribution was the TT (Tourist Trophy) race on the Isle of Man, first held in 1907. For many years it was the most prestigious event in the motorcycling calendar. The Motorcycling World Championships began in 1949, with the TT race counting as the British Grand Prix. But in the early 1970s many leading drivers began to boycott the Manx event on the grounds of safety – since 1907 224 riders have been killed on the island. In 1976 the FIM stripped the race of its world championship status. The British Grand Prix is now held at Donington.

Basketball

It is a truth almost universally acknowledged that three of the four supposedly indigenous American sports have a British origin. Baseball is based on an English game well known to Jane Austen, American football evolved from a British sport and the first recorded games of ice hockey were played by British soldiers in Canada. Basketball is the only major sport to have been invented on US soil – by a Canadian. In 1891, Dr James Naismith was a clergyman working as a physical education instructor at the YMCA training school in Springfield, Massachusetts. That autumn he and others were asked by the head of the athletics department to try to come up with a lively and exciting game that could be played indoors to keep their students fit during the long New England winters, something that was more interesting than gymnastics and apparatus work.

Naismith took the challenge seriously. He looked at the other sports of the day, most of which were played outside and were difficult to transfer indoors. Then he worked out what attributes he wanted his new game to have. He wanted it to be a team game; he wanted it to be fair to all, easily learned and playable by average men and women; and he wanted it to be free of rough play. From this starting point he worked out five principles that still underpin the game today:

- There should be a ball which is large, light and played only with the hands. He didn't want bats or sticks to be used and he didn't want the ball to be kicked. He wanted it to be thrown through the air.

- There was to be no running with the ball in hand because that would necessitate tackling and rough play. So the only way to move the ball was by passing or by dribbling – running while bouncing the ball with one hand.

- No member of either team was to be restricted from getting the ball at any time that it was in play.

- Both teams were to occupy the same space but there was to be no personal contact. Any kind of rough play would bring immediate disqualification and a penalty.

- Finally, Naismith had observed that there was a lot of jostling in defence of the net, the goal or the goal line in other sports. For this reason he wanted the 'goal' to be horizontal and elevated so that it could not be guarded. He remembered a local game from his schooldays called 'duck on a rock' which involved a lobbed arcing shot. That's how people would shoot in his new game.

Based on these principles, Naismith prepared a simple set of thirteen rules. His plan had been to nail square boxes at either end of the elevated track around the Springfield gymnasium. But he couldn't find any boxes so instead used two half-bushel peach baskets. Hence the name of the sport. On 21 December 1891, Naismith gathered a class of eighteen students, explained his new rules and asked two of them, Frank Mahan and Duncan Patton, to pick teams of nine. The game was under way. After initial doubts – Naismith later recorded in his diary that he was really worried they wouldn't take to his idea – the students became enthusiastic. After a lot of running and shouting, William R. Chase became the first person to score in basketball with a 25-foot midcourt shot. The students went home for Christmas to tell everyone about the new game.

It spread like wildfire. In the New Year, numerous local YMCAs wrote to Naismith to ask for a copy of the rules. It was taken up by colleges and universities around the land. Five of the players in the original game were Canadians, so it is not surprising that Canada was the first country outside the US to adopt the game. By 1893, it had reached France. In 1894, it was demonstrated in London. Soon afterwards it had reached Australia, China, India, Brazil and Japan. Slightly adapted rules for women's basketball were published in 1895. The first intercollegiate game took place in 1896 between the University of Iowa and the University of Chicago. Chicago won 15–12.

It took a while to standardize the rules and how many people there should be on each team (it's now five) and to sort out the equipment. The peach baskets were replaced in many places in 1892 by a heavy wire basket, then by an iron hoop with a hammock-style basket underneath. In those early days a ladder was required to retrieve the ball after a successful throw. Then a pole was used to poke the ball out, then a chain attached to the bottom of the basket which hung down so that an official could reach it. It wasn't until 1912–13 that someone had the bright idea of having a net which was open at the bottom to allow the ball to fall through.

In the fateful Berlin Games of 1936, basketball became an Olympic sport. US college coaches and teams raised enough money by subscription to take James Naismith, then 75, to Germany to throw the ball for the first game. He died three years later.

Fencing

The earliest record we have of a fencing match is a relief carving in the temple of Madinat Habu near Luxor in Upper Egypt built by

Rameses III around 1190 BC. The fencers are wearing masks and body protection, they have narrow shields attached to their left arms for parrying and the tips of their swords are blunted. The presence of judges, indicated by feathered wands, suggests that this was a tournament rather than simply a practice match.

The modern sport evolved out of European swordsmanship. During the time of full armours, swords were large bludgeoning instruments which required more strength than skill to use effectively. But the introduction of gunpowder in the fourteenth century made heavy armour redundant. Swords became much lighter and easier to manipulate. As a result, skilful swordsmanship became a necessity. Guilds of fencing masters were formed all over Europe to develop the art. In the sixteenth century, the Italians developed the rapier, which relied on the dextrous use of the point rather than the edge of the blade. This required a nimble and controlled style which relied on skill and speed rather than strength. But these new swords were still too heavy to use in defence, so swordsmen held daggers in their left hands to parry attacks. This new form of fencing quickly spread throughout Europe.

The next major development came not from fighting but from fashion. The long trailing rapier had been fine when men wore doublet and hose, top boots and cloaks. But the court of the Sun King in France favoured silk stockings, breeches and brocaded coats which could not accommodate the rapier. So gentlemen took to wearing short 'court' swords. It quickly became apparent that these new swords were ideal close-quarter weapons which only required the use of one hand, using the point to attack and the blade to defend. Proficiency in the use of the small sword became an essential requirement for a gentleman, and to help him train, a new practice sword called a 'foil' – because the tip was 'foiled' or blunted – was introduced. To minimize the risk of injury, rules and conventions were introduced which are reflected in modern regulations.

Around 1750, the French master La Boessière finally cottoned on to what the Egyptians had developed nearly three thousand years before and 'invented' the mask. This allowed a much more complex form of

*Illustrations from a treatise on fencing by the French fencing
master Le Sieur Labat, published in 1696*

swordplay and fencing with foils became a stylized and enjoyable art
rather than a form of combat. But this was an era when duels were still
common; faced at dawn with an opponent with a heavier sword and no
regard for conventional niceties, skill with a foil wasn't a great help. So
in the middle of the nineteenth century, the *épée de combat* was evolved, a
proper duelling sword but one which could also be used in competition
in conditions as close to duelling as protective clothing allowed.

The final member of the trio of modern fencing instruments was
introduced by the Hungarians in the late eighteenth century. They
took the Eastern scimitar and turned it into the curved sabre for their
cavalry. Others later adapted it as the cutlass for the navy. It was the
Italians who developed the light sabre as both a duelling and a fencing
weapon. The modern sport, long established in schools and colleges
but formalized through agreed rules and national associations only in
the late nineteenth century, still features these three weapons: the foil,
épée and sabre.

The British have always been ambivalent about fencing. We were reluctant to give up the English broadsword when the rapier first came in, even though it was ludicrously cumbersome. The earliest prizefights featured swords and cudgels as well as fists, but early on the 'Fancy' decided that fists were the manly thing; swords were prissy and French. Fencing has been an Olympic sport since the first modern games in 1896, but Britain has rarely featured among the medals.

Gymnastics

Gymnastics was never going to be a British sport. In its early form it was disciplined, formalized, collective and non-competitive. And it was good for you. That was not designed to appeal to gamesters such as the British. For a start, how did you bet on it? So we left it to the Swedes and the Germans.

In the ancient world, gymnastics evolved from the training exercises that athletes undertook to prepare themselves for strenuous sports like wrestling, boxing and athletics. A primitive form of modern gymnastics appeared in the later years of the ancient Olympic Games. After the Games came to an end, the idea of the systematic training of the body effectively disappeared. It re-emerged in the nineteenth century when gymnastics came to be seen as both recreational and therapeutic, a pleasant way of developing discipline of both mind and body. The first gymnastic societies were founded in Germany and in Bohemia, then part of the Austro-Hungarian Empire. They were followed by Switzerland and France – the French were convinced that they had lost the Franco-Prussian War because their young men were not fit enough to fight and they encouraged gymnastics to remedy this deficiency.

Modern gymnastics has developed from two major systems. In Sweden a system of free-flowing ground exercise was developed to accentuate rhythm of movement, whereas the Germans developed formal apparatus work designed to develop the muscles. In the 1920s the Fédération Internationale de Gymnastique, founded in 1881 to formalize international competitions, worked out a way of blending the fluency of the Swedish system with the precision of the German approach to produce the form of gymnastics that we know today.

Shooting

You may have noticed that a recurring theme in this book has been the attempts of kings and councils to ban ancient sports because they were distracting people from the practice of archery, vital for the defence of the realm. It is tempting to suggest that as soon as the longbow was made redundant as a weapon by the introduction of firearms, the British characteristically turned archery into a sport, based on the very practice they had apparently spent centuries trying to avoid; and then tried to bunk off shooting practice. In fact, archery was a popular pastime throughout the period when the longbow was an important weapon. But we were not the first to embrace shooting with guns as a sport.

All ancient societies on all continents (with the curious exception of Australia) used bows and arrows for both hunting and warfare. In the Middle Ages, the longbow was a major element in England's military power, playing a crucial role in such famous victories as Crécy, Poitiers and Agincourt. When its importance as a weapon began to decline, enthusiasts continued to use it as a means of hunting and as an enjoyable and skilful pastime. Henry VIII, himself no mean exponent of the art, was keen that the skills of archery be maintained. When Roger Ascham, a Cambridge academic and future tutor to Elizabeth I, wrote a book on the subject called *Toxophilus, the Schole of Shooting*, Henry was so pleased he gave him a pension of £10 a year. Ascham had been keen on archery when he was a boy and returned to it at Cambridge after a bout of illness. He received so much criticism from his fellow academics for indulging in such an unintellectual activity that he wrote his book – the first ever written in English about a pastime – as a defence. For him, archery was a wholly worthwhile relaxation:

How honest a pastime for the mind; how holesome an exercise for the body; not vile for great men to use, not costly for poor men to sustayne, not lurking in holes and corners for ill men at their pleasure to misuse it, but abiding in the open sighte and face of the worlde.

In 1539, Henry founded what was to become the Honourable Artillery Company to encourage the science of artillery through the use of 'long bowes, cross bowes and handgunnes'. Its members used to practise in Finsbury Fields, part of which came to be known as the Artillery Ground. In 1590, as the longbow was effectively discarded for military purposes, some members of the Company formed the Finsbury Archers so they could continue the activity they loved. A few years

A 'ticket' from the Finsbury Archers, which
members bought to enter a competition

later they initiated the first of three annual competitions – the Easter Target, Whitsuntide Target and the Eleven Score Target – which were to continue until 1761. With the dissolution of the Finsbury Archers in that year, the future of archery as a sport looked bleak. But in 1780 a Lancashire landowner, sportsman and natural historian called Sir Ashton Lever helped found the Toxophilite Society, which became the 'Royal Tox' when the Prince of Wales, later George IV, became its patron in 1787. It is not the oldest surviving archery society – that honour goes to the Royal Company of Archers in Edinburgh, founded as the King's bodyguard in Scotland in 1676 – but it is the most influential.

In 1844, the first of the Grand National Archery Meetings – the British Championships – was held at York. Five years later the Grand

National Archery Society was founded as the national governing body of the sport in Britain. International competition began with annual matches between England and France before World War I. The governing body of international archery was formed in 1931 and predictably has a French name: the Fédération Internationale de Tir à l'Arc (FITA). Archery featured in a number of the early modern Olympic Games, and then after a long break became a regular Olympic sport in 1972. For a few years after that the Americans did very well, but now the sport is dominated by South Korea. Britain wins medals regularly, but is no longer a leading archery nation.

Nor are we particularly good at shooting. Target shooting with guns is much older than one might imagine. The first shooting match that we know of took place in Eichstadt in Germany in 1477. There is a painting of rifle shooting in Switzerland which shows contestants firing at targets from enclosed shooting booths; beside each target is a hut which conceals a target marker who comes out after each shot with a pole to show the marksman – and the judges, who are also pictured – where the bullet hit. There are even flags to show the direction of the wind. The picture dates from 1504.

From that point on rifle shooting became immensely popular, particularly in Germany. A contemporary account talks of there being a 'shooting park' in every German village by 1517. From there, shooting spread throughout Europe, including Russia. In America, rifles were an essential part of life on the frontier and by the early nineteenth century most frontier villages were holding shooting matches every weekend. By 1830 shooting clubs were becoming popular in the major cities of the east. The National Rifle Association was formed in 1871. The international governing body of shooting, initially the International Shooting Union but now renamed the International Shooting Sport Federation, was set up in 1907.

Shooting has featured in every modern Olympics since 1896, largely because the founder of the modern games, Baron Pierre de Coubertin, was a French pistol-shooting champion. Most, but certainly not all, the medals are won by European countries. Britain is a regular competitor and wins the occasional medal, but cannot claim to be a major shooting country.

Weightlifting

Trials of strength have been a human obsession throughout history. The traditional test of manhood among many early societies was to lift a particular special rock. Such rocks, inscribed with the names of the people who first lifted them, have been found all over Greece. Such 'manhood' rocks have also been found in Scottish castles dating from the Middle Ages.

Modern weightlifting began in the nineteenth century, inspired by the exploits of professional strongmen from Russia, Germany and France. Formal competition started in the late 1800s, and the first open world championship was held at the Café Monico in London in 1891. It was won by an Englishman called Lawrence Levy.

Weightlifting featured in the first modern Olympic Games in Athens in 1896, when the one-hand lift was won by another Briton called Launceston Elliot. It featured again in Los Angeles in 1904 but did not become a regular Olympic sport until 1920, when the International Weightlifting Federation was formed. Since then the most successful lifters have tended to come from Eastern Europe and the Middle East. After a good start, Britain has not really pulled its weight in weight-lifting.

Wrestling

Wrestling in some form or another appears in the art and literature of almost every ancient civilization, from China to South America, dating back in some cases to as early as 3000 BC. Wrestling was the most popular sport among the ancient Greeks and was an important part of the original Olympic Games. The Romans were never as keen on wrestling as the Greeks and when the ancient Olympics finally came to an end in the late fourth century AD, wrestling disappears from view in

Europe for a while. But it still thrived in the Middle East, especially with the Turks, and in the Far East.

References to wrestling of many different styles reappear in Europe in the Middle Ages. Wrestling matches took place in London in 1222 and folk wrestling of different kinds thrived throughout Britain for many centuries – and still does in some areas. In 1520, at the Field of the Cloth of Gold, Henry VIII fought a private match with the French King Francis I. In the nineteenth century it was the French who developed wrestling as a professional sport in a style known as Greco-Roman, although there is no direct connection with the classical sport. The fame and popularity of the leading wrestlers of the day inspired the establishment of hundreds of amateur clubs across Northern and Eastern Europe, all using the Greco-Roman style. Formal amateur competitions began soon afterwards.

Meanwhile in America various European styles had been tried. Around 1880, a new style emerged which was distinctly American but evolved directly from the English Lancashire style called 'catch-as-catch-can'. It was the precursor of the current 'international freestyle' wrestling which was codified by the sport's governing body, the Fédération Internationale de Lutte Amateur (FILA) in 1920.

Greco-Roman wrestling featured in the first modern Olympics in Athens in 1896, while freestyle wrestling was included in the Los Angeles games in 1904 and the London games of 1908. Since 1920, both forms have been included at every Olympics. Great Britain, however, has not sent any wrestlers to the Olympics since 1984.

Equestrian sports

Britain has long been a major force in the equestrian sports at events such as the Olympic Games, but we cannot claim to have invented them. There are three main disciplines: showjumping, dressage and three-day eventing, which combines the first two with a cross-country element. The riding schools of Austria, France and Italy were all influential in developing the ideas and techniques used, but it is the French who can claim the credit for developing equestrianism as a sport.

Showjumping grew out of fox-hunting. As land everywhere became more enclosed, hunters needed their mounts to be able to jump hedges and fences. As their skills developed, they wanted to show them off. The first competitions were held in France in the middle of the nineteenth century. Initially the competing horses were paraded in front of the audience and then set off around the country, which didn't please the spectators much. Very quickly the jumps were positioned in an arena so that everyone could see them. The French held the first Grand Prix showjumping event in Paris in 1860. The Irish tried it at the Dublin Horse Show in 1869. By the end of the nineteenth century it was appearing at British horse shows. The first major showjumping event in Britain was held at Olympia in 1907.

Dressage and three-day eventing both have military origins. Riding schools such as the Imperial Spanish School in Vienna developed dressage – a French word meaning 'training' – as a way of teaching horses to be obedient, which was obviously vital on the battlefield. Three-day eventing began life as something of an endurance test for military horses. But it was gradually refined into something the French initially called *raids militaires*, a true test of a horse's (and rider's) stamina and ability.

Equestrian sports first appeared in the Olympics in 1900 in Paris. They then disappeared for a couple of games and returned in 1912. Since then, they have been included in every Olympics. Up until 1952, only male military officers were allowed to compete a clear sign of the sport's military origins. Since this time, it has been one of the very few Olympic sports where men and women compete together on an equal basis. It has been one of our most successful Olympic sports.

Winter sports

It is hardly surprising that Britain did not invent most winter sports. What is surprising is how much influence we had over their development. And there is one Winter Olympic event which the British, or at least the Scottish, did invent.

Skiing began in Scandinavia at least 4000 years ago. The oldest skis we know of, which were found in bogs in Sweden and Finland, are between 4000 and 5000 years old; and a rock carving of skiing found in Norway near the Arctic Circle dates from 2000 BC. For most of this time skiing was used mainly as a practical way of getting around in snow. It wasn't until the 1840s that the Norwegians held the first skiing competition – a cross-country race at Tromsö. The Norwegians were also responsible for introducing skiing to the Alps, where downhill skiing was developed. Norway can also claim credit for inventing ski-jumping. Competitive skiing began in California in 1860.

Ice-skating probably began in Scandinavia some 2000 years ago, with blades made of bone. The word *skate* is derived from the Dutch word *schaats*, which dates from the sixteenth century. But the sport of figure skating is much later. The first known account of figure skating was written by Englishman Robert Jones in 1772. Competitions were held in the 'English style' of skating, which was very stiff and formal and quite unlike skating today, in the nineteenth century. But the sport was transformed into the fluid and expressive style we know now by the great American skater Jackson Haines in the 1860s. Britain won consecutive gold medals in the men's figure skating in 1976 and 1980 with John Curry and Robin Cousins and another gold in the ice dancing with Jayne Torvill and Christopher Dean in 1984. The same pair won bronze ten years later, which was the last British medal.

Bobsleigh is the result of a cooperative effort between adventurous English tourists and an entrepreneurial hotelier called Caspar Badrutt, who owned the Krup Hotel in St Moritz in Switzerland and subsequently built the Palace Hotel. He constructed the Cresta Run, the first natural ice half-pipe, towards the end of the nineteenth century for the use of his English guests. They developed the skeleton (the small head-first sledge), the luge (lying down with feet first) and the first bobsleigh. The first organized competition was held in St Moritz in 1898. Bobsleigh was included in the first winter Olympics in 1924. Great Britain has had some success at bobsleigh and lies ninth in the Olympic medal table.

Curling, which to the annoyance of those who play it is often described as being a bit like bowls played on ice with large, smooth

The rights (left) and wrongs (right) of figure skating:
from a manual published in 1869

Curling was a hugely popular sport in Scotland
from the late middle ages

granite stones, was developed in Scotland in the late Middle Ages. The
first club was formed at Kilsyth, near Glasgow, in 1510. A stone
marked 1511 was found when an old pond near Dunblane was
drained. It was beside another one marked 1551. In 1541, the notary
John McQuhin recorded a challenge involving throwing stones across
ice between a monk at Paisley Abbey and a relative of the abbot. From
that time on there are growing numbers of references to the game. By
the end of the eighteenth century, curling was played throughout the
Lowlands of Scotland.

The game was widely celebrated by Lowlands poets. We don't
know whether Robert Burns was a curler, but he certainly knew all
about the sport, as these two stanzas from 'Tam Samson's Elegy'
clearly show:

> When Winter muffles up his cloak,
> And binds the mire like a rock;
> When to the loughs the curlers flock,
> Wi' gleesome speed,
> Wha will they station at the cock?
> Tam Samson's dead!
>
> He was the king o' a' the core.
> To guard, or draw, or wick a bore,
> Or up the rink like Jehu roar
> In time o' need;

> But now he lags on Death's hog-score –
> Tam Samson's dead!

The 'cock' was the tee or permanently marked target at which curlers aim. The other technical terms would be familiar to modern-day curlers. The sport was also elegantly described in the *Statistical Account of Scotland*, which gives us so much valuable information about life north of the border. The Minister at Muirkirk in Ayrshire wrote this about the importance of curling to his parishioners:

Their chief amusement in winter is curling, or playing stones on smooth ice. They eagerly vie with one another who shall come nearest the mark, and one part of the parish against another, one description of men against another, one trade or occupation against another, and often one whole parish against another, – earnestly contend for the palm, which is generally all the prize, except that perhaps the victors claim from the vanquished the dinner and bowl of toddy, which, to do them justice, both commonly take together with great cordiality, and generally without any grudge at the fortune of the day; wisely reflecting, no doubt, that defeat as well as victory is the fate of war. Those accustomed to this amusement, or that have acquired dexterity in the game, are extremely fond of it. The amusement itself is healthful; it is innocent; it does nobody harm; let them enjoy it.

In 1838, what is now the Royal Caledonian Curling Club was formed to act as the national regulatory body for the sport and standardize the rules, which were different in different parts of the country. From that date the sport exploded in popularity. By the end of the nineteenth century, almost every parish had its own curling pond. The Scots, as is their wont, then proceeded to export the game to every country which had a suitable climate. In 1966, what is now the World Curling Federation was established. It is based in Perth in Scotland.

Curling was included in the first Winter Olympics in 1924 and then re-introduced in 1998 for both men's and women's teams. British men won the gold medal in 1924 and, much to the delight of the whole of Scotland, British women won gold in 2002.

Cycling

Britain had a lot of influence over the development of cycling as a sport but it was the French who actually started it. The very first bicycle race took place on 31 May 1868 over 1200 metres in the Parc St-Cloud in Paris. It was organized by the Olivier brothers, the managers of the Michaux factory which had built the first real bicycle by attaching

Thomas McCall's published designs for rear-wheel
driven velocipedes from 1869

pedals to the axle of the front wheel in 1861. The race was won by an Englishman called James Moore. The first English cycle race took place the following day at Hendon in Middlesex. Later, in 1868, the first town-to-town cycle race took place over the 80-odd miles between Paris and Rouen.

Some believe the first bicycle that you could propel without putting your feet on the ground had been built in 1839 by a blacksmith from Dumfriesshire called Kirkpatrick Macmillan. It is said to have had two swinging cranks mounted at the front that the rider could push back and forth to drive the rear wheel. Others doubt this story. Either way, the idea never caught on, whereas the *vélocipède* built by the Michaux family was an instant hit. By 1865 they were making more than 400 a year and in 1866, their chief mechanic Pierre Lallement emigrated to America and took out the first patent there.

The Michaux bicycle had a large front wheel and a small rear one – an English version was immediately nicknamed the penny-farthing. These were awkward machines to ride and were also known as 'bone-shakers' because of their solid tyres and springless frame. In 1874, an Englishman called H. J. Lawson developed a bike which had two even-sized wheels and was driven by the now familiar chain attached to the rear wheel. It was called the safety bicycle because it was much more stable. In 1888, a Scottish vet working in Belfast called John Boyd Dunlop developed the first pneumatic tyre, which made cycling much more comfortable and much more popular. The first cycle race using pneumatic tyres was held in 1891 from Bordeaux to Paris. Strangely, it was reserved for British amateur riders and was won by one G. Mills.

The combination of the safety bicycle with Dunlop's pneumatic tyres helped cycling take off. The first cycle-racing tracks, or velodromes, appeared in Paris, London and New York and made possible a whole range of new events. At the same time road racing was flourishing. In 1903 the Tour de France, the greatest bike race of them all, was founded by Henri Desgrange, the manager of *L'Auto*, the forerunner of the French daily sports newspaper *L'Équipe*. Three years earlier the Union Cycliste Internationale had been formed, which was to give modern international cycling its rules and races. Cycling has been an Olympic sport since 1896. Britain has not until recently had much success in the major road races, but in the last few years the British team has established itself as one of the major forces – if not the major force – in track cycling. In the Beijing Olympics of 2008, they won seven out of the available ten gold medals.

Postscript

So the big question is: why aren't the British better at the sports they invented? If there was an easy answer, of course, the problem would have disappeared long ago. But I do have some thoughts.

The first is painfully obvious. The fact that you invented a sport doesn't mean you're bound to excel at it. Take motor racing. As we've seen, the French developed it with a passion, whereas the British became involved really rather late on. Yet France has produced just one world champion driver to Britain's eight. On the other hand, inventing a sport can lead to dangerous arrogance and complacency. In the 1920s and 1930s, when British football was refusing to have anything to do with FIFA, an official said that putting countries such as Uruguay and Brazil on the same level as England, Scotland, Wales and Ireland was a case of 'magnifying the midgets'. He hadn't noticed that those countries were developing levels of skill British footballers arguably have still not yet attained. The English team didn't take part in the World Cup until 1950.

Then there is what I will call the Will Carling issue. The English rugby captain once famously described the Rugby Football Union committee as '57 old farts', a comment which briefly cost him his job. But there was undoubtedly truth in it. The Victorian concept of the gentleman amateur still lingers in the administration of many British sports.

The idea that it's not the winning but the taking part that matters is

still strong. That's why the quote from Kipling can still be seen above
the players' entrance to the Centre Court at Wimbledon:

> If you can meet with Triumph and Disaster
> And treat those two impostors just the same

You wouldn't find those words above the door in the changing room
of the Australian Test cricket team. But that doesn't mean to say that
it's not right.

And that brings us to the attitude of the British people. Do we expect
to win when our national team plays? Not really. We're delighted if
they do, or if an individual British sportsperson does. But if they don't,
we regard it just as business as usual. And we don't really mind (except,
perhaps, if it's as humiliating as not qualifying for Euro 2008). The
British, polyglot nation though we now are, are quite comfortable with
their own identity. We know who we are. We don't need success on the
playing field to tell us. Not like those Australians.

There is another characteristic I think is very important. The British
are playful. We like to play with words, for instance. This is not
something which all other nations share. If you try making a pun to a
French person or a German, the chances are they won't have a clue
what you're doing or why you're doing it. We like playing games. But
as an eminent sports sociologist – there are such things – has said, when
sport becomes professional it ceases to be play and becomes work. We
aren't always happy with that. We like people such as Denis Compton,
David Gower and Ian Botham because they made it fun. When you've
got their talent, it doesn't matter much. But we like it in lesser mortals
as well. We can't be doing with Geoffrey Boycott all the time.

So it seems to me that the differing attitudes that drove the development of sport in Britain in the two phases we identified in the introduction have had an impact. The first was that sport was fun and a
great excuse for gambling. The second was that sport is good for you
and that winning is not necessarily what it's all about. Those ideas,
which are probably still there at the back of our minds, may well have
held us back in today's ruthlessly competitive sporting world. But it was

those attitudes that led us to invent the whole idea in the first place. The world should be grateful.

And anyway, there are signs that things may be changing. The British track cycling team achieved their astonishing medal haul in the 2008 Olympics in Beijing by adopting some very un-British attitudes. They got the structure right, they got the coaching right and they concentrated their lottery money on winners. UK Sport offered funding for forty plus cyclists. But the team said they weren't interested in people who might come fourth, fifth, sixth, seventh or eighth. They wanted to concentrate on potential medalists. They persuaded UK Sport to give them the same amount of money for just twenty three cyclists. So much for de Coubertin's idea that it's not the winning but the taking part that matters. The result was that all but one of the cyclists came home with a medal.

In other sports too, especially sailing and rowing, the British team showed a real desire to win. The sight of British athletes distraught because they had only won an Olympic silver medal became almost a sub-theme of the Games. So we are still a strong sporting nation. We are not and probably never will be again as dominant as we once were, but there's still life in the old bulldog yet.

APPENDIX:
SURVIVING TRADITIONAL SPORTS EVENTS

Cricket

Broadhalfpenny Down: Cricket is still played regularly on the original home of the Hambledon Club by the Broadhalfpenny Brigands, who run the ground on behalf of the owners, Winchester College. The Hambledon Club still exists, but now play on Ridge Meadow, nearer the village.

Sailing

Cowes Week: Still takes place every summer. Traditionally it starts on the first Saturday after the last Tuesday in July, except when the tides make this impractical.

Football

Many traditional folk football games still survive. What follows is not an exhaustive list, but a good starting point. The games are listed in chronological order.

Haxey, Lincolnshire: The Haxey Hood takes place on 6 January, the twelfth day of Christmas. It generally involves around two hundred players from Haxey and the neighbouring village of Westwoodside, but there are no formal teams. At 3.00 pm the 'Sway Hood' – a rolled hessian sack that is sewn up so it doesn't unravel – is thrown into the air. A huge rugby-style scrum then forms around it, known as the 'Sway'. The idea is to drive the Sway

Hood, which cannot be thrown or run with, to one of the four local pubs, which can take several hours. The game ends when the Hood reaches one of the pubs and is touched by the landlord from his front step. The winning pub then keeps the Hood until the following year.

St Ives, Cornwall: Not called football but, in the Cornish tradition, hurling. Takes place on the first Monday after 3 February, the feast day of the town's patroness St Ia. It begins at 9.30 am with the blessing of the silver ball at St Ia's sacred well and ends at midday.

Alnwick, Northumberland: A traditional game called 'Scoring the Hales' takes place on Shrove Tuesday in a field called The Pasture below Alnwick Castle, between the parishes of St Michael and St Paul. There are usually around 150 men on each side and the winner is the first team to score three 'hales' or goals. Starts at 2.00 pm.

Ashbourne, Derbyshire: Home of possibly the oldest and best-known Shrovetide game. It takes place on Shrove Tuesday and Ash Wednesday. The 'pitch' is three miles long and two miles wide, with the town of Ashbourne in the middle. All able-bodied men, women and children are encouraged to take part. Those born on the north side of the Henmore River form the 'Up'ards' team, those from the south side are the 'Down'ards'. Each day the game starts at 2.00 pm and can continue until 10.00 pm.

Atherstone, Warwickshire: A different Shrove Tuesday football game, which is thought to date back more than 800 years. It is played along Watling Street, the old Roman road, at the point where it forms the main street of Atherstone town. There are no teams and no goals. The game lasts from 3.00 pm to 5.00 pm and the winner is the person who has the ball when the game ends. After 4.30 pm the ball can be deflated or hidden (or both).

St Columb Major, Cornwall: Another hurling game, held on Shrove Tuesday and then again on the second Saturday following, between teams from 'Town' and 'Country'. Confined to the town centre for the first hour, the game then moves towards the 'place assigned' of one or other team.

Sedgefield, County Durham: The 'Ball Game' starts at 1.00 pm, when the leather ball is passed three times through a 'bull ring' in the centre of the village. For the next three hours it is kicked around the village. As in Atherstone, there are no teams. The first person to get the ball to any of the local pubs receives a free drink. After 4.00 pm, the aim is to 'ally' the ball at the goal – a beck in the south of the village. Whoever achieves this then has to return the ball to the centre of the village and pass it through the bull ring three more times.

Hobkirk, Roxburghshire: The annual Ba' event takes place in this border town on the Monday after Shrove Tuesday between the 'Uppies' and the 'Downies'. It lasts from mid-afternoon until well after dark. The aim is to score as many 'hails' or goals as possible.

Jedburgh, Roxburghshire: The Jethard Handba' game takes place in this border town every February, with a noon start for boys and a 2.00 pm start for men. Between ten and fifteen games can be played during the course of the day. The 'Uppies' score by 'hailing' the ball over Jedburgh Castle wall, the 'Doonies' by getting the ball into Skiprunning Burn.

Ancrum and Denholm, Roxburghshire: More border town Ba' games, again held in February, and again featuring the 'Uppies' and the 'Doonies'.

Workington, Cumberland: A series of three games which take place on Good Friday, Easter Tuesday and the following Saturday. The 'Uppies' were traditionally colliers, while the 'Downies' were sailors. The goals are a mile apart: the sailors try to 'hale' the ball over a capstan at the harbour, while the colliers target is the wall of Workington Hall.

Hallaton, Leicestershire: Known as the 'Hallaton Hare Pie Scramble and Bottle Kicking', this event takes place every Easter Monday. The two teams – one from Hallaton, the other from the neighbouring village of Medbourne – gather on Hare Pie Hill. After scrambling for pieces of pie thrown into the crowd, the competitors hold up three small barrels. Two are full of beer, the third is solid wood. The solid barrel – known as the 'bottle' – is then thrown into the air three times. When it lands for the final time, the game begins. Hallaton try to get the bottle over the stream close to their village, Medbourne aim for the stream next to theirs. There are no rules and no time limit.

Duns, Berwickshire: The Duns Ba' game takes place in July as part of the Duns summer festival or 'Reivers Week'. The married men of the village take on the bachelors. The goals are at opposite corners of the market square.

Kirkwall, Orkney: the Kirkwall Ba' takes place twice a year, on Christmas Day and New Year's Day, between the 'Uppies' and the Doonies'. Which team you were in used to depend on your place of birth, but now it's a matter of family tradition. The Uppies try to touch the ba' against a wall in the south end of the town, while the Doonies' aim is to get it into the waters of Kirkwall Bay. The game start at 1.00 pm and can last for up to eight hours.

Rowing

Doggett's Coat and Badge Wager: Still takes place every year. It is believed to be the oldest continuous sporting event in the world. It takes place in late July – the exact date and time depend upon the tide. The course is from London Bridge to Chelsea.

Bumping races: Still take place at Oxford and Cambridge. 'Eights Week' in Oxford is the fifth week of the Trinity (summer) term. 'May Bumps' in Cambridge actually take place in June, at the end of the summer term after exams are over.

Athletics

The Wenlock Olympian Games: Take place every year in July. Go to www.wenlock-olympian-society.org for details and dates.

Robert Dover's Cotswold Olimpick Games: Take place every year on the first Friday after the Spring Bank Holiday at Dover's Hill, above Chipping Camden and overlooking the Vale of Evesham. They include races and events such as the final of the British shin-kicking championship, plus a torch-light procession. See www.olimpickgames.co.uk.

Swimming

The Serpentine Swimming Club: Holds its annual 'Peter Pan Christmas Day Race' at 9.00 am on Christmas morning. It has been going since 1864. The 'Bridge to Bridge' race in July is even older – it started in 1837.

Bowls

The Southampton Old Bowling Green: In continuous use since 1299, it hosts the 'knighthood' competition every year, starting on the third Wednesday in August. It can last for up to ten days. The winner is dubbed a 'knight-of-the-green' and can never take part again.

NOTES ON ILLUSTRATIONS

The author and publisher have made every effort to trace copyright holders, and to obtain their permission for the use of copyright material. The publisher apologizes for any errors or omissions and would be grateful to be notified of any corrections that should be incorporated in future editions of the book.

Most of the illustrations in this book are based on contemporary engravings, prints and cartoons.

Page xxii: *Tom Brown's Schooldays*, 1869 edition; p.2: *Athletics of the Ancient World*, Gardiner, 1910; p.4 (top): *Athletics of the Ancient World*, Gardiner, 1910; p.4 (bottom) *Antike Turngerathe*, Juthner, 1896; p.6: *Pugilistica*, 1906; p.7: *Pugilistica*, 1906; p.9: eighteenth-century engraving; p.11: eighteenth-century engraving; p.15, eighteenth-century print; p.16: eighteenth-century print; p.18: eighteenth-century engraving; p.19: eighteenth-century engraving; p.20: print from *Annals of Sporting and The Fancy Gazette*; p.21: eighteenth-century engraving; p.24: eighteenth-century engraving; p.26: eighteenth-century print; p.27: eighteenth-century print; p.31: nineteenth-century photograph; p.32: nineteenth-century photograph; p.35: *Athletics of the Ancient World*, Gardiner, 1910; p.37, by permission of Trinity College, Dublin; p.41, seventeenth-century engraving; p.44: seventeenth-century etching; p.45: print after painting by Wooton, 1728; p.47: eighteenth-century engraving; p.48 (top): eighteenth-century engraving; p.48 (bottom): eighteenth-century print; p.51: eighteenth-century cartoon; p.52: eighteenth-century print; p.54: eighteenth-century print after Dighton; p.55: eighteenth-century engraving after Rowlandson; p.62: *Pierce Egan's Book of Sports*, 1832; p.64: nineteenth-century print; p.68: nineteenth-century photograph; p.71: Guildford Borough Court Book, 1586–1675, Guildford Borough Council; p.72: children's book illustration, 1611; p.75: eighteenth-century engraving; p.78: eighteenth-century engraving; pp.83, 85, 86: by permission of the MCC; p.89: photo by Henry Dixon (1820–1893) of painting then owned by the Lord family; p.93: eighteenth-century engraving; p.97: eighteenth-century engraving; p.98: eighteenth-century engraving; p.100: eighteenth-century engraving; p.101: eighteenth-century engraving; p.105: nineteenth-century photograph; p.110: nineteenth-century photograph; p.117: from a fourteenth-century manuscript book of prayers; p.118: by permission of the British Museum; p.120: nineteenth-century engraving; p.121: nineteenth-century engraving; p.123: nineteenth-century sketch; p.125: eighteenth-century drawing; p.129, photo by H. M. Cowie, by permission of St Andrews University; p.132: nineteenth-century photograph; p.134: *Illustrated London News*, 1870; p.136: nineteenth-century engraving by Frederick Gilbert; p.142: seventeenth-century engraving; p.143: seventeenth-century engraving; p.146: nineteenth-century sketch; p.149: *Pierce Egan's Book of Sports*, 1832; p.153: nineteenth-century engraving; p.158: by permission of the National Football Museum; p.158: nineteenth-century print; p.165: nineteenth-century etching; p.168: nineteenth-century engraving; pp.173, 186: *Badminton Library, Football*; p.176: nineteenth-century photograph; p.198: *Illustrated London News*, 1871; p.199: *Illustrated London News*; p.200: *The Graphic*, 1870; p.202: nineteenth-century engraving; p.205: from a painting by W.B. Wooton; p.207: nineteenth-century drawing; p.209: nineteenth-century photograph; p.213: nineteenth-century photograph; pp.230, 231, 233, 243, 246: *Badminton Library, Boating*, 1889; p.235: *Badminton Library, Rowing and Punting*, 1898; p.237: eighteenth-century engraving; p.242: by permission of Tyne and Wear Museums; p.248: nineteenth-century photograph; p.251: nineteenth-century photograph; p.253: contemporary photograph; p.257: *Children's Amusements*, 1820; p.259: *The Book of Sports*, 1832; p.261: *Mary's Book of Sports*, 1832; p.263: nineteenth-century photograph; p.264: nineteenth-century drawing; p.266: nineteenth-century photograph; p.268: *A Little Pretty Pocket Book*, 1744; p.271: seventeenth-century engraving; p.274: by permission of the British Library; p.278: seventeenth-century engraving; p.281: nineteenth-century print; pp.283, 286: *Rules of Sphairistike*, 1874; p.290: nineteenth-century engraving; p.291: nineteenth-century photograph; pp.296, 297: *Badminton Library, Tennis*, 1890; p.299: *Sports and Pastimes of the People of England*, Strutt, 1801; p.303: *Journal of Hellenic Studies*, 1922; p.304: fourteenth-century manuscript, by permission of the British Museum; p.305: *The Book of Games*, 1810; p.307: nineteenth-century engraving; p.308: nineteenth-century engraving; p.311: by permission of Mercian Sports; p.318: *Athletics of the Ancient World*, Gardiner, 1910; pp.320, 324, 325 (top), 325 (bottom): *Badminton Library, Athletics*, 1887; pp.320, 323: Chambers Book of Days, 1864; p.327: *Pugilistica*, 1906; pp.343, 344, 348, 358: *Badminton Library, Swimming*, 1893; p.346: nineteenth-century drawing; p.349: *Illustrated London News*; p.353: nineteenth-century photograph; p.354: *Illustrated London News*, 1875; p.355: Bryant and May, 1876; p.356: nineteenth-century publicity drawing; p.363: thirteenth- and fourteenth-century drawing, *Sports and Pastimes of the People of England*, Strutt, 1801; p.364: *Quarles's Emblems*, 1635; p.365: Victorian engraving; p.368: Victorian photograph; p.370: eighteenth-century engraving; p.371: *Badminton Library, Billiards*, 1896; p.378: contemporary poster; p.383: contemporary photo; p.385: *The Motor*, 1923; p.390: seventeenth-century illustrations; p.393: *Badminton Library, Archery*, 1984; p.399: nineteenth-century illustrations; p.402: nineteenth-century drawings.

BIBLIOGRAPHY

Introduction

Hughes, Thomas, *Tom Brown's Schooldays*. Macmillan: London, 1857
Birley, Sir Derek, *Sport and the Making of Britain*. Manchester University Press: Manchester, 1993

Boxing

Ford, John, *Prizefighting: The age of Regency boximania*. David and Charles: Newton Abbott, 1971
Gee, Tony, *Up to Scratch: Bareknuckle fighting and the heroes of the prize-ring*. Queen Anne Press: Harpenden, 2001
Miles, Henry Downes, *Pugilistica, being 144 years of the history of British boxing (3 vols)*. Weldon: London, 1880

Horse racing

Cook, Sir Theodore Andrea, *A History of the English Turf (3 vols)*, H. Virtue and Company: London, 1901–4
Longrigg, Roger, *The History of Horse Racing*. Macmillan: London, 1972
Mortimer, Roger, *The Jockey Club*. Cassell: London, 1958
Thompson, Laura, *Newmarket: From James I to the present day*, Virgin Books: London, 2000
Vamplew, Wray, *The Turf: A social and economic history of horse racing*. Allen Lane: London, 1976

Cricket

Altham, A.H., *A History of Cricket*. Allen & Unwin: London, 1926

Ashley-Cooper, F.S., *The Hambledon Cricket Chronicle, 1772–1796*. H. Jenkins, London, 1924

Bailey, Trevor, *A History of Cricket*. Allen & Unwin: London, Boston, 1978

Birley, Sir Derek, *A Social History of English Cricket*. Aurum Press: London, 1999

Bowen, Rowland, *Cricket: A history of its growth and development throughout the world*. Eyre and Spottiswoode: London, 1970

Green, Stephen, *Lords: The cathedral of cricket*. Tempus: Stroud, 2003

Lewis, Tony, *Double Century: The story of the MCC and cricket*. Hodder and Stoughton: London, 1987

Major, John, *More Than a Game: The story of cricket's early years*. HarperSport: London 2007

Nyren, John, *John Nyren's The Cricketers of my Time, the Original Version, published for the first time since 1832, introduced and edited by Ashley Mote*. Robson Books: London, 1998

Wynne-Thomas, Peter, *The History of Cricket: From the Weald to the Wold*. Stationery Office: Norwich, 1997

Golf

Browning, Robert, *A History of Golf*. Dent: London, 1955

Clark, Robert, *Golf: A Royal and Ancient game*. Macmillan: London, 1899

Darwin, Bernard (et al), *A History of Golf in Britain*. Cassell: London, 1952

Hutchinson, Horace G. (et al), *Golf (Badminton Library of Sports and Pastimes)*, Longmans, Green: London, 1890

Yachting

Heaton, Peter, *A History of Yachting in Pictures*. Tom Stacey: London, 1972

Heaton, Peter, *Yachting: A history*. Batsford: London, 1955

Phillips-Birt, Douglas, *The Cumberland Fleet: Two hundred years of yachting, 1775–1975*. Bodley Head: London, 1978

Football

Davies, Hunter, *Boots, Balls and Haircuts: An illustrated history of football from then 'til now*. Cassell Illustrated: London, 2004

Goldblatt, David, *The Ball is Round: A global history of football*. Viking: London, 2006

Hornby, Hugh, *Uppies and Downies: The extraordinary football games of Britain*. English Heritage: Swindon, 2008

Walvin, James, *The People's Game: The history of football revisited*. Mainstream: Edinburgh, 1994

Shearman, Montague (et al), *Athletics and Football (Badminton Library of Sports and Pastimes)*. Longmans: London, 1889

Young, Percy M., *A history of British football*. Paul: London, 1968

Rugby

Dunning, Eric, *Barbarians, Gentlemen and Players: A sociological study of the development of rugby football*. M. Robertson: Oxford, 1979

Gate, Robert, *Rugby League: An illustrated history*. Barker: London, 1990

Macrory, Jennifer, *Running with the ball*. Collins Willow: London, 1991

Richards, Huw, *A Game for Hooligans: The history of rugby union*. Mainstream: Edinburgh, 2006

Titley, U.A. and McWhirter, Ross, *Centenary History of the Rugby Football Union*. Rugby Football Union, 1970

Rowing

Cleaver, Hylton, *A History of Rowing*. H. Jenkins: London, 1957

Dodd, Christopher, *The Story of World Rowing*. Stanley Paul: London 1992

Halladay, Eric, *Rowing in England: A social history*. Manchester University Press: Manchester, 1990

Rowe, R.P.P. and Pitman, C.M., *Rowing (Badminton Library of Sports and Pastimes)*. Longmans, Green: London, 1898

Whitehead, Ian, *The Sporting Tyne: A history of professional rowing*. Portcullis Press and Gateshead Council: Gateshead, 2002

Woodgate, Walter Bradford, *Boating (Badminton Library of Sports and Pastimes)*. Longmans, Green: London, 1888

Baseball

Block, David, *Baseball Before We Knew It: A search for the roots of the game.* University of Nebraska Press: Lincoln, 2005

Brasch, Rudolph, *How Did Sports Begin?: A look at the origins of man at play.* McKay: New York, 1970

Kirsch, George B., *Baseball and Cricket: The creation of American team sports 1838–72*. University of Illinois Press: Urbana, 2007

Lawn Tennis

Aberdare, Baron Morys George Lyndhurst Bruce, *The Story of Tennis*. S. Paul: London, 1959

Alexander, George F., *Wingfield: Edwardian Gentleman*. Peter E. Randall: Portsmouth, New Hampshire, 1986

Gillmeister, Heiner, *Tennis: A cultural history*. Leicester University Press: London, 1997

Heathcote, C.G., *Lawn Tennis (Badminton Library of Sports and Pastimes)*. Longmans, 1890

Morgan, Roger, *Tennis: The Development of the European Ball Game*. Ronaldson Publications: Oxford, 1995

Robertson, Max, *Wimbledon 1877–1977*. Barker: London, 1977

Todd, T., *The Tennis Players*. Vallency Press: Guernsey, 1979

Hockey

Howells, M.K., *The Romance of Hockey's History*. M.K.Howells: Milton Keynes, 1996

Miroy, Nevill, *The History of Hockey*. Lifeline: Laleham on Thames, 1986

Nicholson Smith, J. and Robson, Philip A., *Hockey: Historical and Practical (The Isthmian Library)*. Innes: London, 1899

Athletics

Llewellyn Smith, Michael, *Olympics in Athens 1896: The invention of the modern Olympic Games*. Profile Books: London, 2004

Lovesey, Peter, *The Official Centenary History of the Amateur Athletics Association*. Guinness Superlatives: Enfield, 1979

Shearman, Montague, *Athletics (The Badminton Library of Sports and Pastimes)*. Longmans, Green: London, 1901

Thom, Walter, *Pedestrianism; or, an account of the performances of celebrated pedestrians during the last and present centuries*. Aberdeen, 1813

Swimming

Jarvis, Margaret A., *Captain Webb and 100 years of Channel Swimming*. David & Charles: Newton Abbot, 1975

Love, Christopher, *A Social History of Swimming in England*. Routledge: London, 2008

Sinclair, Archibald and Henry, William, *Swimming (The Badminton Library of Sports and Pastimes)*. Longmans, Green: London, 1903

Pub Games

Brown, Derek, *Guinness Book of Darts*. Guinness Superlatives: Enfield, 1982

Everton, Clive, *Guinness Book of Snooker*. Guinness Superlatives: Enfield, 1982

Everton, Clive, *The History of Snooker and Billiards*. Partridge Press: Haywards Heath, 1986

Manson, James, *The Complete Bowler*. Adam and Charles Black: London, 1912

The Ones That Got Away

Burke, Edmund H., *The History of Archery*. Heinemann: London, 1958

Hilton, Christopher, *Grand Prix Century*. Haynes Publishing: Yeovil, 2005

Kerr, John, *A History of Curling*. David Douglas: Edinburgh, 1890

Longman, C.J. and Walrond, Col. H., *Archery (Badminton Library of Sports and Pastimes)*. Longmans, Green: London, 1894

INDEX

ALLEN LANE
an imprint of
PENGUIN BOOKS

Recently Published

Sebastian Seung, *Connectome: How the Brain's Wiring Makes Us Who We Are*

Callum Roberts, *Ocean of Life*

Orlando Figes, *Just Send Me Word: A True Story of Love and Survival in the Gulag*

Leonard Mlodinow, *Subliminal: The Revolution of the New Unconscious and What it Teaches Us about Ourselves*

John Romer, *A History of Ancient Egypt: From the First Farmers to the Great Pyramid*

Ruchir Sharma, *Breakout Nations: In Search of the Next Economic Miracle*

Michael J. Sandel, *What Money Can't Buy: The Moral Limits of Markets*

Dominic Sandbrook, *Seasons in the Sun: The Battle for Britain, 1974-1979*

Tariq Ramadan, *The Arab Awakening: Islam and the New Middle East*

Jonathan Haidt, *The Righteous Mind: Why Good People are Divided by Politics and Religion*

Ahmed Rashid, *Pakistan on the Brink: The Future of Pakistan, Afghanistan and the West*

Tim Weiner, *Enemies: A History of the FBI*

Mark Pagel, *Wired for Culture: The Natural History of Human Cooperation*

George Dyson, *Turing's Cathedral: The Origins of the Digital Universe*

Cullen Murphy, *God's Jury: The Inquisition and the Making of the Modern World*

Richard Sennett, *Together: The Rituals, Pleasures and Politics of Co-operation*

Faramerz Dabhoiwala, *The Origins of Sex: A History of the First Sexual Revolution*

Roy F. Baumeister and John Tierney, *Willpower: Rediscovering Our Greatest Strength*

Jesse J. Prinz, *Beyond Human Nature: How Culture and Experience Shape Our Lives*

Robert Holland, *Blue-Water Empire: The British in the Mediterranean since 1800*

Jodi Kantor, *The Obamas: A Mission, A Marriage*

Philip Coggan, *Paper Promises: Money, Debt and the New World Order*

Charles Nicholl, *Traces Remain: Essays and Explorations*

Daniel Kahneman, *Thinking, Fast and Slow*

Hunter S. Thompson, *Fear and Loathing at Rolling Stone: The Essential Writing of Hunter S. Thompson*

Duncan Campbell-Smith, *Masters of the Post: The Authorized History of the Royal Mail*

Colin McEvedy, *Cities of the Classical World: An Atlas and Gazetteer of 120 Centres of Ancient Civilization*

Heike B. Görtemaker, *Eva Braun: Life with Hitler*

Brian Cox and Jeff Forshaw, *The Quantum Universe: Everything that Can Happen Does Happen*

Nathan D. Wolfe, *The Viral Storm: The Dawn of a New Pandemic Age*

Norman Davies, *Vanished Kingdoms: The History of Half-Forgotten Europe*

Michael Lewis, *Boomerang: The Meltdown Tour*

Steven Pinker, *The Better Angels of Our Nature: The Decline of Violence in History and Its Causes*

Robert Trivers, *Deceit and Self-Deception: Fooling Yourself the Better to Fool Others*

Thomas Penn, *Winter King: The Dawn of Tudor England*

Daniel Yergin, *The Quest: Energy, Security and the Remaking of the Modern World*

Michael Moore, *Here Comes Trouble: Stories from My Life*

Ali Soufan, *The Black Banners: Inside the Hunt for Al Qaeda*

Jason Burke, *The 9/11 Wars*

Timothy D. Wilson, *Redirect: The Surprising New Science of Psychological Change*

Ian Kershaw, *The End: Hitler's Germany, 1944-45*

T M Devine, *To the Ends of the Earth: Scotland's Global Diaspora, 1750-2010*

Catherine Hakim, *Honey Money: The Power of Erotic Capital*

Douglas Edwards, *I'm Feeling Lucky: The Confessions of Google Employee Number 59*

John Bradshaw, *In Defence of Dogs*

Chris Stringer, *The Origin of Our Species*

Lila Azam Zanganeh, *The Enchanter: Nabokov and Happiness*

David Stevenson, *With Our Backs to the Wall: Victory and Defeat in 1918*

Evelyn Juers, *House of Exile: War, Love and Literature, from Berlin to Los Angeles*

Henry Kissinger, *On China*

Michio Kaku, *Physics of the Future: How Science Will Shape Human Destiny and Our Daily Lives by the Year 2100*

David Abulafia, *The Great Sea: A Human History of the Mediterranean*

John Gribbin, *The Reason Why: The Miracle of Life on Earth*

Anatol Lieven, *Pakistan: A Hard Country*

William Cohen, *Money and Power: How Goldman Sachs Came to Rule the World*

Joshua Foer, *Moonwalking with Einstein: The Art and Science of Remembering Everything*

Simon Baron-Cohen, *Zero Degrees of Empathy: A New Theory of Human Cruelty*

Manning Marable, *Malcolm X: A Life of Reinvention*

David Deutsch, *The Beginning of Infinity: Explanations that Transform the World*